Removing A Badge of Slavery

Dedicated to the Memory of My Parents . . .
and for Sylvia and Marvin Davis

REMOVING A BADGE OF SLAVERY

The Record of
Brown v. Board of Education

EDITED
BY
MARK WHITMAN

Markus Wiener Publishing, Inc.
Princeton & New York

For information write to:
  Markus Wiener Publishing, Inc.
  114 Jefferson Road, Princeton, NJ 08540

Library of Congress Cataloging-in-Publication Data

Removing a badge of slavery: the record of Brown v. Board of
  Education/Mark Whitman, ed.
    Includes bibliographical references and index.
    ISBN 1-55876-049-0 (cloth) ISBN 1-55876-058-X (paper)
    1. Discrimination in education—Law and Legislation—United
States—History. 2. Segregation in education—Law and
legislation—United States—History. 3. Brown, Oliver, 1918-
—Trials, litigation, etc. 4. Topeka (Kansas). Board of Education—
Trials, litigation, etc. I. Whitman, Mark, 1937- .
KF4155.R46 1992
344.73'0798—dc20
[347.304798]   92-15367
                                                         CIP

Printed in The United States of America on acid-free paper

Amendment Fourteen

Section 1.   All persons born or naturalized in the United States, and subject to the jurisdiction thereof, are citizens of the United States and of the State wherein they reside. No State shall make or enforce any law which shall abridge the privileges or immunities of citizens of the United States; nor shall any State deprive any person of life, liberty, or property, without due process of law; *nor deny to any person within its jurisdiction the equal protection of the laws.*

Preface

THERE ARE FEW areas of intellectual endeavor in which the general reader and the undergraduate student are urged more fervently to "go to the source" than American constitutional law or history. It seems eminently sensible to ground one's knowledge of a Supreme Court case on the actual text of the Court's decision, rather than on a second-hand account. Excerpts from Court opinions appear routinely in the daily newspapers. Marvelous casebooks abound.

Much less material exists, however, which seeks to give the reader a detailed look at how landmark Supreme Court controversies actually develop—during their trial stage, in lower court decisions, and in the briefs filed, and the oral arguments conducted at the bar of the Supreme Court itself. Professor Alan Westin's outstanding books on the steel seizure case and the *United States* v. *Nixon* demonstrate the value of such an exercise.

No Supreme Court case can be illuminated more usefully through an examination of its record than *Brown* v. *Board of Education*. This is not only because of *Brown's* preeminent place in the history of American constitutional law. The sheer complexity of the case—the fact that it is really five separate controversies blended into one—means that the original documents can serve a clarifying function not essential to less multifaceted constitutional disputes. Furthermore, the very fact that so much has been written about *Brown*, and that readers have been exposed already to some of the trial testimony or legal argumentation, suggests that a larger acquaintance with its majestic record might carry for them a special intellectual impact.

I have tried, therefore, to let the record of *Brown* speak for itself in this book to the greatest degree possible. My introductory material and annotations precede the excerpts I have chosen and do not intrude upon them, except where absolutely necessary.

In discussing this record, people whom I admire greatly might use the term "African-American," with its emphasis upon a rich and unique cultural heritage. I normally use the term myself. But we are dealing here with an era in American history in which there was a tragic obsession with race and color as ends in themselves, when a hateful and irrational stigma often attached to them. *Brown* is part of the story of how we began to efface this shameful strain on American life. Therefore, with all respect, I have chosen to use the term "black" in my annotations.

I have acquired many intellectual and personal debts in the course of this work.

The project would not exist but for the friendship, encouragement, and shrewd advice offered by my colleague, Professor Patricia Romero. If she has consistently overrated my abilities, it was, she would say, in a good cause.

The same is true of Professor Myron Scholnick, the kind, supportive colleague and friend whom every academic dreams of having, and few in fact ever run into.

I have been fortunate to teach for over twenty years in the History department at Towson State University, a model of collegiality and commitment to undergraduate education. The delightful atmosphere in which we work was established and nourished by our former chairperson, Professor Mary Catherine Kahl, and has been maintained under her successor, Professor Douglas Martin.

I should single out all my colleagues no doubt. I know it will be understood if I give special thanks to Laura Eldridge, Karl Larew, Fred Rivers, and Garry Van Osdell. My typist and grammatical arbiter, Janet Himes, is in line for the civilian equivalent of the purple heart. Finally, I am especially grateful for the supportive ties of family: Sandy and Steve Winters; my nephews, Gary Winters, Andy Winters and his wife Laura; and my cousins, Penny and Sol Love, Rita and Irv Sherman, and Marlene and Bernie Whitman.

Of course anyone who writes about *Brown* owes an immeasurable debt, both intellectual and spiritual, to Richard Kluger's magisterial work, *Simple Justice*. Those who have yet to read this great book are fortunate in one sense; there lies ahead of them a magnificent experience.

Contents

General Introduction

Brown v. *Board of Education of Topeka, Kansas* is the formal name of a specific controversy in American constitutional law. Yet it is also the "generic" name, as it were, for five separate lawsuits, filed independently of each other, but consolidated for their argument in the Supreme Court of the United States. Together these suits challenged the constitutionality of legally enforced segregation in America's elementary and secondary schools. The cases were first heard before the Court in December, 1952. The Justices ordered that they be reargued the next year, and handed down their judgment on the legality of segregation on May 17, 1954. Another opinion, dealing with the implementation of the 1954 decision, followed on May 31, 1955; it is usually called *Brown II*.

Three of the lawsuits decided in the 1954 opinion, including *Brown* v. *Board of Education*, originated in federal district courts. *Briggs* v. *Elliott* challenged educational segregation in Clarendon County, South Carolina; *Davis* v. *County School Board of Prince Edward County* concerned practices in Virginia. In all three cases the complainants asserted that segregation by its very nature violates the equal protection clause of the fourteenth amendment. They sought the destruction, in public education at least, of the doctrine which had reigned since the 1896 case of *Plessy* v. *Ferguson*: that separate facilities for the races do not constitute a denial of the equal protection of the laws so long as the facilities are approximately equivalent. These three cases form the primary focus of this volume (which will conclude with the deciding of *Brown I*).

A fourth case, *Belton* v. *Gebhart*, originated in the state courts of Delaware and also involved equal protection claims. But *Bolling* v. *Sharpe*, though argued with the other four, stood apart from them in large measure because *Bolling* attacked the school segregation sanctioned under federal law in the District of Columbia. Such an attack could not rest on the equal protection clause, which applies only to the states. Consequently, *Bolling* has a history somewhat separate from the rest, and was resolved by the Court in a separate opinion.

It was the cases decided under the rubric of *Brown* v. *Board of Education*, however, which attracted by far the greatest attention. Indeed *Brown* ranks as probably the most far-reaching and the most morally significant Supreme Court decision in American history. Invalidation of the school segregation statutes of seventeen states was the prelude by the Court to a rapid destruction of officially imposed segregation in all areas of our national life—in public parks, in recreation facilities, in transportation. But *Brown* also served as a catalyst for the modern civil rights movement, which won momentous victories over discrimination during the next decade and a half. In the longer run, the decision set off forces which produced the constitutional dilemmas of the 1970s and of today—busing and quotas. Moreover, *Brown* foreshadowed an era in which the Supreme Court under Earl Warren would exert, for better or worse, an influence on American society more profound than any exerted by the judiciary since the time of John Marshall.

Yet surprisingly enough, *Brown* does not ring with timeless eloquence. Its tone is low-key and matter-of-fact. And the legal processes which lay behind the opinion have a curiously elliptical quality to them.

Thus the practice overturned in *Brown* was one which the Court had never actually affirmed in a precedent relating specifically to education. There had never been a case up through 1952 in which the Justices heard a direct challenge to separate but equal schools, and then endorsed the validity of educational segregation. Conversely, those who sought to end separate schools in 1952 and 1953 were convinced until the eleventh hour that they could best achieve their goal by not insisting that *Plessy* be overruled.

I

To understand how this all came about, we need to go back to *Plessy* v. *Ferguson*, the wellspring of the separate but equal doctrine. *Plessy* was not an education case at all. The case involved transportation, specifically a Louisiana law which segregated blacks and whites in railway carriages. The Court's decision went well beyond the facts of the case, however, and upheld the general authority of the state to impose such segregation. Legalized separation of the races, said Justice

Henry Brown, constituted a "reasonable" form of regulation, consistent with "the established usages, customs, and traditions of the people."[1]

In fact, the "most common instance" of this recognized power, Justice Brown pointed out, "is . . . the establishment of separate schools for white and colored children."[2] The Justice called particular attention to the case of *Roberts* v. *Boston* (1849), in which the Massachusetts Supreme Court had turned aside the pleas of the great abolitionist leader (and later Senator) Charles Sumner, and upheld the validity of segregation in Boston schools. The separate but equal principle in education first emerged, then, as merely one example of a broadly accepted state power. Therefore the majority in *Plessy* did not find it necessary to examine or to expatiate upon educational separation, especially since some of Homer Plessy's lawyers drew a sharp distinction between education and transportation, essentially conceding segregation to be valid with respect to the former. Justice John Marshall Harlan's prophetic dissent in the *Plessy* case contains not a single reference to education, an ominous omission, it soon became clear.

Later decisions upholding educational segregation dealt with the general subject at least, but never with a direct challenge to the separate but equal doctrine. And their affirmation of *Plessy* was often inferential and obscure. The first of these cases, *Cummings* v. *County Board of Education* (1899), involved the refusal even to honor *Plessy*. The defendant school board in question had shut down its black high school entirely, pleading economic exigency, while maintaining support of the white high schools. The black plaintiffs in the case stayed within the confines of *Plessy*, arguing merely that they were entitled to equal treatment. Only during oral argument in the Supreme Court, when it was procedurally too late, did their attorneys challenge the legality of segregation itself. The attorneys asked as well for a rather odd remedial application of the *Plessy* standard. Instead of demanding that county officials provide a black high school equivalent to the white ones, they demanded that the white institutions also be shut down.

Justice Harlan's opinion for a unanimous Court explicitly noted that "[W]e need not consider . . . in this case . . . . the argument that the vice in the common-school system of Georgia [is] the requirement that the white and colored children of the state be educated in separate schools."[3] Harlan then rejected the plaintiffs' remedy as too extreme, since it would deprive white students of educational opportunities without doing anything to provide them for black students.

Different issues might have arisen, the Justice claimed, had the plaintiffs set out merely to compel the board of education to reestablish the black high school. Yet the deeper thrust of his opinion suggested that even a plea for separate but equal facilities would meet rejection. So long as a local school board did not act in "bad faith," he indicated, or out of an open "hostility to the colored race," the Supreme Court could not countermand its actions (despite the fact that the actions were blatantly inconsistent with *Plessy*).

> [T]he education of the people in schools maintained by state taxation is a matter belonging to the respective states, and any interference on the part of Federal authority with the management of such schools cannot be justified except in the case of a clear and unmistakable disregard of rights secured by the supreme law of the land. We have no such case to be determined.[4]

Clearly, a state or locality which was constitutionally empowered to disregard *Plessy* was empowered to act in accordance with it.

The second case testing educational segregation concerned a private institution, and nothing in its pleadings or opinions disputed *Plessy*'s applicability to public institutions. *Berea College* v. *Kentucky* (1908) involved a state statute which forbade any "person, corporation, or association"[5] from operating an integrated school. The Court upheld the statute as applied to Berea College, long a center of integrated education, because the college was a corporation and subject therefore to almost unrestricted state regulation. The majority expressed grave doubts as to whether the statute could validly be applied to individuals, or to private associations which were unincorporated, but held that these putatively unconstitutional aspects of the law were separable from its restrictions on corporate entities.

Justice Harlan dissented, arguing that the provisions of the Kentucky law were obviously inseparable from one another, served a common purpose, and that the Court was obliged therefore to strike them down together. He thought it "a reflection upon the common sense of legislators"[6] to assume that they would have prohibited a private corporation from offering integrated instruction, yet left individuals and unincorporated groups free to do so. "It was the teaching . . . of the two races *together*, . . . no matter by whom or under whose authority, which the legislature sought to prevent."[7]

The Justice went out of his way to note, however, that he was talking about Berea College, not Berea High School. "Of course, what I have said has no reference to regulations prescribed for public schools, established at the pleasure of the state and maintained at the public expense."[8]

Gong Lum v. Rice (1927) affirmed the Plessy doctrine in education more explicitly. But the plaintiff in the case wished to operate within the segregation system, rather than to challenge that system's validity. Martha Lum was a nine-year-old girl of Chinese descent whose father sought to enroll her in a white Mississippi school; officials informed him, however, that since his daughter was not a white Caucasian she must go to a black school. Gong Lum instituted a suit, claiming that his daughter had a constitutional right to be reassigned, since "she is not a member of the colored race."[9] This scarcely qualified as a ringing challenge to Plessy's underlying rationale. Still, the plaintiff was denying that a state possessed the undiluted authority to classify students by race and assign them to schools accordingly.

However, the Court, which included Oliver Wendell Holmes, Louis Brandeis, and Harlan Fiske Stone, pronounced the issue in Gong Lum old-hat, even though the Justices had never squarely examined that issue.

"Were this a new question," said Chief Justice William Howard Taft, "it would call for very full argument and consideration, but we think that it is the same question which has been many times decided to be within the constitutional power of the state. . . ."[10] The Chief Justice cited Plessy and Roberts v. Boston to support this contention, which was understandable in light of the references to them in previous cases. The fact remained that Plessy never discussed educational segregation as such, and that Roberts was decided almost twenty years before ratification of the fourteenth amendment.

II

If the doctrine of separate but equal remained judicially unexplored in the late 1920s, it loomed as a palpable reality in American education. What segregation was producing in fact was grotesque inequality. In 1929, for instance, the state of Alabama spent $36 a year per white student on schools, and $10 per black student. In Arkansas, blacks constituted 23% of the school enrollment, yet received 12% of the funds. In Florida, Georgia, and Louisiana, the ratio was more than 4 to 1 in favor of white education. That figure typified the South as a whole. In 1930, per capita expenditures for black education were only 28% of the amount spent on whites.

It was at this point that the National Association for the Advancement of Colored People (the NAACP) commenced the long legal struggle against educational segregation, the struggle which led to *Brown*—and beyond. Founded in 1909 by an alliance of civic leaders and intellectuals, both white and black, the NAACP had emerged by the 1920s as the nation's most influential voice for black Americans, and their staunchest champion in the courts. Until his retirement in 1928, the Boston aristocrat Moorfield Storey led a cadre of volunteer NAACP lawyers who carried on an incessant battle against racial injustice in America. Storey, who was the Association's first president, and a one-time president of the American Bar Association, won a series of historic victories before the Supreme Court. These included decisions which invalidated criminal convictions obtained in a lynch-mob atmosphere (*Moore* v. *Dempsey*, 1923); outlawed local ordinances creating racially-restrictive residential zoning (*Buchanan* v. *Warley*, 1917); and struck down state primary laws disenfranchising blacks by use of the infamous "grandfather clause," a provision extending suffrage only to those whose ancestors had been able to vote before 1866 (*Guinn* v. *United States*, 1915).

Beginning in 1929, the NAACP moved in a new direction. A charitable organization named the Garland Fund bestowed upon the Association a long-term grant of $100,000 (only $20,000 of which actually materialized) to finance a coordinated campaign against segregation in America, especially in elementary and secondary schools. The Fund recommended the filing of taxpayers suits in selected counties of those states which most flagrantly discriminated against black education. The suits would not actually challenge the constitutionality of state segregation laws. Complainants would demand only that local officials follow *Plessy* and correct massive educational inequalities. But the theory was that over the long run successful suits of this kind would render the cost of a dual school system so prohibitive as to cause the abolition of segregation.

However, Nathan Ross Margold, a Harvard Law School graduate chosen to shape the NAACP campaign in 1930, suggested a different approach. Margold thought county-by-county suits too time-consuming and expensive. Instead, he contended, NAACP lawyers should attack state segregation statutes directly. This did not mean that they should argue as yet that these statutes were intrinsically unconstitutional. But they could make a strong case that the statutes were invalid nonetheless, because of the blatantly discriminatory manner in which they were drafted or administered. A number of the statutes, for example, did not even mention the need for an equitable division of funds between white and black schools. Because of successful attacks on these statutes, Margold believed, southern officials would have to choose between reconstructing the entire pattern of segregated education on an equitable basis, or abandoning it as too costly.

The approach actually pursued in the 1930s and into the 1940s turned out to be more cautious and at the same time more bold than the one suggested in the Margold Report. It was the work of Charles H. Houston, who took over as the NAACP's first full-time legal counsel in 1935 (indeed at that time its entire legal staff). A product of Washington, D.C.'s middle-class black community, an honors graduate of Amherst and of the Harvard Law School, Charles Houston played a shaping and often neglected role in the struggle for legal equality in America. "He was," said one of his successors, "the Moses of [our] journey."[11]

Houston did not attack the separate but equal doctrine head-on at first; he did not contest the constitutionality of state segregation statutes—either inherently or as applied. Yet he worked on a state-wide .canvas, as the Margold Report advised. More important, his real goal from the outset was not simply equalization of facilities, though this is ostensibly what he sought. The goal was integration.

Houston could do these things because he focused his attack initially at the graduate and professional school level. There, facilities for black students often did not exist at all; and if established, they could be attacked as so irremediably inadequate as to make continued segregation impossible. Anyone could see, presumably, that it was well-nigh impossible to whip together in a short time the physical and instructional equivalent of the University of Virginia Medical School or the University of North Carolina Graduate School of Arts and Sciences. Houston's strategy meant that not only would he be filing lawsuits against a state rather than a mere city or county. Above all, the strategy would force states which maintained segregated professional education into a seemingly impossible choice: either launch extravagantly expensive crash programs to attain equality, or be vulnerable to the charge that they could never satisfy *Plessy* and must admit black students to white schools.

Houston achieved his initial success with this strategy in collabora-

tion with the man who would become his successor as NAACP Chief
Counsel in 1939. He was Thurgood Marshall, then in private practice
in Baltimore, but devoting more and more of his time to NAACP
work. Together, Houston and Marshall took on the case of Donald
Murray, a brilliant graduate of Amherst College who had applied to
the University of Maryland Law School in 1934. Despite his obvious
qualifications for admission, university officials turned him down,
citing the state's policy of educational segregation. Nor did they endeavor to establish a separate law school for him, though they did
helpfully call his attention to a state scholarship program established
the previous year to finance black students who consented to go to
school out of state. The Maryland legislature had not bothered at this
point to appropriate any money for the scholarships; but after Murray
filed his suit, they came up with $10,000 to fund a grand total of
fifty $200 grants. Three hundred eighty black students immediately
requested application forms, and 113 applications had been filed by
the time the program was three weeks old.

Murray refused to participate in the program. And at Houston's
and Marshall's urging, the trial court, and then the Maryland Court
of Appeals ruled that the "rather slender chance for any one applicant
. . . to attend an outside law school, at increased expense, falls short
of providing for students of the colored race facilities substantially
equal to those furnished to . . . whites."[12] Thus Donald Murray must
immediately be admitted to the University of Maryland Law School.

The *Murray* case was a triumph, if only in a single state court. But
in 1938 Houston carried his strategy to the Supreme Court. Appropriately enough, he got the Justices to address a question left hanging in
the *Murray* case: whether even an unlimited kitty for scholarships
justified sending black students out of their home state. Lloyd Gaines,
a black applicant to the University of Missouri Law School, was rejected, but told that he could take advantage of a statute which virtually guaranteed him funds for out-of-state study. However, Chief
Justice Evans Hughes pronounced such an arrangement unconstitutional. "[T]he obligation of the State to give the protection of equal
laws can be performed only where its laws operate," he said. "It is an
obligation the burden of which cannot be cast by one state upon
another. . . ."[13] The Gaines case, it should be noted, marked the first
time the Justices had ever seriously analyzed the issue of segregation
in public education.

Unlike Maryland, Missouri did set up an allegedly "equivalent"

black law school, in a building in St. Louis which the school shared
with a hotel and a movie theater. Houston and his colleagues now
confidently expected to spring the other prong of their trap, to prove
that the segregated law school was physically inadequate. But Lloyd
Gaines unfortunately had disappeared, and the case was never pursued. At about this time, Thurgood Marshall took over as chief counsel of the NAACP, and, for tax purposes among other things, its
legal efforts were now concentrated in a separate organization—the
NAACP Legal Defense and Educational Fund.

III

In 1946, Marshall began a case which would take to the Supreme
Court the questions left hanging by *Gaines. Sweatt* v. *Painter* originated in the Texas courts and went to a full-scale trial in 1947. The
plaintiff, Herman Marion Sweatt, had applied to the University of
Texas Law School and been rejected on racial grounds. As in Missouri, however, state officials quickly set up a separate facility for
blacks in Houston. By the time of the trial they had replaced that
one with a more elaborate arrangement in Austin. Represented by
Marshall, and some of the other lawyers who now joined him on the
NAACP's national staff, Sweatt went into state court to challenge the
legality of this alternative legal institution.

Housed in three rooms in the basement of an Austin office building,
the black school was slated to have a faculty of three instructors from
the regular University Law School for its projected enrollment of ten
students. The library contained 10,000 volumes, as opposed to 65,000
volumes in the Texas law library. This added up to a strong case of
physical inequality, but Marshall did not regard the case as entirely
unassailable. The black law school contained as much floor space per
student as the white one, and its faculty was composed after all of
Texas Law School teachers. Furthermore, students in the segregated
institution were given access to the facilities of the state law library,
which had essentially the same holdings as the Texas library. In the
rudimentary stages of providing black legal education, it now appeared, a state was not wholly precluded from claiming some sem-
blance of physical respectability—especially in a southern courtroom.

There was a deeper concern as well. Even as Marshall moved to
demonstrate concrete inequities in *Sweatt,* he and his associates were
coming to doubt that such efforts paid sufficient dividends. These
efforts might aim eventually at the destruction of Jim Crow at the

graduate level. But inherently they constituted only "a tangential approach to this legal problem," as Marshall later told a symposium at Howard University; they could not, therefore, "produce results in keeping with [the] time, effort and money expended."[14]

Because of these considerations, both tactical and strategic, Marshall placed his primary emphasis at the *Sweatt* trial on arguments which exhibited a grander sweep, though hints of these arguments could be found in earlier cases. The really decisive differences between the black law school and the white one, he now contended, went beyond physical or curricular characteristics. They involved unmeasurable but decisive aspects of legal education, which could never be divided equally between black and white students. There were, for example, extracurricular activities such as moot court and law review, clearly unavailable in a student body numbering only ten. There was the prestige in the community which radiated from the University of Texas Law School. Most important, perhaps, there was the isolation of black students from the lawyers and future judges with whom they would later have to work.

Such shortcomings, it was suggested, harmed a black student's education even more fundamentally than did inadequate buildings or library capacity. A number of eminent law school professors and deans testified on these points at the *Sweatt* trial.

Sociological evidence of this type, relatively common by 1950 in constitutional law cases, had been legitimated early in the century by the celebrated "Brandeis brief," presented to the Supreme Court in the case of *Muller* v. *Oregon* (1908). Through the use of masses of hygiene statistics and industrial reports, Louis Brandeis had persuaded the Justices to uphold an eight-hour day for women. In *Sweatt*, the sociological data buttressed the NAACP's assertion that there were intangible factors which made segregated legal training, indeed any professional training, inherently unequal, no matter what the physical facilities.

Such arguments still rested within the confines of *Plessy*, comprising in essence an end-run around separate but equal where graduate education, and possibly other forms of education, were concerned. They pointed toward the possibility that it might not be necessary to overrule *Plessy* totally in order to achieve integration of schools, simply to demonstrate the decision's inapplicability to the educational process. Yet the approach in *Sweatt* could be viewed as broadly subversive of the *Plessy* doctrine, because it dealt with evils which were endemic to the whole process of segregation.

In any event, the atmosphere of the late 1940s allowed a more candid assertion to be added to the plaintiff's cause. The quickening pace of Supreme Court decisions, the changing mood of the nation, and the shifting temper of America's black community drove Marshall and his associates in Texas to put forth the argument they had always wanted to make: that segregation in education, and by implication anywhere else in American life, was unconstitutional *per se*, that *Plessy* should be overruled.[15]

The Court's decisions since *Gaines* certainly pointed in this direction, striking ever more insistently at racial discrimination in general and Jim Crow laws in particular. Beginning in 1939, for example, the Justices effectively set aside a rule of long standing which had made it easy for states and localities to exclude blacks from juries. The rule placed upon black plaintiffs who were contesting such treatment the heavy, not to say impossible burden of proving that their exclusion resulted from deliberate discriminatory acts by government officials.

But in *Pierre* v. *Louisiana* (306 US 354), and later in *Hill* v. *Texas* (316 US 400, 1942), the Justices reversed the current. They ruled that a total absence of blacks from juries over a long period of time created a strong presumption of racial discrimination, and this presumption shifted to the state the burden of proving that its acts were *not* discriminatory.

In 1944, the Court overturned a precedent of less than a decade's standing and outlawed the stratagem which had replaced the "grandfather clause" as the South's leading device for restricting black suffrage in state elections, the white primary. This contrivance flowed from the notion that the Democratic party in the South was actually a private organization, akin to a country club, and could pick and choose the members who participated in its affairs. The party "chose," of course, to exclude all blacks from the Democrats' intramural election, the only one which mattered in southern politics. The Justices had actually sanctioned this constitutional ruse in the 1936 case of *Grovey* v. *Townsend* (295 US 45). But in *Smith* v. *Allwright* (321 US 649), they held that because primaries were the prelude to a general election scheme endorsed by the state, with choices in that election limited effectively to party nominees, the discriminatory practices of a political party equated with the action of the state itself.

The Court was even beginning to erode *Plessy* directly, in the area of its primary relevance. In *Morgan* v. *Virginia* (328 US 373, 1946), an eight-man majority struck down a Virginia statute requiring buses engaged in interstate transportation to institute segregation once they crossed state lines—though Justice Stanley Reed's opinion in the case relied on the commerce clause rather than the fourteenth amendment to achieve its end. The plethora of state Jim Crow laws, Justice Reed argued, interfered with the uniformity and free flow of interstate commerce. (Reed cited as precedent for his position the 1878 case of *Hall* v. *DeCuir* (95 US 485), in which the Court had invalidated as an invasion of the commerce power a Louisiana law *prohibiting* racial discrimination in all public carriers which entered the state.)

Even when racial categories were permitted, the Court expressed its distaste for them. During World War II, a majority upheld as a matter of military necessity the disgraceful program which sanctioned the deportation of Japanese-American citizens from California to internment camps in other states. But the Justices went out of their way to note that as a general rule distinctions based upon race or national origin were "odious to a free people whose institutions are founded upon the doctrine of equality." Such distinctions "are immediately suspect," and the "courts must subject them to the most rigid scrutiny."[16]

The Japanese exclusion issue concerned federal law, and therefore did not involve analysis under the equal protection clause. But the Justices had conveyed an unmistakable attitude toward racial categories, which was potentially relevant to any aspect of future constitutional adjudication. Normally the fourteenth amendment standard for judging legislative classifications by the states which meted out disparate treatment to individuals or groups was the so-called rational basis test: if there was any reasonable explanation for the dissimilar treatment, if it was plausibly related to a valid legislative end, the classification was constitutional. (An obvious example of a valid classification would be one singling out the visually impaired for special drivers' tests.) The Court was now suggesting, however, that racial distinctions would be judged by a harsher, more suspicious standard.

The most important of the Court's equal protection decisions during the 1940s was *Shelley* v. *Kraemer* (1948). A unanimous vote of the six Justices who participated in the case held that the fourteenth amendment barred state courts from enforcing restrictive covenants on property—deeds which precluded an owner from selling that prop-

erty to blacks, or to other racial or religious groups. Judicial enforcement of the covenants, said Chief Justice Fred Vinson, constituted
"state action . . . in the full and complete sense of the phrase," use
of "the full panoply of state power."[17] In granting such enforcement a
state was clearly denying the equal protection of the laws. The Chief
Justice's facile definition of "state action" mystified even constitutional
scholars sympathetic to the Court's result. But the outcome was an
unmistakable triumph for racial equality.

Shelley's significance lay not only in the Supreme Court's disposal
of the case. The executive branch chose the occasion to come openly
to the support of black America. Solicitor General Phillip Perlman
filed a legal memorandum in *Shelley* urging the destruction of restrictive covenants. This was partly in response to a path-breaking report,
To Secure These Rights, issued by President Truman's Committee on
Civil Rights at the end of 1947. The report called for the end of
legally-enforced segregation in American life, and specifically urged
the Department of Justice to intervene in the *Shelley* case.

Such actions showed a heightened sensitivity on the part of the
Truman administration to the tragedy of racial discrimination, a sensitivity greater than that ultimately displayed by its predecessor. Indeed
the President's support for civil rights helped precipitate a southern
walk-out at the 1948 Democratic convention and the organization of
a regional third party, the so-called "Dixiecrats," under the leadership
of Gov. Strom Thurmond of South Carolina. The subsequent election
highlighted the importance of the President's black support, which
aided him enormously in his upset victory over Thomas E. Dewey.

Meanwhile in 1944, the Swedish economist and sociologist Gunnar
Myrdal brought forth his classic indictment of American racism, gran-
diose in its scope, pitiless in its accumulation of detail. Critics hailed
An American Dilemma from the time of its publication as "the most
penetrating and important book on our contemporary American civili-
zation that has been written." In the book, said sociologist Robert
Lynd, "We Americans are revealed clad in our patchwork 'American
Way,' attempting to live along with the vast and ugly reality of what
Dr. Myrdal calls our 'greatest failure.'"[18]

IV

None of these factors transforming American life moved the trial
court in Texas, which held the black law school to be substantially equal
to the University's facility. Therefore in 1950—the year of Charles

Houston's death—Thurgood Marshall carried to the Supreme Court what was essentially a three-layered argument against segregation.

The top layer of Marshall's written brief for the Court consisted of the declaration that *Plessy* v. *Ferguson* must be overruled. *Plessy's* unconstitutional application to legal training, he argued, comprised but one example of how utterly grotesque were its assertions of the "reasonableness" of separate but equal. The Court had insinuated that racial categories were seldom if ever consistent with the fourteenth amendment, that they must pass a test sterner than mere rational basis. But "[e]ven if we assume . . . that there are circumstances in which a state has the power to make race or color the basis of a legislative classification *(a proposition which we reject in its entirety)*," the classification perpetrated by Texas *"bears no rational relationship to any valid legislative end,* and hence constitutes that form of differential treatment which contravenes the equal protection clause."[19] Clearly, such reasoning applied to many things besides law schools.

The brief's general indictment of segregation drew upon Myrdal and other social scientists, as well as upon the President's civil rights report. "[T]he most irrevocable and deleterious effect of segregation . . . is that it imposes a badge of inferiority upon the segregated group. . . . , recognized not only by the minority group, but by society at large. [Gunnar] Myrdal has pointed out . . . 'Booker T. Washington's famous remark, that the white man could not hold the Negro in the gutter without getting in there himself.'"[20]

Not only had *Plessy* set up a system of racial separation which inherently violated the equal protection of the laws. The system was also one in which the promise of separate but equal would always remain a myth, never attainable in actual fact. Gross inequalities were especially visible in higher education, but they abounded in all segregated institutions. "[T]hat physical equality has not resulted, when the 'separate but equal' doctrine has been applied, is no accident. Segregation is grounded in a belief in Negro inferiority."[21] Thus, "If this Court considers *Plessy* v. *Ferguson* applicable here, that case should now be reexamined and overruled."[22]

Yet Marshall's argument also contained a bottom layer which conformed totally with *Plessy*, because it centered on those physical inequalities which segregation was said inevitably to produce. The plaintiffs continued to press their claim that the black law school in Texas fell short of the University in plant, library, and faculty. "The Negro school . . . opened [only] in March, 1947 and was not accredited by any agency. . . . It [is] freely admitted that 'there is no fair comparison in monetary value' between the two schools. "[23]

In between the top and bottom layers, Marshall lodged those arguments which showed how unimportant physical equality really was, arguments which undercut more broadly *Plessy's* applicability to graduate education, perhaps to education in general, though still without calling for its demise. A group called the Committee of Law Teachers Against Segregation in Legal Education articulated especially well the intangible harms of forced separation, in a memorandum which they filed with the Court.

> If . . . legal education is something alive and vital; if the measure is not cubic feet of air space but the intellectual atmosphere within the walls; . . . if education is in large part association; if research and practice are part of the job of legal training—if any of these things, then certainly Texas (colored) is a mockery of legal education and of the equal protection of the laws. . . . By sending Sweatt to a raw, new law school without alumni or prestige, Texas deprives him of economic opportunity which its white students have. [24]

"In making this argument," the law professors noted, "*Plessy* v. *Ferguson* becomes our direct support. "[25]

A unanimous Supreme Court affirmed this middle approach. The Justices refused to reach Marshall's contention "that Plessy v. Ferguson should be reexamined in the light of contemporary knowledge respecting . . . the effects of racial segregation. "[26] But Chief Justice Vinson's opinion stressed that not only was the black law school inferior to the University of Texas in tangible, physical terms. "What is more important, the University of Texas Law School possesses to a far greater degree those qualities which are incapable of objective measurement but which make for greatness in a law school. "[27] Such qualities included the eminence of the faculty, the clout of the alumni, prestige in the community, tradition, and the like. These differences precluded the possibility that anyone "who had a free choice between [the] law schools would consider the question close. "[28] It was now inconceivable that separate legal education, or graduate education of any kind, would ever pass constitutional muster, because the Court had concentrated for the first time on the inherent inequalities between educational institutions, and in a broader sense on the reality of segregation itself.

The companion case to *Sweatt* focused even more directly on segregation in the raw. George McLaurin was a 68-year-old doctoral candidate in education, whom state officials had reluctantly admitted to the University of Oklahoma Graduate School. Potentially then, he enjoyed access to the same advantages, tangible and intangible, with which white students were favored. But the state decreed that his education within the University must proceed "upon a segregated basis."[29] He was required to sit at a desk in an anteroom outside his classrooms, was given a segregated library carrel in the mezzanine, behind a load of newspapers, and ate in the University cafeteria at a different hour from the white students.

The Court unanimously condemned these practices, which unquestionably "handicapped" McLaurin in his quest for an education. "Such restrictions impair and inhibit his ability to study, to engage in discussions and exchange views with other students, and, in general, to learn his profession. . . . State-imposed restrictions which produce such inequalities cannot be sustained."[30]

But here the inequality which the Justices identified did not lie in prevalence of books or access to faculty, nor even in the differences of prestige and tradition which inhered between institutions physically separated by race. The inequality consisted of the harm which flows from the *very act* of segregating a minority from a dominant majority.

In yet a third case, argued along with *Sweatt* and *McLaurin*, the Court also condemned segregation directly, though reverting to the commerce clause in order to do so. The unanimous decision in *Henderson* v. *United States* (339 US 816) outlawed forced separation of the races in the dining car facilities of railroads engaged in interstate commerce. The United States Government used the three cases to cross the Rubicon on segregation. Having condemned the specific practice of restrictive covenants in *Shelley*, the Solicitor General now filed memoranda which called flatly for the overturning of *Plessy*, in education and elsewhere.

The Court's triple-barreled charge of 1950 convinced many observers that such an action loomed ahead. Some even pronounced it an accomplished fact. "[S]egregation as a way of life is clearly doomed,"[31] said *The New Republic* magazine. The editors of the *Alabama Law Review* concluded that despite the failure of *Sweatt* and *McLaurin* to confront *Plessy*, "the attitude of the Court must be interpreted definitely to be that segregation is unconstitutional *per se*."[32]

V

In the meantime, events were not proceeding as dramatically with regard to elementary and secondary education. During the decade of the 1940s, Marshall and his colleagues on the NAACP national staff were hesitant about attacking segregation on the public school level. This was because the same kind of equalization suit which had proved so successful in *Gaines* and *Murray* took on different implications when applied to grade schools or high schools. Suits concerning these schools proceeded against only a single county or town, as Nathan Margold had pointed out. And whatever its long-term effect might be, the demand for equalization of facilities and of curriculum in a fourth-grade or a ninth-grade setting usually constituted an attempt to achieve just that and nothing more, not to break down the barrier of segregation by oblique means.

It was more readily possible, of course, to provide equal educational resources in a county junior high school than in a state medical college. Faced with gross inequalities in a local system, therefore, southern judges might be persuaded to order equalization of facilities, precisely because to do so would avoid admitting black youngsters to white schools, would preserve the barrier of *Plessy*. At the public school level, equalization was not the weapon for integration which it was in graduate school litigation.

Nonetheless, assessing the realities of the South in the 1940s and the desperate needs of black school children, a number of local NAACP leaders and attorneys accepted equalization suits as an interim strategy, even though these suits would fall short of the results in *Murray* and *Gaines,* and would fail to mount the kind of general attack on state segregation statutes contemplated under the Margold approach. Activity centered in Virginia, where Spottswood Robinson, the NAACP special counsel in the state, and his law partner, Oliver Hill, carried a heavy load of equalization cases.

Marshall and his staff helped to supervise and to finance some of the equalization efforts. Yet the national organization displayed negative feelings toward these suits. Indeed the annual conference of the NAACP stated flatly in 1948 that "it is our policy . . . not [to] undertake any case or cooperate in any case" which recognized "the validity of segregation statutes," or which sanctioned the continuation of "segregated public facilities." Equalization suits in public schools, lawyers were told the next year, must encompass the demand that the only acceptable remedy for the inequalities which they documented was "admission of blacks to white schools." Furthermore, "in each instance," such suits "should make a direct challenge of the segregation statutes involved."[33]

The national staff did push the concept of equalization in the area of teachers' salaries; as early as 1940 Marshall had won a major victory decreeing that school authorities must pay black teachers on the same basis as white teachers (*Alston* v. *School Board of Norfolk*, 112 F.2d 992.) Furthermore, equalization suits at the undergraduate level moved forward with the expectation that they, like graduate school suits, would actually lead to integration. In 1949, Assistant NAACP Counsel Jack Greenberg joined with local lawyers in Delaware to challenge the reality of separate but equal at Delaware State College. This resulted in a state court decision, issued just after *Sweatt* and *McLaurin*, ordering integration at the University of Delaware, the first decision anywhere which breached the segregation barrier in undergraduate education. Up to 1950, however, the NAACP national staff held back from public school litigation.

But after *Sweatt* and *McLaurin*, the picture changed. Everything now pointed toward a direct constitutional assault on *Plessy's* last educational bastion. The graduate school decisions seemed to strike at the heart of all Jim Crow practices. Their logic certainly encouraged the expectation of a judgment declaring *Plessy* totally unsuitable to education. Indeed constitutional law professors would ask their students in later years, "After *Sweatt* and *McLaurin*, was there anything left for the Court to decide in *Brown?*"[34]

Yet the decision to proceed with a direct attack did not come automatically. The *institutional* gap between a decree outlawing segregation in graduate school and one outlawing it in grade school was still "appallingly wide"; and according to his friend, Professor Alfred Kelly, Thurgood Marshall initially doubted that he and his associates "could cross" such a gap.[35] Failure to move, however, meant reliance on the vain hope that equalization of educational opportunity would ever occur under segregation.

In July of 1950, therefore, Marshall convened an NAACP conference to set up "the legal machinery" for an "all-out attack" on segregated education.[36] Equalization suits which countenanced permanent separation of the races ceased to be a live option. Admission of individual blacks to white schools would be urged only as a last resort, with lower court decisions to that effect subject to the right of appeal. Destruction of state segregation statutes was the goal. Said Marshall, "[W]e are going to insist on nonsegregation in American public education from top to bottom—from law school to kindergarten."[37]

The three-layered strategy of *Sweatt* and *McLaurin* would form the mode of operation for the test cases which developed over the next year. Marshall and his colleagues planned to persist, quite naturally, in the argument that *Plessy* should be overruled in regard to education (and to everything else), because racial classifications were patently unreasonable, and equality unattainable while they existed. On the other hand, complainants were certain to discover in many instances gross physical inequities in the facilities for white and black students; if all else failed, they could demand integration as the only efficacious and immediately available remedy for that condition.

But the greatest emphasis, especially at the trial phase of the cases, would be directed toward a final extension of *Sweatt* and *McLaurin*. After some hesitation, Marshall, prodded by his chief assistant, Robert Carter, decided to place a heavy weight on documenting the proposition that segregation in grade school and high school, no less than law school, inflicted harm upon black students which went beyond the mere lack of physical amenities. Many of these disadvantages were obviously the same at all educational levels, especially isolation from the majority group and lack of prestige in the community. But it was possible to strike new themes in the public school context. During the *Sweatt* trial, Marshall had produced powerful testimony from sociology professor Robert Redfield of the University of Chicago, who articulated the overwhelming opinion of the scientific community: "[D]ifferences in intellectual capacity or inability to learn have not been shown to exist as between negroes and whites. . . ."[38] To demonstrate, therefore, that segregation was responsible in part for the lower achievement averages of black youngsters, that it retarded their ability to learn and damaged their personalities, could kill off *Plessy* in the field of education, without the need for a formal interment.

The intellectual mechanisms for implementing such an approach were left over from the graduate school cases. The plaintiffs had only to retool them for their final job. As Professor Mark Tushnet puts it in his brilliant analysis of NAACP legal strategy, "[Their lawyers] had only to substitute a few experts in child psychology for a few experts in the legal profession, and the structure of the desegregation cases would be complete."[39]

Defense lawyers would deride this social science testimony as "pseudo-science," and as "psychology (or sociology), not law." They were not the only people who tended toward such a view. Members of the NAACP legal team, augmented for the school cases by a battery of prominent attorneys and legal scholars, expressed skepticism about the use of a myriad of psychologists, psychiatrists, and sociologists at trial.

One of the authors of the NAACP's Supreme Court brief in *Brown v. Board of Education* later admitted that in characterizing some of the psychological evidence, "I may have used the word 'crap'. . . . I didn't want us to build our case on a gimmick."[40]

But Marshall argued that in utilizing the testimony of social scientists, he was simply following standard trial procedures. "I told the staff," he said, "that we had to try this case just like any other one in which you would try to prove damages to your client. If your car ran over my client, you'd have to pay up, and my function as an attorney would be to put experts on the stand to testify to how much damage was done. We needed exactly that kind of evidence in the school cases."[41]

Notes

[1]*Plessy* v. *Ferguson*, 163 US 537 (1896), at 550.

[2]*Ibid.*, at 544.

[3]*Cumming* v. *County Board of Education*, 175 US 528 (1899), at 543.

[4]*Ibid.*, at 545.

[5]*Berea College* v. *Kentucky*, 211 US 45 (1908), at 54.

[6]*Ibid.*, at 62.

[7]*Ibid.*

[8]*Ibid.*, at 69.

[9]*Gong Lum* v. *Rice*, 275 US 78 (1927), at 81.

[10]*Ibid.*, at 86.

[11]Quoted in Herbert Hill and Jack Greenberg, *Citizen's Guide to Desegregation* (Boston, 1955), frontispiece.

[12]*University of Maryland* v. *Murray*, 169 Md. 478, at 487.

[13]*Missouri ex rel. Gaines* v. *Canada*, 305 US 337, at 350.

[14]Thurgood Marshall, "An Evaluation of Recent Efforts to Achieve Racial Integration in Education Through Resort to the Courts," *Journal of Negro Education* (Vol. 21, 1952), 316, 318.

[15]These arguments concerning intangible differences in legal education and the inherent unconstitutionality of racial categories were put forward during this same period in another case, *Sipuel* v. *Board of Regents of the University of Oklahoma*, 332 US 631 (later named *Fisher* v. *Hurst*, 333 US 147). Indeed it was in *Sipuel* that Marshall first presented the Supreme Court with the argument that segregation was unconstitutional *per se*—in February 1948. The Court did not address this argument, however, because the original complaint in the case had been predicated upon the separate but equal theory of *Gaines*. And at that point in the procedural posture of *Sipuel*, the state of Oklahoma had not yet set up its separate law school. In any event,

Marshall does not seem to have regarded the efforts in *Sipuel* as adequate. In his Howard University address, he speaks of *Sweatt* as the "first case filed in this program" of launching "an all out attack against segregation in public education," 319, 318.

[16]*Hirabayashi v. United States*, 320 US 81 (1943), at 100 (Chief Justice Stone); *Korematsu v. United States*, 323 US 214 (1944), at 216 (Justice Black).

[17]*Shelley v. Kraemer*, 334 US1 (1948), at 19.

[18]Robert S. Lynd, "Prison for American Genius," *Saturday Review of Literature*, Vol. 27, No. 5 (April 22, 1944), p. 5.

[19]*Brief for Petitioner, Sweatt v. Painter*, p. 9, (Italics added).

[20]*Ibid.*, pp. 27–28.

[21]*Ibid.*, p. 67.

[22]*Ibid.*, p. 52.

[23]*Ibid.*, p. 71.

[24]*Brief of Amicus Curiae, Sweatt v. Painter*, pp. 29, 28.

[25]*Ibid.*, p. 22.

[26]*Sweatt v. Painter*, 339 US 631 (1950), at 636.

[27]*Ibid.*, at 634.

[28]*Ibid.*

[29]*McLaurin v. Oklahoma State Regents*, 339 US 637 (1950), at 639–40.

[30]*Ibid.*, at 641.

[31]*The New Republic*, Vol. 122, No. 25 (June 19, 1950), p. 4.

[32]Note, *Alabama Law Review* (Vol. 3, 1950), 181, 182.

[33]Quoted in Mark Tushnet, *The NAACP's Legal Strategy Against Segregated Education, 1925–1950* (Chapel Hill, 1987), p. 115.

[34]Stone, Seidman, Sunstein, Tushnet, *Constitutional Law* (Boston, 1986), p. 461.

[35]Alfred H. Kelly, "The School Desegregation Case," in John Garraty, editor, *Quarrels That Have Shaped the Constitution* (New York, 1987), p. 321.

[36]Quoted in Tushnet, p. 136.

[37]*Ibid.*

[38]*Record of Trial, Sweatt v. Painter*, p. 193.

[39]Tushnet, p. 141.

[40]Quoted in Richard Kluger, *Simple Justice* (New York, 1975), p. 555.

[41]*Ibid.*, p. 316.

PART ONE

Prelude:
The Forebears
of *Brown*

I.
Charles Sumner: Argument in *Roberts* v. *City of Boston* (1849)

IN THE 1840s, the state of Massachusetts was moving to efface the racial prejudice so eloquently denounced by abolitionist reformers such as William Lloyd Garrison. The law forbidding intermarriage was repealed in 1843, and railroads were forced to abandon segregation. Separate schools were also abolished in most of the state.

But the city of Boston held on grimly to its segregated educational system. A separate school had first been established there in 1798 at the urging of black parents, who argued that otherwise prejudice would prevent their children from attending school at all. Supported at first by private donations, because the city refused to fund it, the black institution was eventually enfolded into the public school system.

In 1846, Boston's black community, urged on by the Massachusetts Anti-Slavery Society, petitioned the school committee to do away with segregated education. But over the dissent of two of its abolitionist members, the committee refused.

In response, Benjamin Roberts, one of the black leaders in the battle against segregation, challenged the constitutionality of the school committee's policy. Four times Roberts had attempted to enroll his daughter in a white elementary school, and each time her application was rejected, notwithstanding the fact that she passed five white schools on the way to the segregated one.

The decision in *Roberts* v. *City of Boston* (59 Mass. 198) was written by Chief Justice Lemuel Shaw of the Massachusetts Supreme Court, one of the towering figures of nineteenth century American jurisprudence. In upholding the school committee's power to segregate, Chief

3

Justice Shaw was the first to enunciate, at least with regard to education, the principle which animated *Plessy* v. *Ferguson:* authorities could separate children by race so long as facilities were provided for them on an equal basis. But Charles Sumner, soon to embark upon his historic career in the United States Senate, provided a classic rejoinder to the separate but equal doctrine, one which anticipated with remarkable prescience some of the arguments presented by the lawyers in *Brown.*

Long before *Brown* or *Plessy,* however, the matter of school segregation was moot in Boston. A Massachusetts statute of 1855 abolished such practices totally in the Commonwealth.

EQUALITY BEFORE THE LAW*

Separate Schools Are in The Nature of Caste

The separation of children in the Schools, on account of race or color, is in the nature of *Caste,* and, on this account, a violation of Equality. The case shows expressly that the child was excluded from the school nearest to her dwelling . . . "on the sole ground of color." The . . . Report presented to the School Committee . . . presents the grounds of this discrimination with more fulness, saying, "It is one of *races,* not of *colors* merely. The distinction is one which the All-wise Creator has seen fit to establish; and it is founded deep in the physical, mental, and moral natures of the two races. No legislation, no social customs, can efface this distinction." Words cannot be chosen more apt than these to describe the heathenish relation of Caste. . . .

Strange that here, under a State Constitution declaring the Equality of all men, we should follow the worst precedents and establish among us a Caste. Seeing the discrimination in this light, we learn to appreciate its true character. In India, Brahmins and Sudras, from generation to generation, were kept apart. If a Sudra presumed to sit upon a Brahmin's carpet, his punishment was banishment. With similar inhumanity here, the black child who goes to sit on the same benches with the white is banished, not indeed from the country, but from the school. In both cases it is the triumph of Caste. But the offence is greater with us, because, unlike the Hindoos, we acknowledge that men are born equal. . . .

---

*Reprinted in Charles Sumner, *Works* (Boston, 1900), Vol. 3, pp. 51–100.

Separate School Not an Equivalent for Common School

But it is said that the School Committee, in thus classifying the children, have not violated any principle of Equality, inasmuch as they provide a school with competent instructors for colored children, where they have advantages equal to those provided for white children. It is argued, that, in excluding colored children from Common Schools open to white children, the Committee furnish an *equivalent*. . . .

[I]n point of fact the separate school is not an equivalent. We have already seen that it . . . inflict[s] upon child and parent the stigma of Caste. Still further,—and this consideration cannot be neglected,—the matters taught in the two schools may be precisely the same, but a school exclusively devoted to one class must differ essentially in spirit and character from that Common School known to the law, where all classes meet together in Equality. It is a mockery to call it an equivalent.

3. But there is yet another answer. Admitting that it is an equivalent, still the colored children cannot be compelled to take it. Their rights are found in Equality before the Law; nor can they be called to renounce one jot of this. They have an equal right with white children to the Common Schools. A separate school, though well endowed, would not secure to them that precise Equality which they would enjoy in the Common Schools. The Jews in Rome are confined to a particular district called the Ghetto, and in Frankfort to a district known as the Jewish Quarter. It is possible that their accommodations are as good as they would be able to occupy, if left free to choose throughout Rome and Frankfort; but this compulsory segregation from the mass of citizens is of itself an *inequality* which we condemn. It is a vestige of ancient intolerance directed against a despised people. It is of the same character with the separate schools in Boston. . . .

Evils of Separate Schools

But it is said that these separate schools are for the benefit of both colors, and of the Public Schools. In similar spirit Slavery is sometimes said to be for the benefit of master and slave, and of the country where it exists. There is a mistake in the one case as great as in the other. This is clear. Nothing unjust, nothing ungenerous, can be for the benefit of any person or any thing. . . . The whites themselves are injured by the separation. Who can doubt this? With the Law as their monitor, they are taught to regard a portion of the human family, children of God, created in his image, coequals in his love, as a separate and degraded class; they are taught practically to deny that grand revelation of Christianity, the Brotherhood of Man. Hearts, while yet tender with childhood, are hardened, and ever afterward testify to this legalized uncharitableness. Nursed in the sentiments of Caste, receiving it with the earliest food of knowledge, they are unable to eradicate it from their natures. . . . Their characters are debased, and they become less fit for the duties of citizenship. . . .

Who can say that this does not injure the blacks? Theirs, in its best estate, is an unhappy lot. A despised class, blasted by prejudice and shut out from various opportunities, they feel this proscription from the Common Schools as a peculiar brand. Beyond this, it deprives them of those healthful, animating influences which would come from participation in the studies of their white brethren. It adds to their discouragements. It widens their separation from the community, and postpones that great day of reconciliation which is yet to come.

The whole system of Common Schools suffers also. It is a narrow perception of their high aim which teaches that they are merely to furnish an equal amount of knowledge to all, and therefore, provided all be taught, it is of little consequence where and in what company. The law contemplates not only that all shall be taught, but that *all* shall be taught *together*. They are not only to receive equal quantities of knowledge, but all are to receive it in the same way. All are to approach the same common fountain together; nor can there be any exclusive source for individual or class. The school is the little world where the child is trained for the larger world of life. It is the microcosm preparatory to the macrocosm, and therefore it must cherish and develop the virtues and the sympathies needed in the larger world. And since, according to our institutions, all classes, without distinction of color, meet in the performance of civil duties, so should they all, without distinction of color, meet in the school, beginning there those relations of Equality which the Constitution and Laws promise to all. . . .

But the colored children, placed apart in separate schools, are deprived of this peculiar advantage. Nothing is more clear than that the welfare of classes, as well as of individuals, is promoted by mutual acquaintance. Prejudice is the child of ignorance. It is sure to prevail, where people do not know each other. Society and intercourse are means established by Providence for human improvement. They remove antipathies, promote mutual adaptation and conciliation, and establish relations of reciprocal regard. Whoso sets up barriers to these thwarts the ways of Providence, crosses the tendencies of human nature, and directly interferes with the laws of God.

II.
Plessy v. *Ferguson* (1896): The Bad Seed

SEGREGATION OF THE races in transportation facilities did not take hold at once in the post-Reconstruction South. It was not until the late 1880s that legislation of this sort was passed, beginning with Florida in 1887. Louisiana's law ordering blacks to ride in separate railroad cars was passed in 1890; separation was required irrespective of whether the passenger's destination was out of state or within Louisiana itself.

The black community of New Orleans, the most cosmopolitan and educated in the South, mounted a legal challenge to the statute. The Citizens' Committee to Test the Constitutionality of the Separate Car Law raised $1,500 during 1891, and engaged as counsel one of the legendary figures of the Reconstruction era. Albion Tourgée had been a key figure in the Republican carpetbagger regime of North Carolina, serving for six years as a state judge. Beginning in 1879, he had published half a dozen novels about his Reconstruction experiences, most notably A *Fool's Errand*. Tourgée, who served without fee in the Louisiana case, was assisted by a New Orleans lawyer, James C. Walker.

Walker preferred to challenge the Louisiana law as an unconstitutional regulation of interstate commerce, and a test case was brought involving a black passenger who held a ticket for Mobile, Alabama. But before this controversy could come to trial, the issue it posed was abruptly settled. A state supreme court decision in a wholly independent case declared the segregation statute invalid insofar as it applied to interstate travel.

Tourgée and Walker now moved to attack the statute as a violation of the equal protection clause. On June 7, 1892, Homer Adolph

Plessy, who was an octoroon (seven-eighths Caucasian and one-eighth African blood), boarded the East Louisiana Railroad bound for Covington, Louisiana, and seated himself in the white coach. He was arrested for explicitly refusing to move to the black car, though people of his complexion were in fact seldom bothered by railway officials. This suggests that the East Louisiana Railroad was cooperating in bringing the test case. The railroads generally opposed the segregation law because of the additional expense it entailed.

The statute was initially upheld by Judge John H. Ferguson of the New Orleans Criminal Court. When Tourgée and Walker appealed his decision to the Louisiana Supreme Court in late 1892, the case took the name of *Plessy* v. *Ferguson* (163 US 537). The state supreme court also affirmed the law, and after a delay of three years *Plessy* v. *Ferguson* reached the United States Supreme Court.

Tourgée filed the principal brief in behalf of the plaintiff, but he was joined in the Supreme Court by Samuel F. Phillips, an old friend from North Carolina and a former Solicitor General of the United States. (James Walker also filed a supplemental brief.)

All of these documents convey the searing sense of humiliation which black Americans felt in the presence of segregation (although Phillips' brief did concede the possible validity of segregated education). The lawyers for Homer Plessy were under no illusions as to what lay behind the demand for racial separation.

In contrast, Justice Henry Brown's majority opinion in *Plessy* indulged the illusions of those who saw segregation as a "benefit" to both races. The celebrated dissent of Justice John Marshall Harlan, however, echoes the sentiments of Tourgée and Phillips.

1. Brief for Plaintiff—Albion Tourgée*

IV

The plaintiff . . . contends that the provisions authorizing the officers of a train to require parties to occupy the particular cars or compartments set apart for distinct races, is a statutory grant of authority to interfere with natural domestic rights of the most sacred character.

A man may be white and his wife colored; a wife may be white and her children colored. Has the State the right to compel the husband

---

*Reprinted in Kurland and Casper (eds.), *Landmark Briefs and Arguments of the Supreme Court* (Arlington, Va., 1975, Vol. 13, pp. 27–63.)

to ride in one car and the wife in another? Or to assign the mother to one car and the children to another? Yet this is what the statute in question requires. In our case, it does not appear that the plaintiff may not have had with him a wife belonging to the other race, or children differing with him in the color of their skins? Has a State the right to order the mother to ride in one car and her young daughter, because her cheek may have a darker tinge, to ride alone in another? Yet such things as these, the act in question not only permits, but actually requires and commands to be done under penalty of fine and imprisonment, for failure or neglect. Are the courts of the United States to hold such things to be within the purview of a State's right to impose on citizens of the United States? . . .

IX

The prime essential of all citizenship is *equality* of personal right and the *free* and secure enjoyment of all public privileges. These are the very essence of citizenship in all free governments.

A law assorting the citizens of a State in the enjoyment of a public franchise on the basis of race, is obnoxious to the spirit of republican institutions, because it is a legalization of *caste*. Slavery was the very essence of caste; the climax of unequal conditions. The citizen held the highest political rank attainable in the republic: the slave was the lowest grade of existence. ALL rights and privileges attached to the one; the other had *no legal rights*, either of person or property. Between them stood that strange nondescript, the "free person of color," who had such rights only as the white people of the state where he resided saw fit to confer upon him, but he could neither become a citizen of the United States *nor of any State*. The effect of the words of the XIVth Amendment, was to put *all* these classes on *the same level of right*, as *citizens*; and to make this Court the final arbiter and custodian of these rights. The effect of a law distinguishing between citizens as to race, in the enjoyment of a public franchise, is to legalize caste and restore, in part at least, the inequality of right which was an essential incident of slavery. . . .

XV

. . . . The act in question . . . . is an act of race discrimination pure and simple. The experience of the civilized world proves that it is not a matter of public health or morals, but simply a matter intended to re-introduce the caste-ideal on which slavery rested. The court will take notice of a fact inseparable from human nature, that, when the law distinguishes between the civil rights or privileges of two classes, it always is and always must be , to the detriment of the weaker class or race. A dominant race or class does not demand or enact class-distinctions for the sake of the weaker but for their own pleasure or enjoyment. This is not an act to secure *equal* privileges; these were already enjoyed under the law as it previously existed. The object of such a law is simply to debase and distinguish against the inferior race. Its purpose has been properly interpreted by the general designation of "Jim Crow Car" law. Its object is to separate the Negroes from the whites in public conveyances for the gratification and recognition of the sentiment of white superiority and white supremacy of right and power. . . .

XVII

. . . . The act in question . . . proceeds upon the hypothesis that the State has the right to authorize and require the officers of a railway to assort the citizens who engage passage on its lines, according to race, *and to punish the citizen if he refuses to submit to such assortment.*

The gist of our case is the unconstitutionality of the assortment; *not* the question of equal accommodation. . . . We insist that the State has no right to compel us to ride in a car "set apart" for a particular race, whether it is as good as another or not. Suppose the provisions were that one of these cars should be painted white and the other black; the invidiousness of the distinction would not be any greater than that provided by the act.

But if the State has a right to distinguish between citizens according to race in the enjoyment of public privilege, by compelling them to ride in separate coaches, what is to prevent the application of the same principle to other relations? Why may it not require all red-headed people to ride in a separate car? Why not require all colored people to walk on one side of the street and the whites on the other? Why may it not require every white man's house to be painted white and every colored man's black? Why may it not require every white man's vehicle to be of one color and compel the colored citizen to use one of different color on the highway? Why not require every white business man to use a white sign and every colored man who solicits custom a black one? One side of the street may be just as good as the other and the dark horses, coaches, clothes and signs may be as good or better than the white ones. The question is not as to the *equality* of the privileges enjoyed, but *the right of the State to label one citizen as white and another as colored* in the common enjoyment of a public highway as this court has often decided a railway to be. . . .

XIX

The criminal liability of the individual is not affected by inequality of accommodations.

While the act requires the accommodations for the white and black races to be "equal but separate," it by no means follows as a fact that they always are so. [T]he man who should refuse to go out of a clean and comfortable car into one reeking with filth at the behest of the conductor, would under this act be equally guilty of misdemeanor as if both were of equal desirability. . . . Equal or not equal, the refusal to obey the conductor's behest constitutes a crime. There is no averment in this case of equality of accommodation, but merely that the Plaintiff in Error was assigned "to the coach reserved for the race to which he the said Homer A. Plessy belonged" and that he "did then and there unlawfully insist on going into a coach to which by race he did not belong."

It does not appear to what race he belonged or what coach he entered, but . . . it is asserted that he did not belong to the *same race as the coach*. It is not asserted that the coach to which he was assigned was equal in accommodation to the one which it is alleged he committed a crime in entering. . . .

XX

The exception which is made in section four of the Act in question should not be passed over without consideration: "Nothing in this act shall be construed as applying to nurses attending children of the other race."

The court will take notice of the fact that if there are any cases in the state of Louisiana in which nurses of the white race are employed to take charge of children of the colored race, they are so few that it is not necessary to consider them as a class actually intended to be favored by this exception. Probably there is not a single instance of such relation in the state. What then is the force and effect of this provision? It simply secures to the white parent travelling on the railroads of the state, the right to take a colored person into the coach set apart for whites in a menial relation, in order to relieve the passenger of the care of the children making the journey with the parents. In other words, the act is simply intended to promote the comfort and sense of exclusiveness and superiority of the white race. They do not object to the colored person in an inferior or menial capacity—as a servant or dependent, ministering to the comfort of the white race—but only when as a man and a citizen he seeks to claim equal right and privilege on a public highway with the white citizens of the state. The act is not only class-legislation but class-legislation which is self-condemned by this provision, as intended for the comfort and advantage of one race and the discomfort and disadvantage of the other. . . .

XIII

. . . . Suppose a member of this Court, nay, suppose every member of it, by some mysterious dispensation of providence should wake tomorrow with a black skin and curly hair—the two obvious and controlling indications of race—and in traveling through that portion of the country where the "Jim Crow Car" abounds, should be ordered into it by the conductor. It is easy to imagine what would be the result, the indignation, the protests, the assertion of pure Caucasian ancestry. But the conductor, the autocrat of Caste, armed with the power of the State conferred by this statute, will listen neither to denial or protest. "In you go or out you go," is his ultimatum.

What humiliation, what rage would then fill the judicial mind! How would the resources of language not be taxed in objurgation! Why would this sentiment prevail in your minds? Simply because you would then feel and know that such assortment of the citizens on the line of race was a discrimination intended to humiliate and degrade the former subject and dependent class—an attempt to perpetuate the caste distinctions on which slavery rested—a statute in the words of the Court "tending to reduce the colored people of the country to the condition of a subject race."

Because it does this the statute is a violation of the fundamental principles of all free government and the Fourteenth Amendment should be given that construction which will remedy such tendency and which is in plain accord with its words.

2. Brief for Plaintiff—Samuel F. Phillips[*]

[T]he discrimination [created by this law] is along the line of the late institution of slavery, and is a distinct disparagement of those

---

[*]Reprinted in Kurland and Casper, Vol. 13, pp. 3–26.

persons who thereby are statutorily separated from others because of
. . . Color. . . . It therefore amounts to a *taunt by law* of that previous
condition of their class—a taunt by the State, to be . . . perpetually
repeated . . . *in word* by railroad employees, in places of public business resort within Louisiana.

*It is also submitted that in such a case it is not of the smallest
consequence that the car or compartment set apart for the Colored is
"equal" in those incidents which affect physical comfort to that set
apart for the Whites.* These might even be *superior,* without such
consequence! . . . Whatever legally disparages and whatever is incident to legal disparagement is offensive to a properly constituted mind.
The White man's *wooden* railway benches, if the case were such,
would be preferred to any *velvet cushions* in the Colored car. If Mr.
Plessy be Colored, and has *tasted of* the advantages of free American
citizenship, and has responded to its inspirations, he abhorred the
equal accommodations of the car to which he was compulsorily assigned! . . .

[L]et us suppose that this [statute] had required all persons of Celtic
race to be associated with the Colored in one car or compartment,
and White persons other than those of Celtic race to be placed in
another; would not such a division have been explosively resented and
effectively redressed at once by the Celts, and that with loud applause
from everybody? And *Why?* except for reasons which under free institutions [should] apply to one citizen as well as to another. The above
hypothesis is only an illustration of a suggestion which we submit,
that in discussing . . . the place and rights of Colored citizens, White
citizens are apt, sometimes insensibly, to fall into a lower tone of
thought and discussion than for other citizens. . . .

[But] if, instead of the old plan of allowing parents to educate
children as they choose, government steps in and takes [this] matter
into its own hands, no constitutional objection upon mere general
grounds can be made to provisions by law which respect . . . a prevailing parental sentiment of the community upon this interesting and
delicate subject. In educating the young government steps *"in loco
parentis,"* and may therefore in many things well conform to the will
of natural parents. This is all a part of *Marriage* and *The Family,* and
should be treated conformably therewith.

Separate cars, and *separate schools,* therefore, come under different
orders of consideration. A conclusion as to one of these does not
control determinations as to the other. . . .

3. Majority Opinion of Justice Henry Brown*

So far, then, as a conflict with the Fourteenth Amendment is concerned, the case reduces itself to the question whether the statute of Louisiana is a reasonable regulation, and with respect to this there must necessarily be a large discretion on the part of the legislature. In determining the question of reasonableness it is at liberty to act with reference to the established usages, customs and traditions of the people, and with a view to the promotion of their comfort, and the preservation of the public peace and good order. Gauged by this standard, we cannot say that a law which authorizes or even requires the separation of the two races in public conveyances is unreasonable, or more obnoxious to the Fourteenth Amendment than the acts of Congress requiring separate schools for colored children in the District of Columbia, the constitutionality of which does not seem to have been questioned, or the corresponding acts of state legislatures.

We consider the underlying fallacy of the plaintiff's argument to consist in the assumption that the enforced separation of the two races stamps the colored race with a badge of inferiority. If this be so, it is not by reason of anything found in the act, but solely because the colored race chooses to put that construction upon it. The argument necessarily assumes that if, as has been more than once the case, and is not unlikely to be so again, the colored race should become the dominant power in the state legislature, and should enact a law in precisely similar terms, it would thereby relegate the white race to an inferior position. We imagine that the white race, at least, would not acquiesce in this assumption. The argument also assumes that social prejudices may be overcome by legislation, and that equal rights cannot be secured to the negro except by an enforced commingling of the two races. We cannot accept this proposition. If the two races are to meet upon terms of social equality, it must be the result of natural affinities, a mutual appreciation of each other's merits and a voluntary consent of individuals. . . . Legislation is powerless to eradicate racial instincts or to abolish distinctions based upon physical differences, and the attempt to do so can only result in accentuating the difficulties of the present situation. If the civil and political rights of both races be equal one cannot be inferior to the other civilly or politically. If one race be inferior to the other socially, the Constitution of the United States cannot put them upon the same plane. . . .

Affirmed.

---

*163 US 537, at 550–51.

4. Justice John Marshall Harlan, Dissenting*

. . . I deny that any legislative body or judicial tribunal may have regard to the race of citizens when the civil rights of those citizens are involved. Indeed such legislation as that here in question is inconsistent, not only with that equality of rights which pertains to citizenship, national and state, but with the personal liberty enjoyed by every one within the United States.

The 13th Amendment. . . . not only struck down the institution of slavery as previously existing in the United States, but it prevents the imposition of any burdens or disabilities that constitute badges of slavery or servitude. It decreed universal civil freedom in this country. . . . But that amendment having been found inadequate to the protection of the rights of those who had been in slavery, it was followed by the 14th Amendment, which added greatly to the dignity and glory of American citizenship, and to the security of personal liberty . . . .

These notable additions to the fundamental law . . . . removed the race line from our governmental systems. . . .

It was said in argument that the statute of Louisiana does not discriminate against either race, but prescribes a rule applicable alike to white and colored citizens. But . . . . [e]veryone knows that the statute in question had its origin in the purpose, not so much to exclude white persons from railroad cars occupied by blacks, as to exclude colored people from coaches occupied by or assigned to white persons. . . . The thing to accomplish was, under the guise of giving equal accommodation for whites and blacks to compel the latter to keep to themselves while traveling in railroad passenger coaches. No one would be so wanting in candor as to assert the contrary. The fundamental objection, therefore, to the statute, is that it interferes with the personal freedom of citizens. . . . If a white man and a black man choose to occupy the same public conveyance on a public highway, it is their right to do so, and no government, proceeding alone on grounds of race, can prevent it without infringing the personal liberty of each. . . .

If a state can prescribe as a rule of civil conduct, that whites and blacks shall not travel as passengers in the same railroad coach, why may it not so regulate the use of the streets of its cities and towns as to compel white citizens to keep on one side of the street and black citizens to keep on the other? Why may it not, upon like grounds,

---

*163 US 537, at 554–55, 557–62.

punish whites and blacks who ride together in street cars or in open vehicles on a public road or street? Why may it not require sheriffs to assign whites to one side of a court-room and blacks to the other? And why may it not also prohibit the commingling of the two races in the galleries of legislative halls or in public assemblages convened for the political questions of the day? Further, if this statute of Louisiana is consistent with the personal liberty of citizens, why may not the state require the separation in railroad coaches of native and naturalized citizens of the United States, or of Protestants and Roman Catholics? . . .

The white race deems itself to be the dominant race in this country. And so it is, in prestige, in achievements, in education, in wealth, and in power. So, I doubt not that it will continue to be for all time, if it remains true to its great heritage and holds fast to the principles of constitutional liberty. But in view of the Constitution, in the eye of the law, there is in this country no superior, dominant, ruling class of citizens. There is no caste here. Our Constitution is color-blind, and neither knows nor tolerates classes among citizens. In respect of civil rights, all citizens are equal before the law. The humblest is the peer of the most powerful. The law regards man as man, and takes no account of his surroundings or of his color when his civil rights as guaranteed by the supreme law of the land are involved. . . .

In my opinion, the judgment this day rendered will, in time, prove to be quite as pernicious as the decsion made by this tribunal in the *Dred Scott Case.* . . . Sixty millions of whites are in no danger from the presence here of eight millions of blacks. The destinies of the two races in this country are indissolubly linked together, and the interests of both require that the common government of all shall not permit the seeds of race hate to be planted under the sanction of law. What can more certainly arouse race hate, what more certainly create and perpetuate a feeling of distrust between these races, than state enactments which in fact proceed on the ground that colored citizens are so inferior and degraded that they cannot be allowed to sit in public coaches occupied by white citizens? That, as all will admit, is the real meaning of such legislation as was enacted in Louisiana.

The sure guaranty of the peace and security of each race is the clear, distinct, unconditional recognition by our governments, national and state, of every right that inheres in civil freedom, and of the equality before the law of all citizens of the United States without regard to race. State enactments, regulating the enjoyment of civil rights, upon the basis of race, and cunningly devised to defeat legitimate results of the war, under the pretense of recognizing equality of rights, can have no other result than to render permanent peace impossible and to keep alive a conflict of races, the continuance of which must do harm to all concerned. . . .

The arbitrary separation of citizens, on the basis of race, while they are on a public highway, is a badge of servitude wholly inconsistent with the civil freedom and the equality before the law established by the Constitution. It cannot be justified upon any legal grounds.

III.
Brief by Charles H. Houston and Thurgood Marshall: *University of Maryland* v. *Murray* (1936)

THIS FIRST TRIUMPH over segregated legal education was a carefully chosen example of Charles Houston's strategy. By 1934, Thurgood Marshall was anxious to attack racial separation at the University of Maryland Law School, but had not yet settled on a definite case. Meanwhile, a Washington, D.C., attorney, Belford V. Lawson, wanted help from the Baltimore NAACP chapter in a suit he was planning to bring against the University of Maryland undergraduate school at College Park.

Houston, however, threw his weight decisively behind a challenge at the graduate level, and directed Marshall to the case of Donald Murray. The ultimate victory was especially sweet for Marshall, who had not even applied to the Maryland Law School in 1929, realizing how futile it would be.

In 1980, Maryland dedicated a new law library. It was named for Supreme Court Justice Thurgood Marshall.

Brief for Appellee[*]

This scholarship act of 1935 is a special experimental limited act providing $10,000 for the total of scholarships for Negro collegiate,

---

[*]169 Md. 478. The person against whom a legal appeal is taken, i.e. the defendant in an appeal. In this case, the State of Maryland was appealing the Baltimore City

graduate and professional education. The act was interpreted to provide scholarships for tuition only. . . .

[Donald Murray] does not concede that it is constitutional for a State to exile one set of its citizens beyond its borders to obtain the same education which it is offering to citizens of different color at home. It is not without significance that all the "free scholarships" which the State provides for its white citizens are in Maryland colleges and universities. Only its Negro citizens are exiled.

But granting for the sake of argument, that the Act is not void for constitutional reasons regardless of its money provisions, it still does not furnish appellee the equivalent of a course in law at the School of Law of the University of Maryland.

1. Even though his tuition charges of $135.00 in the Howard University School of Law would be paid by the State of Maryland, and he himself would have to pay $203.00 to attend the Day School of the School of Law of the University of Maryland, appellee would still be the loser to attend the Howard University School of Law.

a. If he commuted from his home in Baltimore to Washington and returned each school day, commutation would cost him approximately $15.00 per month for 9 months; he would have to buy at least one meal per school day in Washington; he would lose four hours per school day on the road from home to school and back again, or approximately 840 hours during the school year which he might otherwise use in relaxed, uninterrupted work on his courses. Then there would be the physical energy expended in the travel back and forth catching early and late trains.

b. If he lived in Washington he would have to pay for separate room and board, whereas attending the School of Law of the University of Maryland he could live at home with no maintenance expense. The question whether he can be forced into exile has already been noted.

2. Since appellee desires to practice law in Baltimore, the $135.00 scholarship would be no equivalent for loss of the opportunity to observe the courts in Baltimore during his law school career which would be possible if he attended the School of Law of the University of Maryland; no equivalent for the familiarity and drill he would get in Maryland law through the special emphasis laid on it in the instruc-

---

Court's decision to admit Donald Murray to Maryland Law School. Thus Murray was the appellee in the case. The state was the appellant.

tion given in the School of Law of the University of Maryland; no equivalent for the opportunity he would have to become acquainted with, to appraise the strength and weaknesses of the Judges and practitioners of Maryland whom he would have to deal with later in his practice. It must be remembered that the law is a competitive profession, and this matter of equivalent must be judged in part on the basis of the handicap which appellee would have coming from a foreign law school in competitive practice with graduates of the School of Law of the University of Maryland.

3. The $135.00 scholarship is but a tempting mess of pottage held out to induce him to sell his citizenship rights to the same treatment which other citizens of Maryland receive, no more and no less. Equivalents must also be considered in terms of self-respect. Appellee is a citizen ready to pay the same rate of taxes as any other citizen, and to go as far as any other citizen in discharge of the duties of citizenship to state and nation. He does not want the scholarship or any other special treatment. . . .

It is plain that the State of Maryland has not offered appellee the equivalent of the opportunities and advantages which he would have in studying law in the School of Law of the University of Maryland.

IV.
Gunnar Myrdal: *An American Dilemma* (1944)

GUNNAR MYRDAL'S MONUMENTAL work was undertaken in the spring of 1938, under the auspices of the Carnegie Corporation of New York. It was understood from the beginning that while Myrdal would be the director of this "comprehensive study of the Negro in the United States," a staff of scholars and researchers would assist him. (Author's Preface, p. xlix in 1962 edition.) In late 1938, Myrdal decided to undertake "an exploratory journey" through the South. "Without it," he told his sponsors, "our later studies will have no concrete points at which to be fixed." (pp. xlix, 1.) Some of his experiences on the trip are tellingly related in *An American Dilemma*.

The project was expected to take a minimum of two years, but actually stretched out longer than expected because Myrdal felt that "my duty was to go home to Sweden" after the Nazi invasion of Denmark and Norway in April 1940. (p. lii.) He returned to the United States a year later.

Brilliant and comprehensive as it was, *An American Dilemma* was scarcely a revelation to the black community or to the NAACP legal team. But as the book gained widespread public approval its insights formed a congenial background for the sociological and historical attack upon segregation. In Professor Mark Tushnet's words, "*An American Dilemma* said nothing new to the NAACP, but it certified to the general public that people should pay attention to what the NAACP said." (*The NAACP's Legal Strategy Against Segregated Education*, p. 119.)

Yet the experience of *Sweatt* v. *Painter* suggested that less embarrassing intellectual revelations might be more effective in destroying racial separation.

21

CHAPTER 28. THE BASIS OF SOCIAL INEQUALITY*

2. The One-sidedness of the System of Segregation

I have heard few comments made so frequently and with so much emphasis and so many illustrations as the one that "Negroes are happiest among themselves" and that "Negroes really don't want white company but prefer to be among their own race". . . . In the South, many liberals are eager to stress this assertion as part of the justification for their unwillingness to give up the Southern doctrine that the Negroes must not be allowed to aspire to "social equality". . . .

For the moment, we shall leave it an open question whether the whites understand the Negroes correctly on this point. We shall start from the evident fact that—quite independent of whether or not, to what extent, and how the Negroes have accommodated themselves—*social segregation and discrimination is a system of deprivations forced upon the Negro group by the white group.* This is equally true in the North and in the South, though in this respect, as in all others, there is more segregation and discrimination in the South, and thus the phenomenon is easier to observe.

That segregation and discrimination are forced upon the Negroes by the whites becomes apparent in the *one-sidedness* of their application. Negroes are ordinarily never admitted to white churches in the South, but if a strange white man enters a Negro church the visit is received as a great honor. The guest will be ushered to a front seat or to the platform. The service will often be interrupted, an announcement will be made that there is a "white friend" present, and he will be asked to address the Negro audience, which will loudly testify its high appreciation. Likewise, a white stranger will be received with utmost respect and cordiality in any Negro school, and everything will be done to satisfy his every wish, whereas a Negro under similar circumstances would be pushed off the grounds of a white school. Whenever I have entered a Negro theater in the South, the girl in the ticket office has regularly turned a bewildered face and told me that "it is a colored movie." But she has apparently done this because she thought I was making a mistake and wanted to spare me embarrassment. When I answered that I did not care, the ticket office girls usually sold the

---

*Excerpts from *An American Dilemma* by Gunnar Myrdal, Vol. II, pp. 575–76, 586–88. Copyright 1944, 1962 by Harper & Row, Publishers, Inc. Reprinted by permission of HarperCollins Publishers.

ticket and received my visit as a courtesy. I have never been refused service in a Negro restaurant in the South.

When the white conductor in a train has told me occasionally that I was in the wrong car, the underlying assumption has also been the same, that the separation was made in order to save white people from having to tolerate Negro company. Contrary to the laws—which are all written on the fiction of equality—he has, with a shrug of his shoulders, always left me where I was after I told him I had gone there purposely to have a look at the Negroes. A Negro who would disclose a similar desire to observe whites would, of course, be dealt with in quite another way. In the streetcars and buses the separation seems to be enforced fairly well in both directions. When, however, the conductor tells me, a white man, that I have taken the wrong seat, it is done in a spirit of respect and in order to help me preserve my caste status. The assumption is that I have made a mistake with no intention of overstepping the rules. In the case of a Negro the assumption is usually the contrary, that he is trying to intrude. . . .

The rules are understood to be for the protection of whites and directed against Negroes. This applies also to social rituals and etiquette. The white man may waive most of the customs, as long as he does not demonstrate such a friendliness that he becomes known as a "nigger lover"; the reaction then comes, however, from the white society. He can recognize the Negro on the street and stop for a chat, or he can ignore him. He can offer his hand to shake, or he can keep it back. Negroes often complain about the uncertainty they experience because of the fact that the initiative in defining the personal situation always belongs to the white man. It is the white man who chooses between the alternatives as to the character of the contact to be established. The Negro, who often does not know how the white man has chosen, receives surprises in one direction or the other, which constantly push him off his balance.

The white man is not completely free either. He cannot go so far as to "lose caste" or to endanger the color line for the rest of the community. And when he takes certain freedoms, he must not allow the Negro to understand that he, the Negro, can claim them as a right. But each restriction on the white man's freedom is made to appear as a privilege, whereas each restriction on the Negro's freedom is culturally defined as an insult or a discrimination. Thus the one-sidedness of the segregation system is *felt* to hold, even when it does not so appear to the outsider. . . .

6. The Theory of "No Social Equality"

In his first encounter with the American Negro problem, perhaps nothing perplexes the outside observer more than the popular term and the popular theory of "no social equality." He will be made to feel from the start that it has concrete implications and a central importance for the Negro problem in America. . . . One moment it will be stretched to cover and justify every form of social segregation and discrimination, and, in addition, all the inequalities in justice, politics and breadwinning. The next moment it will be narrowed to express only the denial of close personal intimacies and intermarriage. The very lack of precision allows the notion of "no social equality" to rationalize the rather illogical and wavering system of color caste in America.

The kernel of the popular theory of "no social equality" will, when pursued, be presented as a firm determination on the part of the whites to block amalgamation and preserve "the purity of the white race." The white man identifies himself with "the white race" and feels that he has a stake in resisting the dissipation of its racial identity. . . . From this racial dogma will often be drawn the *direct* inference that the white man shall dominate in all spheres. But when the logic of this inference is inquired about, the inference will be made *indirect* and will be made to lead over to the danger of amalgamation, or, as it is popularly expressed, "intermarriage."

It is further found that the ban on intermarriage is focused on white women. For them it covers both formal marriage and illicit intercourse. In regard to white men it is taken more or less for granted that they would not stoop to marry Negro women, and that illicit intercourse does not fall under the same intense taboo. . . . To prevent "intermarriage" in this specific sense of sex relations between white women and Negro men, it is not enough to apply legal and social sanctions against it—so the popular theory runs. In using the danger of intermarriage as a defense for the whole caste system, it is assumed both that Negro men have a strong desire for "intermarriage," and that white women would be open to proposals from Negro men, *if* they are not guarded from even meeting them on an equal plane. The latter assumption, of course, is never openly expressed, but is logically implicit in the popular theory. The conclusion follows that the whole system of segregation and discrimination is justified. Every single measure is defended as necessary to block "social equality" which in its turn is held necessary to prevent "intermarriage."

The basic role of the fear of amalgamation in white attitudes to the race problem is indicated by the popular magical concept of "blood." Educated white Southerners, who know everything about modern genetic and biological research, confess readily that they actually feel an irrational or "instinctive" repugnance in thinking of "intermarriage." These measures of segregation and discrimination are often of the type found in the true taboos and in the notion "not to be touched" of primitive religion. The specific taboos are characterized, further, by a different degree of excitement which attends their violation and a different degree of punishment to the violator: the closer the act to sexual association, the more furious is the public reaction. Sexual association itself is punished by death and is accompanied by tremendous public excitement; the other social relations meet decreasing degrees of public fury. Sex becomes in this popular theory the principle around which the whole structure of segregation of the Negroes— down to disfranchisement and denial of equal opportunities on the labor market—is organized. The reasoning is this: "For, say what we will, may not all the equalities be ultimately based on potential social equality, and that in turn on intermarriage? Here we reach the real *crux* of the question." In cruder language, but with the same logic, the Southern man on the street responds to any plea for social equality: "Would you like to have your daughter marry a Negro?"

This theory of color caste centering around the aversion to amalgamation determines, [then], the white man's rather definite rank order of the various measures of segregation and discrimination against Negroes. The relative significance attached to each of those measures is dependent upon their degree of expediency or necessity—in the view of white people—as means of upholding the ban on "intermarriage." In this rank order, (1) the ban on intermarriage and other sex relations involving white women and colored men takes precedence before everything else. It is the end for which the other restrictions are arranged as means. Thereafter follow: (2) all sorts of taboos and etiquettes in personal contacts; (3) segregation in schools and churches; (4) segregation in hotels, restaurants, and theaters, and other public places where people meet socially; (5) segregation in public conveyances; (6) discrimination in public services; and, finally, inequality in (7) politics, (8) justice and (9) breadwinning and relief.

The degree of liberalism on racial matters in the white South can be designated mainly by the point on this rank order where a man stops because he believes further segregation and discrimination are not necessary to prevent "intermarriage."

V.
The NAACP's Brief:
Sweatt v. Painter (1950)

THE BRIEF IN *Sweatt* v. *Painter* laid the basis for the approach followed in *Brown*. But the atmosphere surrounding *Sweatt*, and *McLaurin* v. *Oklahoma State Regents* as well, was very different from the atmosphere which suffused the later cases.

Two thousand members of the University of Texas educational community staged a rally in Austin in support of integration at the law school, and an all-white local chapter of the NAACP was formed. By the time George McLaurin first attended classes at the University of Oklahoma Graduate School, officials had modified their order requiring him to occupy an antechamber outside the classroom, but his seat was now surrounded by a railing marked "Reserved for Colored." Enraged fellow students tore the railing down.

Brief for Petitioner*

ARGUMENT

I

The State of Texas is forbidden by the equal protection clause of the Fourteenth Amendment to the United States Constitution to deny petitioner's admission to the University of Texas solely because of considerations of race and color. . . .

---

*Herman Sweatt and his lawyers had filed a formal legal petition, requesting the Supreme Court to hear his case. Officially it is called a petition for a writ of certiorari. This made Sweatt the petitioner in the case. The University of Texas, through its President, Theophilus Painter, was the respondent.

27

A. In making admission to the University of Texas School of Law dependent upon applicant's race or color, Texas has adopted a classification wholly lacking in any rational foundation. Therefore, it is invalid under the equal protection clause.

Under Texas law, only whites, or more accurately all racial or color groups other than Negroes, may attend the University of Texas School of Law. Negroes must secure whatever legal educational opportunities Texas offers to them at a separate institution. Even if we assume, *arguendo*, that there are circumstances in which a state has the power to make race or color the basis of a legislative classification (a proposition which we reject in its entirety), nevertheless, we submit, that the difference in treatment, of which petitioner here complains, is one which bears no rational relationship to any valid legislative end, and hence constitutes that form of differential treatment which contravenes the equal protection clause. . . .

1. There is no valid basis for the justification of racial segregation in the field of education. Enforced racial segregation aborts and frustrates the basic purposes and objectives of public education in a democratic society. . . .

We submit that there is no rational connection between racial differences and any valid legislative objective which a state may attempt to promote in providing public education. In this area, therefore, identical treatment of the races is mandatory. . . .

[Thus] racial separation, as it relates to a function as vital to the maintenance of democratic institutions as education, endangers devotion to the very ideals which education is supposed to instill. The segregated citizen cannot give full allegiance to a system of law and justice based on the proposition that "all men are created equal" when the community denies that equality by compelling his children to attend separate schools. Nor can a member of the dominant group fail to see that the community at large is daily violating the very principles in which he is being taught to believe.

It is essential for the successful development of our country as a nation of free people that the understanding and tolerance which we wish practiced in later life be fostered in the classroom. . . .

Nor can it be argued that separation is a more effective and economical method of providing educational advantages. It is generally agreed

that the duplication which segregation requires makes the maintenance of a dual system of education more expensive and in general
lessens the quality of education which would be available to all under
an unsegregated system. . . .

The conclusion, therefore, that the use of race or color as a classification for the purpose of determining the availability of educational
institutions bears no relation to the state's objective is inescapable. . . .

4. *State ordained segregation is a particularly invidious policy which*
    needlessly penalizes Negroes, demoralizes whites and tends to
    disrupt our democratic institutions. . . .

a. [S]egregation prevents both the Negro and white student from
obtaining a full knowledge and understanding of the group from which
he is separated. It has been scientifically established that no child at
birth possesses either an instinct or even a propensity towards feelings
of prejudice or superiority. These prejudices, when and if they do
appear, are but reflections of the attitudes and institutional ideas evidenced by the adults about him. The very act of segregation tends to
crystallize and perpetuate group isolation, and serves, therefore, as a
breeding ground for unhealthy attitudes. . . .

Qualified educators, social scientists, and other experts have expressed their realization of the fact that "separate" is irreconciliable
with "equality". There can be no equality since the very fact of segregation establishes a feeling of humiliation and deprivation to the group
considered inferior.

b. Probably the most irrevocable and deleterious effect of segregation upon the minority group is that it imposes a badge of inferiority
upon the segregated group. This badge of inferior status is recognized
not only by the minority group, but by society at large. As Myrdal
has pointed out:

> "Segregation and discrimination have had material and moral
> effects on whites, too. Booker T. Washington's famous remark,
> that the white man could not hold the Negro in the gutter with-
> out getting in there himself, has been corroborated by many
> white Southern and Northern observers. Throughout this book
> we have been forced to notice the low economic, political, legal,
> and moral standards of Southern whites—kept low because of
> discrimination against Negroes and because of obsession with the
> Negro problem. Even the ambition of Southern whites is stifled

partly because, without rising far, it is so easy to remain 'superior'
to the held-down Negroes." (p. 643) . . .

The lawyer, as has been demonstrated above, enjoys a peculiar and
important role of leadership and guidance in the community. But a
professional man who has received his legal education in a "separate"
or "segregated" school must necessarily reflect the attitudes of and bear
the psychological scars of the society which has arbitrarily placed upon
him the onus of being "different"—a difference which carries with it
the tacit taint of inferiority. The effect upon the community-at-large
as well as upon the Negro professional cannot fail to minimize and
abort the value that such a person might have in the role of a lawyer
and public servant. . . .

Since all available evidence controverts the theory that Negroes
have an inferior mental capacity to whites, and moreover, since when
permitted, the two groups work well together and to their mutual
advantage, it must be concluded that any claim of inferiority is motivated solely by a desire to perpetuate segregation *per se*.

It has been demonstrated, we submit, that Texas cannot show
any rational relationship between racial segregation and the accomplishment of a legitimate legislative purpose. Therefore, its refusal
to admit petitioner to the University of Texas has deprived him of
the equal protection of the laws, under the broadest standard with
which this Court measures compliance with that constitutional
requirement.

B. **Under the test applicable to governmental action based upon
race and color a denial of admission to the University of Texas
to petitioner is a clear and unwarranted deprivation of constitutional rights.**

Respondents' action is unconstitutional for an additional reason. By
making race and color the sole basis for its refusal to admit him to
the University of Texas, Texas has rendered its activities subject to
even stricter tests of constitutionality than would ordinarily be the
case. . . .

Thus, at the very least, this Court requires a stronger showing
of the *real difference* on which the classification rests, and a more
pertinent relationship to the subject matter than is normally the
case. . . .

Since Texas cannot justify [its] practice in terms of any overwhelming public necessity or emergency, we submit that here as in *Oyama v. California*, ". . . there is absent the compelling justification which would be needed to sustain discrimination of that nature." (332 US 633, at 640.)

Thus, under both measurements, the state has subjected petitioner to an unconstitutional deprivation, and the judgment of the court below should be reversed. . . .

IV.

This record discloses the inevitability of discrimination under the "separate but equal" formula. . . .

When we examine the concept "equally" semantically, we find that it is a purely relative term. One cannot compare a state-supported law school, whose student body is composed solely of Negroes, to a state-supported law school whose student body includes various groups (with the exception of Negroes)—whose study of the law is benefitted by a mutual interchange of ideas and attitudes. Even if, for the sake of argument, the physical facilities offered at both schools *were* the same, "not even the most mathematically precise equality of segregated institutions can properly be considered equality under the law." (*To Secure These Rights*, 82) . . .

Conclusion

Historically, the prevailing ideology of our democracy has been one of complete equality. The basic law of our land, as crystallized in our Constitution, rejects any distinctions made by government on the basis of race, creed, or color. This concept of true equality has become synonymous with what is generally defined as "the American Creed". Moreover, this creed has become a symbol of hope for people everywhere.

In petitioner's state of Texas, the educational facilities available to him are governed by the "separate but equal" doctrine. He is asked to believe, in spite of the overwhelming evidence to the contrary, that he can secure "equal" educational opportunities in a school set apart from his fellow citizens. For him, the American Creed is but an attractive idea—not a reality.

Education is not a passive concept. The acquisition of information and special skills, transmitted through the medium of education, enables a citizen to live intelligently as well as productively. To the extent that petitioner is in any way denied the same educational facilities available to other citizens of his state, both he and his fellow citizens are limited in their opportunity to fully participate in our democratic way of life. Petitioner contends that a complete and proper education cannot be attained under the "separate but equal" doctrine of *Plessy v. Ferguson*.

VI.
Sweatt v. Painter (1950) and McLaurin v. Oklahoma State Regents (1950)

Sweatt*

[W]E CANNOT FIND substantial equality in the educational opportunities offered white and Negro law students by the State. In terms of number of the faculty, variety of courses and opportunity for specialization, size of the student body, scope of the library, availability of law review and similar activities, the University of Texas Law School is superior. What is more important, the University of Texas Law School possesses to a far greater degree those qualities which are incapable of objective measurement but which make for greatness in a law school. Such qualities, to name but a few, include reputation of the faculty, experience of the administration, position and influence of the alumni, standing in the community, traditions and prestige. It is difficult to believe that one who had a free choice between these law schools would consider the question close.

Moreover, although the law is a highly learned profession, we are well aware that it is an intensely practical one. The law school, the proving ground for legal learning and practice, cannot be effective in isolation from the individuals and institutions with which the law interacts. Few students and no one who has practiced law would choose to study in an academic vacuum, removed from the interplay of ideas and the exchange of views with which the law is concerned.

---

*339 US 629, 1950.

The law school to which Texas is willing to admit petitioner excludes from its student body members of the racial groups which number 85% of the population of the State and include most of the lawyers, witnesses, jurors, judges and other officials with whom petitioner will inevitably be dealing when he becomes a member of the Texas Bar. With such a substantial and significant segment of society excluded, we cannot conclude that the education offered petitioner is substantially equal to that which he would receive if admitted to the University of Texas Law School.

It may be argued that excluding petitioner from that school is no different from excluding white students from the new law school. This contention overlooks realities. It is unlikely that a member of a group so decisively in the majority, attending a school with rich traditions and prestige which only a history of consistently maintained excellence could command, would claim that the opportunities afforded him for legal education were unequal to those held open to petitioner. . . .

[P]etitioner may claim his full constitutional right: legal education equivalent to that offered by the State to students of other races. Such education is not available to him in a separate law school as offered by the State. We cannot, therefore, agree with respondents that the doctrine of Plessy v. Ferguson requires affirmance of the judgment below. Nor need we reach petitioner's contention that Plessy v. Ferguson should be reexamined in the light of contemporary knowledge respecting the purposes of the Fourteenth Amendment and the effects of racial segregation. . . .

We hold that the Equal Protection Clause of the Fourteenth Amendment requires that petitioner be admitted to the University of Texas Law School.

McLaurin*

[McLaurin] was . . . admitted to the University of Oklahoma Graduate School. [But] . . . his admission was made subject to "such rules and regulations as to segregation as the President of the University shall consider to afford to Mr. G. W. McLaurin substantially equal educational opportunities. . . ." Thus he was required to sit apart at a designated desk in an anteroom adjoining the classroom; to sit at a designated desk on the mezzanine floor of the library, but not to use

---

*339 US 637, 1950.

the desks in the regular reading room; and to sit at a designated table and to eat at a different time from the other students in the school cafeteria. . . .

In the interval between the decision of the court below and the hearing in this Court, the treatment afforded appellant was altered. For some time, the section of the classroom in which appellant sat was surrounded by a rail on which there was a sign stating, "Reserved For Colored," but these have been removed. He is now assigned to a seat in the classroom in a row specified for colored students; he is assigned to a table in the library on the main floor; and he is permitted to eat at the same time in the cafeteria as other students, although here again he is assigned to a special table.

It is said that the separations imposed by the State in this case are in form merely nominal. McLaurin uses the same classroom, library and cafeteria as students of other races; there is no indication that the seats to which he is assigned in these rooms have any disadvantage of location. He may wait in line in the cafeteria and there stand and talk with his fellow students, but while he eats he must remain apart.

These restrictions were obviously imposed in order to comply, as nearly as could be, with the statutory requirements of Oklahoma. But they signify that the State, in administering the facilities it affords for professional and graduate study, sets McLaurin apart from the other students. The result is that appellant is handicapped in his pursuit of effective graduate instruction. Such restrictions impair and inhibit his ability to study, to engage in discussions and exchange views with other students, and, in general, to learn his profession.

Our society grows increasingly complex, and our need for trained leaders increases correspondingly. Appellant's case represents, perhaps, the epitome of that need, for he is attempting to obtain an advanced degree in education, to become, by definition, a leader and trainer of others. Those who will come under his guidance and influence must be directly affected by the education he receives. Their own education and development will necessarily suffer to the extent that his training is unequal to that of his classmates. State-imposed restrictions which produce such inequalities cannot be sustained. . . .

We conclude that the conditions under which this appellant is required to receive his education deprive him of his personal and present right to the equal protection of the laws. . . . We hold that under these circumstances the Fourteenth Amendment precludes differences in treatment by the state based upon race. Appellant, having been admitted to a state-supported graduate school, must receive the same treatment at the hands of the state as students of other races.

PART TWO

The Trial Level

Introduction

AS WE HAVE noted, the assaults on the school segregation statutes of seventeen states, which would end up eventually in the Supreme Court, centered on four geographic locations (with a related suit for the District of Columbia). One focus was the Chancery Court of Delaware, where a relatively gratifying result was achieved. We will concern ourselves mainly, however, with the cases filed in the federal district courts of South Carolina, Kansas, and Virginia.

All four of these lawsuits sought the same constitutional goal: the dismantling of Jim Crow education as a violation of the equal protection of the laws. Furthermore, all of them utilized a procedural technique which could broaden their impact. The suits proceeded not only on behalf of the specific plaintiffs in each controversy, school children and their parents, but on behalf of all others in the various communities who were "similarly situated." In short, the pleadings spoke for every black youngster within a given jurisdiction who was subjected to segregated schools. This transformed the controversies into what are known as "class action" suits. The courts sanction class action suits when it is obvious that the interests of those involved in certain litigation coincide with the interests of those who do not happen to be involved.

From the standpoint of judicial economy, such suits save the time and expense of repetitious trials. From the NAACP's point of view, class action suits were not crucial to the overriding goal of the moment; a single plaintiff could challenge the constitutionality of school segregation laws. But if the courts struck down those laws, or ordered integration even on the basis of *Plessy*, the number of children entitled to relief—to a court-ordered remedy for their segregated status—would greatly expand under the class action technique.

Not that the plaintiffs anticipated victory in the lower courts, certainly not a complete victory. Despite *Sweatt* and *McLaurin*, no one finally expected decisions from any of those courts which overruled or set aside Supreme Court precedent.

The four cases evinced strong similarities, therefore, in strategy and approach. Yet each indigenous situation and each trial manifested its own peculiarities. The disputes were in no way nurtured by the NAACP as part of some master plan for dispatching segregation. As with all of the school cases of this period, the initiative in the four communities came from courageous local citizens and attorneys, with the national NAACP entering the picture upon request. Indeed if Thurgood Marshall and his assistants had been afforded the luxury of choosing the battlegrounds on which to wage a legal campaign, these are not the four they would necessarily have chosen.

This is certainly true of the lawsuit which arose in Clarendon County, South Carolina. *Briggs* v. *Elliott* commenced on November 11, 1949, before the decisions in *Sweatt* and *McLaurin*. Hence it began as an equalization suit (the only suit of this kind, apparently, which Thurgood Marshall ever took a hand in initiating). By the time the case came to trial, however, in the spring of 1951, equalization had been rejected as a strategy in favor of the "all-out attack" on segregated education.

Yet Clarendon County, a wholly rural area, possessed the highest percentage of black citizens of any county in the state, approximately 70%. In the tiny school district against which the suit was actually filed, School District No. 22, there were 870 black pupils and 276 white ones. If the NAACP contemplated a desegregation suit in the deep South, it would be shrewder by far to bring the case in an urban center, where blacks were a minority and whites less openly homicidal toward those who hinted of integration. Furthermore, Marshall felt he had an obligation to the people of the county, who had shown great courage in bringing the suit. He felt that they deserved the decent schools which an equalization approach could readily obtain for them. Finally however, he changed the pleadings in the case to call for the invalidation of segregation laws in South Carolina, or, at the least, admission of blacks to superior white schools.

The driving force behind the original complaint in *Briggs* v. *Elliott* was a minister and teacher in the Clarendon County schools named J. S. DeLaine. For roiling the waters, school officials promptly dismissed DeLaine from his teaching position, then offered him a principal's job if he promised to put a lid on his parishioners' protests. DeLaine's wife, also a teacher, lost her job as well. Harry Briggs, an auto mechanic whose name led alphabetically the list of plaintiffs in the school suit, got the same treatment from his employer and had his credit cut off by the local banks.

The condition these people protested against was as cruel as the treatment they received for protesting it. District 22 maintained three black schools, two elementary schools and an elementary-high school combination. There was a white elementary school and a white high school in the district. The three black institutions together cost $10,900. The white elementary school alone cost $40,000. Furnishings and fixtures at the black schools were valued at $1,800; at the white schools, $12,000.

Two of the three black schools lacked water fountains; at one, students carried the water from the home of a nearby minister. None of the black schools had inside toilets. One of them had no desks. Twenty teachers taught 870 black pupils; twelve teachers taught the 276 white pupils. At the white elementary school there was one teacher for each 28 children, at the black elementary schools one teacher for each 47 children. The white high school maintained only a single class with an enrollment as high as 24; classes in the black high school ranged from 33 to 47.

By the time of the *Briggs* trial, state authorities were making sweeping promises about correcting these conditions, which were endemic throughout South Carolina. In 1951, the state legislature passed a comprehensive school improvement law, funded by a new sales tax. Governor James F. Byrnes vowed that separate *and* equal would truly become a reality in his state, but warned that any court decision requiring "compulsory integration" would lead to the closing down of the public school system.

In line with Byrnes' actions, the school board attorney in *Briggs*, Robert Figg, conceded at the outset of the trial that equality did not exist in the District 22 schools. He guaranteed, however, that the board would speedily rectify the situation. This meant that Figg was now seeking the same goal to which many black plaintiffs had limited themselves in the past: authentic equality, but continued segregation.

The situation in Topeka, Kansas differed markedly from the one prevailing in South Carolina. The laws of Kansas did not absolutely require segregation in all public schools, nor even permit it in some of them. The state's basic statute on the subject, which dated back to 1868, gave communities having a population of 15,000 or more the local option of requiring segregation if they wished, but in their elementary schools only. High schools could not practice forced racial separation, except in Kansas City, which obtained this authority in 1949.

Nine of the twelve communities whose populations qualified them to institute segregation had done so, a pretty good tip-off as to the original reason for the Kansas statute, and the reason for its continued vitality in 1951. Less than 4% of Kansas citizens were black, but 90% of them lived in urban areas, 35% in Kansas City alone. Topeka's black population numbered 8,000. That constituted 10% of the state's black residents, 7.5% of the total population of the city. Six hundred fifty-eight pupils attended Topeka's four black elementary schools; 6,019 pupils went to the eighteen white schools.

The plaintiffs who filed suit against the Kansas law in February, 1951, under the leadership of the local NAACP chapter, maintained that the black schools were inferior to the white ones in facilities and curriculum. But the differences were not of great magnitude, and the issue of physical inequality was not pressed particularly hard at trial. Here then was the purest challenge to the legality of segregation *per se*.

Thurgood Marshall's obligations in South Carolina made it impossible for him to participate in *Brown*. Robert Carter directed the Topeka case, joined by local counsel John and Charles Scott, and Charles Bledsoe. Lester Goodell, a veteran trial attorney, represented the Topeka School Board.

One segment of the black community in Topeka refused to join the suit: the thirty to fourty teachers who taught in the city's segregated schools. Their inhospitable attitude pointed up a ticklish, even agonizing situation, by no means unique to Kansas. Basically the black teachers feared that integrated schools would lead to a massive loss of jobs, since white parents would never submit to having their children taught by black teachers, and white school administrators would inevitably bow to demands with which most of them sympathized anyway.

The fears of the black teachers merited sympathetic understanding, particularly since suits to desegregate faculties were a thing of the future. But so did the aspirations of their fellow citizens. One of the plaintiffs in *Brown* summed up these aspirations in unforgettable fashion early in the trial:[1]

THE WITNESS [SILAS HARDRICK FLEMING]: I would ask . . . for a few minutes to explain why I got into the suit whole soul and body. . . .

JUDGE HUXMAN [PRESIDING JUDGE]: You want to tell the Court why you joined this lawsuit?

THE WITNESS: That's right.

JUDGE HUXMAN: All right, go ahead and tell it.

THE WITNESS: Well, it wasn't for the sake of hot dogs. It wasn't to cause any insinuations that our teachers are not capable of teaching our children, because they are supreme, extremely intelligent, and are capable of teaching my kids or white or black kids. But my point was that not only I and my children are craving light; the entire colored race is craving light. And the only way to reach the light is to start our children together in their infancy and they come up together.

The Virginia case, *Davis v. County School Board of Prince Edward County*, had an unusual and inspiring background. The driving force behind the lawsuit lay in the actions of the students of the county themselves.

Prince Edward County, part of the state's "black belt," was 59% black in population. Moton High School, its only secondary school for black students, typified the mockery of separate but equal in southern education. Built to accommodate 180 pupils, the school housed more than 450 by 1951, thanks to the addition of three "temporary" annexes—shacks covered by tarpaper and heated by stoves. This whole arrangement cost $131,000. Meanwhile, the 384 white pupils in the county attended two high schools, one valued at $500,000. Overall the county invested $.18 per black pupil for every $1.00 spent on a white child's education.

Moton had no gymnasium, showers, dressing rooms, or cafeteria. The curriculum was ridiculously inadequate, lacking such subjects as physics, world history, advanced typing, and stenography, all of them taught in the white schools. Efforts by the local NAACP chapter and the Moton PTA to secure from the school board a commitment for a new building got nowhere.

So the students of Moton took matters into their own hands, led by a remarkable 16-year-old junior named Barbara Rose Johns. Her uncle was the Reverend Vernon Johns, one of the great forerunners of the modern civil rights movement, and at that time pastor of the Dexter Avenue Congregation in Montgomery, Alabama. (When Johns left in 1954, the Congregation chose as his successor the Rev. Martin Luther King, Jr.) Under Barbara Johns' leadership, the entire student body went out on strike in April of 1951, vowing to stay out until they were given a decent school.

The students also contacted Spottswood Robinson and Oliver Hill, the NAACP legal team in Virginia. Knowing that Marshall was already embroiled in Clarendon County, Robinson and Hill shied away at first from a desegregation suit in another majority black area. But Hill later described his reaction when he got to Prince Edward County:[2]

> We knew nothing about this strike until we got a letter asking us to come up there because the children were out on strike. . . . On the way up there our idea was to tell the children to go back to school. I want to be frank with you. When I walked into that church and those little children got up and expressed their grievances and talked about what their parents had tried to do and what they were suffering, I didn't have the nerve. I thought I would have been—well I don't know what I thought I would have been, but I did not have the nerve to even indicate to those children that I thought they should go back to school . . . after that, we took hold of the case and they didn't go back until we told them to go back.

The lawyers made it clear that the day of the pure equalization suit had passed. This suit must challenge segregation itself. Both the students and their parents enthusiastically assented, and on May 23, 1951, Robinson and Hill initiated *Davis v. County School Board of Prince Edward County* in the Federal District Court for the Eastern District of Virginia.

Joining the two Virginia attorneys for the *Davis* trial was Robert Carter of the NAACP national staff. The county's lawyers, Archibald Robertson and T. Justin Moore, headed Richmond's largest and most prestigious law firm. After a pre-trial inspection of Moton High School, they quickly conceded the issue of actual inequality.

But the ultimate issue in all of the federal cases was the constitutionality of state segregation statutes. This meant that all three trials would be conducted before special three-judge tribunals set up specifically to hear such constitutional challenges. The tribunals are composed of one judge from a circuit court of appeals, who presides over the trial, and two district court judges. The decision of this panel can be appealed directly to the Supreme Court.

The jurists on the three panels who heard the school segregation cases varied in ability and reputation. The group in South Carolina exhibited the greatest degree of ideological diversity. Presiding at the trial, held in Charleston on May 28 and 29 of 1951, was the South's most revered jurist, Judge John J. Parker of the Fourth Circuit Court of Appeals. Appointed to the bench in 1925, Parker might be thought to bear a grudge against the NAACP; for in 1930 the organization had formed the linchpin of a coalition which defeated Judge Parker's nomination to the Supreme Court. NAACP opposition at that time stemmed from some racist remarks made by Parker during the course of a 1920 political campaign, pronouncing blacks unfit to participate in politics.

But at no time did anyone regard Judge Parker as a racial extremist. His civil rights decisions from the bench showed him to be moderate, even mildly progressive, though no one expected that he would vote to disturb *Plessy*. He was the author of the 1940 decision mandating equalization of teachers' salaries. And in 1947, Judge Parker affirmed a district court decision which prevented South Carolina from reinstituting the white primary, through the simple expedient of repealing all of its state primary laws (*Rice* v. *Elmore*, 165 F.2d 387.)

The author of that district court opinion, and one of Judge Parker's colleagues on the panel in *Briggs*, was the South's most outspoken judicial liberal, Waites Waring of South Carolina. A Charleston aristocrat, Judge Waring converted to the cause of racial equality only in later life. (He was 70 in 1951.) But his sense of outrage at discrimination grew increasingly evident, expressed more and more openly from the bench. In the white primary opinion, he pointedly told his state's officials, "It is time for South Carolina to rejoin the Union. It is time . . . to adopt the American way of conducting elections."[3] Such sentiments were unlikely to impress the third member of the panel, District Judge George Bell Timmerman, a staunch segregationist.

No one thought the panel in the *Brown* case as prepossessing as the one in *Briggs*, though eventually it would provide the biggest surprise. Circuit Judge Walter Huxman presided at the trial, which began June 25, 1951. Huxman had been a Democratic governor of Kansas from 1936 to 1938, prior to his appointment to the Tenth Circuit in 1939. At his swearing-in ceremony, Judge Huxman expressed a judicial philosophy which would be put to the test in *Brown*. "I hope to be sound, just, progressive with the times," he said, "and adapt myself to changing conditions. The Constitution is pliable, but it must be approached with a sense of responsibility."[4]

The district judges on the panel were Arthur Mellott, chief judge of the Kansas district, and Delmas Hill, another Democrat, who served as the party's state chairman before his appointment to the bench in 1949. Hill would succeed Mellott as chief judge in 1957, and eventually would succeed Huxman on the Tenth Circuit in 1961.

The Virginia trial did not commence until February, 1952. Its presiding judge, Armistead Dobie of the Fourth Circuit, was a celebrated professor and Dean of the University of Virginia Law School when President Roosevelt named him to the district court in 1939; the President acted at the behest of his son, James, one of Dobie's former students. A year later, Dobie moved up to the circuit court. He joined Judge Parker in the white primary opinion, and twice participated in decisions which demanded equalization of public school facilities. But no one expected any surprises from him in the *Davis* case.

District Judge Sterling Hutcheson also found for Robinson and Hill in an equalization suit of 1948. A former United States Attorney for the Eastern District of Virginia, Hutcheson had served on the bench since 1944.

The other district judge, Albert V. Bryan, was chosen in 1947, and ultimately moved on to the Fourth Circuit in 1961. All three of the judges on the *Davis* panel graduated from the University of Virginia Law School. All were Episcopalians.

The Delaware case, *Belton v. Gebhart*, took place in the state's Court of Chancery in October 1951. A single judge handled the matter, Chancellor Collins J. Seitz, the only Catholic involved in deciding any of the desegregation cases. It was Chancellor Seitz who had required that black undergraduate students be admitted to the University of Delaware the previous year, the first court order desegregating a public college.

Belton involved challenges to segregated education at both the elementary and high school levels. As in South Carolina and Virginia, noticeable inequalities existed between the white and black schools in question, though in Delaware the defendants refused to acknowledge them.

The brilliant Wilmington attorney, Louis Redding, a long-time champion of civil rights in his state, led the plaintiffs' case. Joining him was Assistant NAACP Counsel Jack Greenberg, later selected as the organization's chief counsel. Delaware's Attorney General G. Albert Young presented the state's case.

Notes

[1]*Record of Trial, Brown* v. *Board of Education of Topeka*, pp. 109–110.

[2]Quoted in Herbert Hill and Jack Greenberg, *Citizen's Guide to Desegregation* (Boston, 1955), p. 84.

[3]*Elmore* v. *Rice*, 72 F. Supp. 516 (1947), at 528.

[4]"In memory of the Honorable Walter A. Huxman," 474 F.2d (1973), p. 13.

I.
The Doll Man and His Critics

SINCE INEQUALITY OF physical facilities was not pressed as an issue in Kansas, and was conceded in both South Carolina and Virginia, all three of the federal trials centered on the legitimacy of segregation *per se* in elementary and secondary schools. And despite the negative comments of some of the NAACP legal team, Thurgood Marshall and his chief assistants felt that psychological and sociological testimony would materially aid their cause. Such testimony formed a critical part of their presentation in the federal courts, and in Delaware as well, despite the greater need in that case to document physical inequalities.

The mostly hotly-debated of this psychological evidence came from Professor Kenneth Clark of the City College of New York, who testified in all but the Kansas trial. Professor Clark and his wife had done pioneering work on a series of projective psychological tests, designed to isolate the harms which segregation inflicted on black youngsters. The most distinctive test involved the use of two sets of dolls, or pictures of dolls, colored pink and brown. The tests were administered to sample groups of children aged three to seven, in both North and South. The northern children attended both integrated and segregated schools. These tests formed the basis for a paper which Clark delivered to the White House Conference on Children and Youth, held in 1950. Marshall and Robert Carter engaged Clark to conduct similar tests where possible on the children involved in the segregation cases.

NAACP legal advisers retained their doubts about this sort of thing. "Jesus Christ, those damned dolls! I thought it was a joke," said William Coleman, who had been law clerk to Justice Felix Frankfurter in 1949 (and later would serve as Secretary of Transportation under

President Ford). Coleman's comment was symptomatic of the criticisms directed at Clark's methods and conclusions during the next few years—by those who favored the eventual outcome in *Brown*, like Professor Edmond Cahn of New York University Law School, as well as by those less sympathetic to the result, such as Ernest van den Haag, Professor of Philosophy at N.Y.U.

Professor Clark replied vigorously to these criticisms, but his intellectual honesty required him to state frankly what his research could and could not do with regard to school segregation.

The doll tests provided heartbreaking illustrations of the effects of state-imposed school separation. But their nationwide sweep and the experimental techniques which they utilized not only opened the tests to sharp rebuttal. Their emphasis on individual psychological reactions inevitably turned attention away from a systemic analysis of the southern caste system.

1. Testimony of Kenneth Clark—*Briggs* Trial*

Q. Now, Mr. Clark, you had occasion, did you not, to test the reactions of the infant plaintiffs involved in this case by the use of the methods that determine sensitivity to racial discriminations?

A. Yes, I did.

Q. Now, will you tell us when you made these tests and what you did?

A. I made these tests on Thursday and Friday of this past week at your request, and I presented it to children in the Scott's Branch Elementary school, concentrating particularly on the elementary group. I used these methods which I told you about—the Negro and White dolls—which were identical in every respect save skin color. And, I presented them with a sheet of paper on which there were these drawings of dolls, and I asked them to show me the doll—— May I read from these notes?

Judge Waring: You may refresh your recollection.

The Witness: Thank you. I presented these dolls to them and I asked them the following questions in the following order: "Show me the doll that you like best or that you'd like to play with," "Show me the doll that is the 'nice' doll," "Show me the doll that looks 'bad',"

---

*Record of Trial, p. 87 ff. *Records and Briefs of the United States Supreme Court*, 349 US 294, Part 2. (Hereafter, *Records and Briefs*.)

and then the following questions also: "Give me the doll that looks
like a white child," "Give me the doll that looks like a colored child,"
and "Give me the doll that looks like you."

By Mr. Carter:

Q. "Like you?"

A. "Like you." That was the final question, and you can see why.
I wanted to get the child's free expression of his opinions and feelings
before I had him identified with one of these two dolls. I found that
of the children between the ages of six and nine whom I tested, which
were a total of sixteen in number, that ten of those children chose the
white doll as their preference; the doll which they liked best. Ten of
them also considered the white doll a "Nice" doll. And, I think you
have to keep in mind that these two dolls are absolutely identical in
every respect except skin color. Eleven of these sixteen children chose
the brown doll as the doll which looked "bad." This is consistent with
previous results which we have obtained testing over three hundred
children, and we interpret it to mean that the Negro child accepts as
early as six, seven or eight the negative stereotypes about his own
group. And, this result was confirmed in Clarendon County where
we found eleven out of sixteen children picking the brown doll as
looking "bad," when we also . . . take into account that over half of
these children, in spite of their own feelings,—negative feelings—
about the brown doll, were eventually required on the last question
to identify themselves with this doll which they considered as being
undesirable or negative. It may also interest you to know that only
one of these children, between six and nine, dared to choose the white
doll as looking bad. . . . To show you that that was not due to some
artificial or accidental set of circumstances, the following results are
important. Every single child, when asked to pick the doll that looked
like the white child, made the correct choice. All sixteen of the sixteen
[picked] that doll. Every single child, when asked to pick the doll that
was like the colored child; every one of them picked the brown doll.
My opinion is that a fundamental effect of segregation is basic confusion in the individuals and their concepts about themselves conflicting
in their self images. That seemed to be supported by the results of
these sixteen children, all of them knowing which of those dolls was
white and which one was brown. Seven of them, when asked to pick
the doll that was like themselves; seven of them picked the white doll.

This must be seen as a concrete illustration of the degree to which the [pressures] which these children sensed against being brown forced them to evade reality—to escape the reality which seems too overburdening or too threatening to them. . . .

Q. Well, as a result of your tests, what conclusions have you reached, Mr. Clark, with respect to the infant plaintiffs involved in this case?

A. The conclusion which I was forced to reach was that these children in Clarendon County, like other human beings who are subjected to an obviously inferior status in the society in which they live, have been definitely harmed in the development of their personalities; that the signs of instability in their personalities are clear, and I think that every psychologist would accept and interpret these signs as such.

Q. Is that the type of injury which in your opinion would be enduring or lasting?

A. I think it is the kind of injury which would be as enduring or lasting as the situation endured, changing only in its form and in the way it manifests itself.

Mr. Carter: Thank you. Your witness.

Cross-examination.

By Mr. Figg: . . . .

Q. Do you recognize that there is an emotional facet in the problem of two different races living in large numbers together in the same area?

A. I have just given you results which indicate the consequences of that kind of emotional tension.

Q. Well, did you examine any white children while you were up there?

A. I did not examine any white children in Clarendon County.

Q. Have you ever made any examination on what the effect would be in taking into account the present conditions at the present time in South Carolina of forcibly mixing the two races, say between the ages of seven and fourteen in the public schools?

A. I have no direct knowledge of that, sir, because I don't know that.

Q. You haven't made any study of that?

A. May I ask for clarification of your question?

Q. I say, have you ever made any study sufficient to form an opinion as to what would be the effect psychologically upon the white children at the present time and under present conditions forcing them together in mixed schools—children of two races in such a place as School District 22 in Clarendon County?

A. Would you care for me to answer that question in terms of my opinion?

Q. I say, have you ever gone into that subject to determine what the contrary effect would be?

A. No, I could only give you an opinion as to what I believe would happen, but I couldn't tell you what I know would happen. . . .

Q. Has [your test] been used by anybody else that you know of?

A. Yes, sir, it has.

Q. Where was that?

A. A graduate student at Columbia University has used our method with white children. Unfortunately I have not gotten those results, but I have permitted her to use our dolls and our methods on a master's thesis which she was using.

2. Edmond Cahn—"Jurisprudence" (1955)*

When a scientist is engaged in demonstrating a fact of common knowledge (e.g., that fire burns, that a cold causes sniffles, or that segregation degrades), it is not easy to pass a fair judgment on the validity of his proof. Our minds tend to supply his conclusion before he is ready to deduce it. . . . [Thus] the most I can do here is present Professor Clark's evidence . . . , together with the comments that suggest themselves to an untrained but interested observer. . . .

General Comments.—We are not provided here with any proof of the numerical adequacy of the sampling or of its being a representative cross-section. . . . Among these 16 children (or 300, including other groups mentioned) there would probably be a certain proportion with untypical private experiences. In such a strikingly small sample, the results could easily mislead.

Moreover, if one follows the arithmetic in Professor Clark's testimony—which is not easy for me—some of his interpretations seem to be predetermined. For example, if Negro children say a *brown* doll

*New York University Law Review, Vol. 150, 1955.

is like themselves, he infers that segregation has made them conscious of race; yet if they say a *white* doll is like themselves, he infers that segregation has forced them to evade reality.

Perhaps the main point is that this test does not purport to demonstrate the effects of *school* segregation, which is what the court was being asked to enjoin. If it disclosed anything about the effects of segregation on the children, their experiences at school were not differentiated from other causes. Considering the ages of the children, we may conjecture they had not been long at school.

Comment on the Opening Questions: ["Show me the doll that you like best or that you'd like to play with." "Show me the doll that is the 'nice' doll"]—We do not know how the children took these questions. If Professor Clark had offered to give real dolls instead of showing pictures of dolls, the reaction might have been more serious. In any case, I do not think any certain inference follows from 10 out of 16 pointing to the picture of the white doll. Habituation with *dolls* (as distinguished from people) should be allowed for. Manufacturers and commercial fashions practically restrict a child's concept of what a "nice" doll would look like. Many white children of certain generations were taught to prefer "Topsy" or other colored dolls. [An accompanying footnote states: Professor Clark testified that a graduate student at Columbia had used the test on white children with his permission, but he had not obtained the results. Yet it would seem that trying the test on white children would be the very first and most obvious way to begin ascertaining whether it had any probative value when given to Negro children]. . . .

Comment on the "Bad Doll" Question.—Here, it seems to me, the children were tricked. Perhaps that is how some of them felt. There had been no previous question about a "good doll," only about a "nice" one, which the children clearly understood meant one "you'd like to play with." What is a "bad doll"? Some children might consider this a term of preference for play purposes: all little "mothers" love to rebuke and punish naughty dolls. Other children, on hearing the question, would be simply bewildered by the sudden, unexpected introduction of moral or disciplinary references. . . . But I hope the children asked themselves: Why must there be a "bad" doll at all? Why cannot both dolls be "nice"? We observe that [four] children declined to answer this question. Probably they felt it unfair or at least very confusing in the circumstances.

Comment on the Remaining Questions.—It is noteworthy that

seven Negro children picked the white doll "when asked to pick the
doll that was like themselves." Professor Clark leaps to infer that they
were evading reality. This I doubt. Although his testimony does not
make me clear on the point, I gather that these seven children were
among the ten who had previously chosen the white doll as "nice."
Were they wrong, then, to claim that the white doll was very much
"like themselves" because they too were "nice"? No one can state
positively what these children were thinking at the time; but if they
did have perception enough to insist to themselves that the "niceness"
was decisive and not the color, lo and behold! this would be wisdom
indeed! "Out of the mouths of babes and sucklings"? Perhaps, merely
perhaps. In any event, I cannot see that the opposite interpretation
(Professor Clark's) is so evident that it deserves to rank as scientific
proof. . . .

When scientists set out to prove a fact that most of mankind already
acknowledges, they may provide a rather bizarre spectacle. Fifty years
ago, certain biologists who were engaged in just this sort of enterprise,
provoked George Bernard Shaw to denounce their "solemnly offering
us as epoch-making discoveries their demonstrations that dogs get
weaker and die if you give them no food; that intense pain makes
mice sweat; and that if you cut off a dog's leg the three-legged dog
will have a four-legged puppy." Then Mr. Shaw called the scientists
a number of fearful names (beginning with "dolts" and "blackguards"),
none of which would be remotely applicable to the psychologists and
psychiatrists who testified in the desegregation cases. So far as I can
judge, all of these are fine, intelligent, dedicated scholars. Yet one
can honor them as they deserve without swallowing their claims.

3. "Grade School Segregation: The Latest Attack on Racial Discrimination"—*Yale Law Journal* (1952)*

In the *Briggs* case, efforts were made to demonstrate the effects of
segregation by introducing into evidence the results of psychological
projective tests given to sixteen Negro school children involved in the
controversy. The tests were similar to tests previously given to a larger
sample of Negro children three to seven years old from both mixed
and segregated nurseries and schools in the North and South. . . .

*Reprinted by permission of the Yale Law Journal Company and Fred B. Rothman
& Company from *The Yale Law Journal*, Vol. 61, 730–744.

The unhealthy symptoms revealed by the doll tests cannot, however, be traced with certainty to educational segregation. A North-South breakdown of the results fails to establish any statistically significant difference in the preference for the white doll or self-identification with it. [An accompanying footnote states: 72% of the northern children preferred to play with the white doll compared with 62% of the southern children. Sixty-eight percent of the northern children chose the white doll as "nice" compared with 52% of the southern. The only statistically significant differential was that 71% of northern children chose the colored doll as "bad" compared with only 49% of the southern children. . . . These figures at first glance would seem to indicate that the South with its segregated schools provides a healthier environment for Negro children]. [Furthermore] analysis of the tests by age groups shows that Negro children are already aware of race and accompanying value judgments at the preschool age. This rules out the possibility that the schools play an initiating role in creating psychological conflicts.

4. Ernest van den Haag and Ralph Ross—*The Fabric of Society* (1957)*

It is not hard to guess why in his court testimony Professor Clark did not attempt to compare his tests of Negro children in segregated schools with those in unsegregated schools. If Professor Clark had taken both his "scientific" experiments seriously. . . , he would have had to tell the Court that his evidence proves *desegregation* harmful to Negro children. Instead he insisted that *segregation* is. He might be right—provided his own evidence is wrong. . . . That the Southern lawyers who cross-examined Clark when he appeared as an expert witness did not manage to discover so obvious a discrepancy makes one wonder whether Negroes who want to attend Southern law schools have any motive other than to improve them.

Professor Clark presented drawings of dolls to the children, identical except that some dolls had dark and others white skin color. After making sure that the children had noted the difference, he questioned them as to which dolls were "nice" or "bad"; and as to which dolls were like themselves. The majority of the Negro children found the

*Harcourt, Brace and Company (New York, 1957), pp. 165–66. Reprinted by permission of Ernest van den Haag.

white dolls "nice." And about half picked the "nice" white doll as being like themselves. Professor Clark concluded that prejudice had led them to identify white and nice; and even to identify with the white dolls despite their own dark color.

Professor Clark does not mention the possibility that once a child identifies "white" with "nice" he will identify himself with white if he thinks of himself as nice. This is remarkable. His general interpretation—that the identification of "white" with "nice" is a result of anti-Negro prejudice—is truly astounding, however. Suppose dark-haired white children were to identify blonde dolls as nice; or suppose, having the choice, they identified Teddy bears as nice rather than any dolls. Would this prove injury owing to (nonexistent) segregation from blondes? or communal prejudice against humans? Professor Clark's logic suggests that it would.

Control tests—which unfortunately were not presented—might have established an alternative explanation for the identification of white with nice, and black with bad: in our own culture and in many others, including cultures where colored people are practically unknown and cultures where white people are unknown, black has traditionally been the color of evil, death, sorrow, and fear. People are called blackguards or blackhearted when considered evil; and children fear darkness. In these same cultures, white is the color of happiness, joy, hope, purity, and innocence. We need not speculate on why this is so to assert that it is a fact, and that it seems utterly unlikely that it originated with segregation (though it may have contributed to it). Professor Clark's findings then can be explained without any reference to injury by segregation or by prejudice. The "scientific" evidence for this injury is no more "scientific" than the evidence presented in favor of racial prejudice.

The cause of science as well as the cause of Negroes, is much better served if we simply stick to the facts: prejudice exists, it is painful to those against whom it is directed—we need only ask them—and we call it prejudice because it rests on no respectable argument, scientific, or moral. Let us try to eliminate it then. We need not try "scientifically" to prove that prejudice is clinically injurious. This is fortunate, for we cannot.

5. Reply by Kenneth Clark—*Prejudice and Your Child* (1963)*

On the surface, [our] findings might suggest that northern Negro children suffer more personality damage from racial prejudice and discrimination than southern Negro children. However, this interpretation would seem to be not only superficial but incorrect. The apparent emotional stability of the southern Negro child may be indicative only of the fact that through rigid racial segregation and isolation he has accepted as normal the fact of his inferior social status. Such an acceptance is not symptomatic of a healthy personality. The emotional turmoil revealed by some of the northern children may be interpreted as an attempt on their part to assert some positive aspect of the self.

[An accompanying footnote states: The conclusion that the future personality adjustment of the northern Negro is healthier than that of the southern Negro may be supported by an examination of the statistics of admissions of Negroes to a northern state hospital for the mentally ill. These figures show that the annual rate of admission of northern-born Negroes is 40 per 100,000, compared to 186 per 100,000 for those Negroes who were born and lived in the south. These figures, striking in themselves, become even more significant when they are compared with the annual rate of admission of 45 for northern-born whites].

*   *   *   *   *   *   *   *   *

Professor Cahn presents a novel concept of the relationship between common knowledge and scientific knowledge. The logic of his position rests upon the premise that science concerns itself with one order of reality which is distinct from other forms of reality or truth—that a scientific "fact" has different attributes or characteristics than a "fact" of common knowledge. Another related theme which runs through his comments is that a "legal fact" is distinct from both a "scientific fact" and a "fact of common knowledge."

Cahn's pluralistic approach to the nature of "facts," while not a novel philosophical position, seems to involve a mystical semantic confusion which is inconsistent with the assumptions imperative for a scientific approach to the understanding of the nature of man, his society, and his environment. . . .

---

*From *Prejudice and Your Child* by Kenneth Clark, p. 45 ff. Copyright (c) 1963 by Beacon Press. Reprinted by permission of Beacon Press.

Science is essentially a method of controlled observation and veri-
fication for the purpose of reducing human errors of observation,
judgment, or logic. Science begins with observation and ends by testing its assumptions against experience. It is not a creation of another
order of reality. In a very basic sense there cannot be a "legal fact" or
a "fact of common knowledge" which is not at the same time a "scientific fact." Whenever this appears to be true, one or the other type of
"fact" is not a fact.

* * * * * * * * *

When the lawyers of the NAACP, in their understandable zeal to
develop the strongest possible case, asked the social scientists whether
it was possible to present evidence showing that *public school segregation*, in itself, damaged the personalities of Negro children, it was
pointed out to them that the available studies had so far not isolated
this single variable from the total social complexity of racial prejudice,
discrimination, and segregation. It was therefore not possible to testify
on the psychologically damaging effects of segregated schools alone.
Such specific evidence, if available at all, would have to come from
educators and educational philosophers. Some of the more insistent
lawyers felt that only this type of specific testimony would be of value
to them in these cases. It was pointed out to these lawyers that if this
were so then the social psychologists and other social scientists could
not be of any significant, direct help to them.

II.
The Social Scientists Speak

KENNETH CLARK'S DOLL tests attracted extensive attention, but there was a considerable amount of other social science testimony introduced in the school segregation trials.

Some of it followed in Professor Clark's experimental vein. Some expounded upon the clinical methods used for probing the effects of forced separation upon the psyches of black children; this testimony was occasionally technical and speculative in nature. Much of the evidence, however, was designed to deal with the more practical down-to-earth disadvantages of segregation—social isolation and congenital cultural inequalities.

Even where it dealt with psychological effects, a good deal of the testimony was less elaborate than Professor Clark's, more akin in approach and tone to *An American Dilemma* (though neither Professor Clark nor any of the other social scientists who testified denied in any way the validity of Myrdal's analysis, Clark, himself, having been part of the research team which produced the work).

Indeed many of the statements made by the social psychologists and sociologists seemed to be formalized versions of what might strike people as ordinary common sense—the systematic demonstration of those "facts of common knowledge" which "most of mankind already acknowledge."

1. Louisa Holt*—*Brown* Trial

Q. Mrs. Holt, are you at all familiar with the school system in Topeka?

---

*Louisa Holt was Assistant Professor of Psychology at Kansas University.
(Note: Trial Record references in Sections II and III are found in List of Detailed Sources.)

59

A. Yes; I have one child who entered that system this last year and another who enters next September.

Q. You are then aware of the fact that the schools are operated on a segregated basis.

A. I am.

Q. Based upon your experience and your knowledge, taking the segregated factor alone in the school system in Topeka, in your opinion does enforced legal separation have any adverse effect upon the personality development of the negro child?

A. The fact that it is enforced, that it is legal, I think, has more importance than the mere fact of segregation by itself does because this gives legal and official sanction to a policy which inevitably is interpreted both by white people and by negroes as denoting the inferiority of the negro group. Were it not for the sense that one group is inferior to the other, there would be no basis, and I am not granting that this is a rational basis, for such segregation.

Q. Well, does this interference have any effect, in your opinion, on the learning process?

A. A sense of inferiority must always affect one's motivation for learning since it affects the feeling one has of one's self as a person, as a personality or a self or an ego identity. . . . That sense of ego identity is built up on the basis of attitudes that are expressed toward a person by others who are important. First the parents and then teachers, other people in the community, whether they are older or one's own peers. It is other peoples reactions to one's self which most basically affects the conception of one's self that one has. If these attitudes that are reflected back and then internalized or projected, are unfavorable ones, then one develops a sense of one's self as an inferior being. That may not be deleterious necessarily from the standpoint of educational motivation. I believe in some cases it can lead to stronger motivation to achieve well in academic pursuits, to strive to disprove to the world that one is inferior since the world feels that one is inferior. In other cases, of course, the reaction may be the opposite and apathetic acceptance, fatalistic submission to the feeling others have expressed that one is inferior and therefore any efforts to prove otherwise would be doomed to failure.

Q. Now these difficulties that you have described, whether they give a feeling of inferiority which you were motivated to attempt to disprove to the world by doing more or whether they give you a feeling of inferiority and therefore cause you to do less, would you say that the difficulties which segregation causes in the public school system interfere with a well—development of a well-rounded personality?

A. I think the maximum or maximal development of any personality can only be based on the potentialities which that individual himself possesses. . . . [Thus] the instances I cited of those whose motivation to succeed in academic competition is heightened may very well not be fulfilling their own most basic, most appropriate potentialities but seeking, rather, to tilt against windmills, to disprove something which there was no valid reason, in my opinion, to think was so anyhow, namely, the feeling of their inferiority. So even when educational success is achieved that still may not denote the most self-realization of the person. . . .

Q. Now, Mrs. Holt, you are aware of the fact that segregation is practiced in Topeka only for the first six grades. Thereafter, the child goes to high school and junior high school apparently without regard to race or color. You have described difficulties and interferences with the personality development which occurs by virtue of segregation at the first six grades. Is the integration of the child at the junior high school level, does that correct these difficulties which you have just spoken of, in your opinion?

A. I think it's a theory that would be accepted by virtually all students of personality development that the earlier a significant event occurs in the life of an individual the more lasting, the more far-reaching and deeper the effects of that incident, that trauma, will be; the more—the earlier an event occurs, the more difficult it is later on to eradicate those effects.

Q. Your opinion would be that it would be more difficult to eradicate those effects at the junior high school level, is that it; merely because you integrate them at the junior high school level——

A. . . . . There is evidence emerging from a study now going on at Harvard University that the later achievement of individuals in their adult occupational careers can be predicted at the first grade. If that is true, it means that the important effects of schooling in relation to later achievement are set down at that early age, and I therefore don't think that simply removing segregation at a somewhat later grade could possibly undue those effects.

Cross-examination:

By Mr. Goodell:

Q. You mean, Mrs. Holt, there is a serious study being made now to project in the future whether a child in the first grade is going to be a flop or a success?

A. I do.

Q. You have confidence in that do you? . . .

A. I certainly do.

Q. You made a comment in your testimony I would like to call your attention to again; this segregation in some cases would spur, act as a whiplash, on the child to spur him on and make him achieve, and that would be a bad thing.

A. Yes.

Q. You mean it's a bad thing, for example, for a poor boy, because he is poor, the whiplash of poverty makes him work harder to rise higher; that is a bad thing?

A. I mean that that can be at the expense of healthy personality development, self-actualization, self-realization of the most basic fundamental and appropriate kind for that person, and we have plenty of evidence of people who burn themselves out with various emotional or perhaps psychosomatic diseases in whose cases that can be attributed to this overweening striving for competitive success to overcome feelings of inferiority.

2. David Krech*—*Briggs* Trial

Q. Now Mr. Krech, assume that segregated public schools are required by law for Negroes, have you formed any opinion as to what effect this situation will have upon the Negro child?

A. Very definite, and if I may say considered opinion.

Q. Will you kindly say what that opinion is and on what do you base it?

A. My opinion is that legal segregation of education is probably the single, most important factor to wreak harmful effect[s] on the emotional, physical and financial status of the Negro child, and may I also say, it results in a harmful effect on the white child.

Q. Would you explain in a little more detail this harmful effect that you describe, emotionally, financial and physical.

A. Well, the reason why I make such a statement, and I realize it

---

*David Krech was Professor of Psychology at the University of California.

is a rather strong statement [is] that in my opinion legal segregation is the most significant factor to promote, encourage and enhance racial prejudice and racial segregation of all kinds. The reason for that psychologically is primarily this: No one, unless he is mentally diseased, no one can long maintain any attitude or belief unless there are some objective supports for that belief. We believe, for example, that there are trees. We would not long continue to believe that there are trees if we never saw a tree. Legal segregation, because it is legal, because it is obvious to everyone, gives what we call in our lingo environmental support for the belief that Negroes are in some way different from and inferior to white people, and that in turn, of course, supports and strengthens beliefs of racial differences, of racial inferiority. I would say that legal segregation is both an effect, a consequence of racial prejudice, and in turn a cause of continued racial prejudice, and insofar as racial prejudice has these harmful effects on the personality of the individual, on his ability to earn a livelihood, even on his ability to receive adequate medical attention, I look at legal segregation as an extremely important contributing factor. . . .

Q. These injuries that you say come from legal segregation, does the child grow out of them? Do you think they will be enduring, or is it merely a sort of temporary thing that he can shake off?

A. It is my opinion that except in rare cases, a child who has for 10 or 12 years lived in a community where legal segregation is practiced, furthermore, in a community where other beliefs and attitudes support racial discrimination, it is my belief that such a child will probably never recover from whatever harmful effect racial prejudice and discrimination can wreak.

Q. Mr. Krech, assume another situation, assume that . . . segregated public schools . . . which Negroes attend are inferior to white schools, will education in that situation have any adverse effect on the Negro child?

A. Very definitely. . . . I do not hold with some people who suggest the white man, who is prejudiced against the Negro, has no cause to be so prejudiced. I would say that most white people have cause to be prejudiced against the Negro, because the Negro in most cases is indeed inferior to the white man, because the white man has made him [that] through the practice of legal segregation. There is no psychologist that I know of who would maintain that there is any biological, fundamental difference between the two groups of people, but through the practice of inadequate education, that was a hypothetical

situation that you gave me, as a consequence of inadequate education
we build into the Negro the very characteristic, not only intellectual,
but also personality characteristics, which we then use to justify prejudice.

3. M. Brewster Smith*—*Davis* Trial

Q. Dr. Smith, as a social psychologist have you had any occasion
to examine and study the effect of legal segregation on the individual?
A. I have. . . .
Q. As a result of your examination and study, what conclusions
have you reached on that?
A. . . . . In the first place, we can say that there is definite impairment or deficit for the member of the segregated against group, the
Negro, in regard to intellectual development and educational development. There are several respects in which this is an inevitable consequence of segregation. One very important respect arises from the
following considerations: The society that we live in, with its values,
with its sources of recognition and prestige, is predominantly a white
society. The Negro came here under circumstances that meant that
to the extent to which the Negro has a culture of his own, it is the
white culture at secondhand. Now any pattern of human relationships
that involves cutting off a segment of the group, the Negro, from full
participation in this predominantly white culture that we live in, with
its historical continuity of values, is, in itself, bound to be impover-
ishing so far as the intellectual and educational development of the
individual is concerned. . . .
[T]he effects of segregation in this sphere are such as to make the
Negro, on the average, more like the common prejudiced conception
of a Negro, as a stupid, illiterate, apathetic but happy-go-lucky person.
In other words, the effects of segregation in this sphere are such as to
help perpetuate the pattern of segregation and prejudice out of which
these effects arise.
Secondly, I would like to refer to effects in the sphere of emotional,
moral, spiritual—if you will, development of the individual. Segregation, although by law imposed upon both white and the Negro groups,
means different things, depending upon whether the individual is on

---

*M. Brewster Smith was Professor of Psychology at Vassar College.

the top or bottom side of the line of segregation. For the individual who is segregated against, this is inevitably going to be understood— perhaps not formally but still understood at some psychological level— as meaning that I, the person segregated against, am someone that has to be quarantined, somebody that has to be kept, from associating with people because I am not good enough, and this is inherently an insult to the integrity of the individual. In psychological studies of personality development, one of the most widely accepted propositions is that self respect, self esteem, being on good terms with one's self, is crucial for effectiveness in personality. It is also a widely established proposition that we form our pictures of ourselves, we form the basis for this self respect from the way in which we see others regarding us. Children, whether they be white, Negro, or any background, who grow up knowing that they are despised by the people around them, are thought not as good as the people around them, are going to grow up with conceptions of themselves as being, in some way, not worthy. And this is going to have any variety of consequences all of which I think would be agreed by anybody to be harmful and detrimental to the best interests of the individual.

Here again, . . . it should be pointed out, I believe, the effects of segregation are such as to maintain a vicious circle which perpetuates the prejudice in segregation itself. The Negro coming out of this set of experiences is less likely to be effective in advancing his position. He is more likely to be apathetic, or, perhaps in some rare cases, rebellious. He is less capable of cooperative, effective collaboration in the solution of his problems realistically, and, furthermore he presents to the white person the characteristic picture of the so-called Negro stereotype of an individual who brings on himself the prejudice of the majority white group. . . .

Q. . . . . Are there any ways in which this adverse effect impairs the learning process of the child who is subjected to it?

A. Very definitely, it does impair the learning processes of the child. . . . Of course, it is manifestly impossible to disentangle completely the effects of segregation in the schools from the entire pattern of experience which the child undergoes in a segregated society. The school is a tremendously important part of this child's experience, and . . . segregation in the school imposed by the official authority of the State has somewhat different weight perhaps from segregating experiences where they are up to the preferences of the individuals. So that the school is an instance where the general effects of segregation are going to come home to the child in a particularly important way. I think one might also add that the high school years, which of course are pertinent to the particular case at hand, are of particular importance. For a great many of those students, that will be the last contact with the formal school situation before they go out into society at large. This is the last chance of the educational system to prepare them for citizenship in the outer world. By that token, I think this becomes an even more important aspect of their total lives. . . .

Cross-examination.

By Mr. Moore: . . . .

Q. It is your contention here with regard to this high school situation in Prince Edward County, Virginia, that we are here dealing with, that regardless of how excellent were the buildings and equipment; regardless of how excellent were the teachers, their education, their experience, their qualifications; regardless of their salaries; regardless of school bus equipment; assuming all curricula were just the same, or better than in any of the white schools,—it is your opinion that you do not believe that the Negro child in the new Negro high school could obtain equal opportunities and educational advantages?

A. It sounds awfully nice, sir, but my answer would be, unequivocally, No, . . . "The gold bars on a cage don't make it any less a cage." I think psychologically that is a most important point.

Q. In these places that you are familiar with, in New York, where there is no segregation by law or separation by law, do you not know as a fact that separation, I will call it, is generally practised in the public school system?

A. That frequently occurs as a result of residential segregation. I think there is this to be said, which makes the crucial difference: that where segregation occurs with the official sanction of the State, it is an official insult, whereas, when it occurs because the Negroes in this neighborhood go to this school, to be sure, there is the deprivation of opportunity for adequate human relations all along the line, but there is not the official insult. I think that is the major difference.

Q. In other words, you are undertaking to draw the distinction between what you call an official insult and a private insult?

A. Yes. I think that is an important distinction.

Q. Did it ever occur to you that perhaps there might be a corresponding insult to people in Virginia and some of these other southern states if the southern system were done away with? Do you think that would be of any importance so far as the development of the school system is concerned?

A. I do not see how being told that one cannot [relegate] a group . . . to a position of inferiority is in any reasonable sense . . . an insult to the integrity or self-respect of the white Southerner.

4. Wilbur B. Brookover*—*Brown* Trial

In American society we consistently present to the child a model of democratic equality of opportunity. We teach him the principles of equality; we teach him what kind of ideals we have in American society and set this model of behavior before him and expect him to internalize, to take on, this model, to believe it, to understand it. At the same time, in a segregated school situation he is presented a contradictory or inharmonious model. He is presented a school situation in which it is obvious that he is a subordinate, inferior kind of a citizen. He is not presented a model of equality and equal opportunity and [the] basis of operating in terms of his own individual rights and privileges. Now, this conflict of models always creates confusion, insecurity, and difficulty for the child who can not internalize a clearly defined and clearly accepted definition of his role. . . . This frustration that results may result in a delinquent behavior or otherwise criminal or socially abnormal behavior. Now the negro child is constantly presented with this dual definition of his role as a citizen and the segregated school perpetuates this conflict in expectancies, condemns the negro child to an ineffective role as citizen and member of society. . . .

Cross-examination.

By Mr. Goodell:

Q. Doctor, I will just ask you one question: Have you ever heard of these people, all negroes: Mary McLeod Bethune of Sumter, South Carolina, who is president of the college there, Bethune-Cookman College, Daytona Beach, Florida.

---

*Wilbur B. Brookover was Professor of Sociology at Michigan State University.

A. I have heard of someone by the name of Bethune. I am not sure that I know.

Q. Richard Wright, Greenwood, Mississippi and Jackson, Mississippi, author of Native Son, negro.

A. I have.

Q. Charles Johnson of Bristol, Virginia.

A. Charles Johnson, that I know.

Q. Sociologist and president of Fisk University.

A. I think that is in Tennessee.

Q. Perhaps so. Walter White, of Atlanta, Georgia, Executive Secretary of National Association for the Advancement of Colored People.

A. I have heard of him; don't know him.

Q. George Washington Carver, Neosho, Missouri, residence.

A. I have heard of him.

Q. Langston Hughes, poet and author; I believe from Kansas.

A. I have heard of him; don't know him.

Q. W. E. B. DuBois who was an author, I believe connected with Fisk University at Nashville.

A. I know a DuBois who is an anthropologist. I don't know if this is the one.

Q. Mordecai Johnson, Paris, Tennessee, president of Howard University, Washington, D.C., negro university.

A. I know the name; I don't know him at all.

Q. William Grant Still, a composer of Little Rock, Arkansas.

A. Don't know him. . . .

Q. Some of these men you know. Assuming they were all educated—got their preliminary education in segregated schools, a large part of them in the south, would you—did you consider that in arriving at your opinion here?

A. Certainly did. The fact that occasionally a person is able to overcome, through various readjustments and other experiences, the conflict of roles, the conflict of models, does not disturb the generalization which I make, in the least. Certainly there are individual cases which either through psychotherapy or other experiences, the individual is able to overcome such difficulties. But this is not the general case at all.

5. Isidor Chein*—*Davis* Trial

Q. . . . . [D]oes segregation on the basis of race in education have any adverse effect on the educational content of the segregated child—what he gets out of the school?

A. I would say, definitely, Yes. . . . [T]he school is to a child . . . one of the representatives, and one of the important representatives, of authority.

I can put it in these terms: Interestingly enough—and this complicates the problem from the point of view of adjustment of the segregated child—Negroes have, by and large, not developed feelings of hostility toward the form of government or the institutions of the United States as such, or of their individual states. They feel a deep sense of loyalty in so far as I can determine, to these institutions. The effect is that they cannot say to the State or to the Federal Government, as they can say with regard to an individual person on a purely social plane who discriminates against them, who holds them in contempt, and so on. . . . They cannot say . . . , "You are a bad cousin, and I don't care what you say or what you think about me." There is a defense mechanism which is available in terms of social prejudice which is not available in terms of such official expressions of prejudice. So, they have this authority system saying to them, "You are not good enough." . . .

So, the school inherently, and segregation in the school inherently, means infinitely more than the effects of prejudice elsewhere and has the effect of stamping-in these other effects and saying they are right. . . .

Cross-examination.

By Mr. Moore: . . . .

Q. Do you mean to say that . . . in a State where there was segregation on a voluntary basis, as compared with a State where segregation was, as in Virginia, on a lawful basis, on a statutory basis, that it is your view, as you presented to the Court, that you consider that this personality warping or damage to the child is substantially different in

---

*Isidor Chein was Director of the Commission on Community Interrelations, American Jewish Congress.

the case where there is a statutory scheme as compared with other situations? . . .

A. Yes, that is my opinion, that it is the official sanction which says to the child, "It is not only a matter of I, Joe Doaks, don't like you," but it says to the child that the government of the State of Virginia thinks that you are not fit to associate with white children. This is an authority source, and the effect of such authority is to inevitably make more impressive what is involved in the basic fact of segregation.

Q. Do you not realize this fact, that if the average child in a State like Virginia grows up in a home where, based on custom and tradition the child becomes accustomed to certain ways and certain attitudes, with respect to persons of another race or group, that the existence of a statute or no statute, on the subject of segregation is going to have very little difference on the fundamental attitude of that child? Don't you recognize that?

A. I do not believe that, . . . exactly for the reason which I have stated in direct testimony, which it is purely a social matter that can be rationalized away in a great many ways. Where the child has a basic respect for the authority of the State, where he has a basic loyalty to the State, he cannot rationalize it away. He cannot say, "You are a bad man, you have no sense." To the authority of the State, he has only one possible response, "You must be right."

6. Hugh W. Speer*—*Brown* Trial

Q. Dr. Speer, did you examine the curriculum in the schools in the City of Topeka?

A. Yes.

Q. Tell the Court what you mean by "curriculum." . . .

A. By "curriculum" we mean something more than the course of study. As commonly defined and accepted now, "curriculum" means the total school experience of the child. Now, when it comes to the mere prescription of the course of study, we found no significant difference. But, when it comes to the total school experience of the child, there are some differences. In other words, we consider that education is more than just remembering something. It is concerned

---

*Hugh W. Speer was Professor of Education at the University of Kansas City.

with a child's total development, his personality, his personal and social adjustment. Therefore it becomes the obligation of the school to provide the kind of an environment in which the child can learn knowledge and skills such as the three "R's" and also social skills and social attitudes and appreciations and interests, and these considerations are all now part of the curriculum.

Q. I see, Dr. Speer. Do you have anything further to say?

A. Yes. And we might add the more heterogeneous the group in which the children participate, the better [they] can function in our multi-cultural and multi-group society. For example, if the colored children are denied the experience in school of associating with white children, who represent 90% of our national society in which these colored children must live, then the colored child's curriculum is being greatly curtailed. The Topeka curriculum or any school curriculum cannot be equal under segregation. . . .

Cross-examination.

By Mr. Goodell: . . . .

Q. What do you mean by total curriculum?

A. I mean the total school experience of the school child, what the instructions, what the books are, what the surroundings of the buildings are, what his associations with the other children are.

Q. Well, eliminating that feature, the associations with the other children, which is the racial feature. . . .

A. In professional circles we have a term called the great "gestalt" which means the sum is greater—the whole is greater than the sum of the parts and, when we start taking into account only the parts one by one, we destroy our "gestalt", and we cannot make a wise comparison.

Judge Mellott: What was that word?

The Witness: (Spelling) G-e-s-t-a-l-t. . . .

Judge Huxman: I think Dr. Speer has made it quite clear from his evidence—he has to me at least, if I understand it—that segregation, racial segregation, is the prime and controlling factor of the equality of the whole curriculum, and that these physical factors are secondary, and that his testimony, as it registered with me, is that aside from racial segregation he perhaps would not testify that there was any such inequality in the physical properties as would deny anybody an equal educational opportunity. Do I understand your testimony correctly?

The Witness: If I may say, Your Honor, I think I would sum up this way: That there is, in my opinion, some inequality in physical facilities between the groups in Topeka, but, in addition to that, there is also the difference of segregation itself which affects the school curriculum. . . .

By Mr. Goodell:

Q. . . . . It's your opinion, then, that you can't have separate schools in any public school system and have equality, is that right?

A. Yes

Q. And that is predicated on the—on your philosophy or your theory that merely because the two races are kept apart in the educational process, isn't that right, mere separation causes inequality.

A. That is one of the things which causes inequality, yes, sir.

III.
Rebuttal in Virginia

WHILE THE NAACP'S expert witnesses were cross-examined in all of the trials, only in Virginia did the defendants produce social scientists as rebuttal witnesses, to endorse the separate but equal principle. The most eminent of these witnesses was Professor Henry Garrett, chairman of the Department of Psychology at Columbia, a nationally renowned experimental psychologist, and a native of Virginia. The other rebuttal witnesses were native northerners. Dr. William H. Kelly, a child psychiatrist and director of the Memorial Foundation and Guidance Clinic in Richmond, was born and educated in Michigan. John Nelson Buck of Lynchburg State Colony, a state-operated mental hospital, came from Philadelphia and Swarthmore College. None of these experts, it turned out, fervently supported Jim Crow education, but all of them took a dim view of the psychological effects of court-ordered integration. They also offered criticisms of the work of Kenneth Clark and of other social scientists who had testified in the Virginia trial.

Virginia's lawyers unashamedly invoked *Plessy* to buttress their position, as their counterparts in other states had done. But they were especially assiduous in documenting the view that educational separation was "reasonable," because it comported with the "established usages, customs, and traditions of the people." They also encouraged their witnesses to offer grim assessments of the social dislocation which would result if these customs were upset. The star witness in this regard was W. Colgate Darden, former Governor of the state and President of the newly integrated University of Virginia. Darden's testimony was backed up by Prof. Lindley Stiles, head of the University's Department of Education.

Most of Virginia's defense witnesses, however, were prodded into significant concessions during cross-examination.

1. John Nelson Buck*

Q. [F]rom your studies, will you state whether you consider that [the problems of integrating schools] differ at different educational levels; and, if so, what is the most acute period?

A. Yes; I think problems at various levels do differ very sharply. It seems to me that at the graduate and professional school levels it has been very capably demonstrated that there is almost no friction existing between Negroes and whites. . . .

Let us reverse the scale, and let us consider the elementary school level—I am speaking now of the situation in Virginia, not the ideal situation, because we don't have that. As the situation exists now, I think the problems would be very great at both the elementary and the secondary school levels. I don't know whether you can say at one level they would be greater than the other. I think the problems at both levels would be great. I say that, because, in my opinion, the average child, whether Negro or white, by the time he has entered school, has pretty well crystallized his racial attitudes, and I think that this would be very sharply reflected in his relationships in an intimate educational association.

At the high school level, you would have the additional question, of course, of all the psychological problems of adolescence. . . .

Q. Now, having in mind the history of separateness of schools for Negroes and whites in Virginia, with which I am sure you are familiar, will you state whether you consider that segregation in the Virginia public schools is a normal or an abnormal thing?

A. Well, segregation in Virginia must be regarded as a normal thing, since, in the entire life of the school system, no other situation has obtained.

Q. Well, do you think that has a substantial bearing—the normalcy of it—upon the attitudes of white parents and children, on the one hand, and Negro parents and children, on the other?

A. I do, sir. I think, that in attempting to change a traditional status or state, it must be done in a gradual, orderly sort of fashion. I think that we have to take extreme care that in correcting what we may see as a social ill, we do not in the correction produce a greater illness.

Q. I think it appears here that we have had this system for some 80 years in this Commonwealth. I wish you would state, as an expert in your field, what you consider would be the effect on the personali-

---

*John Nelson Buck was Clinical Psychologist at Lynchburg State Hospital.

ties involved, if suddenly, by court decree, the system of separateness that we have were done away with? . . .

A. May I state, first, that I do not know of any instance in history where a social ill was corrected by coercion or by a dramatic or sudden change, where the results were beneficial to either group or both groups. I don't like to prophesy, but it seems to me that if it were attempted to abolish segregation summarily or immediately in Virginia, the following would take place. . . . It would seem to me, first, that an indeterminable, but probably large, number of white parents would withdraw their children from the public school system and seek to place them in private schools—and there simply aren't enough private schools to take care of them. The respective school boards of the cities and counties would certainly be faced with what might be called "overwhelming" problems of administration. I think that two of the specific problems with which they would be faced would be first, extremely great pressure to abandon the present commendable program of providing better schools—much better schools for the Negroes. Another pressure would be to get them to employ white teachers in place of Negro teachers. . . .

I think, though—and this is one of the more serious things—that the school children, both white and Negro, would express, both overtly and covertly, in the school situation, the attitudes of their parents, to the detriment, largely, of both white and Negro. . . . I . . . subscribe to the idea that this non-adaptability is lessened at the higher cultural levels. There is certainly going to be less tension there. But it must be remembered that in the state of Virginia we have many, many people who are not adaptable in this particular respect. . . .

Q. Right there, from your knowledge of conditions, do you believe that in Virginia, today, by court decree it would be possible for the Negro child to obtain general acceptance in the schools, you were talking about, on the part of the white teachers and the white students?

A. I do not. I am sorry to say, I don't.

Q. What would be, in your opinion, the effect of that on the Negro child as compared to the situation he is in now, where he is in school with his own group?

A. I think it would be fair to say, here, that we are probably faced with the choice of the lesser of two evils. I feel that as an abstract idea, segregation is bad. . . .

Q. Will you state what is your opinion concerning studies that have been done, that you are familiar with, which purport to show that segregation or separation per se is harmful to the white and Negro children?

A. I don't think that any thoroughly objective and sufficiently large study has ever been done. I think there are various reasons for that. Such a study would be extremely difficult to perform. It would involve comparison at two separate educational levels of Negro children in a segregated situation, as against a nonsegregated situation, with approximately the same facilities, caliber of teachers, and so on, and a similar comparison of whites. I think we would also have to consider such variables as size of family. We would have to take into consideration all of the noneducational factors which would affect behavior in the school situation and affect the educability of children in that situation. . . .

Q. Mr. Buck, if we assume that this high school program, which you are familiar with from hearing the evidence in this case, after the construction of the new high school in Prince Edward County is completed as planned, and that the result is that the Negro high school students will have as good or better buildings and facilities as the whites, and if you also assume that the curriculum is as good or better, and the teachers' qualifications, teachers' salaries, and bus facilities, and the other things we have talked about, were just as good or better, in your judgment, can the Negro child attending that school receive as good or better opportunities and advantages for education as the child could if he were over in the white school?

A. I think, in the present situation in Virginia, as I mentioned before, that that would be the case. This would be an interim situation, the duration of which I certainly would not be qualified to prophesy.

Q. Over-all, do you believe that the Negro child would be better-off in such a situation, attending the separate schools, with these facilities and curriculum, and so forth, that I have described, than he would be if he were transferred, or the attempt were made to transfer him over to the white school?

A. I most certainly do.

Cross-examination.

By Mr. Carter:

Q. Dr. Buck——

A. Mr. Buck. Let's keep the record straight. . . .

Q. I think you said that you thought the abrupt change would be harmful?

A. I do.

Q. That aside, for a moment, in your opinion as a clinical psychologist, do you feel that racial segregation has an adverse effect on a healthy personality development?

A. As an abstract statement—as a generality, let us put it that way— I should say Yes. I think that anything that sets up artificial barriers, restricting communication between individuals in a given community, is perhaps, at least theoretically, bad; but I think that such a statement must be modified by the situation which exists, obviously, and there are many, many situations. I don't think a generality can actually be given.

Q. Would it be a fair statement, Mr. Buck, to say that while you feel that segregation has harmful effects on the Negro child, that in so far as you are concerned, it is a question of time, and that you feel that, although this problem can be eliminated and can be handled, it should not be done immediately—it is a question of time?

A. I think that your approach to this problem is bad, if it is an abrupt and direct approach. I think racial relationships in Virginia over the past 80 years have improved immensely. I think it is the sincere desire, certainly of all thinking Virginians, to continue to improve them. I think that such actions as this have an adverse effect, because they tend to arouse an opposition, a resentment on the part of the people, because they don't understand the purpose which you gentlemen may have. I am not questioning the sincerity of the purpose, but I do question the method.

Q. Again, I would like to ask, the disagreement as between this side of the table and yours, on the witness-stand, is on method and not on the actual goal?

A. There is no agreement as to goal, at all. I am not a lawyer, but as I see it, the laws of the State of Virginia, which have stood for the past 80 years, express the wish of the majority of the people. As I understand it, in a democratic situation, the majority of the people are entitled to express a wish, and have that wish carried out by the rest. I am sure the majority does not wish to do an injury to the rest, but it seems to me that the orderly procedure is a legislative procedure. . . .

Q. Would this be a fair statement, Mr. Buck, that the consensus of opinion among people in your profession and related professions, is that racial barriers, barriers based on races, do harm to the individual?

A. Yes, that is the consensus, sir. But, once again, the harm that is done depends on many other circumstances. I do not think that is the sole cause.

Mr. Carter: That is all.
Mr. Moore: Just one question.

Redirect examination.

By Mr. Moore:

Q. Speaking as a clinical psychologist, Mr. Buck, is it your opinion that voluntary segregation would have more serious effects on the personality of the average Negro child than what now exists, that is, segregation under Virginia law?

A. I have never given that too much thought, but I should think that voluntary segregation might well have a very definite inferiority feeling involved because the Negro child who is separated by his own parents from the community, as such, would certainly feel that separation more acutely than separation which is a statutory thing.

Mr. Moore: That is all. You may be excused.

Mr. Carter: I have one more question that I would like to ask Mr. Buck.

By Mr. Carter:

Q. On what do you base that finding?

A. That is—I do not base it on any finding. I base it simply on my opinion, which is very definitely . . . that the impact of individual prejudice, . . . and I think it might well be considered that, is stronger than statutory. In other words, the situation which is extremely well structured from the very beginning is an easier situation to adapt to than a situation in which the child might grow up to a certain point and then have someone say, "Here, you can't associate with the rest of your own people, let alone some one else."

Q. In other words, to borrow from Dean Stiles, "It is a question of the degree of sickness?"

A. That is right.

Q. You would agree that the patient is sick?

A. I think the whole society is sick.

2. Dr. William H. Kelly*

Q. Have you found out in your work that segregation of some sort is really inherent in our everyday life?

A. My answer to that is Yes. I think that a form of segregation occurs in all of the cultures that are exposed to one another; that we have it on social levels; that segregation exists in all cultures. . . .

Q. Do you consider, from a psychiatrist's standpoint on this question of public acceptance, popular acceptance, or segregation or non-segregation, that there is any analogy that may fairly be drawn to the days of prohibition?

A. Yes; I think so. I think it is pretty clear that you can tell people, by an act or law, what they must do, but that doesn't mean that they will do it. . . .

Cross-examination.

By Mr. Carter: . . . .

Q. In your clinic, . . . do white psychiatrists treat Negro children?

A. Yes.

Q. In view of the testimony that you gave, I would just like to ask you this question. Do you feel that the Negro children would get better treatment by a psychiatrist if they were placed in segregated clinics, treated by Negro psychiatrists . . . ?

A. I do not think that would necessarily follow. . . .

Q. As a psychiatrist, do you feel that racial segregation is a social situation which has some effect upon personality development of the individual?

A. Yes, I do.

Q. As a psychiatrist, do you think that social situation is adverse or beneficial to the personality?

A. I would have to say that it is adverse to the personality.

Mr. Carter: That is all.

---

*Dr. William H. Kelly was Director of the Memorial Foundation and Guidance Clinic, Richmond, Virginia.

Redirect examination.

By Mr. Moore:

Q. Do you consider that the adverse effect which you have mentioned would be substantially different in a situation where there was voluntary segregation, as compared with segregation by statute?

A. I think that the fact that segregation would exist would cause the same problem.

3. Henry Garrett[*]

Q. Doctor, I believe your testimony means that for these last 28 years that you have been a graduate professor, you have been moving up in the faculty there at Columbia University in the field of psychology.

A. 28 or 27.

Q. In connection with that development, you have, as a Virginia boy that moved up to the big city, had to do a great deal of study and reading in your field?

A. Well, yes.

Q. Have you found anything in the literature that indicates to your mind that the mere act of segregation by law can be identified as being detrimental or really be the cause or effect which in any material degree differs from the conditions that we all know exist in New York and other sections of the country where segregation is practiced on a voluntary basis? . . .

A. I think I can reach that, perhaps.

I do not think that one can possibly defend separation of one group from another, if the separated group is stigmatized or put into an inferior position. Separation can be of different sorts which does not involve, necessarily, any feeling of inferiority or any stigma. The principle of separation in education, for example, is long and well established in American life. Boys and girls are taught in separate schools, Catholic children in parochial schools, Jewish children in Hebrew schools; we have opportunity classes for those children who are slow; we have classes for those children who are bright. It has been regarded by many people as being non-democratic, but it does not seem to have made a great deal of difference in those children.

---

[*]Henry Garrett was Professor of Psychology at Columbia University.

So long as the facilities which are allowed are equal, the mere fact of separation does not seem to me to be, in itself discriminatory. . . .

Q. May we turn to another point? In Dr. Smith's testimony, he developed his views, including this statement, in referring to segregation from a psychological level. He said:

"This is inherently an insult to the integrity of the individual."

Do you find any sociological or psychological basis for any such comment as that by him as applied to the high school situations in Virginia, and particularly the Prince Edward County High School?

A. The term "insult" to an individual's personality, it seems to me, is fairly strong language in the situation in which it is used. I think an idealistic person, who is likely to let his sympathies go beyond his judgment may be so strongly prejudiced on the side of abstract goodness that he does not temper the application of the general principle with a certain amount of what might be called common sense. The [Virginia] situation is fairly far removed, it seems to me, from an abstract term of that sort. . . .

Q. Doctor, just one final question, which I have put to all of these last witnesses. Assuming that this school program that is proposed and is in the process of execution for Prince Edward County is carried out, . . . is there any reason why the Negro student in that high school should not receive equal opportunities and advantages from an educational standpoint as the white child or as good as the Negro child could get if he were transferred over to the white school?

A. Provided you have equal facilities. It seems to me that in the State of Virginia today, taking into account the temper of its people, its mores, and its customs and background, that the Negro student at the high school level will get a better education in a separate school than he will in mixed schools. . . .

Cross-examination.

By Mr. Carter: . . . .

Q. I think you said, Dr. Garrett . . . that, in your opinion, racial segregation, without a stigma, would be all right?

A. Right. I would like to qualify that, if you don't mind my interrupting you. What I said was that in the state of Virginia, in the year 1952, given equal facilities, that I thought, at the high school level, the Negro child and the white child—who seem to be forgotten most of the time—could get better education at the high school level in separate schools, given those two qualifications: equal facilities, and the state of mind in Virginia at the present time.

Now, I can go on a little with that, and perhaps save you some questions.

If a Negro child goes to a school as well-equipped as that of his white neighbor, if he had teachers of his own race and friends of his own race, it seems to me he is much less likely to develop tensions, animosities, and hostilities, than if you put him into a mixed school where, in Virginia, inevitably he will be a minority group. Now, not even an Act of Congress could change the fact that a Negro doesn't look like a white person; they are marked off, immediately, and I think, as I have said before, that at the adolescent level, children, being what they are, . . . reflect the opinions of their parents, and the Negro would be much more likely to develop tensions, animosities, and hostilities in a mixed high school than in a separate school.

Q. Do you consider, Dr. Garrett, that racial segregation, as presently practised in the United States, and in Virginia, is a social situation which is adverse to the individual?

A. It is a large question. In general, wherever a person is cut off from the main body of society or a group, if he is put in a position that stigmatizes him and makes him feel inferior, I would say Yes, it is detrimental and deleterious to him.

Q. What I would like to ask you is, do you know of any situation involving racial segregation of Negroes in the schools, like that practised in the United States, and in Virginia, where this stigmatism has not been put on the separation?

A. I think, in the high schools of Virginia, if the Negro child had equal facilities, his own teachers, his own friends, and a good feeling, he would be more likely to develop pride in himself as a Negro, which I think we would all like to see him do—to develop his own potentialities, his sense of duty, his sense of art, his sense of histrionics; and my prediction would be that if you conducted separate schools at the high school level for Negroes and whites, one of two things might happen: that the Negroes might develop their schools up to the level where they would not mix, themselves; and I would like to see it happen. I think it would be poetic justice. They would develop their sense of dramatic art, and music, which they seem to have a talent for—athletics—and they would say, "We prefer to remain as a Negro group." The other would be in a mixed school where, as I said, a great many animosities, disturbances, resentments, and hostilities and inferiorities would develop.

I don't think either of those is certain. I am completely out of crystal balls at the present time, and I am not a very good prophet, but it seems to me those are the two lines it might take in the future.

Q. Isn't it the policy of the University at which you are now teaching—isn't it its fundamental policy—that in order to build a strong institution, it must get people of all economic groups, all racial backgrounds, even of all countries?

A. That is right.

Q. Isn't that based on the belief that in that way the institution can give more to the student?

A. That is right. That is a university—not a high school?

Mr. Carter: That is all.

4. Colgate Darden*

Q. . . . .[W]hat in your opinion would be the impact and result upon the educational opportunities and advantages afforded and to be afforded by the existing and projected educational program in Virginia, if the Constitutional and statutory provision relating to mixed schools should be stricken down by judicial decree?

A. . . . I believe it would impair the opportunities for both races.

Q. Would you care to elaborate and give us your reasons for that?

A. The primary reason I think arises out of the difficulty of financial support for public education. As you know, it has been exceedingly difficult to gather together the funds needed to develop a sound system of public instruction in Virginia. I think there is an enormous amount of good will for the public school system now. I think the striking down of the separate facilities would bring on conflict—not violence, but misunderstanding or sharp differences of opinion between the two races in Virginia that would eventuate in a sizable falling off of the funds required for public education. That is what I fear would happen. I may be wrong in that assumption. . . .

Q. Is that good will which you have [described] to the Court . . . , would that be, or not, in your judgment virtually destroyed or weak-

---

*Colgate Darden was President of the University of Virginia, Charlottesville.

ened if the system which now maintains under our Constitution should be stricken down?

A. I do not think it would be virtually destroyed, but I think it would be badly impaired. I think the fabric of good will between the races in Virginia is a very stout fabric; I think it would take a great deal to rend it or tear it apart or to have violence develop. But I think it unquestionably would slow up materially the forward movement that we know of. . . . I think the white children and the colored children would be set back enormously. Those parents who were able and who were of a mind to do it would withdraw their children and place them in private schools. Other people, whites, I think probably following their lead, might be inclined to keep their children at home or to organize them in little groups and provide teachers for them. The net result would be that neither would get the quality of instruction that is now obtainable in the State. . . .

Cross-examination.

By Mr. [Oliver] Hill: . . . .

Q. One final question: Living in a world such as we have, do you not think it is time that we should give consideration to preparing people of different racial groups to live more harmoniously and to think better of each other, and to know more about each other, if we are going to have this peace that we are aspiring to?

A. Yes; I think that, as an abstract principle.

Q. Don't you think that can be better acquired in the laboratory of the public school than anywhere else?

A. I do not. I don't believe that knowing people better necessarily leads you to like them more, nor do I believe that the interchange of information between people will prevent war. Europe is a breeding ground of war, and their people have known one another for centuries. So, I don't believe that knowing a fellow necessarily makes you like him—you may know so much about him that you do not like him. I don't believe that the mixing up of people in the high school makes any better feeling. . . . You realize that this problem we are dealing with is a by-product, and a fearful by-product, of human slavery. We are the inheritors of that system, and we are attempting to deal with it, both white and colored, in what we perceive to be the most likely fashion. It is not something that we deal with in vacuum or theory; it is a hard, practical fact. And I don't believe that the striking down of the separate school by the Federal Government would bring about a forwarding of the educational program of the people of Virginia.

Judge Dobie: Have you any more "final" questions?
Mr. Hill: No, sir.

By Mr. Hill:

Q. Of course, what you have expressed is just your personal opinion?
A. I said that, at the beginning.

IV.
Mr. Moore's Antics

"[His cross examination of Professor Clark] brought the house down. Everyone there enjoyed it—except maybe the other side. . . . But it wasn't done in a nasty way."
Archibald Robertson, Moore's law partner and co-counsel, in *Richard Kluger, Simple Justice, p. 497.*

As any healthy-minded person reads the Virginia trial record, it is impossible not to contrast the altruism and sober dignity of the scientists with the behavior of defendants' counsel, who, by his manner of espousing the old order, exposed its cruelty and bigotry. Here was a living spectacle of what racial segregation can do to the human spirit. The segregated society, as defendants' own expert had said, was "sick"; and the tactics of cross-examination used by defendants' lawyer showed how very sick it was.
Edmond Cahn, in "Jurisprudence," p. 165.

THE VIRGINIA TRIAL also produced moments in which the veneer of politeness which normally prevailed during the litigation was stripped away, and the nastier impulses boiling beneath the surface surged forth. These excursions into ugliness were usually the work of Virginia's combative chief counsel, T. Justin Moore.

Moore was especially rough on Kenneth Clark. In his Virginia testimony, Clark discussed his doll testing techniques at length; but he never actually conducted such tests in Prince Edward County because the plaintiffs were high school students. Instead Clark held interviews with sixteen of the students, asking them a series of questions about educational disparities in the county, what could be done about the situation, and how the young people felt about whites.

Justin Moore, in the words of his co-counsel, responded by putting on "a moronic face and the accent of a little darkey," and launching one of his many brutal counter-attacks against the plaintiffs.

1. Cross-Examination of Kenneth Clark*

Q. As I recall it, you had only six questions [in the interview].

A. Well, as I said—let me see—

Q. We will just play like I am one of these 18-year-olds. Now, you just put on the interview like you did it.

Judge Dobie: "Make me a child again."

Mr. Moore: I would like to be a child again.

Dr. Clark: "Your name, please."

Mr. Moore: "Justin Moore."

Dr. Clark: "How old are you, Justin?"

Mr. Moore: "I will play like I am 18."

Dr. Clark: "What grade are you in?"

Mr. Moore: "I will be in the 10th grade." I have been a little slow.

Dr. Clark: "What school do you go to?"

Mr. Moore: "I go to the Moton School."

Dr. Clark: "What does your mother do?"

Mr. Moore: "She works: she works on the farm, and works every day."

Dr. Clark: "What does your father do?"

Mr. Moore: "He works on the farm, too."

Dr. Clark: "I would just like to ask you some questions. Tell me about your school."

Mr. Moore: "Well, it is not much good.—"

Dr. Clark: "Will you tell me about it?"

Mr. Moore: "Well, we don't have all the things that they have got over at the other school. That is what my parents say."

Dr. Clark: I don't remember one of them saying that, by the way. Not one of them volunteered information.

Mr. Moore: I just want to see how you put on the test.

Dr. Clark: "What about the white school?"

Mr. Moore: "I hear at home that it is fine. I have never been over there.

Mr. Clark: "You hear that it is fine?"

Mr. Moore: "Yes, that is what I hear.—

Dr. Clark: "Why is that?"

Mr. Moore: "Well, they have got more money, I suppose, for it."

Dr. Clark: "Who has more money?"

Mr. Moore: "The School Board."

---

*Davis Trial, p. 280 ff. Records and Briefs, Part 3.

Dr. Clark: "Well, what do you think can be done about it?"

Mr. Moore: "Well, I think we may get a better school if we keep on fighting about it."

Dr. Clark: "Do you think that things will get better?"

Mr. Moore: "Oh, yes, I think they are going to get better if we keep NAACP working for us."

Dr. Clark: "Tell, what do you think of white people?"

Mr. Moore: "Oh, some of them good, some of them bad. I think that is about the way most of my friends feel about it."

Dr. Clark: "What do you think of colored people?"

Mr. Moore: "Oh, the same way—some of them good, some bad."

Dr. Clark: "What do you think we can do to make things better?"

Mr. Moore: "Well, just work harder."

Dr. Clark: "Do you think it will get better eventually?"

Mr. Moore: "Oh, yes, I think it is getting better all the time."

Dr. Clark: That was the briefest interview we have ever had.

Judge Dobie: Dr. Clark, I hope it won't embarrass you by asking you to give Mr. Moore an I. Q. rating. . . .

By Mr. Moore:

Q. Do you seriously contend that a little 3-minute interview like we have had, or if you stretch it out to five minutes, really means anything, carried out on the basis that you have indicated, where a 17-, 18-, or 19-year-old student, who has had this subject discussed day in and day out for nearly a year—do you really seriously contend that that means anything except that they wanted to complain about their school and they wanted to get another school?

A. Mr. Moore, I don't believe that the results of this interview are of any world-shaking importance. . . .

Q. Are you familiar with the fact that one of the primary purposes of the NAACP, as it has been announced repeatedly by their representatives, as reported in the press, has been to stir up and foment critical situations that will call attention to this racial problem?

A. I am not—

Mr. Hill: Just a moment. If counsel is going to ask a question, I think he should ask it accurately, and I challenge Mr. Moore to state any place where NAACP has been reported as being its policy to foment anything. We unquestionably are trying to break up segregation, and everybody will admit that. But if he is going to ask the question, let him ask it fairly.

Mr. Moore: You, yourself, were reported in the Richmond Press
. . . as urging the people in Richmond to create these situations that
focus attention on differences in race treatment, and you know you
were.

Mr. Hill: I dispute that, and I dispute the fact that even the press
reported any such thing. I did say, and I say it now, that I urged
people to exert themselves to carry on their rights, whatever their
rights were, under the law; they should press for them. . . .

Mr. Moore: And you have repeatedly, and the press has reported
it, urged the Negroes in Richmond to try to create a situation in the
public transportation and to tie up all of the policemen they can, and
all the transit operators. You know that it is a fact.

By Mr. Moore:

Q. I ask you, as a matter of fact, do you not know that is one of
the policies of the NAACP?

A. I certainly do not.

Q. Do you deny that?

A. I deny it on the basis of my knowledge.

Q. You do not know of that?

Judge Dobie: I think that is as far as you can go.

(Earlier in the Cross-examination)

Q. Dr. Clark, I would first like to inquire as to several questions
about yourself. Where were you born?

A. I was born in the Panama Canal Zone.

Q. You lived in the Panama Canal Zone until you were of what
age?

A. Until I was, I think, about 4; I am not sure. . . .

Q. In view of your reference to Panama, I must inquire, if you
know—you appear to be of rather light color—what percentage, as
near as you can tell us, are you white and what percentage some
other?

A. I haven't the slightest idea. What do you mean by "percentage"?

Q. I mean, are you half white, or half colored, and half Panama-
nian, or what?

A. I still can't understand you.

Q. You don't understand that question?

A. No.

2. Cross-Examination of Isidor Chein[*]

Q. Dr. Chein, just how do you spell your last name?

A. C-H-E-I-N.

Q. What kind of a name is that? What sort of racial background does that indicate?

A. The name is a poor English version of Hebrew which designates charm.

Q. What is your racial background?

A. I could not give an honest answer to that because of the complexity of the concept. I think what you want to know is am I Jewish.

Q. Are you 100 per cent Jewish?

A. How do I answer that?

Q. I do not know, you know.

A. In all honesty, the framework of the question is not one which can be, as far as I know, intelligently answered. All of my—both of my parents and all of my ancestors, as far back as I know, were Jewish.

A. That answers my question. I simply wanted to find out what was the story about that. Where were you born?

A. In the United States, in New York City.

Q. Were your parents native born in the United States?

A. No.

Q. Where were they born?

A. In Poland.

Q. How long had they lived in this country when you were born? . . .

Q. I take it that in view of your testimony on this question of what you consider to be damage to the Negro child that you would equally advocate the barring of the law such as we have in Virginia, and in other southern States, which would prevent intermarriage between the races. . . .

A. . . . . Fundamentally, it seems to me that the purposes and goals of marriage are not the purposes and goals of education. . . .

Q. Do you not recognize that the existence of these laws, such as in Virginia and many of the southern States, barring marriage of certain groups, carry with it the implication of a difference in [status]?

A. They do . . . . There is a big difference, however, to the child who is 6 years, 10 years, 12 years old, who has to go to school every single day with the exception of week ends and the summer vacations,

---

[*]*Davis* Trial, p. 213 ff. *Records and Briefs*, Part 3.

to be reminded of the fact that he is not good enough for other kinds of association, and the effect on this child of the existence of a law forbidding intermarriage; in terms of the effects on the child, there is no question as to which is the far more significant factor in terms of the weight of the State authority and opinion.

(Prior to the Cross-Examination)

Judge Dobie: Do you want to cross-examine [Dr. Chein]?

Mr. Moore: Yes, sir; we will have some questions.

Judge Dobie: All right. I thought we would adjourn for lunch. Suppose we adjourn now?

Mr. Moore: Oh, yes, let us adjourn now. I think we will all be in a better frame of mind if we adjourn for lunch.

Judge Dobie: All right. We will adjourn until 2:25.

Mr. Robinson: If Your Honor please, I would like to ask an adjournment until about 2:45. Your Honor granted an adjournment yesterday of an hour and fifteen minutes. We have a long way to go to get something to eat. We spend about three-quarters of an hour in traveling, and we have thirty minutes in which to get lunch. The case has moved along rather fast and I don't think it will delay us too much.

Judge Dobie: All right! We will adjourn until 2:45.

(Thereupon, at 1:10 p.m., a recess was taken until 2:45 p.m.)

3. Cross-Examination of John Julian Brooks*

Q. I would just like to get this perfectly clear. Your real contention is that statutes, such as we have in Virginia and throughout the South, in line with your view about this effort to strike down the school provisions, these statutes that relate to intermarriage should also be stricken down to carry out your full theory; is not that your real position?

Mr. Carter: One moment, Your Honor. I think that this case involves the question of equality of opportunity in the schools. I was not aware of the fact that the plaintiffs were here to attempt to attack

---

*Davis Trial, p. 177. Records and Briefs, Part 3. John Julian Brooks was Director of the New Lincoln School, New York.

the intermarriage statutes of Virginia. It seems to me this has no bearing on it.

Mr. Moore: We think you have opened up this whole subject as to making good citizens.

Judge Dobie: I think when you enter the field of miscegenation that is a little far removed.

V.
The Preliminary Decisions

THE DECISIONS OF the three-judge federal panels produced no unexpected results. But they varied greatly in texture and tone.

The lead opinion in the South was written by Judge John Parker. Issued on June 21, 1951, it constituted a powerful and seemingly self-confident defense of *Plessy*, though subtle ambiguities lurked in its reasoning. And *Briggs* produced a powerful dissent by Waites Waring, who soon thereafter resigned from the bench and moved to New York.

Judge Albert Bryan's opinion in Virginia (March 7, 1952) followed Judge Parker's to the letter. Both opinions acknowledged inequalities in plant and curriculum, but both reacted in the same negative way to the demand that integration be ordered to remedy these shortcomings.

The *Brown* decision, issued on August 3, 1951, stuck to the broader issue of *Plessy*'s validity, since physical inequality was not really an issue in Kansas. While coming to the expected conclusion on this matter, Judge Walter Huxman and his colleagues displayed a genuine ambivalence, which they clearly assumed that higher courts would resolve. Their decision also indicated that some of the psychological testimony introduced by Robert Carter had left its mark.

Chancellor Seitz's opinion in Delaware (April 1, 1952) revealed the same perplexities about *Plessy* which troubled Judge Huxman. Yet not unexpectedly, in light of the Chancellor's decision in the University of Delaware case, he took the practical step which the southern judges were unwilling to take. This step, of course, did not end the controversy as far as the plaintiffs were concerned. (As a state court matter, Chancellor Seitz's judgement was initially appealed to the Delaware Supreme Court, which upheld his decision on August 28, 1952.)

1. *Briggs* v. *Elliott**

Judge John J. Parker

The problem of segregation as applied to graduate and professional education is essentially different from that involved in segregation in education at the lower level. . . .

At this level, as good education can be afforded in Negro schools as in white schools and the thought of establishing professional contacts does not enter into the picture. Moreover, education at this level is not a matter of voluntary choice on the part of the student but of compulsion by the state. The student is taken from the control of the family during school hours by compulsion of law and placed in control of the school, where he must associate with his fellow students. The law thus provides that the school shall supplement the work of the parent in the training of the child and in doing so it is entering a delicate field and one fraught with tensions and difficulties. In formulating educational policy at the common school level, therefore, the law must take account, not merely of the matter of affording instruction to the student, but also of the wishes of the parent as to the upbringing of the child and his associates in the formative period of childhood and adolescence. If public education is to have the support of the people through their legislatures it must not go contrary to what they deem for the best interests of their children.

There is testimony to the effect that mixed schools will give better education and a better understanding of the community in which the child is to live than segregated schools. There is testimony, on the other hand, that mixed schools will result in racial friction and tension and that the only practical way of conducting public education in South Carolina is with segregated schools. The questions thus presented are not questions of constitutional right but of legislative policy, which must be formulated, not in vacuo or with doctrinaire disregard of existing conditions, but in realistic approach to the situations to which it is to be applied. . . . The federal courts would be going far outside their constitutional function were they to attempt to prescribe educational policies for the states in such matters, however desirable such policies might be in the opinion of some sociologists or educators. For the federal courts to do so would result, not only in interference with local affairs by an agency of the federal government, but

---

*Volume 98 Federal Supplement 529

also in the substitution of the judicial for the legislative process in what is essentially a legislative matter.

The public schools are facilities provided and paid for by the states. The state's regulation of the facilities which it furnishes is not to be interfered with unless constitutional rights are clearly infringed. . . .

We conclude, therefore, that if equal facilities are offered, segregation of the races in the public schools as prescribed by the Constitution and laws of South Carolina is not of itself violative of the Fourteenth Amendment. We think that this conclusion is supported by overwhelming authority which we are not at liberty to disregard on the basis of theories advanced by a few educators and sociologists. Even if we felt at liberty to disregard other authorities, we may not ignore the unreversed decisions of the Supreme Court of the United States which are squarely in point and conclusive of the question before us. . . .

To this we may add that, when seventeen states and the Congress of the United States have for more than three-quarters of a century required segregation of the races in the public schools, and when this has received the approval of the leading appellate courts of the country including the unanimous approval of the Supreme Court of the United States at a time when that court included Chief Justice Taft and Justices Stone, Holmes and Brandeis, it is a late day to say that such segregation is violative of fundamental constitutional rights. It is hardly reasonable to suppose that legislative bodies over so wide a territory, including the Congress of the United States, and great judges of high courts have knowingly defied the Constitution for so long a period or that they have acted in ignorance of the meaning of its provisions. The constitutional prnciple is the same now that it has been throughout this period; and if conditions have changed so that segregation is no longer wise, this is a matter for the legislatures and not for the courts. The members of the judiciary have no more right to read their ideas of sociology into the Constitution than their ideas of economics.

It is argued that, because the school facilities furnished Negroes in District No. 22 are inferior to those furnished white persons, we should enjoin segregation rather than direct the equalizing of conditions. In as much as we think that the law requiring segregation is valid, however, and that the inequality suffered by plaintiffs results, not from the law, but from the way it has been administered, we think that our injunction should be directed to removing the inequalities resulting from administration within the framework of the law rather than to nullifying the law itself. As a court of equity, we should exercise our power to assure to plaintiffs the equality of treatment to which they are entitled with due regard to the legislative policy of the state. In directing that the school facilities afforded Negroes within the district be equalized promptly with those afforded white persons, we are giving plaintiffs all the relief that they can reasonably ask. . . .

Judge Waites Waring, Dissenting

If a case of this magnitude can be turned aside . . . by the mere . . . admission that some buildings, blackboards, lighting fixtures and toilet facilities are unequal but that they may be remedied by the spending of a few dollars, then, indeed people in the plight in which these plaintiffs are, have no adequate remedy or forum in which to air their wrongs. If this method of judicial evasion be adopted, these very infant plaintiffs now pupils in Clarendon County will probably be bringing suits for their children and grandchildren decades or rather generations hence in an effort to get for their descendants what are today denied to them. If they are entitled to any rights as American citizens, they are entitled to have these rights now and not in the future. And no excuse can be made to deny them these rights which are theirs under the Constitution and laws of America by the use of the false doctrine and patter called "separate but equal". . . .

And so we must . . . face without evasion or equivocation, the question as to whether segregation in education in our schools is legal or whether it cannot exist under our American system as particularly enunciated in the Fourteenth Amendment to the Constitution of the United States. . . .

Let us now come to consider whether the Constitution and Laws of the State of South Carolina are in conflict with the true meaning and intendment of this Fourteenth Amendment. The whole discussion of race and ancestry has been intermingled with sophistry and prejudice. What possible definition can be found for the so-called white race, Negro race or other races? Who is to decide and what is the test? For years, there was much talk of blood and taint of blood. Science tells us that there are but four kinds of blood: A, B, AB and O and these are found in Europens, Asiatics, Africans, Americans and others. And so we need not further consider the irresponsible and baseless references to preservation of "Caucasian blood". So then, what test are we going to use in opening our school doors and labeling them "white" and "Negro"? The law of South Carolina considers a person of one-eighth African ancestry to be a Negro. Why this proportion? Is it based upon any reason: anthropological, historical or ethical? And how are the trustees to know who are "whites" and who are "Negroes"? If it is dangerous and evil for a white child to be associated with another child, one of whose great-grandparents was of African descent, is it not equally dangerous for one with a one-sixteenth percentage? And if the State has decided that there is danger in contact between the whites and Negroes, isn't it requisite and proper that the State furnish a series of schools one for each of these percentages? If the idea is perfect racial equality in educational systems, why should children of pure African descent be brought in contact with children of one-half, one-fourth, or one-eighth such ancestry? To ask these questions is sufficient answer to them. The whole thing is unreasonable, unscientific and based upon unadulterated prejudice. We see the results of all of this warped thinking in the poor under-privileged and frightened attitude of so many of the Negroes in the southern states; and in the sadistic insistence of the "white supremacists" in declaring that their will must be imposed irrespective of rights of other citizens. This claim of "white supremacy", while fantastic and without foundation, is really believed by them for we have had repeated declarations from leading politicians and governors of this state and other states declaring that "white supremacy" will be endangered by the abolition of segregation. There are present threats, including those of the present Governor of this state, going to the extent of saying that all public education may be abandoned if the courts should grant true equality in educational facilities. . . .

[T]he plaintiffs [in this case] brought many witnesses, some of them of national reputation. . . .

From their testimony, it was clearly apparent, as it should be to any thoughtful person, irrespective of having such expert testimony, that segregation in education can never produce equality and that it is an evil that must be eradicated. This case presents the matter clearly for adjudication and I am of the opinion that all of the legal guideposts, expert testimony, common sense and reason point unerringly to the conclusion that the system of segregation in education adopted and practiced in the State of South Carolina must go and must go now.

Segregation is per se inequality.

The courts of this land have stricken down discrimination in higher education and have declared unequivocally that segregation is not equality. But these decisions hve pruned away only the noxious fruits. Here in this case, we are asked to strike its very root. Or rather, to change the metaphor, we are asked to strike at the cause of infection and not merely at the symptoms of disease. And if the courts of this land are to render justice under the laws without fear or favor, justice for all men and all kinds of men, the time to do it is now and the place is in the elementary schools where our future citizens learn their first lesson to respect the dignity of the individual in a democracy.

To me the situation is clear and important, particularly at this time when our national leaders are called upon to show to the world that our democracy means what it says and that it is a true democracy and there is no under-cover suppression of the rights of any of our citizens because of the pigmentation of their skins. And I had hoped that this Court would take this view of the situation and make a clear cut declaration that the State of South Carolina should follow the intendment and meaning of the Constitution of the United States.

2. *Davis* v. *County School Board of Prince Edward County**

Judge Albert V. Bryan
On [the] fact issue the Court cannot say that the plaintiffs' evidence overbalances the defendants'. But on the same presentation by the plaintiffs . . . Federal courts have rejected the proposition, in respect to elementary and junior high schools, that the required separation of the races is in law offensive to the National statutes and constitution. They have refused to decree that segregation be abolished incontinently. We accept these decisions as apt and able precedent. Indeed we might ground our conclusion on their opinions alone. But the facts proved in our case, almost without division and perhaps peculiar here, so potently demonstrate why nullification of the cited sections of the statutes and constitution of Virginia is not warranted, that they should speak our conclusion. . . .

It indisputably appears from the evidence that the separation provision rests neither upon prejudice, nor caprice, nor upon any other

---

*Volume 103 Federal Supplement 337

measureless foundation. Rather the proof is that it declares one of the ways of life in Virginia. Separation of white and colored "children" in the public schools of Virginia has for generations been a part of the mores of her people. To have separate schools has been their use and wont. . . .

In this milieu we cannot say that Virginia's separation of white and colored children in the public schools is without substance in fact or reason. We have found no hurt or harm to either race. This ends our inquiry. It is not for us to adjudge the policy as right or wrong. . . .

On the issue of actual inequality our decree will declare its existence in respect to buildings, facilities, curricula and buses. We will restrain immediately its continuance in respect to the curricula and conveyances. We will order the defendant to pursue with diligence and dispatch their present program, now afoot and progressing, to replace the Moton buildings and facilities with a new building and new equipment, or otherwise remove the inequality in them.

3. *Brown* v. *Board of Education of Topeka**

Judge Walter Huxman

We have found as a fact that the physical facilities, the curricula, courses of study, qualification of and quality of teachers, as well as other educational facilities in the two sets of schools are comparable. . . .

In fact, while plaintiff's attorneys have not abandoned this [challenge to the equality of facilities], they did not give it great emphasis in their presentation before the court. They relied primarily upon the contention that segregation in and of itself without more violates their rights guaranteed by the Fourteenth Amendment.

This contention poses a question not free from difficulty. As a subordinate court in the federal judicial system, we seek the answer to this constitutional question in the decisions of the Supreme Court when it has spoken on the subject and do not substitute our own views for the declared law by the Supreme Court. The difficult question as always is to analyze the decisions and seek to ascertain the trend as revealed by the later decisions. . . .

[In that regard] it is vigorously argued and not without some basis . . . that the . . . decisions of the Supreme Court in *McLaurin* v.

---

*Volume 98 Federal Supplement 797

Oklahoma and *Sweatt* v. *Painter* show a trend away from the *Plessy* and [Gong] Lum cases. . . .

[Indeed] if segregation within a school as in the *McLaurin* case is a denial of due process, it is difficult to see why segregation in separate schools would not result in the same denial. Or if the denial of the right to commingle with the majority group in higher institutions of learning as in the *Sweatt* case and gain the educational advantages resulting therefrom, is lack of due process, it is difficult to see why such denial would not result in the same lack of due process if practiced in the lower grades.

It must however be remembered that in both of these cases the Supreme Court made it clear that it was confining itself to answering the one specific question, namely: "To what extend does the equal protection clause limit the power of a state to distinguish between students of different races in professional and graduate education in a state university?", and that the Supreme Court refused to review the *Plessy* case because that question was not essential to a decision of the controversy in the case.

We are accordingly of the view that the *Plessy* and *Lum* cases have not been overruled and that they still presently are authority for the maintenance of a segregated school system in the lower grades. . . .

FINDINGS OF FACT

IV

There is no material difference in the physical facilities in the colored schools and in the white schools and such facilities in the colored schools are not inferior in any material respect to those in the white schools.

V

The educational qualifications of the teachers and the quality of instruction in the colored schools are not inferior to and are comparable to those of the white schools. . . .

VIII

Segregation of white and colored children in public schools has a detrimental effect upon the colored children. The impact is greater when it has the sanction of the law; for the policy of separating the races is usually interpreted as denoting the inferiority of the Negro [sic] group. A sense of inferiority affects the motivation of a child to learn. Segregation with the sanction of law, therefore, has a tendency to retard the educational and mental development of Negro [sic] children and to deprive them of some of the benefits they would receive in a racial integrated school system. . . .

CONCLUSIONS OF LAW. . . .

IV

The only question in [this] case . . . is whether legal segregation in and of itself without more constitutes denial of due process. We are of the view that under the above decision of the Supreme Court the answer must be in the negative. We accordingly conclude that plaintiffs have suffered no denial of due process by virtue of the manner in which the segregated school system of Topeka, Kansas, is being operated.

4. *Belton* v. *Gebhart**

Chancellor Collins J. Seitz

[P]laintiff's first contention . . . is that the evidence demonstrates that the refusal to permit plaintiffs and members of their class to attend schools for white children similarly situated, results in their receiving educational opportunities markedly inferior to those offered white children. This consequence flows, say plaintiffs, solely from the fact that they are Negroes. Simply stated, plaintiffs contend that the evidence shows that legally enforced segregation in education, in and of itself, prevents the Negro from receiving educational opportunities which are "equal" to those offered whites.

Plaintiffs produced many expert witnesses in the fields of education, sociology, psychology, psychiatry and anthropology. Their qualifications were fully established. No witnesses in opposition were produced. . . .

Defendants say that the evidence shows that the State may not be "ready" for non-segregated education, and that a social problem cannot be solved with legal force. Assuming the validity of the contention, without for a minute conceding the sweeping factual assumption, nevertheless, the contention does not answer the fact that the Negro's mental health and, therefore, his educational opportunities are ad-

---

*Volume 87 Atlantic Reporter, Second Series, 862

versely affected by State-imposed segregation in education. The application of Constitutional principles is often distasteful to some citizens,
but that is one reason for Constitutional guarantees. The principles
override transitory passions.

I conclude from the testimony that in our Delaware society, State-
imposed segregation in education itself results in the Negro children,
as a class, receiving educational opportunities which are substantially
inferior to those available to white children otherwise similarly situated.

But my factual conclusion does not dispose of the question presented. I say this because it is necessary to consider the decisions of
the United States Supreme Court construing the Fourteenth Amendment as they apply to this general problem. . . .

The question which judicial integrity requires me to answer is this:
Has the U. S. Supreme Court by fair or necessary implication decided
that State-imposed segregated education on the grammar and high
school levels, in and of itself, does not violate the Fourteenth
Amendment? . . .

[I think that] by implication, the Supreme Court of the United
States has said a separate but equal test can be applied, at least below
the college level. This Court does not believe such an implication is
justified under the evidence. Nevertheless, I do not believe a lower
court can reject a principle of United States Constitutional law which
has been adopted by fair implication by the highest court of the land.
I believe the "separate but equal" doctrine in education should be
rejected, but I also believe its rejection must come from that
Court. . . .

Under these circumstances [the gross physical inequalities which
Chancellor Seitz found to exist between the black and white schools],
defendants urge that . . . the Court . . . do no more than direct the
defendants to equalize facilities and opportunities, and give them time
to comply with such an order. . . . It is true that in such a situation
some courts have merely directed the appropriate State officials to
equalize facilities. I do not believe that such is the relief warranted by
a finding that the United States Constitution has been violated. It
seems to me that when a plaintiff shows to the satisfaction of a court
that there is an existing and continuing violation of the "separate but
equal" doctrine, he is entitled to have made available to him the State
facilities which have been shown to be superior. To do otherwise is
to say to such a plaintiff: "Yes, your Constitutional rights are being

invaded, but be patient, we will see whether in time they are still being violated." If, as the Supreme Court has said, this right is personal, such a plaintiff is entitled to relief immediately, in the only way it is available, namely, by admission to the school with the superior facilities. To postpone such relief is to deny relief, in whole or in part, and to say that the protective provisions of the Constitution offer no immediate protection.

PART THREE

At the Bar of the Supreme Court: The First Argument

Introduction

THE LOWER COURT decisions in *Briggs* and *Brown* went to the Supreme
Court for reconsideration in the summer of 1951. Since both cases
involved the constitutionality of state law and the decisions of three-
judge panels, they were put before the Court through the method
known simply as appeal. Under the so-called Judges' Bill of 1925, the
legislation which created the Court's modern procedures for handling
litigation, such appeals were supposed to be heard as a matter of right.
They fell into a small category of cases deemed worthy of automatic
Supreme Court review.

It was not necessary therefore in either *Briggs* or *Brown* to resort to
the more common, and presumably more uncertain device for bringing a controversy to the Court's attention, the device called a petition
for a writ of certiorari. The vast majority of litigants who want to
appear at the bar of the Supreme Court must file such a petition,
which literally asks the Justices "to certify" their case, in short to hear
it. The Justices have total discretion in determining which petitions
they will accept, lest they be inundated with work. Marshall, Carter,
and their clients seemed to occupy a more favorable position. Indeed
they now took on a new legal title. They were no longer the plaintiffs,
but the appellants. The school boards were no longer the defendants,
but the appellees.

By 1951, however, a large gap had grown up between the legislative
intent of the Judges' Bill and the Court's actual manner of considering
appeals. Many years earlier, the Justices had concluded that hearing
even the entire appeals docket posed an intolerable burden, and so
they instituted a practice for handling such cases which still obtains
today. They require the parties to an appeal to file a jurisdictional
statement, explaining the nature and importance of their case. The
Court then treats the statement as it would a petition for certiorari,
and feels free to dismiss the appeal unless four Justices think the
matter important enough for full argument.

107

Many complex factors enter into whether an appeal (or a certiorari petition) will be granted. The most basic consideration is that the appeal involve a significant constitutional or statutory issue, that it present what the Court calls a "substantial federal question." As Chief Justice Charles Evans Hughes noted in 1937, "Review by the Supreme Court is in the interest of the law, its appropriate exposition and enforcement, not in the mere interest of the litigants."[1]

In that regard, the *Briggs* and *Brown* cases easily qualified. They were obviously of fundamental constitutional significance. But were the Justices ready to tackle issues of such explosive import? The Court frequently sets aside even the most momentous questions because it feels that the moment has not arrived for deciding them, that the issues they pose are not ripe for adjudication.

The initial handling of the segregation cases suggested hesitancy. The Court took no action on either case until January 28, 1952. This was two weeks after Judge Parker sent on to Washington a report from the Clarendon County school commissioners which he had demanded in his original decision, detailing the progress made during the previous six months toward achieving equalization. In light of this report, the Justices dismissed the *Briggs* suit, at least temporarily, and sent the matter back to the lower court "for further proceedings."[2] Meanwhile, they had not acted at all on the *Brown* appeal.

The "further proceedings" in March of 1952 went about as expected. Thurgood Marshall argued that since the school board's report admitted equality of facilities did not yet exist in Clarendon County, Judge Parker should immediately admit black students to the white schools, even under his holding that the South Carolina segregation law was valid. But Parker and his colleagues (Judge Dobie having replaced Judge Waring) predictably refused Marshall's demand. Clarendon County, said the Judge, had "complied with the decree . . . to equalize conditions as rapidly as was humanly possible." This happy state would be realized by September, and "no good would be accomplished for anyone by an order disrupting the organization of the schools so near the end of the scholastic year."[3]

Briggs was appealed once more, and now things began to happen. On June 9, 1952, the Court granted the appeals in both *Brown* and *Briggs*, joining them together for oral argument in October. (Since *Briggs* fell off the Supreme Court schedule of cases at the time of its dismissal, *Brown* would now head the docket.) But on October 8, 1952, the Court postponed arguments until December 8, because it had granted an appeal in *Davis* v. *County School Board of Prince Edward County*. The Justices now wanted all these cases consolidated.

The consolidation went further. Shortly after the October postponement, Supreme Court Clerk Harold B. Willey instructed the lawyers in the District of Columbia desegregation suit, *Bolling* v. *Sharpe*, that the Court wished to hear their case along with the other three. The Justices regarded this as advisable, apparently, even though *Bolling* involved a federal jurisdiction and raised separate constitutional issues. In the *Bolling* case, a petition for a writ of certiorari was required, and the Court granted certiorari on November 10, 1952.

Finally on November 13, Attorney General Albert Young of Delaware petitioned for a writ of certiorari to contest the state court decisions ordering integration of Delaware's schools. The Court granted the petition, but told the Delaware lawyers that they must present their case along with the other four on December 9, 1952, a day later than originally announced.

In the meantime, a change in the cast of characters who would argue before the Court was taking place. The Topeka school board decided in 1952 that the city would abolish segregation in the near future. Their attorney had written to the Court in early October, therefore, a week before the original date for oral argument, saying that the board would not defend the *Brown* suit. The rescheduling to December did not affect the board's position; but since the statute under attack was a state statute, the Attorney General of Kansas reluctantly agreed to defend it at the Supreme Court level.

The Court which would hear the school segregation cases consisted of five Justices appointed by President Roosevelt and four chosen by President Truman.

The five Roosevelt appointees were:

HUGO L. BLACK (b. 1886). Black was a Senator from Alabama when selected for the Court in 1937. A populist and a staunch supporter of the New Deal, Black's record stamped him as relatively liberal on racial matters for his time and place. Reporters discovered after his confirmation that Black had briefly joined the Ku Klux Klan in the 1920s, but Roosevelt's first appointee refused to resign and rode out the storm of public protest.

STANLEY K. REED (b. 1884). One of two Kentuckians on the Court, Reed was Solicitor General at the time of his nomination in 1938. In that capacity, he performed the unenviable task of defending key New

Deal legislation before some of his hostile predecessors on the bench, once fainting in the middle of a presentation because of overwork.

FELIX FRANKFURTER (b. 1882). A Harvard professor, legal scholar, and confidant to Justices Holmes and Brandeis, Frankfurter functioned as a close personal adviser to President Roosevelt before going on the Court in early 1939. While at Harvard, he sat on the national board of the NAACP. Regarded as the Court's most learned member, he sometimes exasperated colleagues who thought he was treating them as he would a refractory student.

WILLIAM O. DOUGLAS (b. 1898). A former Yale Law School professor, Douglas was serving as chairman of the Securities and Exchange Commission when Roosevelt nominated him to replace Louis Brandeis in 1939. This made him at forty the youngest member of the Court since Joseph Story in the early nineteenth century. Regarded as the Court's most outspoken liberal, Douglas was sometimes accused of hasty judicial craftsmanship in his opinons.

ROBERT H. JACKSON (b. 1892). Jackson gained praise as one of the nation's greatest Solicitors General, a post he held before becoming Attorney General in 1940. F.D.R. nominated him for an Associate Justiceship in 1941, after seriously pondering his selection as Chief Justice. On the bench, Jackson was especially noted for his sparkling, lucid prose style.

The Truman appointees included the incumbent Chief Justice:

FRED M. VINSON (b. 1890). Vinson was Truman's Secretary of the Treasury when the President named him as Chief Justice in 1946. A long-time Congressman from Kentucky and a power on the House Ways and Means Committee, he also served as Roosevelt's Director of Economic Stabilization during World War II. After the hectic tenure of Vinson's predecessor as Chief Justice, former Associate Justice Harlan Fiske Stone, Truman was drawn to the appointment of an outsider with a talent for political compromise. Furthermore, Vinson was not without judicial experience, having been on the Court of Appeals for the District of Columbia from 1938 to 1943.

HAROLD BURTON (b. 1888). Elected as a reform Mayor of Cleveland in 1935, Burton was a Republican Senator from Ohio when Truman chose him for the Court in 1945. This being the new President's first appointment, he seems to have selected Burton in order to dramatize his belief in the non-partisan nature of the institution. Not a profound legal thinker, Burton won the respect of his colleagues nonetheless for his humility and fairness.

TOM C. CLARK (b. 1889). A former Assistant Attorney General in charge of the Criminal Division, Clark had moved up to Attorney General at the time of his selection in 1949. A native Texan, he was one of four southerners on the Court in 1952. Though certainly not a Holmes or a Brandeis, Clark scarcely deserved President Truman's dyspeptic judgment on him in later years. "Tom Clark was my biggest mistake. No question about it. . . . He hasn't made one right decision that I can think of."[4] (This would theoretically include *Brown v. Board of Education*.)

SHERMAN M. MINTON (b. 1890). A native of southern Indiana, Minton turned out to be Truman's final addition to the Court. He became a Truman crony while a member of the Senate from 1935 to 1941. Defeated for reelection, he received an appointment to the Seventh Circuit Court of Appeals, where he was serving at the time of his Supreme Court nomination in 1949. It was not regarded as a distinguished selection.

The hope that Chief Justice Vinson would function as a soothing influence on the Court was quickly disappointed. The postwar Justices remained bitterly divided on personal as well as ideological grounds. All of the Roosevelt appointees were united in their low opinion of Vinson as a jurist. Frankfurter, in turn, disliked Black and Douglas, whom he accused of lacking the impartial temperament necessary to Supreme Court service. He was especially venomous in his attitude toward Douglas, believing that his colleague was using the Court to maneuver himself into the Presidency. Meanwhile, Jackson expressed bitter enmity toward Hugo Black, believing that Black had destroyed any hope of his elevation to Chief Justice in 1946 by threatening to resign from the Court if President Truman chose Jackson (a charge which Black denied).

Yet whatever their differences, the Justices appeared united in the area of civil rights and equal protection. They had decided the *Sweatt—McLaurin—Henderson* trio of cases by a unanimous vote, *Shelley* by 6–0. Justice Burton alone dissented in *Morgan v. Virginia*.

The picture was actually more complicated. However much the final product in *Sweatt* and *McLaurin* pointed toward the demise of segregation, at least in educational institutions, several Justices expressed views at the time of those decisions which boded ill for the appellants in *Brown*. The Justices focused on a matter which would eventually loom large in the disposition of the school segregation cases: the original intent of the fourteenth amendment.

Thus Chief Justice Vinson argued initially that the issues in *Sweatt* and *McLaurin* were "settled by [the] legislative history surrounding [the] adoption of [the] 14th amend[ment]."[5] Segregated schools, he noted, existed in most of the states after the Civil War; and while not bearing directly on the intent of the fourteenth amendment, it was significant that Congress had condoned segregation in the District of Columbia schools. "[W]hen we have all this historical background, it is hard for me to say schools should not be separate."[6] Because of this evidence, Vinson was inclined at first to deny relief to either Sweatt or McLaurin. "How can you have [a] constitutional provision *as to graduate* but *not as to elementary* [schools]?"[7]

Justice Reed took much the same view. "It is hard for me to say something that has been constitutional for years is suddenly bad. The 14th Amendment was not aimed at segregation. . . . It would be unfortunate at this time for us to say segregation [is] unconstitutional."[8] Unlike his two colleagues, Justice Robert Jackson favored granting relief to Sweatt and McLaurin because of the obvious inequalities involved in their situations. But he could find nothing in the fourteenth amendment to suggest that it applied to segregated schools, or indeed to education at all. "In effect, we [would be] amending the Constitution."[9]

Vinson and Reed acquiesced, of course, in the final disposition of the graduate school cases, Vinson even writing the opinions. But it is highly unlikely that the Chief Justice viewed those opinions in the same light as did the liberal admirers of *Sweatt* and *McLaurin*—as a de facto repudiation of *Plessy*. Here was an instance in Supreme Court jurisprudence which was akin to a situation often noted in literature. The intention of the words and the intention of the author did not necessarily square. Along with Reed and Jackson, Vinson no doubt maintained a straight face when he rejected the "contention that Plessy v. Ferguson should be reexamined in the light of contemporary knowledge."

Clearly then, three of the Justices of 1952 were of doubtful mien regarding the constitutional contentions being pressed in the *Brown* cases. Some might automatically place this number at four, because Tom Clark had voted 90% of the time with Vinson since coming on the Court. In fact, however, Clark inclined toward a tougher approach to segregation. His comments at the time of *Sweatt* and *McLaurin* do display a marked hesitancy to confront the matter in elementary and secondary schools. But he expressed no doubts about the graduate school issue and no regrets over the possibility of *Plessy's* eventual demise. "I join with those who would reverse these cases upon the ground that segregated graduate education denies equal protection of the laws. . . . If some say this undermines *Plessy* then let it fall, as have many Nineteenth Century oracles."[10]

Four of the other Justices who were to hear the *Brown* cases in 1952—Black, Douglas, Frankfurter, and Burton—were more inclined toward outlawing educational segregation; Justice Minton's views were unknown. But for all of the Justices such a decision presented grave practical difficulties. Parts of the South were bound to greet it with outrage, even with defiance. And any successful show of disobedience to the Court's orders exposed its fragility as an institution in American society, threatened the delicate balance on which its function in our constitutional system depends.

Under that system, the Court is in the literal sense of the word *Supreme*: the final, authorized interpreter of the Constitution, with authority to direct that Senators and Presidents obey judicial mandates. But the Justices command no army or nuclear arsenal which compels obedience to those mandates. No popular endorsement in a recent election backs them up when they rule. In that sense the Supreme Court is in Alexander Hamilton's words the "least dangerous" branch.[11] The efficacy of its judgments rest upon moral consent. If it gets too far out of step with the realities of American society, the executive branch may find itself unable or unwilling to enforce Court decrees, no matter how legally correct the Justices (and the law professors) believe them to be. Such a situation nourishes the erosion, not to say the destruction of the Court's constitutional role.

No Justice articulated this sense of the Court's fragility so well as Felix Frankfurter. For him indeed, the entire rule of law was infinitely fragile. "His fear," said one of his Harvard colleagues, was "not of authority but of the breakdown of authority, of the letting loose upon society of the dread war of each against each."[12] As Frankfurter himself once put it:

> The most prized liberties themselves presuppose an independent judiciary through which these liberties may be . . . vindicated. If one man can be allowed to determine for himself what

is law, every man can. That means first chaos, then tyranny.
Legal process is an essential part of the democratic process.[13]

Frankfurter no doubt favored a decision in *Brown* invalidating Jim
Crow education. He certainly agonized over the prospect of judicial
supervision in a sensitive area of social policy, exactly the kind of
interference with legislative prerogatives he normally deplored. But
an undated fragment found in his papers, entitled "Segregation,"
shows the direction of his thinking. "Stare decisis means respect for
decisions." But "Society keeps changing or rots through stagnation.
Human needs gradually emerge into consciousness . . . and assert
themselves with such impact that they become absorbed into the existing framework of law."[14]

The Justice believed it essential, however, to proceed in the school
cases in a manner which avoided the chaos he so feared. He wanted
a unanimous decision of the Court, if that was at all possible. In
preparation for the oral arguments, he also began to ponder the kind
of decree for implementing segregation likely to cause the least adverse
reaction in the South. Clearly, Frankfurter's greatest fear was a decision which would be disobeyed; his overriding goal was to see that
this did not happen.

Hugo Black shared the concern of his frequent antagonist. He told
his colleagues frankly that a decision scuttling *Plessy* in education,
much as he favored it, would unloose southern racial demagoguery
and would probably have to be implemented in places by force. With
such uneasy sentiments stirring, the Justices prepared to consider
Brown and its companion cases in December, 1952.

There are basically two stages in which a case is argued before the
Supreme Court. The oral argument, to which we have already alluded, normally constitutes the final stage. Before that, however, the
parties submit written briefs to the Court. These briefs trace in some
detail the factual background of the case. Most important, they ex-
pound point by point the major legal or constitutional contentions
which each side feels should determine the outcome. The appellant's
brief is due three weeks before the Court hears the case; the appellees
must file one week before the hearing.

In 1952, no rule limited the length of Supreme Court briefs. Some
of them, even in ordinary anti-trust cases, ran to more than 300 pages.
The United States government brief in the important steel seizure
case, heard in June of 1952, consumed 175 pages; the steel company's
brief, 104 pages. Eventually, the Court's growing case load, and the

conviction of many Justices that briefs were too long anyway, produced a rule in 1980 which restricts all written briefs to fifty pages. Such restrictions would not have hampered any of the litigants in the state segregation controversies. The longest brief in those cases, the Kansas brief in *Brown* v. *Board of Education of Topeka*, covered only 43 pages. The NAACP brief in *Brown* was but 13 pages.

Length notwithstanding, Supreme Court rules require counsel to provide the busy Justices with several learning aids to the briefs they submit. Every brief has to start with a three or four page summary of the argument it is about to make, and the main body of the argument itself must contain boldface headings at the beginning of each section. The definitive guide to the intricacies of the Court's rules, *Supreme Court Practice* by Robert Stern and Eugene Gressman, admits frankly that these summaries and boldface headings are designed for men "who may not have had time to read the entire brief before oral argument."[15] But the Justices surely read the documents in the school cases.

In character, the briefs filed for the Justices' benefit differ from the type filed in lower courts. There the piling up of legal citations, especially citations from Supreme Court cases, is thought decisive, since lower courts are closely bound by precedent. But Stern and Gressman remind lawyers that the high court "is not bound by authorities to any greater extent than it wishes to be, and . . . is much freer to reach what it regards as the correct or wise decision than any subordinate tribunal."[16] This means that while attorneys cannot ignore authority, they can attempt more openly to persuade the Justices "on grounds of reason and principle. . . . The first and most important factor for counsel to remember is that he is writing for a *supreme court.* . . ."[17]

Individuals or organizations not involved in a case, but wishing to make their views known, may file an *amicus curiae* (friend of the court) brief. Until 1949, anyone could freely do this. But because of the 21 amicus briefs which descended upon the Court in *Shelley* v. *Kraemer,* the Justices modified the rule, requiring consent of the parties to a case, or an order of the Court itself, before friendly parties can intervene. Seven friends of the Court, including the government of the United States, filed briefs supporting the appellants in the state cases grouped under *Brown.*

The oral argument is the climactic phase of the advocate's role before the Supreme Court, and the only part of the legal drama which the public can witness. Under the rules prevailing in 1952, each side in a case received one hour of argument, reduced in 1970 to half an hour. But both then and now, the Court may extend this allotment. In the steel seizure case each side was given two and one half hours of oral argument. The lawyers in the school segregation cases got the standard one hour for each side. Since there were five related cases, however, that meant ten hours of oral argument.

There is one cardinal principle which governs all oral presentations. Attorneys must not read their argument verbatim, as if they were declaiming in an oratory contest. Rather, they should speak naturally and conversationally, using notes as a guide. "The oral argument," say Stern and Gressman, "should not be a mere recitation of the contents of the brief. It should be adapted . . . to whatever the Court does not seem to understand or appreciate. . . . In the Supreme Court, flexibility is . . . essential."[18] Above all, advocates should be prepared to engage in a dialogue with the Justices, who question them vigorously as a rule about the nuances of their case. Many Justices see this Socratic function as the most important aspect of public argumentation. Justice Frankfurter, a tough and persistent questioner, once noted that the Court, sitting for oral argument, was "not designed as a dozing audience for the reading of soliloquies, but as a questioning body, utilizing oral arguments as a means of exposing the difficulties of a case with a view to meeting them."[19]

Lawyers are prone to view the Court's questioning as an unwelcome intrusion on their carefully designed pattern of argument. But the questions also present an opportunity to allay doubts which trouble a wavering Justice, or to better arm one already sympathetic to your cause. Justice Jackson, a great advocate before the Court as Solicitor General prior to his appointment, could see both sides of the issue. He admitted that questions from the bench often "upset the plan of argument before the lawyer has fairly started."[20] Nonetheless, "it seemed to me that I could make no better use of my time than to answer any doubt which a judge would do me the favor to disclose. Experience in the Court teaches that a . . . . lively dialogue may be a swifter and surer vehicle to truth than a dismal monologue."[21] Engaging in such a dialogue meant standing up to the Justices at times, Jackson thought. "Be respectful, of course, but also be self-respectful, and neither disparage yourself nor flatter the Justices. We think well enough of ourselves already."[22]

Stern and Gressman conclude that many attorneys regard oral argument before the Court as a useless ritual, once a case is thoroughly briefed. But the Justices who have commented on the matter take a different view. Justice Jackson felt that his colleagues "would answer unanimously that . . . they rely heavily on oral presentations. Most of them form at least a tentative conclusion from it in a large percentage of . . . cases."[23] Chief Justice Hughes was even more emphatic. Except in very complex litigation, he asserted, "the impression that a judge has at the close of a full argument accords with the conviction which controls his final vote."[24]

The Supreme Court's method of considering cases underlines the possible importance of oral argument. The Justices meet in conference soon after the oral presentation to deliberate on their decision, at a time when the presentation remains fresh in their minds. In 1952, the Court's practice was to convene on Saturday and consider the cases argued that week. When it met on Saturday, December 13, to talk about the school segregation cases, the members had been deluged with oral argument on Tuesday, Wednesday, and Thursday.

But whether those arguments played the decisive role which Jackson and Hughes suggest they usually play is doubtful. Extensive study and reflection was going on among the Justices before the oral presentation of *Brown* and its companions. When that happens, the impressions created by dialogue will likely recede in importance. Phillip Elman, who was Special Assistant to the Attorney General at the time of the *Brown* arguments in 1952, has noted, "[T]he greater the issues involved in a case, the less oral arguments are likely to affect it."[25]

Notes

[1] Quoted in Anthony Lewis, *Gideon's Trumpet* (New York, 1964), p. 25.
[2] *Briggs v. Elliott*, 342 US 350 (1952), at 351.
[3] *Briggs v. Elliott*, 103 F. Supp. 920 (1952), at 922.
[4] Harry Truman, *Plain Speaking* (New York, 1973), p. 225.
[5] Dennis Hutchinson, "Unanimity and Desegregation: Decisionmaking in the Supreme Court, 1948–1958," *Georgetown Law Journal* (Vol. 68, 1979), 1, 22.
[6] *Ibid.*
[7] *Ibid.*, p. 23.
[8] *Ibid.*
[9] *Ibid.*, p. 24.
[10] *Ibid.*, p. 22.

[11]Alexander Hamilton, "Federalist 78," in Clinton Rossiter, editor, *Federalist Papers* (New York, 1961), p. 465.

[12]Louis Jaffe, "Justice Frankfurter's Judicial Universe," *Harvard Law Review* (Vol. 62, 1949), 357, 410.

[13]*United States* v. *United Mine Workers*, 330 US 258 (1947), at 311–12.

[14]Quoted in Bernard Schwartz, *Super Chief* (New York, 1983), p. 77.

[15]Robert L. Stern, Eugene Gressman, Stephen M. Shapiro, *Supreme Court Practice*, Sixth Edition (Washington, D.C., 1986), p. 556.

[16]*Ibid.*, p. 560.

[17]*Ibid.*, pp. 560, 559.

[18]*Ibid.*, p. 606.

[19]Felix Frankfurter, *Of Law and Men* (New York, 1956), p. 321.

[20]Robert H. Jackson, "Advocacy Before the United States Supreme Court," *Cornell Law Quarterly* (Vol. 37, 1951), 1, 6.

[21]*Ibid.*, p. 12.

[22]*Ibid.*, p. 4.

[23]*Ibid.*, p. 2.

[24]Charles Evans Hughes, *The Supreme Court of the United States* (New York, 1928), p. 61.

[25]Quoted in Richard Kluger, *Simple Justice* (New York, 1975), p. 551.

I.

Brown v. Board of Education of Topeka

BECAUSE THE PLAINTIFFS had all but conceded that black and white schools in Topeka were equal in terms of facilities and curriculum, the NAACP brief in the *Brown* case could not invoke the three-layered strategy of *Sweatt*. But like its companions in South Carolina and Virginia, the brief followed the earlier trial by placing its heaviest emphasis upon the "middle strategy"—articulation of the psychological harms caused by segregation.

Such a course was particularly appropriate in *Brown* considering Judge Huxman's cryptic but potentially explosive finding of fact in the lower court decision. The body of the brief did not present social science evidence in detail, however. Instead an appendix, signed by 35 prominent social scientists, gave a rather diffuse but often incisive summary of the accumulated knowledge concerning "The Effects of Segregation and the Consequences of Desegregation." This appendix was formally attached to all of the state appeals. But it is found in the published record immediately following the brief in *Brown* v. *Board of Education*.

These social science findings inspired the NAACP to take the conservative route to destroying separate but equal in education. The brief's central contention was that the *Plessy* decision did not have to be overruled in this area, because the state of scientific knowledge, as well as the logic of *Sweatt* and *McLaurin*, rendered *Plessy* inapplicable to educational facilities. The appellants buttressed their point with a shrewd put perhaps over-ingenious argument from history: *Plessy* was not controlling for the *Brown* cases because its doctrine had never been at issue in a case involving educational institutions until *Sweatt* and *McLaurin*; and there the Justices denied the state's authority to set up the racial classifications in question.

Standing in isolation, such arguments could be taken as the converse of the ones made by Homer Plessy's lawyers in 1896. They had insinuated that separate but equal *was* applicable to education, but maintained that it did not necessarily apply elsewhere.

In any event, the appellants' view of *Plessy* was sharply challenged in the Kansas brief, composed by the state's Assistant Attorney General Paul Wilson; and the Justices vigorously pursued the matter at oral argument.

1. Appellants' Brief*

ARGUMENT

I

The State of Kansas in affording opportunities for elementary education to its citizens has no power under the Constitution of the United States to impose racial restrictions and distinctions.

While the State of Kansas has undoubted power to confer benefits or impose disabilities upon selected groups of citizens in the normal execution of governmental functions, it must conform to constitutional standards in the exercise of this authority. These standards may be generally characterized as a requirement that the state's action be reasonable. Reasonableness in a constitutional sense is determined by examining the action of the state to discover whether the distinctions or restrictions in issue are in fact based upon real differences pertinent to a lawful legislative objective. . . .

When the distinctions imposed are based upon race and color alone, the state's action is patently the epitome of that arbitrariness and capriciousness constitutionally impermissive under our system of government. *Yick Wo v. Hopkins*, 118 U.S. 356; *Skinner v. Oklahoma*, 316 U.S. 535. A racial criterion is a constitutional irrelevance, *Edwards v. California*, 314 U.S. 160, 184, and is not saved from condemnation even though dictated by a sincere desire to avoid the possibility of violence or race friction. *Buchanan v. Warley*, 245 U.S. 60; *Morgan v. Virginia*, 328 U.S. 373. Only because it was a war

---

*Reprinted in Kurland and Casper, Vol. 49, pp. 27–61.

measure designed to cope with a grave national emergency was the federal government permitted to level restrictions against persons of enemy descent. *Hirabayashi* v. *United States*, 320 U.S. 81; *Oyama* v. *California*, 332 U.S. 633. This action, "odious," *Hirabayashi* v. *United States, supra,* at page 100, and "suspect," *Korematsu* v. *United States,* 323 U.S. 214, 216, even in times of national peril, must cease as soon as that peril is past. *Ex Parte Endo,* 323 U.S. 283.

This Court has found violation of the equal protection clause in racial distinctions and restrictions imposed by the states in selection for jury service, *Shepherd* v. *Florida,* 341 U.S. 50; ownership and occupancy of real property, *Shelley* v. *Kraemer,* 334 U.S. 1; *Buchanan* v. *Warley, supra;* gainful employment, *Takahaski* v. *Fish and Game Commission,* 334 U.S. 410; voting, *Nixon* v. *Condon,* 286 U.S. 73; and graduate and professional education. *McLaurin* v. *Board of Regents; Sweatt* v. *Painter.* The commerce clause in proscribing the imposition of racial distinctions and restrictions in the field of interstate travel is a further limitation of state power in this regard. *Morgan* v. *Virginia,* 328 U.S. 373.

Since 1940, in an unbroken line of decisions, this Court has clearly enunciated the doctrine that the state may not validly impose distinctions and restrictions among its citizens based upon race or color alone in each field of governmental activity where question has been raised. . . .

It follows, therefore, that under this doctrine, the State of Kansas which by statutory sanctions seeks to subject appellants, in their pursuit of elementary education, to distinctions based upon race or color alone, is here attempting to exceed the constitutional limits to its authority. For that racial distinction which has been held arbitrary in so many other areas of governmental activity is no more appropriate and can be no more reasonable in public education.

II

The court below, having found that appellants were denied equal educational opportunities by virtue of the segregated school system, erred in denying the relief prayed.

The court below made the following finding of fact:

"Segregation of white and colored children in public schools has a detrimental effect upon the colored children. The impact is greater when it has the sanction of the law; for the policy of

> separating the races is usually interpreted as denoting the inferiority of the negro group. A sense of inferiority affects the motivation of a child to learn. Segregation with the sanction of law, therefore, has a tendency to retard the educational and mental development of negro children and to deprive them of some of the benefits they would receive in a racially integrated school system."

That these conclusions are the consensus of social scientists is evidenced by the appendix filed herewith. . . .

Under the Fourteenth Amendment, equality of educational opportunities necessitates an evaluation of all factors affecting the educational process. *Sweatt* v. *Painter*; *McLaurin* v. *Board of Regents*. Applying this yardstick, any restrictions or distinction based upon race or color that places the Negro at a disadvantage in relation to other racial groups in his pursuit of educational opportunities is violative of the equal protection clause.

In the instant case, the court found as a fact that appellants were placed at such a disadvantage and were denied educational opportunities equal to those available to white students. It necessarily follows, therefore, that the court should have concluded as a matter of law that appellants were deprived of their right to equal educational opportunities in violation of the equal protection clause of the Fourteenth Amendment.

Under the mistaken notion that *Plessy* v. *Ferguson* and *Gong Lum* v. *Rice* were controlling with respect to the validity of racial distinctions in elementary education, the trial court refused to conclude that appellants were here denied equal educational opportunities in violation of their constitutional rights. Thus, notwithstanding that it had found inequality in educational opportunity as a fact, the court concluded as a matter of law that such inequality did not constitute a denial of constitutional rights. . . .

Gong Lum v. *Rice* is irrelevant to the issues in this [case]. . . .

There the petitioner was not inveighing against the system, but that its application resulted in her classification as a Negro rather than as a white person, and indeed by so much conceded the propriety of the system itself. . . .

In short, she raised no issue with respect to the state's power to enforce racial classifications, as do appellants here. Rather, her objection went only to her treatment under the classification. This case, therefore, cannot be pointed to as a controlling precedent covering the instant case in which the constitutionality of the system itself is the basis for attack and in which it is shown the inequality in fact exists.

In any event the assumptions in the *Gong Lum* case have since been rejected by this Court. In the *Gong Lum* case, without "full argument and consideration," the Court assumed the state had power to make racial distinctions in its public schools without violating the equal protection clause of the Fourteenth Amendment. . . . Language in *Plessy* v. *Ferguson* was cited in support of these assumptions. These assumptions upon full argument and consideration were rejected in the *McLaurin* and *Sweatt* cases in relation to racial distinctions in state graduate and professional education. [So] according to those cases, *Plessy* v. *Ferguson* is not controlling for the purpose of determining the state's power to enforce racial segregation in public schools. . . .

Plessy v. *Ferguson* is not applicable [to this case, therefore]. Whatever doubts may once have existed in this respect were removed by this Court in *Sweatt* v. *Painter*. . . .

Thus, the very basis of the decision in the *Gong Lum* case has been destroyed. We submit, therefore, that this Court has considered the basic issue involved here only in those cases dealing with racial distinctions in education at the graduate and professional levels. . . .

In the *McLaurin* and *Sweatt* cases, this Court measured the effect of racial restrictions upon the educational development of the individual affected, and took into account the community's actual evaluation of the schools involved. In the instant case, the court below found as a fact that racial segregation in elementary education denoted the inferiority of Negro children and retarded their educational and mental development. Thus the same factors which led to the result reached in the *McLaurin* and *Sweatt* cases are present. Their underlying principles, based upon sound analyses, control the instant case.

Conclusion

In light of the foregoing, we respectfully submit that appellants have been denied their rights to equal educational opportunities within the meaning of the Fourteenth Amendment and that the judgment of the court below should be reversed.

APPENDIX TO APPELLANTS' BRIEFS
The Effects of Segregation and the Consequences of Desegregation:
A Social Science Statement

I

The problem of the segregation of racial and ethnic groups constitutes one of the major problems facing the American people today.
It seems desirable, therefore, to summarize the contributions which
contemporary social science can make toward its resolution. There
are, of course, moral and legal issues involved with respect to which
the signers of the present statement cannot speak with any special
authority and which must be taken into account in the solution of the
problem. There are, however, also factual issues involved with respect
to which certain conclusions seem to be justified on the basis of the
available scientific evidence. It is with these issues only that this paper
is concerned. . . .

II . . . .

Segregation imposes upon individuals a distorted sense of social
reality.

Segregation leads to a blockage in the communications and interac-
tion between the two groups. Such blockages tend to increase mutual
suspicion, distrust and hostility.

Segregation not only perpetuates rigid stereotypes and reinforces
negative attitudes toward members of the other group, but also leads
to the development of a social climate within which violent outbreaks
of racial tensions are likely to occur. . . .

On the basis of [our] general fund of knowledge, it seems likely that
feelings of inferiority and doubts about personal worth are attributable
to living in an underprivileged environment only insofar as the latter
is itself perceived as an indicator of low social status and as a symbol
of inferiority. In other words, one of the important determinants in
producing such feelings is the awareness of social status difference.
While there are many other factors that serve as reminders of the
differences in social status, there can be little doubt that the fact of
enforced segregation is a major factor.

This seems to be true for the following reasons among others: (1)
because enforced segregation results from the decision of the majority
group without the consent of the segregated and is commonly so
perceived; and (2) because historically segregation patterns in the

United States were developed on the assumption of the inferiority of the segregated.

In addition, enforced segregation gives official recognition and sanction to these other factors of the social complex, and thereby enhances the effects of the latter in creating the awareness of social status differences and feelings of inferiority. The child who, for example, is compelled to attend a segregated school may be able to cope with ordinary expressions of prejudice by regarding the prejudiced person as evil or misguided; but he cannot readily cope with symbols of authority, the full force of the authority of the State—the school or the school board, in this instance—in the same manner. Given both the ordinary expression of prejudice and the school's policy of segregation, the former takes on greater force and seemingly becomes an official expression of the latter. . . .

The preceding view is consistent with the opinion stated by a large majority (90%) of social scientists who replied to a questionaire concerning the probable effects of enforced segregation under conditions of equal facilities. This opinion was that, regardless of the facilities which are provided, enforced segregation is psychologically detrimental to the members of the segregated group. . . .

IV

The problem with which we have here attempted to deal is admittedly on the frontiers of scientific knowledge. Inevitably, there must be some differences of opinion among us concerning the conclusiveness of certain items of evidence, and concerning the particular choice of words and placement of emphasis in the preceding statement. We are nonetheless in agreement that this statement is substantially correct and justified by the evidence, and the differences among us, if any, are of a relatively minor order.

2. Appellees' Brief*

ARGUMENT

Does a statute which permits but does not require cities of more than 15,000 population to maintain separate school facilities for colored and white students violate the fourteenth amendment to the Constitution of the United States in a situation where a court has

---

*Reprinted in Kurland and Casper, Vol. 49, pp. 70–110.

specifically found that there is no discrimination or distinction in physical facilities, educational qualifications of teachers, curricula or transportation facilities?

Appellees contend that only a negative answer to this question is possible. . . .

Appellants suggest that the Plessy case is not applicable to the situation before us. Admittedly, the question presented in the Plessy case arose out of segregation of white and colored races in railroad cars and not segregation in the public schools. However, the decision of the Court rises above the specific facts in issue and announces a doctrine applicable to any social situation wherein the two races are brought into contact. . . .

Appellants further state that *Gong Lum v. Rice* "is irrelevant to the issues in this case." . . .

[But] we do not believe that appellants [are suggesting] that the rights of the Negro citizens differ from the rights of the Mongolian citizen, Martha Lum. If such an idea is advanced here, this Court should have no more difficulty in disposing of that contention than it did of that phase of the Gong case where it seemed to be contended that a yellow child had different rights than a Negro child. The Court simply held that children of all races have equal rights but that those rights are not infringed upon when the state provides that the different races shall be educated in separate schools of equal facility.

Appellants further contend that whatever force the Plessy and Gong-Lum cases may have had has been overcome by the recent decisions of *Sweatt v. Painter,* and *McLaurin v. Oklahoma.* [We] concede that if there has been any change in the attitude of this Court as to the constitutionality of the separate but equal doctrines as it affects segregation, it must be found in these two cases. Thus, we have examined them carefully. But we find no statement therein that would cause us to believe the Court intended to reverse or modify its earlier decisions. In the Sweatt case, the Court held that a Negro prospective law student could not be denied admission to the renowned University of Texas Law School—"one of the nation's ranking law schools" (p. 663), and be compelled to accept instruction in a new school of perhaps questionable worth, inferior as to faculty, plant and student body. The McLaurin case only found that a Negro graduate student, who had successfully compelled his admission to the University of Oklahoma to do graduate work in education, was still being denied equal rights when he was segregated inside the university as to his seat in class, in the library and in the dining hall. Unquestionably, these cases sustain the position that equal facilities must be provided. However, that point is not at issue in this case. . . .

In the Sweatt and McLaurin cases the Court specifically refused to consider the issue of constitutionality of racial separation in schools of equal facility in view of contemporary knowledge and held only that where the State did not furnish equal facilities for one race, the students of that race were being denied equal protection of the laws. [We] contend that this refusal by the Court to review the Plessy and Gong-Lum doctrines in its later decisions can only be interpreted to support the view that those cases still stand as expressions of the rule established by the Supreme Court upon the question of racial segregation within the public schools. . . .

The District Court's Finding of Fact No. VIII is insufficient to establish appellants' right to injunctive relief and to require reversal of the judgment below. . . .

The only existing Finding of Fact which is relied upon by appellants and the only one quoted in their brief is the District Court's Finding of Fact No. VIII. . . .

We call attention to the fact [however that this] Finding is couched only in broad and general language; it makes no specific or particular reference to any of the appellants, nor to the grade schools in Topeka, nor to racial groups other than Negroes, nor to inequality of educational opportunities between Negroes and other racial groups. The substance of the finding can be summarized in the following statement: "Generally speaking, segregation is detrimental to colored children, and deprives them of some benefits they would receive in a racial integrated school system."

The Finding of Fact No. VIII cannot be stretched, as counsel for appellants apparently would like to stretch it, into a finding that the appellants in this case have "suffered serious harm in being required to attend segregated elementary schools in Topeka" and that "appellants were placed at such a disadvantage (in relation to other racial groups in [their] pursuit of educational opportunities) and were denied educational opportunities equal to those available to white students." . . .

There is no specific finding that segregation has had a personal detrimental effect upon any of the appellants. There is no specific finding that any of the appellants personally has interpreted segregation as denoting inferiority of the Negro group, or that the motivation to learn of any of the appellants has been affected by a sense of inferiority. There is no finding that the educational and mental development of any of the appellants has actually been retained or retarded by reason of segregation in the Topeka schools. In short there is no finding that any of the appellants individually and actually has been harmed by segregation in the Topeka school system. . . .

We believe the court intended the finding to mean simply that colored children would be better off in integrated schools than they are in segregated schools. Conceding that that is the meaning of the finding, it does not amount to a finding of actual discrimination against colored children and in favor of white children upon the facts in this case. . . . The mere fact, if it be a fact, that the Topeka school system could be improved so far as education of colored children is concerned, does not prove discrimination against them.

In the opinion of the District Court no mention is made of Finding of Fact No. VIII. It is clear the District Court did not consider or intend to attach to that finding the same significance which appellants seek to place upon it.

We do not question that if the Finding of Fact No. VIII means everything appellants claim it means, they would be entitled to an injunction and reversal of the judgment, if this court should overrule the "separate but equal doctrine." However, it is clear that the District Court did not intend or consider the finding to mean all the things appellants claim for it.

3. Oral Argument[*]

ARGUMENT ON BEHALF OF THE APPELLANTS

By Mr. Carter. . . .

MR. CARTER: . . . . It is our position that *Plessy* v. *Ferguson* is not in point here. . . .

We . . . take the position that whatever the court below may have felt about the reach of the Plessy case, that the Court in the Sweatt case made it absolutely clear that *Plessy* v. *Ferguson* had nothing to do with the question of education. . . .

[Also], we do not believe that *Gong Lum* can be considered as a

---

[*]Reprinted in Leon Friedman (ed.), *Argument* (New York, 1969), p. 18 ff.

precedent contrary to the position we take here. Certainly it cannot be conceded as such a precedent until this Court, when the issue is squarely presented to it, on the question of the power of the state [to institute segregation], examines the question and makes a determination in the state's favor. . . .

JUSTICE FRANKFURTER: Mr. Carter, while what you say may be so, nevertheless, in its opinion, the Court, in *Gong Lum*, did rest on the fact that this issue had been settled by a large body of adjudications going back to what was or might fairly have been called an abolitionist state, the Commonwealth of Massachusetts.

Going back to the Roberts case—

MR. CARTER: Yes, sir. . . .

JUSTICE FRANKFURTER: . . . Do we not have to face the fact that what you are challenging is something that was written into the public law and adjudications of courts, including this Court, by a large body of decisions and, therefore, the question arises whether, and under what circumstances, this Court should now upset so long a course of decisions?

Don't we have to face that, instead of chipping away and saying, "This was dictum," and "This was a mild dictum," and "This was a strong dictum," and is anything to be gained by concealing that central fact, that central issue? . . .

MR. CARTER: Well, Mr. Justice Frankfurter, I would say on that that I was attempting here to take the narrow position with regard to this case, and to approach it in a way that I thought the Court approached the decision in *Sweatt* and *McLaurin*.

I have no hesitancy in saying to the Court that if they do not agree that the decision can be handed down in our favor on this basis of this approach, that I have no hesitancy in saying that the issue of "separate but equal" should be faced and ought to be faced, and that in our view the "separate but equal" doctrine should be overruled.

But as I said before, as the Court apparently approached *Sweatt* and *McLaurin*, it did not feel it had to meet that issue, and we do not feel it has to meet it here, but if the Court has reached a contrary conclusion in regard to it, then we, of course, take the position that the "separate but equal" doctrine should squarely be overruled. . . .

JUSTICE FRANKFURTER: Are you saying that we can say that "separate but equal" is not a doctrine that is relevant at the primary school level? Is that what you are saying?

JUSTICE DOUGLAS: I think you are saying that segregation may be all right in street cars and railroad cars and restaurants, but that is all that we have decided.

MR. CARTER: That is the only place that you have decided that it is all right.

JUSTICE DOUGLAS: And that education is different, education is different from that.

MR. CARTER: Yes, sir.

JUSTICE DOUGLAS: That is your argument, is it not? Isn't that your argument in this case?

MR. CARTER: Yes.

JUSTICE FRANKFURTER: But how can that be your argument when the whole basis of dealing with education thus far has been to find out whether it, the "separate but equal" doctrine is satisfied?

JUSTICE DOUGLAS: You are talking about the gist of the cases in this Court?

JUSTICE FRANKFURTER: I am talking about the cases in this Court.

ARGUMENT ON BEHALF OF THE APPELLEES

By Mr. Wilson. . . .

JUSTICE FRANKFURTER: May I trouble you before you conclude your argument, to deal with this aspect of the case, . . . namely, what would be the consequences, as you see them, for this Court to reverse this decree relating to the Kansas law, or to put it another way, suppose this Court reversed the case, and the case went back to the

District Court for the entry of a proper decree. What would Kansas be urging should be the nature of that decree in order to carry out the direction of this Court?

MR. WILSON: As I understand your question, you are asking me what practical difficulties would be encountered in the administration of the school system?

JUSTICE FRANKFURTER: Suppose there would be some difficulties? I want to know what the consequences of the reversal of the decree would be, and what Kansas would be urging us the most for dealing with those consequences of the decree?

MR. WILSON: In perfect candor, I must say to the Court that the consequences would probably not be serious.

As I pointed out, our Negro population is small. We do have in our Negro schools Negro teachers, Negro administrators, that would necessarily be assimilated in the school system at large. That might produce some administrative difficulties. I can imagine no serious difficulty beyond that.

REBUTTAL ARGUMENT ON BEHALF OF APPELLANTS

By Mr. Carter

MR. CARTER: We think [the] finding of fact of the court below makes necessary a reversal of its judgment.

Without regard to any other consideration, the court below found that inequality flowed from segregation, and our position, as stated previously, is if there [are inequalities], in fact, that educational opportunities can not be equal in law. . . .

JUSTICE BLACK: Is that a general finding or do you state that for the State of Kansas, City of Topeka?

MR. CARTER: I think I agree with the fact that the finding refers to the State of Kansas and to these appellants and to Topeka, Kansas. I think that the findings were made in this specific case referring to this specific case.

JUSTICE BLACK: [But] if you are going to go on the findings, then you would have different rulings with respect to the places to which this applies, is that true?

MR. CARTER: . . . . . Now, of course, under our theory, you do not have to reach the finding of fact or a fact at all in reaching the decision because of the fact that we maintain that this is an unconstitutional classification being based upon race and, therefore, it is arbitrary.

II.
Briggs v. *Elliott*

IN THE LOWER court proceedings in *Briggs*, Marshall had pursued the three-tiered strategy, culminating with his plea to Judge Parker at the second hearing that integration be ordered to correct Clarendon County's palpable inequities. But at the Supreme Court level, this "last resort" demand for equality was transformed, because of bitter experience, into a much broader attack on segregation, a variation on an argument used in *Sweatt*: School segregation statutes were unconstitutional because true equality of facilities would never materialize under a segregated system. All of the arguments in the *Briggs* brief, therefore, were aimed at the destruction of that system.

The "middle" argument, focusing on psychological and sociological harm, was dominant, of course, and occupied the lead position. Possibly because that argument had met rejection in the South Carolina courts, its constitutional logic was articulated here with more sharpness and more clarity than in *Brown*, where the appellants were intent mainly in calling attention to the lower court's sympathy with such arguments. The social science appendix was attached by implication to *Briggs*; still, the brief itself contained excerpts from the lower court trial, leading off with Kenneth Clark's testimony.

South Carolina finally introduced some social science evidence of its own. During the trial, the school board attorneys sought unsuccessfully to obtain the testimony of the South's leading sociologist, Professor Howard W. Odum of the University of North Carolina, an outspoken enemy of southern racism, but a cautious meliorist on issues of educational integration. As a substitute, Robert Figg tried to place into the trial record the text of a speech which Odum had recently delivered, but Judge Parker would not allow it. Now excerpts from the speech found their way into South Carolina's Supreme Court brief. Some of the other quotations in the brief might be regarded as decidedly less felicitous.

During the briefing stage, and most important at oral argument, Governor Byrnes of South Carolina had secured the services of the man regarded as the nation's most outstanding and experienced advocate before the bar of the Supreme Court. John W. Davis served as Solicitor General of the United States during the administration of Woodrow Wilson, and was the Democratic party's candidate for President in 1924, prior to embarking on a fabulously successful career as a Wall Street corporation lawyer. Now 79, he had participated in over 25 cases before the Supreme Court. The Justices engaged in little dialogue with Davis, who hit hard at the concerns expressed by Vinson and Reed at the time of the *Sweatt* case. Thurgood Marshall, however, was peppered with questions, Justice Frankfurter, as usual, taking the lead.

1. Appellants' Brief*

ARGUMENT

I

Legally enforced racial segregation in the public schools of South Carolina denies the Negro children of the State that equality of educational opportunity and benefit required under the equal protection clause of the Fourteenth Amendment.

In its recent opinions on the constitutionality of racially segregated public education, this Court has refused, on the one hand, to give blanket sanction to such state racism, but refrained on the other hand, from formulating a general rule that all forms of governmentally imposed segregation offend the equal protection clause of the Fourteenth Amendment. Without saying that such racial segregation is *per se* valid or *per se* invalid this Court has tested each complaint against segregated education in terms of whether or not—taking into account the nature, purpose and circumstances of the educational program— the segregated person or group is in some real and significant sense denied educational benefits available to the rest of the community.

In two recent cases, *Sweatt v. Painter,* and *McLaurin v. Oklahoma*

---

*p. 12 ff. *Records and Briefs*, Part 2.

State Regents, this Court considered the question: "to what extent does the equal protection clause of the Fourteenth Amendment limit the power of a state to distinguish between students of different races in professional and graduate education in a state university?" (339 U.S. 629, 631).

In neither case were physical inequalities decisive of the issue. In the *Sweatt* case, there were quantitative differences between the white and Negro law schools with respect to such matters as the number of faculty members, the size of the libraries and the scope of the curricula. This Court, however, laid stress upon those "more important" factors which are "incapable of objective measurement." . . .

In the *McLaurin* case, there was no question of inequality insofar as buildings, faculties or curricula were concerned because McLaurin was actually in the same classroom with the other students. The only issue in that case was whether the enforced racial segregation of McLaurin inherent in his being seated apart from the other students denied to him educational benefits equivalent to those offered other students. This Court held that it did.

Although the Sweatt and McLaurin cases arose in the field of higher education, the constitutional issue is the same at every level of public education: Does state-imposed segregation destroy equality of educational benefits?

The *Sweatt* and *McLaurin* cases teach not only that this is the issue which must be resolved in every case presented for judicial review, but also that in seeking the answer the Court will consider the educational process in its entirety, including, apart from the measurable physical facilities, whatever factors have been shown to have educational significance. And where the record shows that segregation is a major handicap to education, the Court will hold that the difference in treatment is the type of state-imposed inequality which is prohibited by the equal protection clause of the Fourteenth Amendment.

Any other conclusion would be inconsistent with the rule recognized in the *Sweatt* and *McLaurin* cases that where the state-imposed racial restrictions impair the ability of the segregated student to secure an equal education because of the denial of any kind of educational benefits available to other students, the aggrieved student may invoke the protection afforded by the equal protection clause of the Fourteenth Amendment to enjoin the maintenance of state-imposed barriers to a racially integrated school environment.

This rule cannot be peculiar to any level of public education. Public elementary and high school education is no less a governmental function than graduate and professional education in state institutions. Moreover, just as Sweatt and McLaurin were denied certain benefits characteristic of graduate and professional education, it is apparent from this record that appellants are denied educational benefits which the state itself asserts are the fundamental objectives of public elementary and high school education. . . .

. The record in this case emphasizes the extent to which the state has deprived the appellants of these fundamental educational benefits by separating them from the rest of the school population.

Expert witnesses testified that compulsory racial segregation in elementary and high schools inflicts considerable personal injury on the Negro pupils which endures as long as these students remain in the segregated school. These witnesses testified that compulsory racial segregation in the public schools of South Carolina injures the Negro students by: (1) impairing their ability to learn; (2) deterring the development of their personalities; (3) depriving them of equal status in the school community; (4) destroying their self-respect; (5) denying them full opportunity for democratic social development; (6) subjecting them to the prejudices of others and stamping them with a badge of inferiority. . . .

On the basis of like testimony in a similar case another District Court made a finding of fact that segregation in public schools retarded the mental and educational development of the colored children and was generally interpreted as denoting the inferiority of the Negro group. *Brown* v. *Board of Education.* . . .

The application of the rationale of the *Sweatt* and *McLaurin* cases to the record in the instant case requires the conclusion: "that the conditions under which this appellant is required to receive his education deprive him of his personal and present right to the equal protection of the laws. . . . We hold that under these circumstances the Fourteenth Amendment precludes differences in treatment by the state based upon race." (*McLaurin* v. *Oklahoma State Regents*, 339 U.S. 637, 642).

II

The compulsory segregation laws of South Carolina infect its public schools with that racism which this Court has repeatedly declared unconstitutional in other areas of governmental action. . . .

The laws here involved, like all others which curtail a civil right on a racial basis, are "immediately suspect" and will be subjected to "the most rigid scrutiny." *Korematsu* v. *United States*, 323 U.S. 214, 216. . . .

[Furthermore] a state legislative classification violates the equal protection clause of the Fourteenth Amendment either if it is based upon nonexistent differences or if the differences are not reasonably related to a proper legislative objective. Classifications based on race or color can never satisfy either requirement and consequently are the epitome of arbitrariness in legislation. . . .

Segregation of Negroes as practiced here is universally understood as imposing on them a badge of inferiority. It "brands the Negro with the mark of inferiority and asserts that he is not fit to associate with white people." It is of a piece with the established rule of the law of South Carolina that it is libelous *per se* to call a white person a Negro. . . .

South Carolina has made no showing of any educational objective that racial segregation subserves. Nor could it. Efforts to conjure up theories of intellectual differences between races are futile. . . .

Therefore, the compelling conclusion is that the provisions of the Constitution and Code of South Carolina requiring racial segregation in education are no more capable of surviving constitutional onslaught than the invidious classification legislation previously voided by this Court as repugnant to the constitutional guarantee of the equal protection of the laws. . . .

IV

The equalization decree does not grant effective relief and cannot be effectively enforced without involving the Court in supervising the daily operation of the public schools.

The rights here asserted are personal and present.

At the beginning of the first hearing, at the time of the first judgment and at the time of the judgment here appealed from, the appellants and appellees were in agreement that the equal protection of the laws of South Carolina was being denied to the appellants herein— and the District Court twice made this finding.

The appellants were entitled to effective and immediate relief as of the time of the first judgment on June 23, 1951. . . . At the second hearing on March 3, 1952, appellees admitted that, although progress was being made, the physical facilities were still unequal. . . . Appellants then urged that they were entitled to immediate relief by an injunction against the continuation of the policy of excluding them from an opportunity to share all of the public school facilities—good and bad—on an equal basis without regard to race and color. This the District Court refused to do even after a showing that the June, 1951, decree had failed to produce even physical equality after eight months.

Rather, the District Court again ordered an injunction requiring the appellees to make available to appellants and other Negro pupils of the district "educational facilities, equipment, curricula and opportunities equal to those afforded white pupils." Appellees' sole defense has been complete reliance on the segregation laws of South Carolina. As long as the District Court insists on declaring these laws valid and constitutional, appellees will continue to enforce them. The record in this case shows that in the past their action has discriminated against appellants and all other Negroes. Whatever they do in the future will be under the continuing policy of rigid racial segregation. . . .

At some point appellants are entitled to conclude their litigation and enjoy constitutional equality in the public schools. The District Court's decree can accomplish neither objective. It should be annulled, and a decree entered restraining the use of race as the factor determinative of the school which the child is to attend.

Conclusion

In light of the foregoing, we respectfully submit that appellants have been denied their rights to equal educational opportunities within the meaning of the Fourteenth Amendment and that the judgment of the court below should be reversed.

2. Appellees' Brief*

III

The District Court correctly held that the conflicts of opinion regarding the effects of segregation and its abolition present questions of legislative policy and not of constitutional right. . . .

In summary, the opinions of [appellants'] witnesses were to the effect that segregation of Negro and white children in separate schools created psychopathic complexes of inferiority in the Negro and of

---

*p. 19 ff. *Records and Briefs*, Part 2.

superiority in the white; and that the children of both races suffered from such segregation. . . .

Not one of these witnesses, however, has had any responsibility whatever for decisions in the field of public policy. And, with but one exception, no one of them admits any investigation of educational, social, or racial conditions in the State of South Carolina, or . . . in Clarendon County.

The sole exception is the witness Kenneth Clark. . . .

[And] if we assume, with Professor Clark, that the age of starting school is a critical one, surely the question as to whether or not a child of very tender years, so psychologically pre-conditioned, should be placed in a separate school of his own race or in a school with children whom he regards as superior, is a question fraught with difficulty and requiring the most careful and painstaking consideration, necessarily involving study of the accumulated data which the most thorough, impartial and scientific research can supply. This question, we submit, is one for the legislative and educational authorities of the states to decide and not for the courts.

This Court may judicially notice the fact that there is a large body of respectable expert opinion to the effect that separate schools, particularly in the South, are in the best interests of children of both races as well as of the community at large.

The recorded history of South Carolina reveals clearly that the provisions for separate schools came about after the State had had some 12 years of experience with mixed schools in the period from 1865 to 1877. The constitutional convention held in South Carolina in 1866 debated the question of separate or mixed schools, and adopted a provision for the latter. . . .

The unhappy result of the mixed-schools provision [is] . . . summarized in Dr. [Edgar] Knight's article entitled *Reconstruction and Education in South Carolina*, which appeared in *The South Atlantic Quarterly*, Vol. XVIII, No. 4, October, 1919, and Vol. XIX, No. 1, January, 1920.

> "The presence and influence of the negro in political, educational and social affairs also complicated an otherwise unhappy condition. Just how far the promoters of mixed school legislation expected it to extend is a matter of conjecture, but that it was perhaps the most unwise action of the period is a certainty, lending itself to a most unfortunate and damaging reaction for many years after the return to home rule. The principal objection raised

to the school system during this time arose from the fear of mixed schools, a provision which was not demanded by either race. On the contrary, both races were violently opposed to the scheme and the friends of the schools constantly urged the adoption of separate schools. But the agitation in Congress of the Civil Rights Bill in 1872 had here, as in other southern states, the effect of aggravating a prejudice which had begun to develop with the state constitutional provision for mixed schools." (Vol. XIX, p. 61.)

And further:

"It was many years, therefore, before confidence could be restored and the principle of universal and free education could gather sufficient strength to give it wide acceptance and popular approval. Here, as in the other southern states, it has been difficult to recover from the ills inherited from the reconstruction practices following the close of the Civil War, and here, as elsewhere in that region, the stigma and the reproach of the indignities and the injustices of that period have been a deadly upas to the cause of public education. Only in recent years has recuperation been rapid enough to assure promise of a better day in public education." (Vol. XIX, p. 66.)

The propriety of the administrative practice of separate schools at the present time and under present conditions in South Carolina is fully sustained by the opinion and judgment of leading sociologists and educators who, unlike the witnesses for appellants, have the basis, in years of research, observation, and practical experience in states where the two races live in the same areas in great numbers. . . .

Dr. [Howard] Odum's years of research in the field of racial relations in the southern states; his untiring efforts to bring about progress in that field; and his acknowledged freedom from anything which could even remotely be suggested as prejudice or preconceived approach to racial questions, are widely known; and it is believed that he is the best informed authority in the country on southern racial matters and the considerations which must be taken into account in evaluating and dealing with them. . . .

After urging the immediate ending of segregation in graduate and professional schools, [Dr. Odum] stated:

"That this is a structurally different situation from elementary and secondary schools, in the framework of America's private, religious, and public school system will be as manifest to the courts as it is to the executive and legislative units of government and to the practical administrative constituency of American education." . . .

[Indeed] W.E.B. DuBois, the same prominent Negro whose views are quoted at length by Myrdal, has said:

"It is difficult to think of anything more important for the development of a people than proper training for their children, and yet I have repeatedly seen wise and loving colored parents take infinite pains to force their little children into schools where the white children, white teachers, and white parents despised and resented the dark child, made mock of it, neglected or bullied it, and literally rendered its life a living hell. Such parents want their child to 'fight' this thing out,—but, dear God, at what a cost! Sometimes, to be sure, the child triumphs and teaches the school community a lesson; but even in such cases, the cost may be high, and the child's whole life turned into an effort to win cheap applause at the expense of healthy individuality. In other cases, the result of the experiment may be complete ruin of character, gift, and ability and ingrained hatred of schools and men. For the kind of battle thus indicated, most children are under no circumstances suited. It is the refinement of cruelty to require it of them. Therefore, in evaluating the advantage and disadvantage of accepting race hatred as a brutal but real fact or of using a little child as a battering ram upon which its nastiness can be thrust, we must give greater value and greater emphasis to the rights of the child's own soul. We shall get a finer, better balance of spirit; an infinitely more capable and rounded personality by putting children in schools where they are wanted, and where they are happy and inspired, than in thrusting them into hells where they are ridiculed and hated." *Does the Negro Need Separate Schools?*, *Journal of Negro Education*, Vol. 4, pp. 328, 330–31 (1935).

ENDNOTE: W.E.B. DUBOIS—DOES THE NEGRO NEED SEPARATE SCHOOLS?

I know that this article will forthwith be interpreted by certain illiterate "nitwits" as a plea for segregated Negro schools and colleges. It is not . . . .

It means this, and nothing more.

To sum up this: theoretically, the Negro needs neither segregated schools nor mixed schools. What he needs is Education. What he must remember is that there is no magic, either in mixed schools or in segregated schools. A mixed school with poor and unsympathetic teachers, with hostile public opinion, and no teaching of truth con-

cerning black folk, is bad. A segregated school with ignorant place-
holders, inadequate equipment, poor salaries, and wretched housing,
is equally bad. Other things being equal, the mixed school is the
broader, more natural basis for the education of all youth. It gives
wider contacts; it inspires greater self-confidence; and suppresses the
inferiority complex. But other things seldom are equal, and in that
case, Sympathy, Knowledge, and the Truth, outweigh all that the
mixed school can offer. (Page 335.)

3. Oral Argument*

ARGUMENT ON BEHALF OF THE APPELLANTS

By Mr. Marshall. . . .

JUSTICE FRANKFURTER: Do you think that this law was passed
for the same reason that a law would be passed prohibiting blue-eyed
children from attending public schools? You would permit all blue-
eyed children to go to separate schools? You think that this is the case?

MR. MARSHALL: No, sir, because the blue-eyed people in the
United States never had the badge of slavery which was perpetuated
in the statutes. . . .

JUSTICE FRANKFURTER: Do you really think it helps us not to
recognize that behind this are certain facts of life, and the question is
whether a legislature can address itself to those facts of life . . . within
the Fourteenth Amendment, or whether, whatever the facts of life
might be, where there is a vast congregation of Negro population as
against the states where there is not, whether that is an irrelevant
consideration? Can you escape facing those sociological facts, Mr.
Marshall?

MR. MARSHALL: No, I cannot escape it. But if I did fail to escape
it, I would have to throw completely aside the personal and present
rights of those individuals.

JUSTICE FRANKFURTER: No, you would not. It does not follow

---

*Reprinted in Friedman, *Argument*, p. 44 ff.

because you cannot make certain classifications, you cannot make some classifications. . . .

MR. MARSHALL: [But] I think that when an attack is made on a statute on the ground that it is an unreasonable classification, and competent, recognized testimony is produced, I think then the least that the state has to do is to produce something to defend their statutes.

JUSTICE FRANKFURTER: I follow you when you talk that way.

MR. MARSHALL: That is part of the argument, sir.

* * * * * * * * * * * *

JUSTICE FRANKFURTER: You mean, if we reverse, it will not entitle every mother to have her child go to a nonsegregated school in Clarendon County?

MR. MARSHALL: No, sir.

JUSTICE FRANKFURTER: What will it do? Would you mind spelling this out? What would happen?

MR. MARSHALL: Yes, sir. The school board, I assume, would find some other method of distributing the children, a recognizable method, by drawing district lines. . . .

JUSTICE FRANKFURTER: You mean that geographically the colored people can live in one district?

MR. MARSHALL: No, sir, they do not. They are mixed up somewhat.

JUSTICE FRANKFURTER: Then why would not the children be mixed?

MR. MARSHALL: If they are in the district, they would be. . . .

JUSTICE FRANKFURTER: I think that nothing would be worse than for this Court—I am expressing my own opinion—nothing would be worse, from my point of view, than for this Court to make an abstract declaration that segregation is bad and then have it evaded by tricks.

MR. MARSHALL: No, sir. As a matter of fact, sir, we have had cases where we have taken care of that. . . .

JUSTICE FRANKFURTER: It would be more important information in my mind, to have you spell out in concrete what would happen if this Court reverses and the case goes back to the district court for the entry of a decree.

MR. MARSHALL: I think, sir, that the decree would be entered which would enjoin the school officials from segregating on the basis of race or color. Then I think whatever district lines they draw, if it can be shown that those lines are drawn on the basis of race or color, then I think they would violate the injunction. If the lines are drawn on a natural basis, without regard to race or color, then I think that nobody would have any complaint.

For example, the colored child that is over here in this school would not be able to go to that school. But the only thing that would come down would be the decision that whatever rule you set in . . . it shall not be on race, either actually or by any other way. . . .

JUSTICE FRANKFURTER: . . . I think it is important to know, before one starts, where he is going.

ARGUMENT ON BEHALF OF THE APPELLEES

By Mr. Davis. . . .

MR. DAVIS: . . . . [I]f, as lawyers or judges, we have ascertained the scope and bearing of the equal protection clause of the Fourteenth Amendment, our duty is done. The rest must be left to those who dictate public policy, and not to courts. . . .

What was the condition of those who framed the instrument? The resolution proposing the Fourteenth Amendment was proffered by Congress in June, 1866. In the succeeding month of July, the same Congress proceeded to establish, or to continue separate schools in the District of Columbia, and from that good day to this, Congress has not waivered in that policy. It has confronted the attack upon it repeatedly. During the life of Charles Sumner, over and over again, he undertook to amend the law of the District so as to provide for mixed and not for separate schools, and again and again he was defeated.

JUSTICE BURTON: What is your answer, Mr. Davis, to the suggestion . . . that at that time the conditions and relations between the two races were such that what might have been unconstitutional then would not be unconstitutional now?

MR. DAVIS: My answer to that is that changed conditions may affect policy, but changed conditions cannot broaden the terminology of the Constitution, the thought is an administrative or a political question, and not a judicial one.

JUSTICE BURTON: But the Constitution is a living document that must be interpreted in relation to the facts of the time in which it is interpreted. . . .

MR. DAVIS: Oh, well, of course, changed conditions may bring things within the scope of the Constitution which were not originally contemplated, and of that perhaps the aptest illustration is the interstate commerce clause. Many things have been found to be interstate commerce which at the time of the writing of the Constitution were not contemplated at all. Many of them did not even exist. But when they come within the field of interstate commerce, then they become subject to congressional power, which is defined in the terms of the Constitution itself. So circumstances may bring new facts within the purview of the constitutional provision, but they do not alter, expand, or change the language that the framers of the Constitution have employed.

JUSTICE FRANKFURTER: Mr. Davis, do you think that "equal" is a less fluid term than "commerce between the states"?

MR. DAVIS: Less fluid?

JUSTICE FRANKFURTER: Yes.

MR. DAVIS: I have not compared the two on the point of fluidity.

JUSTICE FRANKFURTER: Suppose you do it now.

MR. DAVIS: I am not sure that I can approach it in just that sense.

JUSTICE FRANKFURTER: The problem behind my question is whatever the phrasing of it would be.

MR. DAVIS: That what is unequal today may be equal tomorrow, or vice versa?

JUSTICE FRANKFURTER: That is it.

MR. DAVIS: That might be. I should not philosophize about it. But the effort in which I am now engaged is to show how those who submitted this amendment and those who adopted it conceded it to be, and what their conduct by way of interpretation had been since its ratification in 1868.

JUSTICE FRANKFURTER: What you are saying is, that as a matter of history, history puts a gloss upon "equal" which does not permit elimination or admixture of white and colored in this aspect to be introduced?

MR. DAVIS: Yes, I am saying that.

JUSTICE FRANKFURTER: That is what you are saying?

MR. DAVIS: Yes, I am saying that. I am saying that equal protection in the minds of the Congress of the United States did not contemplate mixed schools. . . .
It is true that the Fourteenth Amendment was addressed primarily to the states. But it is inconceivable that the Congress which submitted it would have forbidden the states to employ an educational scheme which Congress itself was persistent in employing in the District of Columbia.

REBUTTAL ARGUMENT ON BEHALF OF THE
APPELLANTS

By Mr. Marshall. . . .
JUSTICE FRANKFURTER: Do you think it would make any difference to our problem if this record also contained the testimony of

six professors from other institutions who gave contrary or qualifying testimony [on the harmfulness of segregation]? Do you think we would be [in] a different situation?

MR. MARSHALL: You would, sir, but I do not believe that there are any experts in the country who would so testify. [E]ven the witnesses, for example, who testified in the next case coming up, the Virginia case, all of them, admitted that segregation in and of itself was harmful. They said that the relief would not be to break down segregation. But I know of no scientist that has made any study, whether he be anthropologist or sociologist, who does not admit that segregation harms the child. . . .

JUSTICE FRANKFURTER: Of course, if it is written into the Constitution, then I do not care about the evidence. If it is in the Constitution, then all the testimony that you introduced is beside the point. . . .

MR. MARSHALL: I think, sir, that . . . this Court has repeatedly said that you cannot use race as a basis of classification.

JUSTICE FRANKFURTER: Very well. If that is a settled constitutional doctrine, then I do not care what any associate or full professor in sociology tells me. If it is in the Constitution, I do not care about what they say. But the question is, is it in the Constitution?

MR. MARSHALL: This Court has said just that on other occasions. They said it . . . in some of the Fourteenth Amendment cases, going back to Mr. Justice Holmes. . . .

JUSTICE REED: In the legislatures, I suppose there is a group of people, at least in the South, who would say that segregation in the schools was to avoid racial friction.

MR. MARSHALL: Yes, sir. Until today, there is a good-sized body of public opinion that would say that, and I would say respectable public opinion.

JUSTICE REED: Even in that situation, assuming, then, that there is a disadvantage to the segregated group, the Negro group, does the legislature have to weigh as between the disadvantage of the segregated group and the advantage of the maintenance of law and order?

MR. MARSHALL: I think that the legislature should, sir. But I think, considering the legislatures, that we have to bear in mind that I know of no Negro legislator in any of these states, and I do not know whether they consider the Negro's side or not. It is just a fact. But I assume that there are people who will say that it was and is necessary, and my answer to that is, even if the concession is made that it was necessary in 1895, it is not necessary now because people have grown up and understand each other.

They are fighting together and living together. . . . As a result of the ruling of this Court, they are going together on the higher level. Just how far it goes—I think when we predict what might happen, I know in the South where I spent most of my time, you will see white and colored kids going down the road together to school. They separate and go to different schools, and they come out and they play together. I do not see why there would necessarily be any trouble if they went to school together.

JUSTICE REED: I am not thinking of trouble. I am thinking of whether it is a problem of legislation or of the judiciary.

MR. MARSHALL: I think, sir, that the ultimate authority for the asserted right by an individual in a minority group is in a body set aside to interpret our Constitution, which is our Court.

III.
Davis v. County School Board of Prince Edward County

AS IN THE *Davis* trial, Justin Moore and his colleagues took the offensive in the Supreme Court briefs, stressing what they regarded as the special background of their state, and hinting at the dire consequences which might follow a desegregation decree. The appellants' brief took on the aspect of a reply to the appellees.

The *Davis* case had followed a procedural route which set it apart somewhat from *Briggs*. In Virginia there was no interim hearing in the district court on the progress being made toward equalizing schools, a hearing at which the NAACP lawyers could have pressed (and undoubtedly seen the futility of) the last resort argument for integration as the only available form of equalization. The *Davis* brief, therefore, presented such an argument at the Supreme Court level. Yet the final section of the brief, paralleling *Briggs*, shows that this was a last resort argument indeed, that no remedy which tolerated racial classifications was really acceptable. If any further proof of this point is needed, it is found in *Belton v. Gebhart*, where the lower court actually granted the last resort remedy.

1. Appellees' Brief*

ARGUMENT

A

Segregation Does Not of Itself Offend the Constitution. . . .

---

*p. 12 ff. *Records and Briefs*, Part 3.

2

The Guiding Legal Principles. . . .

We assert that the doctrine of *Plessy* v. *Ferguson* has today the vitality here that it had 50 years ago. We believe its doctrine sound. We believe that it will withstand re-examination. But if it is to be re-examined, that should be done in the light of the guiding principles which this Court has established to determine what is the equal protection of the laws.

The equal protection of the laws does not mean that all men at all times must receive the same treatment. The State is entitled to protect its people against the lunatic and the leper. One basic standard is established: if, in making its classifications, the State acts reasonably, its action meets the constitutional test.

The difficulties of application come with the determination of reasonableness. But 2 rules are clear. As Mr. Justice Frankfurter has said:

> "The Fourteenth Amendment did not tear history up by the roots. . . ." (*Goesaert* v. *Cleary*, 335 U.S. 464, 465, 1948)

Thus the historical background is significant; it cannot be disregarded.

Similarly, classifications to be measured against the equal protection standard are not measured in a vacuum: . . . .

> "It is by . . . practical considerations based on experience rather than by theoretical inconsistencies that the question of equal protection is to be answered." (*Railway Express Agency, Inc.* v. *New York*, 336 U.S. 106, 110, 1949)

Thus the action of the State must be viewed in the light of the historical background and of the present practical problem before the question of reasonableness can be determined. When the history and the practicalities in regard to educational segregation in Virginia are examined, the reasonableness of the Virginia action is clear. . . .

3

The Virginia Background

Any problem involving the races in Virginia can be understood only in the light of the history of the last century. Violence breeds resentment in both races. The passage of time has removed violence and substantially removed resentment in Virginia. But it would be idle to say that Virginians of both races—despite scientific tests—do not recognize that differences between them exist. Virginia has established segregation in certain fields as a part of her public policy to prevent violence and reduce resentment. The result, in the view of an overwhelming Virginia majority, has been to improve the relationship between the different races and between individuals of the different races.

One field in which segregation is basic Virginia policy is that of education. . . .

The people of Virginia overwhelmingly believe that segregated education is best for all the people. This must be so. It is crystal clear that segregation is more expensive than amalgamation. Yet Virginia citizens are willing to pay the cost. They are firmly determined to root out factual discrimination; they are equally determined to follow the segregated course.

This was the finding of the Court below, amply supported by the evidence. . . .

When the great majority of the people feel so certain that segregated schooling is desirable in the circumstances under which they live, in what way is it irrational or arbitrary?

4

The Psychological Issue

The Appellants ignore the Virginia background; they say that it is immaterial. They thus disregard this Court's admonitions that matters to be decided under the Fourteenth Amendment must be decided in the light of history and in the practical setting in which the conflict arises.

The testimony they presented in the Court below like the tract they now offer to this Court as an Appendix to their brief discussed segregated education in the air. No definite facts and no particular location affect the vista of the perfect life to come.

They avoid the Virginia situation. . . .

[Such] witnesses, basing their opinions on a lack of knowledge of Virginia and in a field which, they have now so well stated, "is admittedly on the frontiers of scientific knowledge," are the Appellants' case. But they were by no means the only experts who testified before the Court below. The Appellees presented 4 educators, a psychiatrist and 2 psychologists. . . .

Like the witnesses for the Appellants, these experts presented by the Appellees are eminent men. They do not stand alone; they are quite representative of a great number of experts not available for presentation to the Court below. . . . The Court below was plainly justified in its finding that the Appellants' evidence did not overbalance that for the Appellees on this phase of the case. That is almost all that need be said. . . .

We conclude therefore that psychology, a "new science," cannot provide any satisfactory basis for a determination that segregated schooling in the Virginia background is unreasonable. The consensus of social scientists, despite the statement of Appellants and their remarkable polemic (Appendix to Brief), is not as they say it is. At most, there is a conflict. The social traditions of half the nation should not be overthrown on such surmise and speculation.

5

The Effect of Amalgamation

We do not seek here to threaten or to coerce. We seek simply to show that the end of segregation by law will not be the millennium. We say this with expert backing.

Let it be noted at the beginning that there is no precedent that, if high schools in Virginia are amalgamated, interracial difficulties will not arise. The graduate school cases are not in point. As Dr. Garrett said:

> "Whenever there are just a few members of a different racial group, they are . . . not regarded as a distinct minority group— there are too few of them." (R. 565.)

So far in Southern graduate institutions, the Negro is a rarity; it is only when the number becomes a substantial proportion, as it would be in high school, that the problem will become acute.

The main difficulty with amalgamation is that it will result in all children receiving a worse education. The views of the witnesses for the Appellees, the only ones at all familiar with the Virginia problem, were unanimous on this point. . . .

So with the demise of segregation, education in Virginia would receive a serious setback. Those who would suffer most would be the Negroes who, by and large, would be economically less able to afford the private school. . . .

If constitutional determinations were made on a theoretical basis, these considerations might be irrelevant. But they must be made, as this Court has said, on the practical basis of existing conditions. These factors serve to highlight the reasonableness of the Virginia decision under present circumstances to favor segregated high school education.

2. Appellants' Brief*

II

Under the Fourteenth Amendment appellants are entitled to equality in all aspects of the educational process as well as equality in physical facilities and curricula. . . .

Dr. Kelly, Mr. Buck and Dr. Garrett admitted that racial segregation has harmful effects on Negro children. . . . Dr. Darden admitted the possibility of personality damage resulting from segregation. . . .

Appellants' demonstration of the harmful consequences of segregation upon the segregated group was thus substantiated by appellees' own witnesses, and the District Court's conclusion that appellants' evidence does not overbalance appellees' is manifestly erroneous and cannot stand. . . .

Appellees' witnesses also predicted the effects of immediate desegregation by court injunction: The people of Virginia are not ready for the change. They would ignore a desegregation injunction. Those who could afford to do so would send their children to private schools. Financial support for the public schools would diminish, and racial relations would be impaired. Frictions and tensions would develop, although there would be no violence. Employment of Negro teachers would be adversely affected. . . . Subtle forms of segregation would displace statutory separation so that Negro children would not be benefitted by the change but would be better off in a segregated school. . . .

This line of testimony is immaterial. The crux of this case is the impact of a state policy of segregation upon the individual in his pursuit of learning. Appellants say that the effect is discriminatory and injurious because it is the State that imposes it—and the evidence sustains their position. Appellees say the removal of the State's hand will not benefit the Negro student because discrimination imposed by individuals will continue.

Appellees, however, fail to distinguish between constitutionally per-

---

*p. 15 ff. *Records and Briefs*, Part 3.

missible individual activity and constitutionally proscribed governmental action. As this Court said in the *McLaurin* case (pp. 641–642):

> "It may be argued that [McLaurin] will be in no better position when these restrictions are removed, for he may still be set apart by his fellow students. This we think irrelevant. There is a vast difference—a Constitutional difference, between restrictions imposed by the state which prohibit the intellectual commingling of students, and the refusal of individuals to commingle where the state presents no such bar. The removal of the state restrictions will not necessarily abate individual and group predilections, prejudices and choices. But at the very least, the state will not be depriving appellant of the opportunity to secure acceptance by his fellow students on his own merits."

Nor can the segregation laws be successfully defended on the ground that it is in appellants' best interest that they be deprived of their constitutional rights. . . .

The District Court . . . predicated its decision on the ground that the school segregation laws had existed for more than eighty years and [were] declared "one of the ways of life in Virginia." . . . The Fourteenth Amendment was adopted for the express purpose of bringing that "way of life" to an end. . . .

III

The inferiority of the educational facilities and opportunities afforded Negro students requires an injunction restraining appellees from excluding appellants from sharing the superior facilities and opportunities on an equal basis without regard to race or color.

The District Court found that the Negro high school is unequal to the white high schools as to buildings, facilities, curricula and busses. . . .

We are dealing with an exercise of state power affecting rights secured by the Fourteenth Amendment. . . .

The persons whose rights must be determined in this case are Negro high school students. Over many years a vast number of Negroes, including some who attended the Moton High School when suit was brought, have completed their education without having been afforded the educational equality which the Constitution demands. For many this case represents the last opportunity to obtain that equality. Their plight is in no way alleviated by a decree effective—if ever—only at some time subsequent to their graduation.

The Constitution countenances no such moratorium upon the satisfaction of the rights here involved. The rights secured by the equal protection clause of the Fourteenth Amendment are both personal and present. . . .

There being no dispute or controversy as to a present unconstitutional denial of appellants' rights to equality of educational facilities and opportunities, no legal justification exists for its continuance.

In *Belton v. Gebhart,* . . . a similar situation was presented. Inequalities were found at the secondary and elementary school levels. It was urged that the appropriate relief would be a decree directing the school authorities to equalize the facilities while affording them a reasonable time to do so. It was shown that the State was engaged in a building program which by September, 1953, would have the Negro high school facilities equal to those for whites. The court there declined to follow *Briggs v. Elliott,* or the decision of the District Court in this case, and held that the Negro plaintiffs must be admitted to the white school. . . .

This conclusion accords with the decisions of this Court. Appellants must be permitted to share the superior facilities and opportunities in the County on an equal basis without regard to race or color. *Missouri ex rel. Gaines v. Canada.*

IV

An equalization decree cannot be effectively enforced without involving the court in supervision of the daily operation of the public schools. . . .

The history of education in Prince Edward County does not suggest that the school authorities are particularly responsive to legal directives to equalize. Since 1869–70, they have been enjoined by statute to maintain white and Negro schools "under the same general regulations as to management, usefulness and efficiency." The record discloses no historical moment at which the legislative command has been obeyed. It affirmatively shows inequality continuously existent for a period of at least thirty-four years. Yet the District Court essayed to bring about by its equalization decree a result which more than eighty years of legislative injunction has not been able to accomplish.

At some point appellants are entitled to conclude their litigation and enjoy constitutional equality in the public schools. The District Court's decree can accomplish neither objective. It should be annulled, and a decree entered restraining the use of race as the factor determinative of the school which the child is to attend.

3. Oral Argument*

ARGUMENT ON BEHALF OF THE APPELLEES

By Mr. Moore. . . .

JUSTICE REED: . . .[If] your experts had not been so persuasive as they were, . . . and the trial court had accepted their conclusion that [segregation] was detrimental and was injurious to the ability of the Negro child to learn or of the white child to learn, and created great difficulties, what difference does it make which way they decided this particular question?

MR. MOORE: I think you can argue the matter two ways, Your Honor. I think, in the first place, you can argue that the difference, for instance, in the Kansas finding and the Virginia finding point up how important is the legislative policy that is involved, that Mr. Davis talked about so much this morning. It just illustrates how it really is a policy question.

JUSTICE REED: I can understand that. But is it your argument that there are two sides to it?

MR. MOORE: It illustrates there are two sides to it, and it points up that the real crux of the whole matter is that there is involved fundamentally a policy question for legislative bodies to pass on, and not for courts.

Now, in the second place, it emphasizes, I hope, that the historical background that exists, certainly in this Virginia situation, with all the strife and the history that we have shown in this record, shows a basis, a real basis, for the classification that has been made.

JUSTICE REED: There has been a legislative determination in Virginia?

MR. MOORE: That is right, sir.

---

*Reprinted in Friedman, *Argument*, p. 92 ff.

JUSTICE REED: That the greatest good for the greatest number is found in segregation?

MR. MOORE: That is right; with these lawmakers continuously since 1870 doing their job to do their best in the general welfare.

ARGUMENT ON BEHALF OF THE APPELLEES

By Mr. (Lindsay) Almond
(Attorney General of Virginia). . . .
MR. ALMOND: . . . . [Integration] would destroy the public school system of Virginia as we know it today. That is not an idle threat. . . .

THE CHIEF JUSTICE: General, in what way will it destroy it?

MR. ALMOND: It would destroy it, Mr. Chief Justice, because we must have . . . money with which to operate the public school system . . . , and the people would not vote bond issues through their resentment to it.
I say that not as a threat.

ARGUMENT ON BEHALF OF THE APPELLANTS

By Mr. Robinson. . . .
JUSTICE REED: What do you conceive to be the purpose of the Virginia enactment of the statute?

MR. ROBINSON: . . . . Doctor Darden characterized the problem before the court as a by-product, and a fearful by-product, of human slavery, and he went on to say that we are the inheritors of that system.
I think from the historical viewpoint, there is much to sustain the position that the original notion behind the school segregation laws was to impose upon Negroes disabilities which prior to the time of the adoption of the Thirteenth, Fourteenth, and Fifteenth Amendments they labored under. That is the only thing that I can offer to this Court in the way of a justification.

IV
Postscript: *Belton* v. *Gebhart*: What Happens When You Win?

1. NAACP Brief*

I

The Injury Inflicted by Segregation

WE URGE THAT in affirming the judgment of the court below this Court give recognition and legal validity to the facts indisputably established in the record and found by the Chancellor, to the effect that state-enforced racial segregation inflicts a grievous mental injury on the Negro children who are set apart in education. . . .

The Court of Chancery held that the Negroes' mental health and therefore their educational opportunity are adversely affected by state imposed segregation in education. But the Chancellor also held that he could not legally recognize the factual condition because to do so would be in effect to rule that racially segregated facilities for Negroes could never be equal to those set apart for whites and were, therefore, unconstitutional; whereas, this Court had fairly implied that racial segregation in education is constitutional. The Supreme Court of Delaware accepted this legal conclusion. . . .

Stating the matter simply, we do not believe that this Court, in the *Plessy* and *Gong Lum* cases, to which the Chancellor referred, intended to uphold racial segregation irrespective of what could be established concerning its effects. We do not believe that it was intended

---

*pp. 11–13. *Records and Briefs*, Part 5.

that facts which could demonstrate the impossibility of segregated facilities being equal should be ignored. They were not ignored in the *McLaurin* case, and they were not ignored in the *Sweatt* case. . . .

To deny legal validity to what the record has clearly shown and remit plaintiffs to the vicissitudes of an everchanging educational picture would place them under a threat of litigation that would cover all their school years. Where the undisputed testimony, as here, reveals that no matter what physical changes are instituted, Negro children will be disadvantaged by segregation, only a decision based on that ground can fully protect respondents' rights to equality.

II-A

The Judgment Below Should Be Affirmed Because the Nature of the Right Requires Immediate Relief

But even if relief on this ground is denied, we submit that the grounds employed by the court below are reasons why [its] judgment should be affirmed. After all, there is no reason why respondents should be denied the perhaps more measurable opportunities which the State had denied them. An education consists of so many years of schooling and the more time respondents are required to spend in inferior schools, to that degree is their sum total of education inferior. The sooner respondents are admitted the closer can they come to full equality in total education although, unfortunately, there is no way to recoup the losses of earlier segregated years. Immediate admission is an integral part of the right—full equality.

2. Oral Argument—Louis Redding[*]

JUSTICE FRANKFURTER: If we just affirmed this decree below without an opinion, that would be an end of the matter, and the plaintiffs in this case would get all they asked, would they not?

MR. REDDING: No, Sir.

JUSTICE FRANKFURTER: They would be admitted into the school into which they wanted to be admitted.

MR. REDDING: They ask for the equality of educational opportunity.

---

[*]Reprinted in Friedman, *Argument*, pp. 164–65.

JUSTICE FRANKFURTER: That is what they would get if the decree was affirmed.

MR. REDDING: They would get it, sir, but they would get it under the shadow of the threat of the Attorney General that the moment he has shown to the court that facilities are equalized they would then be ejected from the schools.

V.
A Friend of the Court: Brief of the American Jewish Congress

THE APPELLANTS' BRIEFS were detailed and multi-faceted in their indictment of educational segregation. Their emphasis on expert witnesses was dictated no doubt by the imperatives of the adversary process, by the need "to try this case just like any other in which you try to prove damages to your client." Yet the substance of the briefs, especially in the use of experts like Professor Clark and Dr. Holt, was inevitably subject to Professor Cahn's criticism that something was being made very convoluted which was at bottom very simple.

Friends of the court have less constraint on their freedom of intellectual action. They can submit briefs saying things which perhaps the appellants would like to have said. A remarkable brief filed *amicus curiae* by Will Maslow of the American Jewish Congress was cast very much in the mold of *An American Dilemma*. While focusing its attack, quite naturally, on educational segregation, the brief drew a portrait of the southern caste system which automatically called all segregation into question.

ARGUMENT*

When a state establishes racially segregated public schools, it thereby perpetuates inequality between the races and discriminates against the Negro race in violation of the Fourteenth Amendment. . . .

---

*Reprinted in Kurland and Casper, Vol. 49, pp. 215–39.

It is our position that state-imposed racial segregation in public grade schools violates the Fourteenth Amendment because it adopts a classification based on concepts and practices of inequality and, by that adoption, contributes to, extends and deepens the discrimination resulting from the inequality and incorporates that discrimination in the schooling which it provides.

A. The Pre-Existing Inequality of Negroes and Whites

State-imposed segregation stems directly from a vestigial theory of the superiority and inferiority of races inherited as a remnant of the institution of slavery. With the freeing of slaves, attempts were made by the dominant white group to preserve its position of ascendancy by the enactment of discriminatory legislation. Immediately after the Civil War the southern states adopted laws limiting the rights of Negroes to own property, to institute law suits and to testify in judicial proceedings. They imposed different penalties on Negroes and whites for the same offenses and otherwise placed the freedmen under legal restraints. . . . These "Black Codes," as they were called, were a plain reflection of the earlier attitude that Negro slaves, and those descended from them, "had no rights which the white man was bound to respect." *Dred Scott* v. *Sandford*, 60 U.S. (19 How.) 393, 407 (1857). . . .

B. The Constitutional Significance of State-Imposed Racial Segregation on the Lines of a Pre-Existing Social Inequality

The Fourteenth Amendment was intended to and did invalidate the gross discrimination of the Black Codes. . . .

No question would have arisen under the Amendment in the area of education if the states had simply refrained from providing public schools. But if they did provide public schools, they were required to do so in a manner which did not cause unequal treatment. . . .

[And] we submit, *when government gives official sanction to pre-existing social inequality, its action causes a change in both the degree and the nature of the inequality and incorporates it into its own activities.*

This change takes place because once a social classification based on group inferiority is formally adopted by the state, the ensuing official inferiority in turn intensifies and deepens the social inequality from which it stems. . . .

C. The Effect of Racial Segregation
in Public Grade Schools

(1) Enforced segregation in public grade schools stamps the Negro with a badge of inferiority and thereby renders inferior the facilities allocated to him by the state.

It can hardly be disputed that an official regulation declaring that a group is inferior and consequently confining it to separate schools would be discriminatory. That much was virtually conceded in the *Plessy* decision when the Court characterized as a "fallacy . . . the assumption that the enforced separation of the two races stamps the colored race with a badge of inferiority." 163 U.S., at 551. It thereby implied that a different result would have been reached if the contrary were true.

An official declaration that the Negro race is inferior to the white and must therefore be confined to separate schools would necessarily depreciate the value of the Negro schools in the eyes of the community. This is because the value and desirability of property depends not only upon its intrinsic qualities but also upon its association with persons enjoying a certain reputation. The desirability of a beautiful resort may be lessened by its being visited by people deemed of "low" social standing. . . .

We do not have here, of course, an express declaration by the State of Kansas that Negroes are inferior to whites. Yet the same effect is achieved if a state establishes public school segregation along the lines of a pre-existing social inequality. It is plain that that is what public school segregation does.

Examination of the pattern of segregation laws reveals plainly that they are designed not to prevent all contact between the races but to prevent contact on the basis of equality. It is the social definition of the situation that determines its treatment in both law and custom. Merely "shaking a black hand may be very repulsive to a white man if he surmises that a colored man conceives of the situation as implying equality." Johnson, *Patterns of Negro Segregation* (1943), p. 208. Those who insist upon the caste system in our society freely and unstintingly agree to the ritual of equal physical facilities so long as somehow there is also an accompanying communication that the Negro is inferior and is to remain so.

Segregation laws provide the ready vocabulary for that communication. . . .

This primary role of segregation statutes is reflected in the candid admission of a Kentucky court:

> "It is also beyond dispute that the sentiment reflected in this legislation . . . does not find the end or the perfection of its purpose in mere race separation alone. It goes much further in that, as is shown in the general feeling everywhere prevailing, the Negro, while respected and protected in his place, is not and cannot be a fit associate for white girls or the social equal of the white race. To conditions like these that are everywhere about them as a part of the social order and domestic economy of the state, courts cannot shut their eyes. They must . . . notice . . . the position of the races and the attitude of the white race toward the Negro." *Axton Fisher Tobacco Co.* v. *The Evening Post*, 169 Ky. 64 (1916).

That the vocabulary of segregation is effectively understood by the entire community cannot be disputed at this date. Segregation provides a graphic and literal solution to the demand of the white world that Negroes be kept "in their place." To the whites in the community the enforced separation of races . . . is clearly understood as a symbolic affirmation of white dominance, dominance which, to keep it alive, demands as tribute the continuous performance of the racial etiquette. . . . "In this magical sphere of the white man's mind, the Negro is inferior, totally independent of rational proofs or disproofs. And he is inferior in a deep and mystical sense. The 'reality' of his inferiority is the white man's own indubitable sensing of it and that feeling applies to every single Negro . . . the Negro is believed to be stupid, immoral, diseased, lazy, incompetent, and *dangerous*— dangerous to the white man's virtue and social order." Myrdal, *An American Dilemma* (1944), p. 100. . . .

Since both white and Negro view segregation as . . . asserting and reenforcing the inferiority of the latter and since in fact segregation statutes have that effect, this Court should not continue to maintain the erroneous proposition enunciated in *Plessy* v. *Ferguson* that laws requiring separation "do not necessarily imply the inferiority of either race to the other." 163 U.S., at 544. Rather it should find that the schools for Negroes in a segregated system cannot be regarded as the equal of those for whites in respect to their "standing in the community, traditions and prestige." *Sweatt* case, [at 634]. The Fourteenth Amendment plainly condemns the allocation to separate races of such unequal facilities.

PART FOUR

THE SUPREME COURT: REARGUMENT

Introduction

I

THE SUPREME COURT met in conference on Saturday, December 13, 1952, to consider the school segregation cases. This critical part of the Court's work is shielded totally from public view. No formal records are kept of conference deliberations. Only the nine Justices themselves remain in the conference room during discussion of cases and certiorari petitions; the junior Justice serves as the Court's doorkeeper, receiving or dispatching messages.

Hugo Black, among others, felt strongly that the Court's conference deliberations should forever remain secret. Before his death in 1971, Black ordered his son to burn all the notes he had taken at these meetings. Other Justices have been more willing to give citizens and scholars a peek at what goes on around the green baize table in the conference room. Journalists periodically report the "inside story" of recent Supreme Court conferences, courtesy presumably of leaks from the Justices, or their clerks. On a more dignified level, collections of the Justices' private papers often contain notes of the deliberations in which they participated, normally concerning cases decided in the more distant past.

Four accounts exist of the December 13 meeting—by Justices Jackson, Burton, Clark, and Douglas. Generally they are in agreement as to what transpired. Justice Douglas' notes, the most recent to become available, consist of separate memoranda on the state cases and on the District of Columbia case, though in fact discussion of these matters flowed together.

Following a suggestion made by Robert Jackson, the Justices took no formal vote at the conference on *Brown*. But that scarcely hid the divisions which quickly surfaced. The cleavages foreshadowed in *Sweatt* v. *Painter* unmistakably revealed themselves.

Chief Justice Vinson adverted again to the original intent of the fourteenth amendment as reflected in state practice and in the toler-

167

ance by Congress of segregation in the District of Columbia Schools. The Chief Justice, said Clark, found it "Hard to get away from long continued interpretations of Congress ever since the Amendments— and at that time." Or the fact that "Harlan's dissent in [*Plessy* v. *Ferguson*] does not refer to schools." Vinson was also concerned, like many of his colleagues, with the problem of implementing a desegregation decision, especially in the deep South. "More serious when you have large numbers. . . . When you face the complete abolition of public schools in some areas then it is most serious."[1]

Neither Jackson nor Clark record the Chief as saying explicitly how he might vote in the school cases. But Burton marked him down as favoring affirmance of the lower court decisions. With regard to state segregation at least, Douglas wrote of Vinson, "doubts if it can be banned."[2]

Justice Reed's position was stated more bluntly. All the accounts agree that he favored sustaining segregation. Jackson's notes on Reed end with the words, "Uphold segregation as constitutional."[3] Clark records Reed as saying, "I would uphold *separate + equal*."[4]

Tom Clark did not discuss his own views on *Brown*. But the hesitations expressed at the time of *Sweatt* clearly persisted. Clark was not yet ready to take a firm position on elementary and secondary school segregation in December of 1952. Burton assessed his colleague as "inclined to go along with delay."[5] Douglas also has him stating, "if we can delay action it will help," although the Douglas notes indicate, rather surprisingly, that Clark said he could "go along" with a decision proscribing segregation so long as it gave "lower courts the right to withhold relief in light of troubles."[6]

According to Jackson's notes, Clark favored reargument of the District of Columbia case, partly no doubt to put off a final decision. His tentativeness suggested that he might be receptive to having all of the cases reargued. This is further indicated by another comment noted down by Jackson: "Thinks result must be same in all as to segregation."[7] Douglas records the same sentiment.

Jackson himself held a decidedly more complex position. He continued in the view that the fourteenth amendment was not intended to apply to segregated schools. A decision overturning *Plessy* in this area would indeed be "amending the Constitution," a policy pronouncement on the part of the Court rather than a judicial decision. Thus his deepest instinct in *Brown*, reflected initially in his questioning at oral argument, and persisting all the way into 1954, was for the Court to avoid the segregation controversy and leave the responsibility for dealing with Jim Crow education where he felt it properly belonged—in the hands of the Congress.

Jackson's analysis of school segregation looked beyond section 1 of the fourteenth amendment to the oft-neglected language of section 5, which provides that "The Congress shall have power to enforce, by appropriate legislation, the provisions of this article." He believed it possible that Congress possessed the authority under section 5 to set aside *Plessy* and to outlaw segregation in state educational systems as no longer compatible with American concepts of morality and public policy. Congress could take the evolutionary approach to the fourteenth amendment which Jackson was reluctant for the Court to take. Yet the Justices might with honor acquiesce in the judgment of a co-equal branch of government, acting under its constitutional mandate. (The Court did something very much like this fourteen years later in *Katzenbach* v. *Morgan* (384 US 641, 1966), a case involving the racial and ethnic implications of literacy tests for voting.)

Furthermore, Jackson believed, it was the Congress, backed up presumably by the executive branch, which was surely the appropriate agency for effecting such massive social change in America, not the courts. As he put it in a memorandum written in December of 1953:

> I know that for this Court to withhold its process while awaiting legislative action would cause grave disappointment to large sections of the country. My preference for legislative as opposed to judicial action is not a mere desire to pass responsibility to others. It goes to the effectiveness of the remedy and to the use to be made of the judicial process over the next generation. [8]

The Justice's questioning in the 1952 oral argument hinted at his interest in a section 5 approach:

JUSTICE JACKSON: Suppose Congress should enact a statute, pursuant to the enabling clause of the Fourteenth Amendment, which nobody seems to attach any importance to here, as far as I have heard, that segregation was contrary to national policy, to the national welfare, and so on, what would happen?

MR. [JUSTIN] MOORE: Your Honor, we thought of that in here, and that is a big question, as you realize.

JUSTICE JACKSON: That is why I asked it.

MR. MOORE: Our view of the matter is that it should not be held valid in this Court; that the only effective way to accomplish that is to be done through . . . amending the Constitution.

JUSTICE JACKSON: You think that the Fourteenth Amendment would not be adequate to do that?

MR. MOORE: We do not believe so. . . .

JUSTICE FRANKFURTER: But Justice Jackson's question brings into play different questions and different considerations, Mr. Moore, because the enabling act of the Fourteenth Amendment is itself a provision of the Fourteenth Amendment; patently Congress looked forward to implementing legislation; implementing legislation patently looked forward to the future, and if Congress passed a statute doing that which is asked of us to be done through judicial decree, the case would come here with a pronouncement by Congress in its legislative capacity that in its view of its powers, this was within the Fourteenth Amendment and, therefore, it would come with all the heavy authority, with the momentum and validity that a congressional enactment has.

MR. MOORE: That may be so, your Honor, but that is another case.

JUSTICE FRANKFURTER: That is a good answer.

MR. MOORE: Yes, it is another case.

JUSTICE JACKSON: I wonder if it is.[9]

Logically, of course, this ideal solution entailed the Court's refusing to hear the school segregation cases at all. But Jackson was well aware of what the results of such judicial abstinence would be. "I suppose," he later remarked, "that realistically this case is here for the reason that action couldn't be obtained from Congress."[10] There is no indication that the Justice was opposed finally to docketing the school cases.

Once the Court heard the cases and scheduled them for conference, Jackson's position may well have been reflected in a memorandum which bore the signature of one of his law clerks, Donald Cronson (later an overseas executive with the Mobil Oil Company). Cronson argued that the Court should not "overrule *Plessy*," but simply "confess error" in the case, clearing the path "so that Congress may by legislation prohibit segregation." Yet if Congress still refused to act, "even though it is informed by this Court that the present system is Unconstitutional," then manifestly, "this Court should not do so."[11]

A decision limited to confessing error, however, would not settle the actual controversies before the Justices, would not result in specific relief or a denial of relief to Linda Brown or to the children of Harry Briggs. Such a resolution of the matter would amount in essence to what is called an advisory opinion, and the Court has eschewed such pronouncements since the time of the first Chief Justice, John Jay.

Consequently, Jackson's comments in the December 13, 1952 conference are not based on Cronson's memo. The Justice reported to his colleagues the grim news that no judicial basis existed for proscribing educational segregation. But he asserted that he could go along with a frankly political decision, one which did what he would have preferred that the Congress do—reinterpret the fourteenth amendment for a new era in education and race relations. Jackson thought it essential, however, that the South be given time to adjust to such radical change. Desegregation *"must* be done in certain period,"[12] according to Clark's notes. Douglas' notes agree.

If Justice Jackson did not rely on Donald Cronson's memo in the conference of December 13, he certainly did not rely on the views articulated in a memorandum submitted by his other law clerk for the 1952 Supreme Court term. Entitled "A Random Thought on the Segregation Cases," the memo stated flatly that "I think *Plessy* v. *Ferguson* was right and should be re-affirmed."[13] The initials on the document are "whr"—William Hubbs Rehnquist.

This Rehnquist memorandum created a political storm when it was unearthed at the time of the present Chief Justice's confirmation as Associate Justice in 1971. (He was elevated to Chief by President Reagan in 1986.) Rehnquist maintained that the memo reflected Justice Jackson's views, not his own, and was prepared for Jackson's use at the December 13 conference.

The Justice's actual remarks in conference, however, suggest that this proposition is debatable; and it was sharply challenged, both in 1971 and later. (We will review the Rehnquist controversy in more detail in Part I of this section.)

Jackson's comments made one thing clear. Four of the Justices at the December 13 conference were opposed to scuttling *Plessy* in education, or harbored doubts about such a course. Not unexpectedly, three others—Black, Douglas, and Burton—favored striking down school segregation. In his own notes, Burton indicates that he was not averse to setting the District of Columbia case down for reargument. All but Justice Douglas ascribe that same sentiment to him. The Douglas notes on *Bolling* v. *Sharpe*, however, say nothing of reargument, simply stating, "segregation is unconstitutional whether by the states or the Congress."[14] While the "answer [was] simple" for Douglas, therefore, on either the state or federal level, he felt that working out the process of desegregation in the states would be a slow and vexing process. "[T]he application of it," he said, "may present great difficulties."[15] Burton's notes on Douglas state, "Simple—Const. question—will take a long time to work it out."[16]

Burton's own position mixed definiteness with caution. "We have Constitution and must be guided by [it]," Clark records him as saying. "We must not depart. But we can use time."[17] Douglas says of Burton, "he would give plenty of time in this decree."[18]

Justice Black said nothing explicitly about time frames. He reminded his brethren, however, if they needed reminding, of the consequences of taking what he believed to be the necessary action. "*Segregation per se violation?* To so hold would bring drastic things— S.C., etc. One of wor[st] features is courts are put on battle front."[19]

Joining these three was the Court's junior member, Sherman Minton, who was surprisingly strong in his views. Minton pronounced segregation in public schools unconstitutional, and was prepared to vote his convictions immediately. "Can't classify as to race[,] bad— *invidious.* This is a race that grew up in trouble."[20]

Felix Frankfurter knew even before the conference that he would be the man in the middle. For that reason, he was not ready to bare his true preferences. He argued that segregation in the District of Columbia schools should unquestionably be proscribed. But on the state question, Frankfurter spoke in elliptical terms, stressing, as others had, the issue of original intent. He could not accuse past courts of misreading the intentions of those who framed the fourteenth amendment. And while he hinted at a broader method for assessing that intent than the one implied by Jackson, a method which would allow him to get where he wanted to go on school segregation, he was not yet ready to espouse such an approach. Burton has him asking in this regard, "What justifies us in saying that what *was* equal in 1868 is not equal now [?]"[21] According to Douglas, he argued that "equal protection does not mean what *was* equal but what *is* equal—he wants to know why what has gone before is wrong. . . ."[22] Frankfurter preferred to have all of the cases reargued. He spoke initially of scheduling the reargument for March, at the current term of the Court, and would have it focus on the original understanding of the fourteenth amendment, as well as on issues of implementation.

Further discussion of the segregation cases, however, during the ensuing months produced no vote and no definite plan for action. "[N]o one on the Court was pushing it,"[23] Frankfurter noted. He decided, therefore, that his colleagues were ripe for a strategy of putting off the whole matter until the October 1953 term. According to Alexander Bickel, one of his law clerks during 1952–53, "He said it looked as if we could hold off a decision that term, . . . and that if we could get together some questions for discussion at a reargument, the case would be held over. . . ."[24]

Working with Bickel, Frankfurter drafted a series of inquiries to be addressed to counsel in preparation for a reargument of *Brown* during the Court's next session. The questions focused on those issues which were bothering Frankfurter and other Justices the most, and producing the appetite for delay:

> Each of these cases is ordered restored to the docket and is assigned for reargument on Monday, October 12, next. In their briefs and on oral argument counsel are requested to discuss particularly the following questions insofar as they are relevant to the respective cases:
>   1. What evidence is there that the Congress which submitted and the State legislatures and conventions which ratified the Fourteenth Amendment contemplated or did not contemplate, understood or did not understand, that it would abolish segregation in public schools?
>   2. If neither the Congress in submitting nor the States in ratifying the Fourteenth Amendment understood that compliance with it would require the immediate abolition of segregation in public schools, was it nevertheless the understanding of the framers of the Amendment.
>   (a) that future Congresses might, in the exercise of their power under section 5 of the Amendment, abolish such segregation, or
>   (b) that it would be within the judicial power, in light of future conditions, to construe the Amendment as abolishing such segregation of its own force?
>   3. On the assumption that the answers to questions 2 (a) and (b) do not dispose of the issue, is it within the judicial power, in construing the Amendment, to abolish segregation in public schools?
>   4. Assuming it is decided that segregation in public schools violates the Fourteenth Amendment,
>   (a) would a decree necessarily follow providing that, within the limits set by normal geographic school districting, Negro children should forthwith be admitted to schools of their choice, or
>   (b) may this Court, in the exercise of its equity powers,

permit an effective gradual adjustment to be brought about from existing segregated systems to a system not based on color distinctions?

5. On the assumption on which questions 4 (a) and (b) are based, and assuming further that this Court will exercise its equity powers to the end described in question 4 (b),

(a) should this Court formulate detailed decrees in these cases;

(b) if so, what specific issues should the decrees reach;

(c) should this Court appoint a special master to hear evidence with a view to recommending specific terms for such decrees;

(d) should this Court remand to the courts of first instance with directions to frame decrees in these cases, and if so what general directions should the decrees of this Court include and what procedures should the courts of first instance follow in arriving at the specific terms of more detailed decrees?

The Attorney General of the United States is invited to take part in the oral argument and to file an additional brief. . . .[25]

The historical inquiry would center on section 1 of the fourteenth amendment:

All persons born or naturalized in the United States . . . are citizens of the United States and of the State wherein they reside. No State shall make or enforce any law which shall abridge the privileges or immunities of citizens of the United States; nor shall any State deprive any person of life, liberty, or property, without due process of law; nor deny to any person within its jurisdiction the equal protection of the laws.

At a conference on May 29, 1953, the Court accepted Frankfurter's tactic, though Justices Black and Douglas were opposed to it. They favored submitting at most questions 4 and 5 to the parties. This proposal on their part had potentially ominous consequences, in the view of Professor Bernard Schwartz, one of the giants of modern constitutional scholarship and author of the definitive judicial biography of Earl Warren. If Black and Douglas had won their point, Professor Schwartz argues, they would have stripped the reargument order of any questions relating "to the merits of the segregation issue," revealing it, therefore, as a "transparent delaying device." In these circumstances, the Justices probably "would not have voted for reargument and a delayed decision."[26] *Brown* would have come down in June of 1953, the product of a bitterly divided Court. Frankfurter may have had this in mind, Professor Schwartz suggests, when he told his friend Judge Learned Hand in July of 1954, "[I]f the 'great libertarians' had had their way we would have been in the soup."[27]

In any event, none of the other Justices agreed with Black and Douglas. Chief Justice Vinson wanted to go just the opposite way, to include questions 1, 2, and 3, while omitting the last two. But a majority of six approved Frankfurter's proposal, and the segregation cases were set down for reargument at the beginning of the October 1953 term.

The acceptance of this approach was a measure of the Court's uncertainty about *Brown*. But a closer look at the questions directed to counsel indicates that the Justices were at least contemplating a way to relieve one of their most persistent anxieties, their concern about implementing a possible decision in favor of the appellants.

This problem, difficult enough in general, was exacerbated by the fact that under accepted constitutional standards a judgment proscribing segregation in public schools would lead to immediate relief for those whose "personal and present" constitutional rights were being violated; it would lead, in other words, to the prompt desegregation of the school districts in which Jim Crow laws held sway. Resolution of the *Brown* cases would directly affect only those districts in which the original plaintiffs had brought suit, but *Brown* would obviously serve as a model for all of the South and border states. Hugo Black had aptly articulated the dangers of doing what precedent demanded, especially where constitutional rights were at stake.

But questions 4 and 5 intimated that the Justices were inching toward a different, and as it turned out a highly controversial route to compliance, should they need to face the matter. Question 4 presented to the parties for argument a pair of possible alternatives, "Assuming it is decided that segregation in public schools violates the Fourteenth Amendment." One alternative followed out the implications of the view that constitutional rights were personal and immediate; a decree would "necessarily follow" admitting black youngsters to "schools of their choice." The other alternative, however, was disturbingly novel, especially to Thurgood Marshall and his colleagues; for it held out the possibility that the Court could, "in the exercise of its equity powers," allow "*an effective gradual adjustment*" to non-segregated school systems.

Question 5 did nothing to assuage any of the concerns the NAACP may have felt, based as it was on the proposition "that this Court *will exercise its equity powers to the end described in question 4* (b)." By June of 1953, in short, the Justices were cautiously circling the solution to the desegregation riddle which they promulgated two years later: the constitutional rights of school children might be vindicated, yet the necessities of the situation could condone a gradualist approach to implementation which meant that most of the actual plaintiffs would never enjoy those rights. Question 5 also reflected a more obvious point; the Court had no intention of getting involved in the details of desegregation.

This gradualism was first suggested to the Court in the brief filed *amicus curiae* by the United States government. The brief repeated what the government had stated in the *Sweatt* trilogy of cases, that *Plessy* could rightly be overruled. But though remedy was not before the Court in the December 1952 argument, the government's attorneys articulated their view of the matter anyway.

Even if the Court reversed *Plessy,* the brief argued, it need not order the immediate abolition of segregated schools. "The fact that a system or practice is determined to be unlawful does not of itself require the Court to order that it be abandoned forthwith."[28] The whole process of desegregation posed obvious practical difficulties; surmounting them would require a "reasonable period of time."[29] The federal district courts should take charge during this period of adjustment, and they might consider various melioristic approaches to compliance, such as grade-by-grade or school-by-school desegregation. District judges should give to the school authorities the opportunity "to develop a program most suited to their own conditions and needs."[30]

It was not by chance that these views on remedy materialized in the government's brief. The principal author of the document was Phillip Elman, Special Assistant to the Attorney General at the time. Elman had been law clerk to Justice Frankfurter and remained a close confidant of the Justice. He knew of the hesitations and divisions within the Court over *Brown,* and later admitted that he composed the remedial section of the brief with these concerns in mind. "It was entirely unprincipled," he said, "it was just plain wrong as a matter of constitutional law, to suggest that someone whose personal constitutional rights were being violated should be denied relief."[31] But "I was simply counting votes on the Supreme Court."[32] Indeed Elman believes that his remedial arguments firmed up the views of Burton and Minton at the December 1952 conference, and helped to influence the ultimate disposition of *Brown,* by offering "[f]or the first time . . . .

a middle ground, separating the constitutional principle from the remedy."[33]

II

Despite questions 4 and 5, it was clear that the reargument order in *Brown* focused mainly upon an inquiry which the average citizen would have supposed from the outset to be decisive in determining the outcome of the cases: what did those who actually wrote the organic law of our nation, in this case the fourteenth amendment, intend that it should do? The quest for original intent is widely regarded as the only approach to constitutional interpretation which squares with our legal order and our democratic culture. To resolve constitutional disputes, it would seem, we simply find out what the document meant to those responsible for framing it and approving it, using whatever historical materials are relevant to the task. Madison's notes on the Philadelphia convention, the *Federalist Papers*, and the congressional debates on the principal amendments are among the most common guides.

The purpose in using these secondary sources, however, must be to illuminate the actual words of the Constitution. As Professor Leonard Levy, our greatest modern constitutional historian, has aptly pointed out, "The most important evidence of original intent is the text of the Constitution itself, which must prevail whenever it surely embodies a broader principle than can be found in the minds or purposes of its framers."[34]

Indeed the view of constitutional interpretation most in vogue at the time the document was written—what a recent essay calls "The Original Understanding of Original Intent"[35]—deprecated the importance of extrinsic materials. Joseph Story, appointed to the Supreme Court in 1811, and author of the monumental *Commentaries on the Constitution* (1833), felt that "contemporary interpretation must be resorted to with much qualification and reserve," and that even at its best such evidence "can never abrogate the text [of the Constitution], it can never fritter away its obvious sense, it can never narrow down its true limitations, it can never enlarge its natural boundaries."[36] While James Madison believed that the intent of the state ratifying conventions (which it is impossible wholly to obtain) was critical in fixing the Constitution's meaning, he did not ascribe similar value to his own notes from Philadelphia, claiming that they "can have no authoritative character . . . in expounding and applying the provisions of the Constitution."[37] They were not published until 1840, four years after his death. Despite the weightiness of such views, it scarcely seems sensible in our own day *not* to make appropriate use of Madison's remarkable work, and of the fruits of modern historical research, in assessing the import of constitutional texts, so long as it is the text they are illuminating.

The Supreme Court has never dissented from an originalist approach to constitutional adjudication. What was said of the Court in 1939 was certainly true in 1953 and remains valid today: "Whenever the United States Supreme Court has felt itself called upon to announce a theory for its conduct . . . , it has insisted . . . that the end and object of constitutional construction is the discovery of the intention of those parties who formulated the document."[38] In directing the parties in *Brown* to comb the evidence surrounding the adoption of the fourteenth amendment, the Court was mandating a familiar technique for ascertaining constitutional meaning.

Yet the Court's questions were pushing the lawyers toward a confrontation which would demonstrate that original intent is not always the touchstone for resolving disputes it may at first appear to be. Constitutional inquiries of the sort posed by the Justices in 1953 are prone to run into language in the document itself which seems deliberately designed to expose the difficulties of originalist theory.

These difficulties stem from the basic nature of our Constitution. If it supplies us in general with only a broad frame of government, not a day-to-day agenda of action, many of its critical provisions, especially in the bill of rights and the fourteenth amendment, are couched in especially spacious language, which defies an easily fixed meaning or import—terms such as "freedom of speech," "cruel and unusual punishment," "due process of law." Furthermore, we do not possess sufficient evidence concerning framer or ratifier intent to allow us to ascertain the level of generality at which these provisions were supposed to be taken. The House debate on the first ten amendments, for example, is hopelessly sketchy; the Senate debates at that time were held in secret. There is no record at all of any of the ratification proceedings.

In dealing with such broad provisions, therefore, constitutional construction often resolves itself into an overdrawn but nonetheless revealing dichotomy between two views of what comprises original intent, the two views hinted at by the ruminations of Justices Jackson and

Frankfurter. One view holds that we must be faithful to the specific meaning and applications which a constitutional provision had for those who wrote and those who approved it. The provision must mean in our age what it meant in theirs. If the framers of the eighth amendment did not conceive of the death penalty as cruel and unusual punishment at the time they wrote the amendment, we cannot so conceive of it today (though practices of which the framers were not yet aware, such as wiretapping for instance, can be subsumed under the fourth amendment's prohibition against unreasonable search and seizure). Such an approach would preserve strict fidelity to the framers' purposes, and certainly qualifies as defensible. Human nature being what it is, it is not impossible to suppose that the framers disapproved of applications of "their" text different from the ones they contemplated.

But this version of original intent would freeze our Constitution in the political and moral culture of 1789 or 1865. For this reason, courts more frequently adhere to the theory which one analyst has called "moderate originalism,"[39] a view which holds that the intentions of the framers must be inferred from the capacious language which unmistakably characterizes the text. In this view, cruel and unusual punishment, or due process of law, can be a changing, evolving principle, "capable of wider application than the mischief which gave it birth."[40]

Such a view of original intent frees the Justices from a historical straitjacket. But it releases them into an atmosphere where they have enormous and largely unsupervised freedom in doing their work, a freedom which can be unsettling to a democratic society. For conceived as unfolding generalities, the provisions of the bill of rights, and of other parts of the Constitution, often tell the Supreme Court little about how to settle real-life legal disputes. What the Court winds up doing, consequently, is constructing on its own hook an entire jurisprudence out of certain constitutional texts—the first amendment, or the fifth, or the commerce clause.

The dichotomy between judicial literalism and judicial discretion is somewhat of a false one to be sure. History does supply us at times with a frame of reference which can be limiting without being suffocating, even where broad-gauged constitutional commands are involved. The fourth amendment's failure, for example, to mention what shall be done with evidence seized in defiance of its prohibition against unreasonable searches and seizures reflects a clear understanding on the part of its framers that such evidence could be introduced at a criminal or civil trial. The recent Court was following a respectable view of original intent, therefore, when it held that rules excluding illegally seized evidence, while valid, are rules of procedure created by judges, not by the fourth amendment itself.[41]

In addition, few would deny that the exact meaning of the term "establishment of religion," as understood by its authors, is highly relevant in determining the meaning of the phrase today, though there is sharp disagreement over what it actually did mean.[42] The original belief that the death penalty was not a cruel and unusual punishment represented the authentic moral consensus, no doubt, of the men who wrote the eighth amendment. That this consensus has not been reversed in our time constitutes for the modern Court a legitimate, if not a decisive reason for leaving the penalty intact.[43]

Still, the situation very frequently created by the breadth of constitutional texts and the complexity of litigation is one which raises original intent to its undifferentiated level of generality. Those seminal words of the first amendment—"Congress shall make no law . . . abridging the freedom of speech, or of the press"—provide a striking illustration of this generalizing tendency at work. Direct evidence of what the framers or ratifiers meant by these words, is, of course, minuscule or non-existent. Quite possibly, it has been argued, their concern was limited to speech concerning political matters.[44] But we cannot specifically document such an intention, and the text belies it.

Yet even if we assume that the framers did mean to restrict the amendment to political speech—accept a medium range, as it were, of original intent—it would be unthinkable to confine such political expression to the view of it which may well have prevailed in 1789. Late eighteenth century America was steeped in a political culture in which freedom of speech and of the press were deemed not inconsistent with prosecutions for the crime of seditious libel. That is to say, people could go to jail for the kind of strident and malicious criticism of government officials which we tolerate routinely today, unless the critics could prove that their charges were scrupulously true.[45]

Since such a definition of free speech is grotesquely unacceptable in the twentieth century, the courts have followed the broad lines of the constitutional text, and have struggled to draw a sensible line between liberty and license. Thus Justices Oliver Wendell Holmes and Louis Brandeis articulated the view that even those who frankly advocate the overthrow of our democratic system cannot be punished unless their advocacy poses a clear and present danger of illegal acts. In Holmes' celebrated words, dissenting in *Abrams v. United States,*

> [T]he best test of truth is the power of the thought to get itself accepted in the competition of the market. . . . I think that we should be eternally vigilant against attempts to check the expression of opinions that we loathe and believe to be fraught with death, unless they so imminently threaten immediate interference with the lawful and pressing purposes of the law that an immediate check is required to save the country.[46]

The dominant view on freedom of expression into the 1950s, however, was the one pronounced by Justice Edward Sanford in the 1925 case of *Gitlow v. New York.* Sanford argued that advocacy of violence *per se* was punishable by the state consistent with the first amendment:

> The state cannot reasonably be required to measure the danger from every . . . utterance in the nice balance of a jeweler's scale. A single revolutionary spark may kindle a fire that, smoldering for a time, may burst into a sweeping and destructive conflagration. It cannot be said that the state is acting arbitrarily or unreasonably when, in the exercise of its judgment as to the measures necessary to protect the public peace and safety, it seeks to extinguish the spark without waiting until it has enkindled the flame or blazed into the conflagration.[47]

By 1968, the majority on the Court had moved to the view that only those who incite others to concrete acts of violence lose first amendment protection. In *Brandenburg v. Ohio,* the Court ruled that "the constitutional guarantees of free speech and free press do not permit a State to forbid or proscribe advocacy of the use of force or of law violation except where such advocacy is directed to inciting . . . imminent lawless action and is likely to incite or produce such action."[48]

None of these sophisticated theories of the relationship between the individual and the state, between freedom and order, are demonstrably inconsistent with the original intention of the framers, as revealed by their text. But how does original intent arbitrate between these competing visions of the first amendment? Clearly it cannot do so. No one who has seriously thought about these matters, says Professor Lawrence Sager of the N.Y.U. Law School, "believes that the drafters of the Constitution and its amendments, or the generation of Americans on whose behalf these provisions were ratified, had formed in their minds shared principles that would make self-evident the exact application and the modern consequences of the abstract principles embodied in the Bill of Rights."[49]

The Court has in truth openly disregarded the original intentions of the framers on numerous occasions, no matter how we measure that intent. It is disquieting perhaps, but probably inevitable, that a concept so often irrelevant in many areas of constitutional law should be discarded wholly on occasion.

The most important example of where the Justices went beyond the reasonable meaning of the text, and the weight of such historical evidence as surrounds it, involves those words of the fourteenth amendment (adapted from the fifth) which immediately precede the equal protection clause: "No state shall . . . deprive any person of life, liberty, or property, without due process of law." The words seem clearly limited to the *procedures* by which laws are administered. They command fairness of government, but only in the *techniques* it uses to take legal action.

Yet since the 1890s, the Court has employed the due process clause of the fourteenth (and the fifth) amendment to invalidate *any* law which is regarded as an unreasonable restriction on people's life, liberty, or property, no matter how scrupulous the procedures for its enforcement. In the argot of constitutional law, the Justices imparted to the clause a substantive as well as a procedural force, with no serious attempt to ascribe such ambitions to the framers themselves.[50] Into the 1930s, this notion of substantive due process was used principally to defend the rights of property against government regulation, but the Court also included other liberties under its rubric, suggesting at one point that the right to be educated might be among them. (*Meyer* v. *Nebraska*, 262 US 390, 1923.) It is through substantive due process that the guarantees found in the first amendment were imposed as limitations on state action beginning in 1925. By the 1950s, this doctrine, however questionable, was too deeply embedded in constitutional precedent to be excised.

III

The equal protection clause, like much of the rest of section 1 of the fourteenth amendment, is of the broad-sounding, indeterminate variety of constitutional provision. The material bearing on intent is more ample for the fourteenth amendment than for the bill of rights, at least where the congressional debates are concerned. But the debates strike most who have read them as sketchy and confused, and their existence probably multiplies rather than diminishes the conundrums of interpretation.

This guaranteed that the reargument in *Brown* would expose the competing views of original intent. Not surprisingly though, both appellants and appellees agreed on a key point of legal strategy: whatever else they did, they must prove their case on original intent at the lowest level of specificity.

From the beginning, Marshall and his colleagues, who filed one consolidated brief on reargument, believed it essential to demonstrate not only that the framers of the fourteenth amendment intended their definition of equality to be broad and capacious enough to include the evils of segregation. They must also demonstrate that the framers specifically sought by that language to outlaw segregation in public schools. Or, at a minimum, that the framers' understanding of their own language encompassed such a goal, *at the time.*

Neither of these tasks turned out to be easy ones for the small army of scholars who volunteered their services to the NAACP cause in the summer of 1953. The problems began on the question of how broadly the fourteenth amendment swept. Many scholars assumed that the first section of the amendment was designed to "constitutionalize," to make permanent, the guarantees for blacks contained in the path-breaking Civil Rights Act of 1866. The Civil Rights Act removed all doubt that blacks were citizens of the United States, and assured to them on an equal basis a series of specific civil rights, including the "right to make and enforce contracts, to sue, . . . give evidence, to inherit, purchase, . . . and convey . . . property."[51] As originally passed by the Senate, however, the bill also contained an open-ended provision, guaranteeing that "there shall be no discrimination in civil rights or immunities"[52] among citizens. The historians working with the NAACP, such as Professor Alfred H. Kelly of Wayne State University, could readily interpret this language as broad enough to proscribe all segregation statutes.

But Professor Kelly and the others got a shock when they examined the debate over the Civil Rights Bill in the House of Representatives. As a result of that debate, they discovered, the House Judiciary Committee struck out the "no discrimination" clause, precisely because of its fear that the language was broad enough to apply to such things as all-white juries and segregated schools. Worse than that, the author of the motion to strike the "no discrimination" language was none other than Representative John Bingham of Ohio, the framer of section 1 of the fourteenth amendment, the man whom Justice Black once called "the [James] Madison" of the amendment.[53] Bingham did not speak specifically of schools in proposing his alteration of the bill, but he professed himself deeply troubled by the reach of the term "civil rights."

The conclusion, Professor Kelly felt, "was painfully clear." The Civil Rights Act was "specifically rewritten" in order to avoid "the embarrassing question of a congressional attack upon State racial-segregation laws, including school segregation." The fourteenth amendment, which made the act permanent, must suffer from the same limitations. It appeared "as if John W. Davis would win the historical argument hands down!"[54]

But further research and contemplation brought Professor Kelly and his co-workers to a convenient but undoubtedly honest revision of their conclusions. They decided that Bingham wished to narrow the Civil Rights Act not because he opposed its potential application to juries or to schools, but because he thought it could not apply to such institutions *under the existing Constitution*. To achieve this broader purpose, he felt, a constitutional amendment was required, an amendment upon which he was already at work even as he engineered the demise of the "no discrimination" clause. In February of 1866, a month before the House debate on the Civil Rights Act, Bingham had proposed in the Joint Committee on Reconstruction a premonitory version of what became section 1 of the fourteenth amendment:

> The Congress shall have power to make all laws which shall be necessary and proper to secure to the citizens of each State all privileges and immunities of citizens in the several States . . . ; and to all persons in the several States equal protection in the rights of life, liberty, and property.[55]

Kelly and his colleagues could assert, therefore, that Bingham's actions on the Civil Rights Bill were consistent with the capacious language he eventually embodied in the amendment. "The . . . Amendment, we told ourselves, had been necessary to accomplish a vast sweep of purpose far beyond the Civil Rights Act." Its language was deliberately not restricted to the provisions of that act. In fact, while defending the fourteenth amendment in the House, Bingham "had . . . said Congress now was writing a constitutional provision, not drafting a statute."[56] Whatever the statute did or did not encompass, Kelly concluded, the amendment was general enough to outlaw school segregation in America some 85 years after its passage.

Yet the NAACP brief on reargument also maintained that the men responsible for the fourteenth amendment specifically intended it to have such an effect in the context of their own day. These men framed an amendment which sought above all to "deprive the states of the power to impose any racial distinctions in determining when, where, and how its citizens would enjoy [their] civil rights."[57] And though they may not have said so explicitly, the "intentions they expressed were definitely broad enough to proscribe state-imposed racial distinctions in public education, as they knew it," as well as "broad enough to forever bar racial distinctions in whatever public educational system the states might later develop."[58]

Plessy, therefore, had not only been outflanked by the decisions in *Sweatt* and *McLaurin*. History demonstrated that it was erroneous in the first place, a repudiation of the explicit goals of those who sponsored the fourteenth amendment. The brief on reargument no longer focused on merely having separate but equal declared inapplicable to education. The basic doctrine must be repudiated:

> Were these ordinary cases, it might be enough to say that the *Plessy* case can be distinguished—that it involved only segregation in transportation. But these are not ordinary cases, and in deference to their importance it seems more fitting to meet the *Plessy* doctrine head-on and to declare that doctrine erroneous.
>
> Candor requires recognition that the plain purpose and effect of segregated education is to perpetuate an inferior status for Negroes which is America's sorry heritage from slavery. But the primary purpose of the Fourteenth Amendment was to deprive the states of *all* power to perpetuate such a caste system.[59]

Whatever the merits or shortcomings of the appellants' analysis of congressional intent, it remained equally essential for them to demonstrate that those responsible for ratifying the fourteenth amendment understood and approved of what it was doing, especially to their schools. Ratifier intent, especially as to the level of generality on which the amendment was conceived, could be endlessly disputed, since we have the full ratification debates of only two states. But state practices concerning educational segregation in the years when the amendment was approved were obviously ascertainable, and were crucial to determining whether contemporaries understood the new amendment to forbid or condone such practices.

The picture was discouraging from the NAACP point of view. At the time they ratified the fourteenth amendment, or immediately thereafter, only fourteen states had laws forbidding educational segregation, or at least did not practice it. (A fifteenth state, Oregon, got rid of racial separation in its Portland schools in 1871.) Just five of these states had taken action in the wake of the amendment itself— Connecticut, Michigan, Florida, Louisiana, and South Carolina; and the last three, of course, subsequently established Jim Crow education. Meanwhile, 22 states had laws either requiring or permitting segregated public schools.

In their desire to demonstrate specific intent, however, the appellants felt called upon to transform this evidence into a claim that "the State Legislatures . . . which ratified the Fourteenth Amendment contemplated and understood that it prohibited State legislation which would require racial segregation in public schools."[60] The effort was necessarily rather strained, but the NAACP brief did make one arresting argument in the process. The brief noted that eight of the former confederate states (aside from Florida, Louisiana, and South Carolina) which had instituted segregated schools by 1870 did so only *after* they ratified the fourteenth amendment and were allowed to return to the Union. The constitutions which they promulgated *prior* to admission contained no such requirements, and in several of the constitutional conventions provisions mandating segregation were defeated. A southern conspiracy was unmistakably suggested, one which cast a searching light on ratifier intent. At the very time "the South was obliged to redefine the status of the freedmen in conformity with their understanding of the Fourteenth Amendment," state constitutions were approved "which without exception were free of any requirement" of segregated schools. "And no law compelling segregated schools was enacted in any state until after it had been readmitted."[61]

The problem with this argument was that the governments which had both approved the constitutions and instituted the segregation requirements were carpetbagger, Republican-dominated administrations. More important was a point presaged by Justice Jackson's comments during the deliberations on *Sweatt* and *McLaurin*. There was no evidence that the fourteenth amendment itself had played any part in these southern constitutional or educational decisions. It is quite likely that many state officials at the time, in the South and elsewhere, did not think that the amendment applied to the area of education at all. In the South, especially, public school systems existed in barely embryonic form, and many still regarded education as a private rather than a governmental function.

This testimony by silence could even be seen as supporting a narrow, Civil Rights Act interpretation of the fourteenth amendment. But such evidence of intent was obviously murky, and conflicts with the actual text of the equal protection clause. From the 1870s on, therefore, the courts went with the text and treated the clause as pertinent to education. The earliest state court decisions dealing with school segregation upheld the practice to be sure, but explicitly subjected it to equal protection analysis, affirming that this part of the fourteenth amendment was considered applicable to educational policy.[62] Yet the lacunae in the southern discussion of segregation cast serious doubts on the NAACP's efforts to demonstrate the amendment's specific intent.

Some of the other efforts to establish intent were decidedly more tenuous, examples of what critics call "law office history." The treatment of the situation in Ohio is symptomatic. Ohio had compulsory segregation in its schools at the time the state ratified the fourteenth amendment, and the Ohio Supreme Court upheld the practice in 1872. It was not until six years later that the legislature made segregated schools a matter of local option. Only in 1887 did Ohio abolish segregation. The appellants' brief recounted the matter as follows:

> After ratification of the Amendment, the [state] legislature did not immediately modify the school laws. In fact, it did nothing until after the Ohio Supreme Court upheld compulsory segregated schools. . . . *Then* the legislature enacted a statute which permitted rather than required segregated schools. *Later,* it denied local school authorities the power to exericse their discretion in the premises. By this act, all public schools were opened to all children without distinction on account of race or color.[63]

The appellees were spearheaded on reargument by John W. Davis' law firm in New York and Justin Moore's in Richmond, though Kansas and Delaware also filed briefs. All were similar in content. The South Carolina brief was the most polished; like the others, it seized gleefully upon the evidence of ratifier intent. The actions of the states confirmed Davis and his associates in their reading of the congressional proceedings. The Civil Rights Act, South Carolina argued, was carefully amended by the House of Representatives to limit it to the rights "specifically enumerated" in the bill. This was done at the instance of Representative John Bingham, "then on his way to becom-

ing the author of Section 1 of the Fourteenth Amendment."[64] Since
section 1 of the amendment itself "was regarded by its proponents" as
removing "all doubt as to the constitutionality of the Civil Rights Bill,"
it seemed evident that when "the Fourteenth Amendment was adopted
by Congress, it was intended simply to . . . perpetuate the protection
of those rights enumerated in the . . . Bill."[65] Its framers had consciously restricted the text of the amendment to that narrow compass.

These critical facts, according to the South Carolina brief, answered not only question 1 of the Supreme Court's enquiry, but disposed of questions 2 and 3 as well. Neither the framers nor the ratifiers
had allowed leeway for the abolition of segregation "in light of future
conditions," whether under section 5 of the fourteenth amendment
or by judicial fiat, because to do so would go beyond the jurisdictional
boundaries set by the amendment. The specific practices of the ratifying states reflected the limited, unbreachable intentions of the framers. Nor did the judiciary have the power "in construing the
Amendment" to abolish separate schools. The Courts could not revise
the equal protection clause to encompass objects which its authors
did not design it "to embrace. . . . Here the purpose of the framers
is clear."[66] No one, after all, had offered the fourteenth amendment
"as a Trojan horse."[67]

Both appellants and appellees, then, appeared to feel comfortable
within the confines of a literalistic view of original intent. Both urged
the Court to act in accordance with what the framers and ratifiers
understood the fourteenth amendment to require in 1870. They just
happened to set very disparate requirements.

It fell to the United States government's supplemental brief on
reargument to split the difference philosophically between the parties,
though its conclusion, quite naturally, favored the clients of the
NAACP. The government lawyers, led again by Philip Elman, found
evidence that the congressional framers did indeed have sweeping
purposes in drafting section 1 of the fourteenth amendment. The
amendment was "part of a broad and continuing program to establish
full freedom and legal equality for Negroes."[68] In marked contrast to
the southerners, Elman and his researchers found neither side in
the congressional debate over section 1 manifesting "any substantial
disagreement as to [its] broad scope."[69]

The evidence bearing upon specific intent was pronounced inconclusive, however. The congressional history hinted at, but was unable
to establish definitively that the framers understood section 1 to outlaw

racial separation in public schools; "neither its proponents nor its opponents found it necessary . . . to catalog exhaustively the specific application of its general principle."[70] On the other hand, the state materials were simply "too sparse, and the . . . references to education too few,"[71] to support any hypothesis about what the ratifiers thought with regard to school segregation. The assumption, though, which "most logically explains the silence of the available . . . materials"[72] was that the state legislatures "were probably unaware that the Amendment was relevant to education, even to the extent of requiring equal, though separate schools."[73]

But nothing in all of this historical documentation posed a barrier to outlawing segregation, the government argued, so long as the notion of original intent was intelligently conceived. The Court certainly had never "declared . . . that a construction of an amendment which is warranted by its provisions . . . cannot be adopted unless it is also affirmatively supported by specific evidence . . . showing that its framers so 'intended.'"[74] On the contrary, a proper understanding of intention acknowledged that "Constitutional provisions like . . . 'equal protection of the laws' express broad principles of government the essence of which is their vitality and adaptability to the progressive changes and needs of the nation."[75]

Judged by this yardstick of intent, segregated education was glaringly unequal. Just as the Court had decided long ago that education in general fell under the rubric of the fourteenth amendment, whatever the perplexities posed by the historical evidence, so the Justices could now decide that separate schools were in violation of the amendment, whether the framers and ratifiers approved of segregation or not.

In answer to questions 4 and 5, the queries which may well have been influenced by its 1952 brief, the government's brief on reargument needed only to refine the position taken earlier. The cases should be remanded to the district courts, the government argued, under a very general decree which gave district judges the leeway to permit a one-year transition to non-segregated education. The "necessities of the situation" might permit them, however, "to extend such period for a further reasonable time."[76]

There was another important perspective on the historical controversy stirred up by the reargument order. Even before the Court took its action of May 1953, Justice Frankfurter had put his law clerk Alexander Bickel to work analyzing the debates over the fourteenth amendment in the 39th Congress. Bickel did not complete his assignment until the late summer of 1953. His 63-page memorandum, edited by Frankfurter, was circulated to all members of the Court just before the *Brown* reargument.

The NAACP attorneys and historians would have regarded the memo as gloomy news. Bickel pointed out not only that the Civil Rights Act of 1866 had been greatly narrowed in the House of Representatives, at the insistence, among others, of John Bingham. He also argued, most significantly, that Bingham's objections to the "no discrimination in civil rights" clause flowed from considerations of policy as well as of constitutional fastidiousness. While Bingham's statements on the subject were decidedly ambiguous, Bickel admitted, the Congressman may well have believed that civil rights in general, as opposed to the specific guarantees of the Civil Rights Act, should be protected by *neither* federal statute nor constitutional authority. "He raised a constitutioI al issue, but it is fair to conclude that his objection at the time went also to the 'latitudinarian' nature of the provision."[77]

Consistent with this view was the fact that Bingham's revised language for section 1 of the fourteenth amendment, the language ultimately accepted by the Congress, was prepared as a substitute for a draft of the amendment which read, "No discrimination shall be made by any state . . . as to civil rights of persons because of race."[78] These were words about identical to the ones struck from the Civil Rights Bill. Indeed during the final drafting, Bingham's "persistent effort . . . was to avoid the use of a general 'civil rights' provision, at least one standing alone."[79] Furthermore, the desultory floor debate on section 1 conveyed the general understanding "that Congress had previously expressed itself in favor of its purpose by passing the Civil Rights Act."[80]

Yet Bickel's memorandum put one final spin on this historical material. The belief that section 1 embodied the Civil Rights Act represented in his view evidence only of the *specific intent* of those who framed and those who voted for the fourteenth amendment: it reflected only what they thought to be the *immediate applications* of the amendment, not the ultimate potentialities of their enactment. The contemporary espectations of the framers could not and did not restrict the ambit of the constitutional text.

The 39th Congress, Bickel argued, was definitely "on notice that it was enacting vague language of essentially indeterminate reach." No "precise statement" of the "full reach" of section 1 or of section 5 was ever articulated during the congressional debate.[81] Thaddeus Stevens, the great Radical leader in the House of Representatives, closed the debate in fact by imploring his colleagues to "take what we can get now, and hope for better things in further legislation."[82] Bickel concluded, therefore, that Congress "left for the future the solution of a number of painful problems. It cannot be said that it knew what role the language it was enacting should or would play in that solution."[83] Such logic clearly freed the Court to act as the appellants wished it to act.

Two other developments ensued between the first and second arguments in *Brown*, one minor, the other momentous. In August of 1953, Chief Justice Vinson moved the date for oral presentation in the cases forward to December 7. On September 8, 1953, one month before the Court's October term was to begin, the Chief Justice died suddenly of a heart attack. By the time the Court met on the first Monday in October, there was a new Chief Justice of the United States, though he was operating under an interim appointment from President Eisenhower pending confirmation by the Senate. Earl Warren now presided over the Supreme Court.

Notes

[1]"Conference Notes of Mr. Justice Clark on the Segregation Cases," printed as Appendix B of Dennis Hutchinson, "Unanimity and Desegregation: Decisionmaking in the Supreme Court, 1948–58," *Georgetown Law Journal* (Vol. 68, 1979), 1, 91.

[2]William O. Douglas, "Conference 12-13-52: No. 8 *Brown* v. *Board of Education of Topeka*," (p. 1). William O. Douglas Papers, Library of Congress. This quotation, and others from the Douglas Papers, are quoted by permission of the estate of William O. Douglas.

[3]Robert H. Jackson, "Segregation" (Handwritten Notes on Conference of December 13, 1952), (p. 2). Robert H. Jackson Papers, Library of Congress.

[4]"Conference Notes of Mr. Justice Clark," 92.

[5]Quoted in Richard Kluger, *Simple Justice* (New York, 1975), p. 612. Kluger provides the classic account of the December 13, 1952 conference, though he did not yet have access to the Clark or Douglas notes.

[6]Douglas, Conference Notes on *Brown*, (p. 2).

[7]Jackson, "Segregation," (p. 3)

[8]Robert H. Jackson, Memorandum of 12/7/53 (Untitled), p. 11. Jackson Papers, Library of Congress.

[9]Oral Argument (*Davis* v. *Prince Edward County School Board*), December 10, 1952, pp. 30–31.

[10]Oral Argument (*Briggs* v. *Elliott* and *Davis* v. *Prince Edward County School Board*), December 7, 1953, quoted in Wasby, D'Amato, and Metrailer, *Desegregation from Brown to Alexander* (Carbondale, Illinois, 1977), p. 58.

[11][Donald Cronson]. "A few expressed prejudices on the Segregation cases," (p. 3). Jackson Papers, Library of Congress.

[12]"Conference Notes of Mr. Justice Clark," 92.

[13]William H. Rehnquist, "A Random Thought on the Segregation Cases," printed in *Congressional Record*, 92nd Congress, 1st Session—Senate (December 8, 1971), 45440, 45441.

[14]William O. Douglas, "Conference 12-13-52: No 413 *Bolling* v. *Sharpe*," (p. 1). Douglas Papers, Library of Congress.

[15]Douglas, Conference Notes on *Brown*, (p. 2).

[16]Quoted in Kluger, *Simple Justice*, p. 603.

[17]"Conference Notes of Mr. Justice Clark," 92.

[18]Douglas, Conference Notes on *Brown* (p. 2).

[19]"Conference Notes of Mr. Justice Clark," 91.

[20]*Ibid.*, 92.

[21]Quoted in Kluger, *Simple Justice*, p. 601.

[22]Douglas, Conference Notes on *Brown*, (p. 1).

[23]Quoted in Kluger, *Simple Justice*, p. 614.

[24]*Ibid.*

[25]*Brown* v. *Board of Education of Topeka*, 345 US 972 (1953).

[26]Bernard Schwartz, *Super Chief* (New York, 1983), p. 81.

[27]Quoted in Schwartz, *Super Chief*, p. 80.

[28]*Brief for The United States as Amicus Curiae*, Brown v. Board of Education of Topeka, p. 27.

[29]*Ibid.*, p. 29.

[30]*Ibid.*, p. 30.

[31]Phillip Elman, "The Solicitor General's Office, Justice Frankfurter, and Civil Rights Litigation, 1946–1960: An Oral History," *Harvard Law Review* (Vol. 100, 1987), 817, 827.

[32]*Ibid.*, 829.

[33]*Ibid.*, 827.

[34]Leonard Levy, *Original Intent and the Framers' Constitution* (New York, 1988), p. xi.

[35]Jefferson Powell, "The Original Understanding of Original Intent," *Harvard Law Review* (Vol. 99, 1985), 865.

[36]Joseph Story, *Commentaries on the Constitution of the United States* (Boston, 1833), Vol. I, p. 300.

[37]Quoted in Levy, *Original Intent and the Framers' Constitution*, p. 1.

[38]Jacobus ten Broek, "Use by the United States Supreme Court of Extrinsic

Aids in Constitutional Construction," *California Law Review* (Vol. 27, 1939), 399.

[39]Paul Brest, "The Misconceived Quest for the Original Understanding," *Boston University Law Review* (Vol. 60, 1980), 204, 205.

[40]*Weems* v. *United States,* 217 US 349 (1910), at 373.

[41]*United States* v. *Leon,* 468 US 897 (1984).

[42]On this point, contrast Chief Justice Rehnquist's celebrated dissent in *Wallace* v. *Jaffree,* 472 US 38 (1985), with Leonard Levy's *The Establishment Clause* (New York, 1986).

[43]*Gregg* v. *Georgia,* 428 US 153 (1976).

[44]As by Robert Bork in "Neutral Principles And Some First Amendment Problems," *Indiana Law Journal* (Vol. 47, 1971), 1. Judge Bork later renounced this view.

[45]This view is documented by Leonard Levy in *Emergence of a Free Press* (New York, 1985). Some scholars do not agree; see George Anastaplo, *The Constitutionalist: Notes on the First Amendment* (Dallas, 1971).

[46]*Abrams* v. *United States,* 250 US 616 (1919), at 630.

[47]*Gitlow* v. *New York,* 268 US 652 (1925), at 669.

[48]*Brandenburg* v. *Ohio,* 395 US 444 (1969), at 447.

[49]Lawrence Sager, "Back to Bork," *New York Review of Books,* October 25, 1990, pp. 23–24.

[50]It can be argued much more plausibly that the phrase preceding the due process clause in section 1, the privileges and immunities clause, was meant to be an open-ended check on the substance of legislation. But the Court consigned the clause to irrelevance in the *Slaughter-House Cases,* 16 Wall. 36 (1873).

[51]Quoted in Alfred Kelly, "The Fourteenth Amendment Reconsidered: The Segregation Question," *Michigan Law Review* (Vol. 54, 1956), 1049, 1061.

[52]*Ibid.*

[53]See Justice Black's celebrated dissent in *Adamson* v. *California,* 332 US 46 (1947), at 74.

[54]Alfred Kelly, "An Inside View of *Brown* v. *Board of Education,*" paper delivered to annual convention of American Historical Association, December 28, 1961; excerpt printed in *U.S. News and World Report,* Vol. 52, No. 6 (February 5, 1962), p. 87.

[55]Quoted in Kelly, "The Fourteenth Amendment Reconsidered," 1072.

[56]Kelly, "An Inside View of *Brown* v. *Board of Education,*" p. 88.

[57]*Brief for Appellants on Reargument,* pp. 67–68.

[58]*Ibid.,* p. 124.

[59]*Ibid.,* p. 17.

[60]*Ibid.,* p. 139.

[61]*Ibid.*, pp. 142–43, 143.

[62]*State ex rel. Garnes* v. *McCann*, 21 Ohio 198, 1871; *People ex rel. Dietz* v. *Easton*, 13 Abbott (N.S.) 159, 1872, *Ward* v. *Flood*, 48 Cal. 36, 1874; *Cory* v. *Carter*, 48 Ind. 327, 1874.

[63]*Brief for Appellants on Reargument*, pp. 171–72, (Italics added).

[64]*Brief for Appellees on Reargument, Briggs* v. *Elliott*, p. 12.

[65]*Ibid.*, pp. 16, 17.

[66]*Ibid.*, p. 57.

[67]*Ibid.*, *p. 53.*

[68]*Supplemental Brief For The United States On Reargument, Brown* v. *Board of Education of Topeka*, p. 112.

[69]*Ibid.*, p. 114.

[70]*Ibid.*

[71]*Ibid.*, p. 117.

[72]*Ibid.*, p. 107.

[73]*Ibid.*, p. 117.

[74]*Ibid.*, *pp. 125–26.*

[75]*Ibid.*, p. 128.

[76]*Ibid.*, pp. 186–87.

[77]Alexander Bickel, "Prefatory Note to Legislative History Of The Fourteenth Amendment," p. iv. Felix Frankfurter Papers, Harvard Law School Library. (Copies of this memorandum are also found in the Burton, Jackson, and Douglas papers.)

[78]Quoted in Alexander Bickel, "The Original Understanding And The Segregation Decision," *Harvard Law Review* (Vol. 69, 1955), 1, 41.

[79]Bickel, "Prefatory Note," p. iv.

[80]*Ibid.*, p. ii.

[81]*Ibid.*, p. v.

[82]Quoted in Bickel, "The Original Understanding And The Segregation Decision," 55. Stevens' speech is found in the *Congressional Globe*, 39th Congress, 1st Session—House of Representatives (June 13, 1866), 3148–49.

[83]Bickel, "Prefatory Note," p. vi.

I.
The Controversy over "whr"

THE DOCTRINAL THRUST of *Brown* v. *Board of Education* clearly influences developments in our own time. But there is a more personal connection to contemporary America. The present Chief Justice of the United States was a Supreme Court law clerk when the school cases were first argued in 1952. And the "whr" memorandum to Justice Robert Jackson, stating that *"Plessy* v. *Ferguson* . . . should be reaffirmed," is seen today, whether rightly or wrongly, as an ominous portent by those who are unhappy with the direction the Rehnquist Court is taking.

The memo to Justice Jackson was originally uncovered in late November of 1971, just as Rehnquist's nomination to be Associate Justice was scheduled to come to a vote in the United States Senate. In a letter to Senate Judiciary Committee Chairman James O. Eastland, on December 8, Rehnquist claimed that the document was "a statement of *his* (Jackson's) views at the conference of the Justices." But as we have seen, this assertion is open to question, since Justice Jackson said nothing about reaffirming *Plessy* at the December 13, 1952, conference. Indeed Jackson's long-time secretary, Mrs. Elsie Douglas, told a newspaper interviewer at the time that Rehnquist's explanation was "incredible on its face," and "smeared the reputation of a great Justice."

It is fair to say, however, that Jackson did believe *Plessy* to rest on formidable historical and precedential underpinnings, which made outlawing school segregation difficult. Furthermore, Donald Cronson, Jackson's other law clerk in 1952, suggested that Rehnquist may not have been the sole author of the memo endorsing *Plessy*. In a cablegram sent to Rehnquist on December 9, 1971, Cronson asserted

195

that to the best of his recollection the memorandum containing the typed initials "whr" was actually a collaborative effort between himself and his colleague, as was the memo recommending that the Court "confess error" in *Plessy*—the one initialed "DC." Both efforts, said Cronson, were ordered up by Justice Jackson so that he could assess conflicting points of view on *Brown*.

If this is so, it is curious that Rehnquist mentioned no such recollection in his letter to Senator Eastland. Aside from this, an analysis submitted at the conclusion of the confirmation debate by Senator Edward Brooke of Massachusetts claimed that internal evidence in the document signed "whr" belies assertions that it did not express Rehnquist's point of view, though the Brooke memo was composed before Cronson's cable was received, and does not address his version of events directly. (Not knowing of confidential communications to which we are now privy, the memo also overestimates Justice Jackson's hostility to *Plessy*.)

William Hubbs Rehnquist was confirmed as Associate Justice of the Supreme Court on December 15, 1971, by a vote of 68–26.

1. "A Random Thought on the Segregation Cases"*

One-hundred fifty years ago this Court held that it was the ultimate judge of the restrictions which the Constitution imposed on the various branches of the national and state government . . . , [on the basis that there are standards to be applied] other than the personal predilections of the Justices.

As applied to questions of inter-state or state-federal relations, as well to inter-departmental disputes within the federal government, this doctrine of judicial review has worked well. Where theoretically co-ordinate bodies of government are disputing, the Court is well suited to its role as arbiter. This is because these problems involve much less emotionally charged subject matter than do those discussed below. In effect, they determine the skeletal relations of the governments to each other without influencing the substantive business of those governments.

As applied to relations between the individual and the state, the system has worked much less well. The Constitution, of course, deals

Congressional Record, Dec. 8, 1971, 45440–41.

with individual rights, particularly in the First Ten and the Fourteenth Amendments. But as I read the history of this Court, it has seldom been out of hot water when attempting to interpret these individual rights. . . . *Scott* v. *Sandford* was the result of [Chief Justice] Taney's effort to protect slaveholders from legislative interference. After the Civil War, business interest came to dominate the Court, and they in turn ventured into the deep water of protecting certain types of individuals against legislative interference. . . . [T]he high water mark of the trend in protecting corporations against legislative influence was probably *Lochner* v. *N.Y.* [198 US 45, 1905.] To the majority opinion in that case, Holmes replied that the Fourteenth Amendment did not enact Herbert Spencer's Social Statics. . . .*

[E]ventually the Court called a halt to this reading of its own economic views into the Constitution. Apparently it recognized that where a legislature was dealing with its own citizens, it was not part of the judicial function to thwart public opinion except in extreme cases.

In these cases now before the Court, the Court is, as [John W.] Davis suggested, being asked to read its own sociological views into the Constitution. Urging a view palpably at variance with precedent and probably with legislative history, appellants seek to convince the Court of the moral wrongness of the treatment they are receiving. I would suggest that this is a question the Court need never reach; for regardless of the Justice's individual views on the merits of segregation, it quite clearly is not one of those extreme cases which commands intervention from one of any conviction. If this Court, because its members individually are "liberal" and dislike segregation, now chooses to strike it down, it differs from the [earlier] court only in the kinds of litigants it favors and the kinds of special claims it protects. To those who would argue that "personal" rights are more sacrosanct than "property" rights, the short answer is that the Constitution makes no such distinction. To the argument made by Thurgood, not John Marshall that a majority may not deprive a minority of its constitutional right, the answer must be made that while this is sound in theory, in the long run it is the majority who will determine what the constitutional rights of the minority are.

---

*Herbert Spencer (1820–1903) was an English philosopher and sociologist; he expounded the notion of Social Darwinism and was a staunch defender of laissez-faire capitalism.

One hundred and fifty years of attempts on the part of this Court
to protect minority rights of any kind—whether those of business,
slaveholders, or Jehovah's Witnesses—have all met the same fate. One
by one the cases establishing such rights have been sloughed off, and
crept silently to rest. If the present Court is unable to profit by this
example, it must be prepared to see its work fade in time, too, as
embodying only the sentiments of a transient majority of nine men.

I realize that it is an unpopular and unhumanitarian position, for
which I have been excoriated by "liberal" colleagues, but I think *Plessy*
v. *Ferguson* was right and should be re-affirmed. If the Fourteenth
Amendment did not enact Spencer's Social Statics, it just as surely
did not enact Myrdal's American Dilemma.

whr

2. Rehnquist's Letter to Senator James O. Eastland, December 8, 1971[*]

DEAR MR. CHAIRMAN: A memorandum in the files of Justice
Robert H. Jackson bearing my initials has become the subject of discussion in the Senate debate on my confirmation, and I therefore take
the liberty of sending you my recollection of the facts in connection
with it. As best I can reconstruct the circumstances after some nine-
teen years, the memorandum was prepared by me at Justice Jackson's
request; it was intended as a rough draft of a statement of *his* views at
the conference of the Justices, rather than as a statement of my views.

At some time during the October Term, 1952, when the School
Desegregation Cases were pending before the Supreme Court, I recall
Justice Jackson asking me to assist him in developing arguments which
he might use in conference when cases were discussed. He expressed
concern that the conference should have the benefit of all of the
arguments in support of the constitutionality of the "separate but
equal" doctrine, as well as those against its constitutionality. In
carrying out this assignment, I recall assembling historical material
and submitting it to the Justice, and I recall considerable oral discussion with him as to what type of presentation he would make when
the cases came before the Court conference.

The particular memorandum in question differs sharply from the
normal sort of clerk's memorandum that was submitted to Justice

---

[*]*Congressional Record*, Dec. 8, 1971, 45440.

Jackson during my tenure as a clerk. Justice Jackson expected case submissions from his clerks to analyze with some precision the issues presented by a case, the applicable authorities, and the conflicting arguments in favor either of granting or denying *certiorari*, or of affirming or reversing the judgments below. While he did expect his clerks to make recommendations based on their memoranda as to whether *certiorari* should be granted or denied, he very definitely did not either expect or welcome the incorporation by a clerk of his own philosophical view of how a case should be decided.

The memorandum entitled "Random Thoughts on the Segregation Cases" is consistent with virtually none of these criteria. It is extremely informal in style, loosely organized, largely philosophical in nature, and virtually devoid of any careful analysis of the legal issues raised in these cases. The type of argument made is historical, rather than legal. Most important, the tone of the memorandum is not that of a subordinate submitting his own recommendations to his superior (which was the tone used by me, and I believe by the Justice's other clerks, in their submissions), but instead quite imperious—the tone of one equal exhorting other equals.

Because of these facts, I am satisfied that the memorandum was not designed to be a statement of *my* views on these cases. Justice Jackson not only would not have welcomed such a submission in this form, but he would have quite emphatically rejected it and, I believe, admonished the clerk who had submitted it. I am fortified in this conclusion because the bald, simplistic conclusion that *"Plessy* v. *Ferguson* was right and should be re-affirmed" is not an accurate statement of my own views at the time.

I believe that the memorandum was prepared by me as a statement of Justice Jackson's tentative views for his own use at conference. The informal nature of the memorandum and its lack of any introductory language make me think that it was prepared very shortly after one of our oral discussions of the subject. It is absolutely inconceivable to me that I would have prepared such a document without previous oral discussion with him and specific instructions to do so.

In closing, I would like to point out that during the hearings on my confirmation, I mentioned the Supreme Court's decision in *Brown* v. *Board of Education* in the context of an answer to a question concerning the binding effect of precedent. I was not asked my views on the substantive issues in the *Brown* case. In view of some of the recent Senate floor debate, I wish to state unequivocally that I fully support

the legal reasoning and the rightness from the standpoint of fundamental fairness of the *Brown* decision.

> Yours very truly,
> WILLIAM H. REHNQUIST,
> *Assistant Attorney General,*
> *Office of Legal Counsel.*

3. The Brooke Memorandum*

Rehnquist states that the memorandum was prepared "as a statement of Justice Jackson's tentative views for his own use" for the
conference of the Justices in the *Brown* case rather than as a statement
of Rehnquist's own position and recommendation to the Justice.

1. The memorandum does not represent what is known of Justice
Jackson's views on minority rights. It is highly improbable that he at
any time believed that *Plessy v. Ferguson* had been rightly decided.
Justice Jackson had a strong record against racial discrimination. . . .
More telling, perhaps, is that Mr. Justice Jackson ultimately not only
voted with the rest of the Court in *Brown* v. *Board of Education* but
actually left his hospital bed to go directly to the Court to be present
for the announcement of the decision on May 17, 1954. And aside
from his judicial career, Justice Jackson had been America's chief
prosecutor at the Nuremburg trials where his opposition to racism was
manifested and reinforced. . . .

Not only does Justice Jackson's prior record on race repel the attribution of a pro-*Plessy v. Ferguson* view to him, but the memorandum
contains another position which could not possibly have been intended to reflect that of the Justice:

"To the argument made by Thurgood, not John Marshall that a
majority may not deprive a minority of its constitutional right, the
answer must be made that while this is sound in theory, in the long
run it is the majority who will determine what the constitutional rights
of the minority are. One hundred and fifty years of attempts on the
part of this Court to protect minority rights of any kind—whether
those of business, slaveholders, or Jehovah's Witnesses—have all met
the same fate. One by one the cases establishing such rights have been
sloughed off, and crept silently to rest. If the present Court is unable
to profit by this example, it must be prepared to see its work fade in

---

Congressional Record, Dec. 9, 1971, 45815–16.

time, too, as embodying only the sentiments of a transient majority of nine men."

Even if it stood alone, his opinion in *West Virginia Board of Education v. Barnette*, 319 U.S. 624,* would be eloquent testimonial that he believed that the Court can and must protect the rights of minorities, including "Jehovah's Witnesses." . . .

"We set up government by consent of the governed, and the Bill of Rights denies those in power any legal opportunity to coerce that consent. Authority here is to be controlled by public opinion, not public opinion by authority. . . .

"If there is any fixed star in our constitutional constellation, it is that no official, high or petty, can prescribe what shall be orthodox in politics, nationalism, religion, or other matters of opinion or force citizens to confess by word or act their faith therein. If there are any circumstances which permit an exception, they do not now occur to us," Id., at 641–642.

Indeed, Mr. Justice Jackson's entire career repudiates the claim that the memorandum reflected the Justice's view "that where a legislature was dealing with its own citizens, it was not part of the judicial function to thwart public opinion except in extreme cases." . . .

Justice Jackson sometimes disagreed with other members of the Court as to the scope of individual rights under the Constitution, but he yielded to no one in his insistence that the protection of such rights was a primary function of the Supreme Court. To put into his mouth the sentence "One by one the cases establishing such rights have been sloughed off, and crept silently to rest" is to contend that Justice Jackson was willing to repudiate a substantial part of his life's work.

2. There is considerable internal evidence in the memorandum, aside from the views which it expresses, to show that it could not have been intended for the use of Justice Jackson in a conference.

a. Taking the memorandum as a whole, it contains nothing that Justice Jackson did not know, or of which he would have to be reminded by a written memorandum. Doubtless, Justices ask their law clerks to draft summaries of precedents, or arguments of counsel to be used by a Justice at conference. But this memorandum does not

---

*This decision struck down a state law requiring school children to salute the American flag during opening exercises on pain of expulsion. It overruled a decision handed down only three years earlier, *Minersville School District v. Gobitis*, 310 US 586 (1940).

contain that kind of legal analysis. It is, rather, a statement of judicial philosophy and well known, if somewhat one-sided, judicial history. It is doubtful whether any Justice would have needed a memorandum to refresh his recollection of the matters contained in that memorandum, but surely Justice Jackson, who was generally regarded as the most able and eloquent advocate on the Court, was unneedful of this kind of prop and would not have asked for it.

b. The title itself is a giveaway, "A Random Thought on the Segregation Cases." A memorandum drafted for use by a Justice in conference would probably have no title at all, but "random" is hardly an appropriate description of a memorandum written pursuant to instructions and for use in serious deliberations. On the other hand, the title is entirely appropriate if the memorandum is indeed what it otherwise appears to be, a memorandum from Mr. Rehnquist to Justice Jackson expressing the law clerk's views.

c. The history recited in the memorandum is so elementary that it would have insulted the intelligence of the other Justices if it had been recited in conference.

d. The personal references to the Justices are inconsistent with the tone which Mr. Jackson would have used, or could have been expected to use. There are three examples of this in the memorandum. Each of these is sufficiently telling that it merits separate attention.

i. "I would suggest that this is a question the Court need never reach; *for regardless of the Justice's* individual views on the merits of segregation, it quite clearly is not one of those extreme cases which commands intervention from one of any conviction."

If the "I" throughout this memorandum is Justice Jackson (that is, if the memorandum was, as Mr. Rehnquist asserts, a statement of Justice Jackson's own position), then the phrase *"for regardless of the Justice's* individual views on the merits of segregation" does not ring true. Rather, Justice Jackson would have said "I would suggest that this is a question the Court need never reach; for regardless of *our* individual views. . . ." Indeed, the singular "Justice's" is (unless it is a typographical error) evidence that the Justice referred to is Justice Jackson being addressed by Mr. Rehnquist.

ii. "If this Court, because its members individually are 'liberal' and dislike segregation, now chooses to strike it down, it differs from [earlier] court[s] only in the kinds of litigants it favors and the kinds of special claims it protects."

It is at least unlikely that Jackson would have referred to the other members of the Court as "liberal" or that Rehnquist would have thought that this usage was proper for a statement that Jackson would make.

   iii. The third passage leaves little doubt that the "I" is Rehnquist, not Justice Jackson.

"I realize that it is an unpopular and unhumanitarian position, for which I have been excoriated by 'liberal' colleagues, but I think *Plessy* v. *Ferguson* was right and should be re-affirmed."

I know of no evidence that Justice Jackson was ever "excoriated by 'liberal' colleagues," that is, by other members of the Court. Indeed, since Justice Jackson had never previously taken any position suggesting that *Plessy* v. *Ferguson* was correct, there would have been no occasion for such excoriation. Mr. Rehnquist's explanation is questionable also because the "liberal colleagues" are referred to in the third person, which would have been inappropriate if the memorandum was drafted for Justice Jackson to use in conference when only those colleagues would be addressed. If the memorandum was really intended for Justice Jackson's use in conference, it would have read something like "I realize that it is an unpopular and unhumanitarian position, for which I may be excoriated by some of my brethren."

A minor, and perhaps less compelling, point as to the use of the third person is that one member of the Court is more likely to refer to the others as "brethren," and that a clerk writing for a Justice would adopt this formula. On the other hand, the word "colleague" is precisely the one which one would expect if a clerk was complaining about the treatment he was receiving from his fellow law clerks. Finally, it is particularly unlikely that Mr. Justice Jackson, of all people, should have required a law clerk to draft language for him in response to other members of the Court who had excoriated him for his position. Mr. Justice Jackson, as is well known, was entirely able to take care of himself in such intramural debate.

   e. The tone of the memorandum is uncharacteristic of Justice Jackson, but more characteristic of Mr. Rehnquist. Most obvious, perhaps, is the *ad hominem* thrust, "To the argument made by Thurgood, not John Marshall."

3. Evidence of Mr. Rehnquist's subsequent actions strongly suggests that the memorandum is a representation of Mr. Rehnquist's own views.

As I pointed out in an earlier floor speech.

a. The memorandum is entirely consistent with the position Mr. Rehnquist took on racial issues until the time of his nomination. For, even a decade after the *Brown* decision Mr. Rehnquist opposed a local anti-discrimination ordinance, expressing greater concern for the discriminator than those discriminated against. And in 1967 Mr. Rehnquist opposed integration of the Phoenix public schools saying, in that context, "we are no more dedicated to an'integrated' society than we are to a 'segregated' society." It is far more plausible to attribute the views of that memorandum to one with Mr. Rehnquist's unfortunate record on racial matters than to Mr. Justice Jackson.

b. The passage quoted earlier, "I have been excoriated by 'liberal' colleagues," is illuminated by Mr. Rehnquist's article about the practices of law clerks at the Supreme Court. In that article in *U.S. News & World Report* he objected that "the political cast of the clerks as a group was to the 'left' of either the nation or the Court." It would now appear that the article was, in part, Mr. Rehnquist's reaction to the excoriation to which he referred in his memorandum to Justice Jackson.

II.
A Slight Digression: The Matter of Original Intent

THE REARGUMENT IN *Brown* called forth what was probably the most detailed exploration of original intent ever attempted in a Supreme Court case up to that time. Those analyses are the forerunner of a broader debate over originalism, or intentionalism, as it is sometimes called, which has raged with particular intensity over the last decade or so among constitutional scholars and politicians.

All points on the compass have been jogged. Thus Raoul Berger of Harvard has argued for strict fidelity to the intentions of those who framed the Constitution and its amendments. Since the fourteenth amendment was designed in his view to perpetuate the Civil Rights Act of 1866, he can find no justification for *Brown* v. *Board of Education*, intensely sympathetic to the result though he may be. Nor does he see any justification for the abolition of capital punishment by the Supreme Court.

Robert Bork articulates a median position, which rejects any notion that the courts must "apply a constitutional provision only to circumstances specifically contemplated by the framers." Where many provisions of the Constitution are concerned, he argues, judges should look for a "core value," capable of different applications in different eras. Bork praises the *Brown* decision, therefore, but warns against conceiving constitutional guarantees on levels of generality so high that they lose touch with their original core.

Other observers accept the legitimacy of, and certainly the need for, a high level of generality in constitutional interpretation. But some of them, like Leonard Levy and Paul Brest, believe that such a version of original intent gives the courts so little guidance as to render the whole notion of intentionalism largely meaningless.

Original intent also became politicized in the 1980s. President Reagan's Attorney General, Edwin Meese, announced himself a devotee of the concept, and used it to deny, among other things, that the bill of rights applies to the states, or that judicial review is sanctioned by the Constitution. On a more serious level, Robert Bork's views on original intent played a critical part in the Senate's rejection of his nomination to the Supreme Court in 1987.

In the sections which follow, Judge Bork explains his median view of original intent. Professor Terrance Sandalow of Michigan Law School examines the nature and the limits of the entire originalist theory.

1. Robert Bork—"The Constitution, Original Intent, and Economic Rights"(1986)*

The problem for constitutional law always has been and always will be the resolution of what has been called the Madisonian dilemma. The United States was founded as what we now call a Madisonian system, one which allows majorities to rule in wide areas of life simply because they are majorities, but which also holds that individuals have some freedoms that must be exempt from majority control. The dilemma is that neither the majority nor the minority can be trusted to define the proper spheres of democratic authority and individual liberty. The first would court tyranny by the majority; the second, tyranny by the minority.

Over time it has come to be thought that the resolution of the Madisonian problem—the definition of majority power and minority freedom—is primarily the function of the judiciary and, most especially, the function of the Supreme Court. That understanding, which now seems a permanent feature of our political arrangements, creates the need for constitutional theory. The courts must be energetic to protect the rights of individuals, but they must also be scrupulous not to deny the majority's legitimate right to govern. How can that be done?

Any intelligible view of constitutional adjudication starts from the proposition that the Constitution is law. . . . What does it mean to say that the words in a document are law? One of the things it means is that the words constrain judgment. They control judges every bit as much as they control legislators, executives, and citizens.

---

*San Diego Law Review, Vol. 23, 823, 1986. Copyright 1986 San Diego Law Review Association. Reprinted with the permission of the San Diego Law Review.

The provisions of the Bill of Rights and the Civil War amendments not only have contents that protect individual liberties, they also have limits. They do not cover all possible or even all desirable liberties. For example, freedom of speech covers speech, not sexual conduct. Freedom from unreasonable searches and seizures does not protect the power of businesses to set prices. These limits mean that the judge's authority has limits and that outside the designated areas democratic institutions govern.

If this were not so, if judges could govern areas not committed to them by specific clauses of the Constitution, then there would be no law other than the will of the judge. It is common ground that such a situation is not legitimate in a democracy. . . . This means that any defensible theory of constitutional interpretation must demonstrate that it has the capacity to control judges. An observer must be able to say whether or not the judge's result follows fairly from premises given by an authoritative, external source and is not merely a question of taste or opinion. . . .

The only way in which the Constitution can constrain judges is if the judges interpret the document's words according to the intentions of those who drafted, proposed, and ratified its provisions and its various amendments. It is important to be plain at the outset what intentionalism means. It is not the notion that judges may apply a constitutional provision only to circumstances specifically contemplated by the Framers. In such a narrow form the philosophy is useless. Because we cannot know how the Framers would vote on specific cases today, in a very different world from the one they knew, no intentionalist of any sophistication employs the narrow version just described.

There is a version that is adequate to the task. Dean John Hart Ely has described it:

> What distinguishes interpretivism [or intentionalism] from its opposite is its insistence that the work of the political branches is to be invalidated only in accord with an inference whose starting point, whose underlying premise, is fairly discoverable in the Constitution. That the complete inference will not be found there—because the situation is not likely to have been foreseen— is generally common ground.*

In short, all an intentionalist requires is that the text, structure, and

---

*John Hart Ely, *Democracy and Distrust*, (1980), pp. 1–2.

history of the Constitution provide him not with a conclusion but with a major premise. That premise states a core value that the Framers intended to protect. The intentionalist judge must then supply the minor premise in order to protect the constitutional freedom in circumstances the Framers could not foresee. Courts perform this function all of the time. Indeed, it is the same function they perform when they apply a statute, a contract, a will, or, indeed, a Supreme Court opinion to a situation the Framers of those documents did not foresee.

Thus, we are usually able to understand the liberties that were intended to be protected. We are able to apply the first amendment's Free Press Clause to the electronic media and to the changing impact of libel litigation upon all the media; we are able to apply the fourth amendment's prohibition on unreasonable searches and seizures to electronic surveillance; we apply the Commerce Clause to state regulations of interstate trucking.

Does this version of intentionalism mean that judges will invariably decide cases the way the Framers would if they were here today? Of course not. But many cases will be decided that way and, at the very least, judges will confine themselves to the principles the Framers put into the Constitution. Entire ranges of problems will be placed off-limits to judges, thus preserving democracy in those areas where the Framers intended democratic government. That is better than any non-intentionalist theory of constitutional adjudication can do. If it is not good enough, judicial review under the Constitution cannot be legitimate. I think it is good enough.

There is one objection to intentionalism that is particularly tiresome. Whenever I speak on the subject someone invariably asks: "But why should we be ruled by men long dead?" The question is never asked about the main body of the Constitution where we really are ruled by men long dead in such matters as the powers of Congress, the President, and the judiciary. Rather, the question is asked about the amendments that guarantee individual freedoms. The answer as to those amendments is that we are not governed by men long dead unless we wish to cut back those freedoms, which the questioner never does. We are entirely free to create all the additional freedoms we wish by legislation, and the nation has done that frequently. What the questioner is really driving at is why judges, not the public but judges, should be bound to protect only those freedoms actually specified by the Constitution. The objection underlying the question is not to the rule of dead men but to the rule of living majorities.

Moreover, when we understand that the Bill of Rights gives us major premises and not specific conclusions, the document is not at all anachronistic. The major values specified in the Bill of Rights are timeless in the sense that they must be preserved by any government we would regard as free. For that reason, courts must not hesitate to apply only values to new circumstances. A judge who refuses to deal with unforeseen threats to an established constitutional value, and hence provides a crabbed interpretation that robs a provision of its full, fair, and reasonable meaning, fails in his judicial duty.

But there is the opposite danger. Obviously, values and principles can be stated at different levels of abstraction. In stating the value that is to be protected, the judge must not state it with so much generality that he transforms it. When that happens the judge improperly deprives the democratic majority of *its* freedom. The difficulty in choosing the proper level of generality has led some to claim that intentionalism is impossible.

Thus, in speaking about my view of the fourteenth amendment's equal protection clause as requiring black equality, Professor Paul Brest of Stanford said,

> The very adoption of such a principle, however, demands an arbitrary choice among levels of abstraction. Just what *is* "the general principle of equality that applies in all cases"? Is it the "core idea of *black* equality" that Bork finds in the original understanding. . . , or a broader principle of "*racial* equality". . . , or is it a still broader principle of equality that encompasses discrimination on the basis of gender (or sexual orientation) as well?
>
> .   .   .   .   .
>
> The fact is that all adjudication requires making choices among levels of generality on which to articulate principles, and all such choices are inherently non-neutral. No form of constitutional decisionmaking can be salvaged if its legitimacy depends on satisfying Bork's requirements that principles be "neutrally derived, defined and applied."*

I think that Brest's statement is wrong and that an intentionalist can do what Brest says he cannot. Let me use Brest's example as a

---

The Fundamental Rights Controversy: The Essential Contradictions of Normative Constitutional Scholarship, Yale Law Journal, Vol. 90, 1981, 1063, 1091–92.

hypothetical—I am making no statement about the truth of the matter. Assume for the sake of the argument" that a judge's study of the evidence shows that both black and general racial equality were clearly intended, but that equality on matters such as sexual orientation was not under discussion.

The intentionalist may conclude that he must enforce black and racial equality but that he has no guidance at all about any higher level of generality. He has, therefore, no warrant to displace a legislative choice that prohibits certain forms of sexual behavior. That result follows from the principle of acceptance of democratic choice where the Constitution is silent. The same sort of analysis could be used to determine whether an amendment imposes black equality only or the broader principle of racial equality. In short, the problem of levels of generality may be solved by choosing no level of generality higher than that which interpretation of the words, structure, and history of the Constitution fairly support.

The power of extreme generalization was demonstrated by Justice William O. Douglas in *Griswold v. Connecticut*.† In *Griswold* the Court struck down Connecticut's anticontraception statute. Justice Douglas created a constitutional right of privacy that invalidated the state's law against the use of contraceptives. He observed that many provisions of the Bill of Rights could be viewed as protections of aspects of personal privacy. He then generalized these particulars into an overall right of privacy that applies even where no provision of the Bill of Rights does. By choosing that level of abstraction, the Bill of Rights was expanded beyond the known intentions of the Framers. Since there is no constitutional text or history to define the right, privacy becomes an unstructured source of judicial power. . . . A concept of original intent, one that focuses on each specific provision of the Constitution rather than upon values stated at a high level of abstraction, is essential to prevent courts from invading the proper domain of democratic government.

2. Terrance Sandalow—"Constitutional Interpretation" (1981)*

The notion that constitutional interpretation consists of determining the intentions of the framers occupies an important place in the his-

---

†381 U.S. 479 (1965).
Michigan Law Review, Vol. 79, 1033, 1981.

tory of thought about the Constitution. Many persons, including some of the most distinguished members of the Supreme Court, have urged that precisely because it is a constitution we are expounding, there is a duty of fidelity to the intentions of those who drafted and ratified the document. Thus, Chief Justice Taney, in deciding "whether a person of the African race can be a citizen of the United States," wrote:

> No one, we presume, supposes that any change in public opinion or feeling . . . should induce the Court to give to the words of the Constitution a more liberal construction in their favor than they were intended to bear when the instrument was framed and adopted. Such an argument would be altogether inadmissible in any tribunal called on to interpret it. If any of its provisions are deemed unjust, there is a mode prescribed in the instrument itself by which it may be amended; but while it remains unaltered, it must be construed now as it was understood at the time of its adoption. It is not only the same in words, but the same in meaning . . . .*

A century later, Mr. Justice Black developed a similar theme and purported to make it a cornerstone of his constitutional philosophy. Rejecting a claim that the death penalty should be held to violate the eighth amendment's prohibition of "cruel and unusual punishments," he wrote:

> In my view, these words cannot be read to outlaw capital punishment because that penalty was in common use and authorized by law here and in the countries from which our ancestors came at the time the Amendment was adopted. It is inconceivable to me that the framers intended to end capital punishment by the Amendment.†

Views such as those expressed by Taney and Black may at times have influenced constitutional decision, but it is beyond doubt that they do not reflect the course of American constitutional development. Constitutional decision-making has not been confined to a process of discovering the specific intentions of the framers. There are various reasons why this is so, but the most pervasive is that the questions for which subsequent generations have sought answers in the Constitution have been the questions of those generations. Since those questions were, most often, not the ones the framers had specifically addressed,

---

*Scott v. Sandford, 60 U.S. (19 How.) 393, 425, 426 (1857).
†McGautha v. California, 402 U.S. 183, 226 (1971) (separate opinion of Black, J.).

it is not surprising that answers were not to be found in the framers' specific intentions. Even the most prophetic of the men who drafted and ratified the Constitution had no occasion to speculate concerning the role of the federal government, vis-á-vis the states, in the management of an integrated and industrialized national economy. Nor did the men of a later generation, who imposed on each state the obligation to afford every person "the equal protection of the laws," have reason to consider whether those words should be held to prohibit sex-based discrimination at a time when the relations between the sexes would be far different from those they had known or could have imagined. Although these and myriad other issues not anticipated by the framers have over the years pressed for solution, the notion that the meaning assigned to the Constitution ought to turn upon the intentions of the framers has continued to exert a strong attraction. The effort to resolve that dilemma has led to an appreciation that the conception of "intention" is a good deal more ambiguous than the statements of Chief Justice Tarney and Justice Black suggest.

The intentions of the framers can, for example, be described on different levels of generality. On one level, it is entirely accurate to state that the framers intended to allow the death penalty and to deny Congress the authority to regulate the quantity of wheat that a farmer might grow for domestic consumption. And the men who adopted the fourteenth amendment intended to permit legislation that would bar women from certain occupations or in a variety of other ways distinguish between men and women. At the same time, it seems entirely plausible to understand the framers as having intended to prohibit all "cruel and unusual punishments," not merely specific practices with which they were familiar and to which they objected. Similarly, in authorizing Congress to "regulate commerce . . . among the several states," the framers can appropriately be understood as intending to invest it with power to regulate not only specific activities that they knew affected that commerce but any activity that might do so. So also, the guarantee of "equal protection of the laws" can be understood as proscribing not only certain practices directed against blacks, with which the draftsmen were immediately concerned, but also all other practices that arbitrarily distinguish among classes of individuals. To ask, in each instance, whether the framers "intended" the specific or the general is to pose a question that almost invariably is unanswerable. The question assumes that they intended one or the other, but not both. But the issues did not arise for the framers in a way that forced such a choice: they could have intended both simultaneously because viewing them as compatible, they had no reason to choose between them.

The insight that intentions can be understood in general terms has played an important role in the development of constitutional law, for it has provided a means by which to mediate between the belief that the meaning of the Constitution ought to be found in the intentions of the framers and the need to accommodate the Constitution to changing circumstances and values. Armed with the awareness that the "intentions of the framers" need not be understood to denote only their most particular intentions, and that the "important objects" of the Constitution could not be achieved if its meaning were held to be confined to such intentions, courts have generally looked to those "important objects" in interpreting the Constitution, secure in the belief that in doing so they were still construing the Constitution, not creating it. Congressional regulation of agriculture, the virtual abolition of capital punishment, and significant restriction of governmental power to discriminate on the basis of sex may not have been specifically intended by the framers, but each might be thought to have roots in their larger purposes.

The belief that those larger purposes could serve as a touchstone for constitutional interpretation has, of course, been especially important because constitutional development has occurred so largely through the institution of judicial review. The conventional understanding of the courts' warrant for the power they exercise is not that the values of judges are preferable to those of legislators, or that judges are a better barometer of contemporary societal values than legislators, but that the values embodied in the Constitution—the "important objects" of those who framed the document—are best entrusted to their care. It has long been accepted, of course, that the performance of this function requires the appraisal of new circumstances and, hence, additional value choices. But these additional value choices have been viewed as subsidiary to those written into the Constitution by the framers and, therefore, as susceptible to evaluation on the basis of their tendency to serve the larger purposes to which the framers committed the nation. Constitutional theory and the institution of judicial review have thus been seen as mutually supportive: judicial review is necessary to assure fidelity to the intentions of the framers, and it is justifiable, notwithstanding its unrepresentative character, because the values to which courts give expression are those to which the nation is bound by the Constitution. . . .

The view that constitutional interpretation involves primarily an elucidation of the general intentions of the framers is understandably attractive, perhaps not only because it seems to support the institutional arrangements we have established for giving contemporary meaning to the Constitution, but also because it is so comforting. The uneasiness, often the agony, and always the responsibility that accompany a difficult choice are softened by the belief that real choice does not exist. In law, the search for repose leads us to attribute responsibility for decisions to those who have gone before and, in constitutional law, to wise men we call "the framers." They may not have foreseen the world in which we live nor the problems we now face, but the words they wrote nonetheless provide "sufficient guidance" if only we have the wisdom to understand them properly. . . .

Reference to the "important objects" of the framers rather than their specific intentions is, no doubt, a necessity if the evolving needs of the nation are to be served. The amendment process established by article V simply will not sustain the entire burden of adaptation that must be borne if the Constitution is to remain a vital instrument of government. Yet, it must be recognized that the more general the statement of the framers' intentions, the weaker is the claim that those intentions circumscribe present judgment. To begin with, our understanding of the framers' intentions is necessarily distorted if we focus solely upon their larger purposes, ignoring the particular judgments they made in expressing those purposes. Intentions do not exist in the abstract; they are forged in response to particular circumstances and in the collision of multiple purposes which impose bounds upon one another. "[T]o make a general principle worth anything," as Holmes wrote,

> you must give it a body; you must show in what way and how far it would be applied actually in an actual system; you must show how it has gradually emerged as the felt reconciliation of concrete instances. . . . Finally, you must show its historic relations to other principles, often of very different date and origin, and thus set it in the perspective without which its proportions will never truly be judged.*

---

*The Use of Law Schools, in The Occasional Speechs of Justice Oliver Wendell Holmes 34, 41 (M. Howe ed. 1962).

So, too, in understanding the intentions of the framers. By wrenching the framers' "larger purposes" from the particular judgments that revealed them, we incur a loss of perspective, a perspective that might better enable us to see that the particular judgments they made were not imperfect expressions of a larger purpose but a particular accommodation of competing purposes. In freeing ourselves from those judgments we are not serving larger ends determined by the framers but making room for the introduction of contemporary values.

The "assistance of counsel" was indeed viewed by the framers as an important constituent of fair trial. . . . But their intention to safeguard the right to such assistance in all federal criminal trials was shaped in part by a conception of the relationship between government and its citizens, a conception that did not emphasize—that barely recognized—an affirmative responsibility on the part of government to its citizens. Absent a sense of such responsibility, it is not surprising that a trial might be deemed fair so long as the defendant was not prohibited from retaining counsel to assist him. Decisions during the past several decades establishing the right of indigents accused of crime to appointed counsel do not merely promote the framers' purpose to achieve fair trials. They also express a fundamentally altered conception of governmental responsibility and, accordingly, of what constitutes a fair trial. Virtually all Americans accept the balance thus struck between the interests of government and of indigent defendants as both wise and humane, but it is a balance that reflects the values of contemporary America, not those of the framers.

Contemporary constitutional law defining freedom of speech and of the press, similarly, is not simply a more adequate expression of the purpose of the framers than they themselves achieved—purposes somehow disembodied from the specific protections they understood to be within the compass of the first amendment—but a fundamentally different accommodation of the interests affected by principles governing the exercise of governmental power. Public discussion was, to be sure, greatly prized during the constitutional period both as a "natural right" of free men and as essential to democratic government. The literature of the period is filled with statements of its importance. So great is the allure of these expressions that we are apt to forget how different those times were from our own. The framers, we need to remember, . . . had not experienced, and thus had no reason to address, the needs of a nation as pluralistic as the United States was later to become. The political order, both of their own time and of the earlier years in which the ideal of freedom of expression first emerged, was far more fragile than that which has existed in the United States at any time during the twentieth century. To reason solely from their statements concerning the importance of public discussion is to ignore the fact that because of their circumstances and their history they held competing values—stability of government, security of private reputations, a conception of sexual morality, etc.—that also played a role in shaping their understanding of freedom of speech and of the press. We ought not to suppose that because these competing values were less frequently given eloquent expression they were entirely subordinated to public discussion. The competing values were already deeply imbedded in the law. The struggle was to gain recognition of the importance of public discussion. The best evidence of the balance that was struck is not the rhetoric that was employed, but the specific principles by which freedom of speech and the press were understood. When we ignore those principles, stressing instead the importance that the framers attached to public discussion and deemphasizing competing values that carried more weight for them than for us, the purposes we serve are not those of the framers, but our own.

The growth of federal power under the commerce clause may serve as a final illustration of the way in which reliance upon the general intentions of the framers permits the values of the present to dominate those of the past. It is customary to attribute to the framers the purpose of authorizing Congress to regulate "that commerce which concerns more states than one."* In the decentralized, rural economy of the late eighteenth century, that was a relatively limited grant of authority. A considerable volume of economic activity was not within the market economy; much, very likely most, activity that was part of the market economy occurred within the boundaries of a single state and had no discernible consequences outside that state. In these circumstances, the power conferred upon Congress afforded relatively limited opportunity to regulate private activity, and it offered little threat to the retention of very considerable autonomy in the states. Congressional power to regulate "that commerce which concerns more states than one," in the setting of an integrated, industrialized, modern economy strikes a very different balance between that power and the autonomy of states and individuals. Since all commercial activity may have consequences outside the state in which it occurs, the Congress has com-

---

*Gibbons v. Ogden, 22 U.S. (9 Wheat.), I, 85 (1824).

plete power to displace state government as a source of economic policy. The expansion of the market sector of the economy further extends federal power to displace state authority. Both changes in the economic structure, moreover, subject an ever-increasing proportion of life to federal regulatory authority. Lifting the framers' "intentions" out of the context in which they were formed, and employing them to deal with current issues, thus yields consequences very different from those the framers conceivably could have anticipated, and involves an accommodation of competing values that cannot reasonably be attributed to them. The framers did intend to authorize Congress to regulate "that commerce which concerns more states than one," but to separate that intention from their understanding that states and individuals retained substantial autonomy from federal control in the realm of economic activity is to lose "the perspective without which its proportions will never truly be judged." When the framers' intentions are placed in perspective, it is apparent that attribution of the contemporary law of the commerce clause to them is chimerical. . . .

Objectives that were compatible in the latter years of the eighteenth century have ceased to be so during the twentieth. Contemporary constitutional law, in establishing a new order among these objectives, does not reflect the intentions of the framers but a contemporary choice as to how those objectives ought to be ordered.

The law we ascribe to the Constitution is not, in brief, a legacy from the "founding fathers" and the Reconstruction Congress. . . . Contemporary constitutional law does, to be sure, rest upon a conceptual framework and employ a vocabulary that is in large measure derived from the framers. The question whether legislation is within the authority of the federal government must, even now, be decided within a framework which recognizes that that government was constituted as one of enumerated powers. We do not consider ourselves at liberty to ignore the question or to answer it merely by demonstrating that the power can best be exercised by the federal government. Decisions continue to be justified by an analysis which begins with the proposition that the exercise of power must be referable to the "commerce" clause or one of the other heads of federal power. Similarly, legislation is not beyond the power of government simply because it is unwise or unjust. A decision limiting governmental power must be grounded in a limitation of governmental power contained in the Constitution.

In making these decisions, however, the past to which we turn is the sum of our history, not merely the choices made by those who drafted and ratified the Constitution. The entirety of that history, together with current aspirations that are both shaped by it and shape the meaning derived from it, far more than the intentions of the framers, determine what each generation finds in the Constitution. As Holmes put it in *Missouri v. Holland:*

> when we are dealing with words that are also a constituent act, like the Constitution of the United States, we must realize that they have called into life a being the development of which could not have been foreseen completely by the most gifted of its begetters. It was enough for them to realize or to hope that they had created an organism; it has taken a century and cost their successors much sweat and blood to prove that they created a nation. The case before us must be considered in the light of our whole experience and not merely in that of what was said a hundred years ago. . . . We must consider what this country has become in deciding what the Amendment has reserved.*

*   *   *   *   *   *

Constitutional law thus emerges not as exegesis, but as a process by which each generation gives formal expression to the values it holds fundamental in the operations of government. The intentions of the framers describe neither its necessary minimal content nor its permissible outer boundaries. Nor is it surprising that that should be so. The framers were a remarkable group of men, and we are significantly in their debt, but it is a fallacy to suppose that because of their antiquity we can look to them for the wisdom that men seek from their elders. Their experience was more limited than ours. . . . It is we, not the framers, who have the experience of life under the document they wrote and who are familiar with the problems of maintaining a constitutional order. More fundamentally, we live in a world that they could not have contemplated, even in fantasy. . . . In these circumstances, it would be surprising—even remarkable—if the intentions of the framers did control the constitutional law of the present.

---

*252 U.S. 416, 433–34 (1920).

III.
Double Perspectives

ALFRED KELLY AND Alexander Bickel, two important participants in the *Brown* reargument, recorded their personal reactions to the events of which they were a part, as well as the scholarly conclusions which flowed from them.

Professor Kelly delivered a paper at the American Historical Association convention of 1961, aptly entitled "An Inside View of *Brown* v. *Board of Education.*" Five years earlier, he had systematically organized the historical analysis which his paper discusses informally, in a seminal article for the *Michigan Law Review*.

Professor Bickel gave his "unofficial" reaction to the research he was doing for Justice Frankfurter in a letter to the Justice which accompanied submission of his original memorandum on the 39th Congress and the fourteenth amendment. Two years later, Bickel wrote an article for the *Harvard Law Review*, reproducing much of his memorandum, and developing further his view that the correspondence between the Civil Rights Act and the fourteenth amendment was only the correspondence of 1866.

1. Alfred Kelly—"An Inside View of *Brown* v. *Board of Education*" (1961)*

One day in early July, 1953, I received a letter from Mr. Thurgood Marshall, General Counsel of the Legal Defense and Educational Fund of the National Association for the Advancement of Colored People. Would I be willing, Mr. Marshall inquired, to prepare a research paper on the intent of the framers of the Fourteenth Amendment with respect to the constitutionality of racially segregated

---

*Richard Kluger Papers—Manuscripts and Archives, Yale University Library.

schools? The United States Supreme Court, Mr. Marshall explained, had recently heard arguments on a series of school segregation cases, four of them on appeal from the states and one of them from the Supreme Court of the District of Columbia. . . .

Instead of handing down a decision, however, the Court handed the cases back to opposing counsel with a request for reargument on the question of the historical intent of the framers of the Fourteenth Amendment. It was at once apparent that the NAACP and its lawyers had scored a tremendous breakthrough. What the Justices' request really seemed to say, the lawyers and scholars at work on the case presently were to agree, was something like this: "we would like to dispose of the Plessy rule, for once and for all, as constitutionally outmoded and incompatible with the realities of the Negro's role in contemporary American society. But we are fearfully embarrassed by the apparent historical absurdity of such an interpretation of the Fourteenth Amendment, and equally embarrassed by the obvious charge that the Court will be 'legislating' if it simply imposes a new meaning on the Amendment without regard to historical intent. Therefore, learned counsel, produce for us in this Court a plausible historical argument that will justify us in pronouncing, in solemn and awful sovereignty, that the Fourteenth Amendment properly was intended by its authors to abolish school segregation, or at least to sanction its abolition by judicial fiat. Thus fortified, we will declare segregated schools in the states to be unconstitutional as a violation of the Fourteenth Amendment. And school segregation in the District will fall under the parallel construction of federal and state constitutional limitations."

The Court's order immediately produced a wild scramble on both sides for the services of constitutional historians, Reconstruction scholars, experts on public law, and so on. The questions the Court had asked were not the kind that lawyers ordinarily deal with, and in the face of them, the NAACP's lawyers confessed themselves, to the self-satisfied amusement of a number of historians and political scientists, to be substantially helpless. It was a scholar's inquiry which the Court had formulated, and not one within the ordinary purview of a lawyer's brief. The NAACP, by the way, was not alone in its embarrassment; counsel for the various respondent segregated school systems, now marshalled under the formidable legal generalship of veteran constitutional lawyer John W. Davis, were equally embarrassed. On both sides the call went out for historical scholarship. . . .

As a constitutional historian, I knew of course that the Fourteenth Amendment had evolved, in some considerable part, out of the Civil Rights Act of 1866. Accordingly, I went to work on the 1866 volumes of the *Congressional Globe*, reading anew the story of the debates that winter and spring for clues concerning the intent which . . . Bingham, Stevens, and the other congressional radicals might have had with respect to legalized segregation and school segregation in particular. I did not really expect to find very much of anything. As any reasonably competent historian could have told the Court and the lawyers on both sides, the historical questions they had framed did not necessarily have very much relevance at all to the issues that seemed consequential then to the embattled Radicals who had hammered out the Civil Rights Act and the Fourteenth Amendment that spring of 1866. The politicians of ninety-five years ago had other and for them more important matters on their minds. The whole thing was a good example of the way in which the matter of what is politically important and historically significant shifts from one age to another. . . .

To my surprise, the debates reprinted in the 1866 volumes of the *Globe* had a good deal to say about school segregation. Unhappily, from the NAACP's point of view, most of what appeared there at first blush looked rather decidedly bad. . . .

The original Civil Rights Bill, as reported out on the Senate floor . . . early in 1866, had indeed been so broadly worded that it obviously would have struck down and outlawed entirely all state segregation laws—those sanctioning segregated schools as well as Jim Crow transportation facilities, and so on. . . .

But when the Civil Rights Bill reached the House, John A. Bingham, himself a Radical of Radicals and a member of the Committee of Fifteen, bitterly attacked the measure, on the grounds that Congress utterly lacked the power to legislate against legalized segregation. . . . To do so, he said, was grossly unconstitutional. . . . Bingham's attack sent the Bill back to the House Judiciary Committee, where the disputed ambiguous language was stricken out. Thereafter, it was reported to the floor once more, this time in a form which absolutely eliminated the controversial segregation language. The conclusion for any reasonably objective historian was painfully clear: The Civil Rights Act as it passed Congress was specifically rewritten to avoid the embarrassing question of a Congressional attack upon state racial segregation laws, including school segregation. . . .

Now note, if you will, the deadly implications of this situation for the NAACP's brief, at least as we have carried the argument thus far. If the Civil Rights Act, as passed, specifically had been amended so as not to abolish legalized state segregation, and if the First Section of the Fourteenth Amendment had been passed merely to constitutionalize the Civil Rights Act, then it could hardly be argued that the intent of Congress, in submitting the Fourteenth Amendment to the states, had been to knock out legalized racial segregation in the states—in schools, in transportation, hotels, or anything else. It looked as if John W. Davis would win the historical argument hands down. . . .

The paper I prepared for [a September conference of lawyers and scholars organized by the NAACP] was not adequate by any standard. I was trying to be both historian and advocate within the same paper, and the combination, as I found out, was not a very good one. . . . I was facing for the first time in my own career the deadly opposition between my professional integrity as a historian and my wishes and hopes with respect to a contemporary question of values, of ideals, of policy, of partisanship, and of political objectives. . . .

To my relief, I found that the lawyers present did not at all resent the fact that I had exposed a considerable difficulty in the argument they would have to make before the Court. On the contrary, they obviously wanted me to clarify as far as possible the difficulties they would confront were John W. Davis and his staff as well prepared as they might be expected to be.

The central discussion swung around a basic question of strategy: ought the Association's lawyers to use a generalized or a particularistic historical approach in their argument. Robert Ming, a Negro lawyer then in private practice in Chicago who had formerly taught law successively at Howard University and the University of Chicago, argued forcibly that the particularistic historical evidence favorable to the NAACP case was either so scanty or so unconvincing that sound strategy called for the abandonment of any attempt to make an argument based on the framers' immediate historical intent. Dangerous as it was, he said, the Court's request ought to be by-passed and the case argued in terms of . . . the overall spirit of humanitarianism, racial equalitarianism, and social idealism which had dominated the rise of the abolitionist movement and which by implication thereby had determined the objectives of the Radical Republicans who had written the Fourteenth Amendment.

It was a powerful argument, but it had one serious weakness: it would not meet the attack of lawyers for the respondent school boards who might show, with damning particularism, the Amendment's specific intent. Several of us therefore argued in reply that the NAACP's lawyers might find it possible to deal with the historical argument successfully in immediate terms. They would, at all events, be obliged to attempt it or run the risk of incurring the Court's direct censure and loss of the case. Ming, a hard and forceful debater and an incisive legal logician, remained unconvinced. . . .

One side point about the conference is worth making: the conference cost the NAACP, Thurgood Marshall later informed the delegates, upwards of thirty thousand dollars. Apparently, it also cost more than the NAACP officials had bargained for, for on the last day they found themselves a bit short of the cash necessary to meet our expense accounts. Accordingly, Marshall took off for Philadelphia, whose Negro leaders, he said, had not contributed their share so far to the expenses of the big legal battle now under way.

In his own words, "I put the touch on those boys down there and they paid off.". . . In a small way, it was a dramatic reflection of the extraordinary revolution in the Negro's economic and power status in American society that had been underway for the last twenty years, and which had been vastly accelerated by the Second World War. The whole conference, in fact, illustrated the way in which a new Negro elite, ably generaled by the lawyers of the NAACP, was lending its newly found economic power, money, and prestige to the great court battle now underway. A hundred years earlier, by contrast, in the Reconstruction battles over the Negro's status, the freedman had been little more than a helpless pawn in a battle between white politicians. Now the Negro was in command of his own fight for equality, marching on the Supreme Court with an army of lawyers, educators, technical experts, and the like, over which a Negro organization, the New York office of the NAACP, retained firm control.

I left the September Conference expecting to have no more to do with the segregation cases beyond what I might read in the newspapers. Ten days later, early in October, however, I was surprised to receive a phone call from Thurgood Marshall. In the curiously winning manner so characteristic of the man, he informed me that since I wasn't doing anything anyhow, I might as well come on down to New York for four or five days and waste my time there. My help, he said with careful flattery, was needed very badly on the brief. My vanity thus touched to the quick, I came. . . .

[Sometime after I arrived] Marshall called me . . . and when I

reached his office I found him and Robert Ming waiting for me.
Marshall now informed Ming and me that he wanted us to sit down
and hammer out a draft of a brief for the Supreme Court.

To this end he locked us up, so to speak, in an isolated suite of
offices over at the NAACP's main headquarters on West Fortieth
Street. Ming and I spent the next three days there, with no one else
present but a stenographer, walking up and down, dictating, arguing,
and orating to one another. The brief-drafting was mostly Ming and
comparatively little Kelly; in the first place Ming knew how to draft a
brief and I didn't; moreover, I found he had very positive ideas about
what he wanted to say. My role, it appeared, was to challenge him
repeatedly, to fight and quarrel with him, attack his history and constitutional law as unsound, and so on. Since being unpleasant comes
naturally both to lawyers and academicians, we got on famously. . . .
At the end of three days we had a brief which Ming said would do.

After five days, I went home completely exhausted, again expecting
to hear no more of the School Segregation cases. But early in November, Marshall called me, informed me once more that I was wasting
time in Detroit, and this time in effect ordering me to come down to
New York for another five days.

This time a still different task awaited me. . . . I met Thurgood
Marshall in his office, where we were joined by John Frank of the
Yale Law School, a nationally known lawyer and legal historian and
author of a number of leading monographs on the Fourteenth Amendment. Marshall informed the two of us that Ming's draft was fine as
far as it went, but that it didn't go far enough. Ming had proceeded
on the theory, earlier outlined here, that it would not do to get too
far involved in specific historical detail with respect to framer intent
and that the Association's case might best be cast in very generalized
terms with a deliberate avoidance of the particular. This tactic, Marshall now informed us, might get past two or three of the justices for
whom, it was clear, he entertained no very great professional regard,
but it would darn well never get past Frankfurter or Douglas. "I gotta
argue these cases," Thurgood said, "and if I try this approach, those
fellows will shoot me down in flames."

And so in the next few days, using the research that numbers of
scholars had done, we wrestled with the matter of adequate answers
to the deadly questions of the congressional intent in drafting and
modifying the Civil Rights Bill. . . . The central question, all three
of us felt, was that damning speech by Bingham which had forced

modification of the Civil Rights Act. . . . Surely John W. Davis would drive this sequence of events home; if he overwhelmed the Court with them, Marshall felt, the case might be lost.

I am very much afraid that for the next few days I ceased to function as a historian and instead took up the practice of law without a license. The problem we faced was not the historian's discovery of the truth, the whole truth and nothing but the truth; the problem instead was the formulation of an adequate gloss on the fateful events of 1866 sufficient to convince the Court that we had something of a historical case. Never has there been, for me at least, a more dramatic illustration of the difference in function, technique and outlook between lawyer and historian. It is not that we were engaged in formulating lies; there was nothing as crude and naive as that. But we were using facts, emphasizing facts, bearing down on facts, sliding off facts, quietly ignoring facts, and above all interpreting facts in a way to do what Marshall said we had to do—"get by those boys down there."

There was one optimistic element in all this, as Marshall pointed out: it was obvious, as I remarked earlier, that the Court was looking for a plausible historical answer. It needed merely to be convinced that it was possible to say that the idea of segregation might have had something to do with the Amendment, that it was not utterly absurd to argue some connection. . . . In other words, Marshall said, we didn't need to win a historical argument hands down, all we needed was a face-saving draw. "A nothin' to nothin' score," Thurgood put it, "means we win the ball game." I believe, by the way, that this was a correct interpretation of the Court's mood.

This may be the place to observe that it was in these conferences that I came to understand why Thurgood Marshall was such a cunning and powerful strategist in the campaign for Negro rights in America. *The Saturday Evening Post* a few years ago called him a charismatic personality; certainly he is all of that, for his dynamism, personality magnetism, and charm are undeniable, while he radiates a tremendous sense of personal power. But I found even more interesting his slashing and mordant sense of humor, his profoundly moving sense of identity with the Negro's tragic role in America, and his tremendous moral commitment to the work in which he was engaged.

The sudden shifts of mood he displayed on occasion were nothing short of astonishing. One morning in his office, he related to John Frank of Yale and myself, with tears in his eyes and a voice dulled with the cumulative grief of three hundred years, the experiment of a leading sociologist with a group of little colored girls, who were given their choice of playing with two sets of dolls, one white or Caucasian, one black or Negro. Even at three years of age, he said, the little colored girls preferred the white dolls, describing the black dolls as "bad" and "not nice" and the white dolls as "pretty" and "good." As Marshall told the story, he seemed bowed down under an unbearable burden of tragedy. A few moments later, his ebullient hilarity restored, he good-naturedly railed at his secretary's negligence, informing her in a voice deliberately weighted with excess Negro accent not to forget "who d' H. N. is around here" and he found immensely amusing my discomfiture at being told what "H. N." stood for. I shall not tell you here.*

Sometimes Marshall could reveal a mood of sudden savagery and bitterness. Customarily he referred to the Mason and Dixon line as "the Smith and Wesson line." On one occasion he read with savage delight from an Iowa frontier paper which portrayed a local Negro community as a mass of illiterate apes. For him, he made clear, this epitomized the white man's attitude toward his people. On still another occasion at an evening session at which I found myself playing devil's advocate with a bit too much enthusiasm and lack of tact, Marshall stopped suddenly and speaking into the growing silence around the table said: "Alfred, you are one of us here and I like you. But"—and this in a voice of terrible intensity—"I want you to understand that when us colored folks takes over, everytime a white man draws a breath, he'll have to pay a fine." A moment later, the good humor and charm returned. That same evening he told me in a mood of hilarious gaiety how his great grandfather had managed to escape from slavery simply because he was, in Thurgood's words, so completely worthless that his grateful master carefully refrained from catching him again. "From all I know about my grandpappy," Thurgood said, "he was a real no good and his master was right."

Gradually, in the next three days, we hammered out a strategy. I like to believe that I played a major part in developing it, but every one of you knows how easily self-deceit functions in a situation of this kind; a little more objectivity tells me that probably we came to the basic idea together and that it had been implicit in the work of various of the legal and historical scholars who had put in so much spade-work before now. . . . Briefly the strategy we fell upon was to argue that Bingham had attacked [the] Civil Rights Bill not because he

---

*"Kelly recoiled upon learning that H. N. stood for 'head nigger'"; Kluger, p. 643.

objected to banning segregation per se but rather because he thought the powers of Congress inadequate, under the Constitution, to sustain such an enactment, so that a constitutional amendment would be necessary for this purpose. Thus by strong implication we made the Fourteenth Amendment actually a device for making legal that which Bingham attacked in the House debates . . . as hopelessly unconstitutional.

To put it differently, instead of equating the Fourteenth Amendment with the Civil Rights Act, we heavily emphasized the difference. The Amendment, we told ourselves, had been necessary to accomplish a vast sweep of purpose far beyond the Civil Rights Act. Here . . . . we pounced on a phrase [which constitutional historian Howard] Jay Graham had dug up: Bingham, in defending the Amendment in the House, had indeed said Congress now was writing a constitutional provision, not drafting a statute; that statutes are writ sharp and narrow and specific, but constitutions are writ broad for ages yet unborn. In our minds' eye Bingham almost seemed to be speaking for our purposes, saying to the Court in the twentieth century that if your age, far beyond our span of time, sees in this Amendment a new birth of liberty it will be altogether legitimate for you to use it for that purpose.

This is the argument, essentially, that you will find incorporated in the historical portions of the NAACP brief as it went to the Court. This is the argument Marshall used in oral argument in answer to the questions from the justices. At this point, incidentally, I should confess something amusing about myself: I am convinced now, that this interpretation, which we hammered out with anything but historical truth as our objective, nonetheless contains an essential measure of historical truth. History is art as well as fact; everyone in this room knows that the facts do not automatically arrange themselves without the historian's creative leap, which occurs in our craft as well as in the exact sciences, and in any event there are a considerable number of facts to support what I shall call the Graham-Frank theory of the Amendment.

2. Alfred Kelly—"The Fourteenth Amendment Reconsidered: The Segregation Question" (1956)*

The Senate on February 2 passed the [Civil Rights] bill, 33 to 12, with the "no discrimination" clause intact. It was clear, however, that

the . . . broad interpretation of this clause and of the bill generally
had raised many doubts which would have to be resolved before the
measure became law.

The . . . bill now went to the House, where on March 2 it was
reported out on the floor by James Wilson of Iowa, Chairman of the
House Judiciary Committee. [O]n the question of the force and effect
of the "no discrimination" clause he declared for a narrow interpretation of the measure in unequivocal terms:

> "This part of the bill [he said, in reference to the no discrimi-
> nation clause] will probably excite more opposition and elicit
> more discussion than any other; and yet to my mind it seems
> perfectly defensible. It provides for the equality of citizens of the
> United States in the enjoyment of civil rights and immunities.
> What do these terms mean? Do they mean that in all things civil,
> social, political, all citizens, without distinction of race or color,
> shall be equal? . . . No. . . . Nor do they mean that all citizens
> shall sit on the same juries, or that their children shall attend the
> same schools. These are not civil rights or immunities.". . .*

In other words, Wilson attempted to reassure the more moderate
Republicans and Conservatives by adopting a restrictive interpretation
of the "no discrimination" clause. But the Conservatives in the House
also refused to be reassured. Representative Rogers of New Jersey, a
die-hard conservative Democrat . . ., replied to Wilson in a lengthy
speech in which he argued . . . that the "no discrimination" clause
would break down all state statutes which classified on the basis of
race. He cited . . . the Kentucky statute for the unequal punishment
of rape, the anti-miscegenation acts, an Indiana statute forbidding
Negroes to acquire real estate, and the Pennsylvania statute segregating white and Negro school children. Civil rights, he insisted, in fact
included "all the rights that we enjoy." "What broader words than
privileges and immunities," he inquired, "are to be found in the dic-
tionary?" (1122) Representative Delano, of Ohio, another conservative, citing the old Ohio school segregation law, observed that the
statute "did not, of course, place the black population on an equal
footing with the whites, and would, therefore, under the terms of
this bill be void." (158) Michael Kerr of Indiana, challenging the
constitutionality of the bill under the Thirteenth Amendment, asked
rhetorically whether it was slavery or involuntary servitude ". . . to

---

Congressional Globe, 39th Congress, 1st Session (1866), 1117. All of the other
quotations cited are from this source, and page numbers are indicated in the text.

deny to children of free negroes or mulattoes . . . the privilege of attending the common schools of a State with the children of white men?" (1268) Representative Henry Raymond, a moderate New York Republican and editor of the *New York Times*, warned that in his understanding the term "civil rights" covered the whole range of commonly understood liberties and immunities, and that he therefore entertained grave doubts as to the measure's constitutionality. (1267)

These arguments carried the day. On March 9, John A. Bingham of Ohio, then a member of the Joint Committee on Reconstruction which presently was to report the substance of the first section of the Fourteenth Amendment to the Congress, rose in the House to demand that the "no discrimination" clause be struck out of the bill. Accepting the "broad" or Conservative interpretation of the "no discrimination" clause, Bingham argued that civil rights included the entire range of civil privileges and immunities within organized society, excepting only political rights, and then insisted that Congress had no power to enact such legislation merely by benefit of the constitutional powers it derived from the Thirteenth Amendment. The result of the present language, Bingham said, would be to strike down every state law that set up any kind of discrimination against Negroes:

> "If civil rights has this extent, what, then, is proposed by the provision of the first section? Simply to strike down by congressional enactment every State constitution which makes a discrimination on account of race or color in any of the civil rights of the citizen. I might say here, without the least fear of contradiction, that there is scarcely a State in this Union which does not, by its constitution or its statute laws, make some discrimination on account of race or color between citizens of the United States in respect of civil rights." (1291)

Bingham then insisted that he believed that all discriminatory legislation ought to be wiped out. But the proper way to achieve this result, he thought, was "not by an arbitrary assumption of power, but by amending the Constitution of the United States, expressly prohibiting the States from any such abuse of power in the future." (1291)

Wilson at first refused to accept Bingham's "broad interpretations," and tried to defend the language of the . . . bill as it stood:

> "The gentleman from Ohio . . . . knows, as every man knows, that this bill refers to those rights which belong to men as citizens of the United States and none other; and when he talks of setting aside the school laws and jury laws and franchise laws of the States by the bill now under consideration, he steps beyond what

> he must know to be the rule of construction which must apply
> here, and as the result of which this bill can only relate to matters
> within the control of Congress." (1294) . . .

After some maneuvering, Bingham carried the day. His amendment to strike out the "no discrimination" clause was first voted down
113 to 37, but the bill was nonetheless returned to the Judiciary
Committee for restudy. On March 13, Wilson himself, reporting the
bill to the floor once more, moved to strike out the "no discrimination"
clause on the grounds that the words in question "might give warrant
for a latitudinarian construction not intended." (1366) The House
immediately concurred unanimously and without debate—obviously
Bingham's argument had ceased to be a matter of controversy. Immediately thereafter, the House passed the bill, 111 to 38. The Senate
concurred in the Bingham amendment, and the bill went to the President, to become law over Johnson's veto.

It seems highly probable, then, that the Civil Rights Act, as finally
passed, was not intended to ban state racial segregation and classification laws. The main force of the Conservatives' attack on the "no
discrimination" clause was that it would indeed destroy all race classification laws. The supporters of the bill at first insisted that this interpretation was erroneous, but when John A. Bingham dramatically
defended the Conservative interpretation in the face of James Wilson's
declaration of narrow intent, the House finally resolved the element
of doubt by striking out the "no discrimination" clause entirely. . . .

A new question now occurs: what was the relationship of the Civil
Rights Act to the Fourteenth Amendment itself? Was the first section
of the amendment intended merely to remove doubt as to the constitutional status of the Civil Rights Act, or was it the intent of the framers
of the amendment and of Congress to go beyond the restrictive and
enumerative scope of the Civil Rights Act, and to place all civil rights,
in the Bingham sense, under the protection of the amendment?

The evidence on this critical point is somewhat contradictory, but
careful analysis appears to establish the following tentative conclusions: First, the principal Radical leaders concerned with the amendment . . . deliberately sought to go far beyond the guarantees of the
Civil Rights Act and to place all civil rights, in the expansive Bingham
definition, under federal guarantees of equality against state law. Second, for strategic political reasons, the first section of the amendment
was in part, at least, represented on the floor of both houses as intended merely to constitutionalize the Civil Rights Act and to put its

guarantees beyond assault by possible future conservative Congresses. Third, and perhaps most important, the very phrases used in the first section of the amendment were, by virtue of their history and derivation, somewhat vague and amorphous, and not subject to precise legal delineation in debate, and it was not altogether to the Radical interest to attempt such definition.

The intent of certain Radical leaders to go beyond the restrictive enumeration of the Civil Rights Act and to incorporate a series of expansive guarantees in the Constitution is quite clear. In a general sense, the best evidence of this is the language of the guarantees which Bingham and the other authors of the Fourteenth Amendment incorporated in the first section. The guarantees they finally adopted—privileges and immunities, due process and equal protection—were not at all derived from the Civil Rights Act. . . .

When the new amendment reached the floor of Congress on April 30, a curious ambiguity developed in the Radicals' advocacy of the measure. On one hand, the Radical leaders, especially in the House, presented the first section as primarily an attempt to constitutionalize the Civil Rights Act and so either to remove doubts as to its validity or to place the guarantees of the act beyond the assault of future hostile Congresses. At the same time, however, they met the Conservative charges as to the broad and revolutionary scope of the rights to be placed under federal protection neither with affirmation nor denial; instead, Bingham, Stevens, and their associates used the technique of lofty, expansive, and highly generalized language to describe the amendment's potential consequences. It was as though the Radical leaders were avoiding a precise delineation of legal consequences.

This ambiguity was present in Stevens' speech of May 8 [1866] opening debate on the amendment in the House. . . . "[T]he Constitution," he [argued], "limits only the action of Congress, and is not a limitation on the States. This amendment supplies that defect, and allows Congress to correct the unjust legislation of the States, so far that the law which operates upon one man shall operate *equally* upon all. . . . Whatever law protects the white man shall afford 'equal' protection to the black man." (2459) It is worth observing here that Stevens is assuming a comprehensive congressional *legislative* power to enforce the amendment against state law.

Stevens then went on to avow that a principal purpose of the amendment was to place the remedies of the Civil Rights Act beyond assault by future unfriendly Congresses:

"Some answer,'Your Civil Rights Bill secures the same things.'
That is partly true, but a law is repealable by a majority. And I
need hardly say that the first time that the South with their cop-
perhead allies obtain the command of Congress it will be repealed. . . . This amendment once adopted cannot be amended
without two-thirds of Congress. That they will hardly get." (2459)

Subsequent speakers on both sides of the House fell in line with
this theory that the first section was in part at least declaratory of the
Civil Rights Act, and was intended either to remove doubts as to the
constitutionality of the law or to place its guarantees beyond congressional discretion. Thus Democrat William Finck of Ohio twitted the
Radicals with the observation that "all I have to say about this section
is, that if it is necessary to adopt it . . . then the civil rights bill, which
the President vetoed, was passed without authority, and is clearly
unconstitutional." (2461) The response of James A. Garfield of Ohio
was characteristic of the Radical position: "The civil rights bill is now
a part of the law of this land. But every gentleman knows it will cease
to be a part of the law whenever the sad moment arrives when that
gentleman's party comes into power. . . . For this reason, and not
because I believe the civil rights bill unconstitutional, I am glad to
see that first section here." (2462) . . .

All this might well imply that the first section of the proposed
amendment was intended to be merely declaratory of the Civil Rights
Act, and would not go beyond its rather restrictive guarantees. But a
second theme was present in the House debates—the argument that
the phraseology of the first section was expansive and "revolutionary"
in character, so that its precise future meaning was susceptible to
indefinitely broad interpretation. . . .

On May 10th, Senator [Jacob] Howard of Michigan, acting as co-
chairman of the Joint Committee . . ., presented the proposed
amendment to the upper house. Howard's speech, unlike Stevens',
presented in no uncertain terms a powerful and convincing "broad
construction" of the force and scope of the first section. Taking up the
privileges and immunities clause, he first asserted that any attempt at
a precise delineation of rights under the clause would be "a somewhat
barren discussion." (2765) . . .

Howard then presented an extremely latitudinarian interpretation
of the due process [and equal protection clauses], which he asserted
would destroy all state class legislation entirely:

"The last two clauses of the first section of the amendment

disable a State from depriving not merely a citizen of the United States, but any person, whoever he may be, of life, liberty or property without due process of law. . . . This abolishes all class legislation in the States, and does away with the injustice of subjecting one caste of persons to a code not applicable to another. It prohibits the hanging of a black man for a crime for which the white man is not hanged. It protects the black man in his fundamental rights as a citizen with the same shield which it throws over the white man. . . . I look upon the first section, taken in connection with the fifth, as very important. It will, if adopted by the States, forever disable everyone of them from passing laws trenching on those fundamental rights and privileges which pertain to citizens of the United States, and to all persons who may happen to be within their jurisdiction. It establishes equality before the law, and it gives to the humblest, the poorest, the most despised of the race the same rights and same protection before the law as it gives to the most powerful, the most wealthy, or the most haughty. That, sir, is republican government as I understand it, and the only one which can claim the praise of a just Government." (2766)

In the debates which followed, there was a general assumption of the accuracy of Howard's latitudinarian interpretation. This meant in turn that there was less disposition in the Senate than there had been in the House to reassure the moderates that the first section of the amendment involved nothing more than a constitutionalization of the Civil Rights Act. In one significant exchange, . . . [Senator William Pitt Fessenden of Maine], as co-chairman of the Joint Committee, undertook to deny categorically that the first section had been inspired by the Civil Rights Act or indeed had anything to do with it at all. Its contents, he pointed out, were entirely different, and it made "no reference" to the disputed law. (2896) . . .

The amendment . . . passed both houses by large majorities without any resolution of the ambiguous contradiction of the Radicals' assurances that they proposed merely to constitutionalize the Civil Rights Act and their proposal to "abolish all class legislation" in the United States. It is probable that the Radicals in fact had no great desire to resolve that ambiguity, for which there was a highly plausible explanation in the politics of the moment. The political situation in Congress in the Spring of 1866 was not yet entirely clear. President Johnson's influence was rapidly being destroyed, but there was a substantial bloc of moderate Republicans who had not yet committed themselves entirely to the Radical position. Bingham, Stevens, . . .

and the other Radicals were clear enough about what they wanted to accomplish, but if they drove home too far the proposition on the floor that their amendment would undoubtedly consummate the destruction of all caste and class legislation in the states, an important element of moderate Republican support might be alienated and the requisite two-thirds majority necessary to the amendment's adoption might not be obtained. Political strategy called for ambiguity, not clarity. . . .

So the first section of the amendment had a philosophic and expansive character which the Radicals refused to define exactly. As Bingham observed significantly early in the session, "You do not prohibit murder in the Constitution; you guarantee life in the Constitution." (432) There were vast advantages in this, for if the political and social currents of the nation consummated the revolutionary implications of the amendment they were writing, then subsequent judicial and congressional implementation and the overall dynamism of consequent constitutional growth would achieve their ultimate purposes. . . .

Perhaps the final comment on the entire problem of the amendment's meaning is the observation that the amendment was now a part of a living and dynamic constitutional system. Its meaning consequently was ultimately to reflect through the medium of the judicial process the evolution of democratic aspiration, will and myth in the American social order on the question of race and caste.

3. Alexander Bickel—Letter to Justice Frankfurter (August 22, 1953)*

August 22, 1953

Dear Mr. Justice:

There are attached some fifty pages telling, verbosely, how the Fourteenth Amendment got through Congress. . . .

What I did of course is nowhere near complete. Conclusions are not explicitly drawn, although it strikes me that they draw themselves. 1866 was an election year of violent political activity. The issue of the day was the necessary reorganization of the political institutions which were to govern a reunited country. That was the meaning of recon-

---

*Felix Frankfurter Papers, Harvard Law School Library.

struction. . . . On that the Congress went to the country against the President and that was primarily, almost wholly, what the Fourteenth Amendment meant. On that the election of that year turned. No one was wholly focused on Section 1 of the Amendment. And to the extent that they were, the great, central body of opinion . . . took the section to mean that there were to be no more Black Codes. That was about all. When the Civil Rights Bill as first introduced seemed to go farther it was objected to (both on the policy and constitutional grounds) and it was narrowed. Section 1 of the Amendment was passed to the refrain of assurances and accusations that it embodied the Civil Rights Act. Little regard was had for language by a Congress not notable for the presence in its membership of very many brilliant men. A blunderbuss was simply aimed in the direction of existing evils in the South, on which all eyes were fixed. There were a few muted warnings that the language was broad, but in the hurry of it in the end none cared much. The dangers to which broad language might lead were distant anyway. It was preposterous to worry about unsegregated schools, for example, when hardly a beginning had been made at educating Negroes at all and when obviously special efforts, suitable only for the Negroes, would have to be made. Even Northern charitable institutions found upon going into educational work in the South that it was best not to try to set up mixed schools. In any event, it is impossible to conclude that the 39th Congress intended that segregation be abolished; impossible also to conclude that they foresaw it might be, under the language they were adopting. What was in Bingham's mind, God alone knows, and in any event Bingham was unable to impart it to the House, so it does not matter. . . . But all this only means that the legislative history is inconclusive. For the Congress was on notice that it was enacting vague language of indeterminate reach. I think, though it is hard to quote chapter and verse on this, [that] very many men in that Congress, not least of all Thaddeus Stevens, thought that the Amendment would operate principally through implementing legislation by Congress. Hopes both for a broad and a narrow application of the general language being voted were met by this impression. Otherwise the 39th Congress saw the issues of its day, among which one overshadowed the rest, and trusted to the future to solve future problems. It pointed, I think, in Section 1 of the Fourteenth Amendment to the general manner in which problems similar to those with which it was dealing should in future be solved. This I believe is the most that can be said, and it is supported it seems to me by the authority of this Court which has extended the solution of the Fourteenth Amendment to problems—notably jury service—which were as little in focus in 1866 as segregation, and concerning which an even better case can be made out to show that the 39th Congress affirmatively indicated that they were without the scope of the Amendment it was proposing. I think the legislative history leaves this Court free to remember that it is a *Constitution* it is construing. I think also that a charitable view of the sloppy draftsmen of the Fourteenth Amendment would ascribe to them the knowledge that it was a *Constitution* they were writing.

4. Alexander Bickel—"The Original Understanding and the Segregation Decision" (1955)*

The final expression of Republican misgivings [about the Civil Rights Act of 1866] was the most formidable, and it was decisive. It came from John A. Bingham of Ohio, a Radical, and one of the most influential men in the 39th Congress. Bingham was speaking in support of a motion he had offered to recommit with instructions to strike the sentence at the head of section I which forbade all "discrimination in civil rights or immunities," and to substitute for the penal enforcement provisions of the bill language permitting a civil action by aggrieved parties.* He tried at the start to meet an argument which he knew would be advanced against him, as indeed it was:

> Mr. Speaker . . . I venture to say no candid man, no rightminded man, will deny that by amending as proposed the bill will be less oppressive, and therefore less objectionable. Doubting, as I do, the power of Congress to pass the bill, I urge the instructions with a view to take from the bill what seems to me its oppressive and I might say its unjust provisions.

Bingham then proceeded to examine the civil rights provision which he proposed to delete. "What are civil rights?" he asked. It seemed that,

> the term civil rights includes every right that pertains to the citizen under the Constitution, laws, and Government of this country. . . . [A]re not political rights all embraced in the term "civil rights," and must it not of necessity be so interpreted?

Harvard Law Review, Vol. 69, 1, 1955.
Congressional Globe, 39th Congress, 1st Session (1866), 1266, 1271–72.

.... [T]here is scarcely a State in this Union which does not, by its constitution or by its statute laws, make some discrimination on account of race or color between citizens of the United States in respect of civil rights.

. . . .

By the Constitution of my own State neither the right of the elective franchise nor the franchise of office can be conferred . . . save upon a white citizen of the United States.

Coming to the specific rights enumerated in that part of section I which his motion would have left untouched, Bingham noted that they had been denied by many states, and said: "I should remedy that not by an arbitrary assumption of power, but by amending the Constitution of the United States, expressly prohibiting the States from any such abuse of power in the future." He had made no such statement about civil rights in general. . . .

These are words spoken in debate by a man not normally distinguished for precision of thought and statement. . . . They are important because of Bingham's role in drafting section 1 of the fourteenth amendment and his avoidance in all his drafts of the term "civil rights." [O]ne thing is certain. Unless one concludes that Bingham entertained apprehensions about the breadth of the term "civil rights" and was unwilling at this stage, as a matter of policy, not constitutional law, to extend a federal guaranty covering all that might be included in that term, there is no rational explanation for his motion to strike it. There was no illusion in Bingham's mind of removing a constitutional infirmity in this fashion. He was endeavoring merely to make the bill less "oppressive," less "unjust." Constitutional scruples to the side, he wanted a bill that would at least be satisfactory on policy grounds. That was the object of his attempt to remove the penal provisions. What other object could he have had in mind in trying also to eliminate the comprehensive civil rights guaranty, which in his opinion would force a change in the law of his own state? . . .

SUMMARY AND CONCLUSIONS . . . .

The Civil Rights Bill . . . , as brought from the Senate to the House, split the alliance of various shades of Moderates and Radicals which constituted the Republican majority. . . . [A] substantial number of Republicans were troubled by the issue of constitutionality. . . . Bingham, whose position was in this instance entirely self-consistent, thought the bill incurably unconstitutional, its enforcement provisions monstrous, and the civil rights guaranty of very broad application and unwise. The concession these Republicans wrung from the leadership was the elimination of the civil rights formula and thus the avoidance of possible "latitudinarian" construction. The Moderate position that the bill dealt only with a distinct and limited set of rights was conclusively validated.

Against this backdrop, the Joint Committee on Reconstruction began framing the fourteenth amendment. In drafting section I, it vacillated between the civil rights formula and language proposed by Bingham, finally adopting the latter. Stevens' speech opening debate on the amendment in the House presented section I in terms quite similar to the Moderate position on the Civil Rights Bill, though there was a rather notable absence of the disclaimers of wider coverage which usually accompanied the Moderates' statements of objectives. A few remarks made in the Senate sounded in the same vein. For the rest, however, section I was not really debated. . . . In this atmosphere, section I became the subject of a stock generalization: it was dismissed as embodying and, in one sense for the Republicans, in another for the Democrats and Conservatives, "constitutionalizing" the Civil Rights Act.

The obvious conclusion to which the evidence, thus summarized, easily leads is that section I of the fourteenth amendment, like section I of the Civil Rights Act of 1866, carried out the relatively narrow objectives of the Moderates, and hence, as originally understood, was meant to apply neither to jury service, nor suffrage, nor antimiscegenation statutes, nor segregation. This conclusion is supported by the blunt expression of disappointment to which Thaddeus Stevens gave vent in the House. Nothing in the election campaign of 1866 or in the ratification proceedings negatives it. Section I received in both about the attention it had received in Congress, and in about the same terms. One or two "reconstructed" Southern legislatures took what turned out, of course, to be temporary measures to abolish segregation. There is little if any indication of an impression prevailing elsewhere that the amendment required such action.

If the fourteenth amendment were a statute, a court might very well hold, on the basis of what has been said so far, that it was foreclosed from applying it to segregation in public schools. The evidence of congressional purpose is as clear as such evidence is likely to be, and no language barrier stands in the way of construing the section in conformity with it. But we are dealing with a constitutional amendment, not a statute. The tradition of a broadly worded organic law not frequently or lightly amended was well-established by 1866, and, despite the somewhat revolutionary fervor with which the Radicals were pressing their changes, it cannot be assumed that they or anyone else expected or wished the future role of the Constitution in the scheme of American government to differ from the past. Should not the search for congressional purpose, therefore, properly be twofold? One inquiry should be directed at the congressional understanding of the immediate effect of the enactment on conditions then present. Another should aim to discover what if any thought was given to the long-range effect, under future circumstances, of provisions necessarily intended for permanence.

That the Court saw the need for two such inquiries with respect to the original understanding on segregation is clearly indicated by the questions it propounded at the 1952 Term. The Court asked first whether Congress and the state legislatures contemplated that the fourteenth amendment would abolish segregation in public schools. It next asked whether, assuming that the immediate abolition of segregation was not contemplated, the framers nevertheless understood that Congress acting under section 5, or the Court in the exercise of the judicial function would, in light of future conditions, have power to abolish segregation.

With this double aspect of the inquiry in mind, certain other features of the legislative history—not inconsistent with the conclusion earlier stated, but complementary to it—became significant. Thus, section I of the fourteenth amendment, on its face, deals not only with racial discrimination, but also with discrimination whether or not based on color. This cannot have been accidental, since the alternative considered by the Joint Committee, the civil rights formula, did apply only to racial discrimination. Everyone's immediate preoccupation in the 39th Congress—insofar as it did not go to partisan questions— was, of course, with hardships being visited on the colored race. Yet the fact that the proposed constitutional amendment was couched in more general terms could not have escaped those who voted for it. And this feature of it could not have been deemed to be included in the standard identification of section I with the Civil Rights Act. Again, . . . in reporting out the abortive Bingham amendment, the Joint Committee elected to submit an equal protection clause limited to the rights of life, liberty, and property, supplemented by a necessary and proper clause. Now the choice was in favor of a due process clause limited the way the equal protection clause had been in the earlier draft, but of an equal protection clause not so limited: equal protection "of the laws." . . . One would have to assume a lack of familiarity with the English language to conclude that a . . . differ- ence between the Bingham amendment and the new proposal was not . . . perceived, namely, the difference between equal protection in the rights of life, liberty, and property, a phrase which so aptly evoked the evils uppermost in men's minds at the time, and equal protection of the laws, a clause which is plainly capable of being applied to all subjects of state legislation. Could the comparison have failed to leave the implication that the new phrase, while it did not necessarily, and certainly not expressly, carry greater coverage than the old, was nevertheless roomier, more receptive to "latitudinarian" construction? No one made the point with regard to this particular clause. But in opening debate in the Senate, Jacob Howard was frank to say that only the future could tell just what application the privileges and immunities provision might have. And before the vote in the Senate, Reverdy Johnson, a Democrat, to be sure, but a respected constitu- tional lawyer and no rabid partisan, confessed his puzzlement about the same clause. Finally, it is noteworthy that the shorthand argument characterizing the fourteenth amendment as the constitutional em- bodiment of the Civil Rights Act was often accompanied on the Re- publican side by generalities about the self-evident demands of justice and the natural rights of man. This was true both in Congress and in the course of the election which followed. To all this should be added the fact that while the Joint Committee's rejection of the civil rights formula is quite manifest, there is implicit also in its choice of lan- guage a rejection—presumably as inappropriate in a consitutional pro- vision—of such a specific and exclusive enumeration of rights as appeared in section I of the Civil Rights Act.

These bits and pieces of additional evidence do not contradict and could not in any event override the direct proof showing the specific evils at which the great body of congressional opinion thought it was striking. But perhaps they provide sufficient basis for the formulation of an additional hypothesis. It remains true that an explicit provision going further than the Civil Rights Act could not have been carried in the 39th Congress. . . . But may it not be that the Moderates and the Radicals reached a compromise permitting them to go to the country with language which they could, where necessary, defend against damaging alarms raised by the opposition, but which at the same time was sufficiently elastic to permit reasonable future advances? This is thoroughly consistent with rejection of the civil rights formula and its implications. That formula could not serve the purpose of such a compromise. It had been under heavy attack at this session, and among those who had expressed fears concerning its reach were Republicans who would have to go forth and stand on the platform of the fourteenth amendment. Bingham, of course, was one of these men, and he could not be required to go on the hustings and risk being made to eat his own words. If the party was to unite behind a compromise which consisted neither of an exclusive listing of a limited series of rights, nor of a formulation dangerously vulnerable to attacks pandering to the prejudices of the people, new language had to be found. Bingham himself supplied it. It had both sweep and the appearance of a careful enumeration of rights, and it had a ring to echo in the national memory of libertarian beginnings. . . .

It is, of course, giving the men of the 39th Congress much more than their due to ennoble them by a comparison of their proceedings with the deliberations of the Philadelphia Convention. Yet if this was the compromise that was struck, then these men emulated the technique of the original framers, who were also responsible to an electorate only partly receptive to the fullness of their principles, and who similarly avoided the explicit grant of some powers without foreclosing their future assumption. Whatever other support this hypothesis may have, it has behind it the very authoritative voice of Thaddeus Stevens, who held it, and twice gave notice of it in speaking on the fourteenth amendment. It was Stevens who dutifully defined section I more or less in the narrow terms a Trumbull or a Fessenden would have used; it fell short of his wishes. And it was Stevens, his hopes fulfilled, who powerfully and candidly emphasized the political opportunities which the amendment gained for the Radicals, and who looked to the future for better things "in further legislation, in enabling acts or other provisions." Similarly, when it at last emerged, though too late to influence debate, the report of the Joint Committee submitted the amendment "in the hope that its imperfections may be cured and its deficiencies supplied, by legislative wisdom. . . ."* It need hardly be added that in view of Stevens' remarks, and in view also of the nature of the other evidence which supports it, this hypothesis cannot be disparaged as putting forth an undisclosed, conspiratorial purpose such as has been imputed to Bingham and others with regard to protection of

---

*Globe, 3038, 3051.

corporations. Indeed, no specific purpose going beyond the coverage
of the Civil Rights Act is suggested; rather an awareness on the part
of these framers that it was *a constitution* they were writing, which
led to a choice of language capable of growth.

5. Endnote: Kelly's Rebuttal to Bickel (1956)

The precise character of Bingham's argument [on the Civil Rights
Act] has become a matter of some controversy. [Alexander] Bickel . . .
argues that Bingham objected to the "no discrimination" clause as a
matter of policy as well as a matter of constitutional law and that he
was "endeavoring merely to make the bill 'less offensive, less unjust.'"
He does not think that Bingham implied that he would approve the
"no discrimination" clause were the constitutional difficulty removed. . . . [H]e concludes that Bingham did not mean to lend any
support in policy, even by constitutional amendment, for the "no
discrimination" clause.

To the present writer this seems a very doubtful reading of Bingham's position. It ignores his extensive extremist antislavery background as well as his position in Congress as one of the strong Radical
Republicans; it ignores, also, the latitudinarian defense of the force
and scope of his own constitutional amendment with respect to civil
rights which Bingham had presented to the House a few days earlier.
It ignores also the following words of Bingham [in his very speech on
the Civil Rights Bill]: "Now what does this bill propose? To reform
the whole civil and criminal code of every State government by declaring that there shall be no discrimination between citizens on account
of race or color in civil rights or in the penalties prescribed by their
laws. I humbly bow before the majesty of justice, as I bow before the
majesty of that God whose attribute it is, and therefore declare there
should be no such inequality or discrimination . . . ; but what power
have you to correct it? That is the question . . . whence do you derive
power to cure it by congressional enactment?"* It appears probable
that while Bingham entertained grave doubts as to the bill's constitutionality, he had no objection to the discrimination clause as a matter
of policy, and on the contrary he looked forward to curing the constitutional difficulty by amendment. . . . The vital objection to Bickel's

---

Globe, 1293.

interpretation, which, if valid, destroys the argument that Bingham ever sought anything more than a restricted scope of civil rights for the Negro, is that it is contradicted by Bingham's entire career and by his latitudinarian position during the debates on the Fourteenth Amendment.

IV.
Reargument: The Central Conflict

THE MOST EXTENSIVE briefs for the appellees on reargument came from South Carolina and Virginia. The research burden was divided between John W. Davis and his colleagues, who concentrated on the congressional debates, and Justin Moore's firm, which focused on the ratification process. Both briefs, however, offered a comprehensive look at the historical material.

Davis remained confident. He felt, said one of his associates, that "unless the Court was going to disregard all that history and all the judicial precedent, he had the case won." (Kluger, *Simple Justice*, p. 647.)

If the South Carolina brief reflected Davis' precision of thought and language, the Virginia brief flashed some of Justin Moore's combativeness, as it indignantly responded to suggestions by the appellants of a southern conspiracy on ratification of the fourteenth amendment and the subsequent institution of segregated schools.

The NAACP brief made its own incisive, though occasionally ragged historical argument. Yet its most powerful feature was the shift in constitutional emphasis from the previous year, prompted in part to be sure by the immersion in Reconstruction history. The central issue in *Brown* was no longer asserted to be the inapplicability of *Plessy* v. *Ferguson* to public education, but the corrupt nature of the entire separate but equal doctrine. Robert Carter's oral presentation in 1952, leading off the NAACP case, had sought to finesse the matter of *Plessy's* constitutional relevance. Now in 1953, Thurgood Marshall was anxious to attack *Plessy* head-on, unmistakably giving that attack his greatest emphasis.

244

The oral argument in *Briggs* v. *Elliott* marked the last of John W. Davis' 140 appearances before the Supreme Court.

1. *Briggs* v. *Elliott*—Appellees' Brief on Reargument*

II

Second Question

If neither the Congress in submitting nor the States in ratifying the Fourteenth Amendment understood that compliance with it would require the immediate abolition of segregation in public schools, was it nevertheless the understanding of the framers of the Amendment

(A) that future Congresses might, in the exercise of their power under Section 5 of the Amendment, abolish segregation, or

(B) that it would be within the judicial power, in light of future conditions, to construe the Amendment as abolishing such segregation of its own force?

Answer

(A) It was not the understanding of the framers of the Amendment that future Congresses might, in the exercise of their power under Section 5 of the Amendment, abolish segregation in public schools.

(B) It was not the understanding of the framers of the Amendment that it would be within the judicial power, in light of future conditions, to construe the Amendment as abolishing segregation in public schools of its own force. . . .

Again, it will be remembered, throughout the debates upon Section 1 of the proposed Amendment as thus recast, assurances were given by its proponents (1) that it was intended only to protect those civil rights which were dealt with in the Civil Rights Act of 1866; (2) that it was intended to remove any existing doubt regarding the constitutionality of the Civil Rights Act of 1866; and (3) that it was also intended to place repeal of the Civil Rights Act of 1866 beyond the power of future Congresses.

The Civil Rights Act of 1866 was enacted, as we have noted, only after the majority in Congress were satisfied that it would not affect

---

*p. 49 ff. *Records and Briefs*, Part 2.

such matters as the separate school systems of the several States but was limited to the civil rights specifically enumerated in the Bill.

We believe it correct to say, therefore, that the resolution whereby the Fourteenth Amendment was submitted to the States for ratification would never have been adopted by Congress in the absence of these assurances or in the presence of an understanding that, after ratification of the Amendment, future Congresses might enact legislation abolishing or prohibiting segregated public school systems within the States. . . .

Nor was it the understanding of the framers of the amendment that it would be within the judicial power, in light of future conditions, to construe the Amendment as abolishing segregation in public schools of its own force. The members of that Congress did not believe that the proposed Amendment touched the subject of separate schools at all.

While the framers of the Amendment certainly knew that the courts had judicial power to construe the Constitution of the United States, we feel safe in stating that it would have been inconceivable to them that the courts in years to come would give to the Amendment a construction directly opposed to the intention of the framers so clearly and permanently recorded in the Amendment's legislative history. . . .

III

Third Question

On the assumption that the answers to Questions 2(A) and (B) do not dispose of the issue, is it within the judicial power, in construing the Amendment, to abolish segregation in the public schools?

Answer

It is not within the judicial power to construe the Fourteenth Amendment adversely to the understanding of its framers, as abolishing segregation in the public schools. Moreover, if, in construing the Amendment, the principle of stare decisis is applied, controlling precedents preclude a construction which would abolish segregation in the public schools. Even if the principle of stare decisis and the controlling precedents be abandoned, and the effect of the Amendment upon public school segregation be examined *de novo,* under established standards of equal protection the Amendment may not be construed to abolish or forbid segregation as a matter of law and *a priori* in all cases. Rather, each case of such segregation must be decided upon the facts presented in the record of that case; and unless the record establishes by clear and convincing evidence that school segregation could not conceivably be warranted by local conditions in the particular case, the Fourteenth Amendment may not be construed to abolish segregation in that case.

May we note at the outset our difficulty in making the basic assumption on which this third question is founded. For we are convinced that the answers to questions 2(A) and (B) do in fact dispose of the issue by demonstrating beyond peradventure that the framers of the Amendment did not understand that future Congresses or courts might abolish segregation in schools. To hold otherwise would be nothing less than an expansion of the Amendment to embrace a matter which the framers clearly intended to be beyond its reach—whether then or in the future.

A. It is not within the judicial power to construe the Fourteenth Amendment adversely to the understanding of its framers, as abolishing public school segregation.

It is, of course, within the judicial power of this Court to construe the Constitution—indeed that is its first and highest function. *Marbury v. Madison,* 1 Cranch 137 (1803). But in construing—by the very meaning of the term—the function of the Court is to interpret the language under scrutiny in accordance with the understanding of the framers. That is fundamental:

> "It is never to be forgotten that, in the construction of the language of the Constitution here relied on, as indeed in all other instances where construction becomes necessary, we are to place ourselves as nearly as possible in the condition of the men who framed that instrument." *Ex parte Bain,* 121 U.S. 1, 12 (1887). . . .

The equal protection clause of the Fourteenth Amendment should be interpreted so as not to include those subjects, and specifically the issue of segregation in public schools, which the framers clearly did not intend the language of the Amendment to embrace. If segregation is to be eliminated, this must be accomplished through legislative action by the States or by constitutional amendment. The Court will give the language of the Fourteenth Amendment only as broad a meaning as its framers meant it to have—especially where, as here, the subject is one specifically considered by the framers. This is no more than a recognition that the concern of the Court is with what "the framers sought to achieve." *Shelley* v. *Kraemer*, 334 U.S. 1, 23 (1948).

Here the purpose of the framers is clear, as we have shown. There is therefore no room for appellants to invoke the principle that the Constitution is often construed as applying to new matters wholly unknown or not familiar to the framers. . . . Cases in that category are examples of interpretation of the words of the Constitution to further the presumed intent of the framers that broad provisions should be adapted to new subject matters. In contrast, to interpret the Fourteenth Amendment as abolishing segregation in public schools would frustrate the expressed intent of the framers. Segregation in schools takes essentially the same form today that it has throughout our history. It was a condition well known to those who framed the Fourteenth Amendment and one that they had no intention of abolishing through the adoption of the Amendment.

Finally, there is no escape from the fact that essentially appellants claim for the Court a power which we believe it will be quick to disavow—a supranatural gift of omniscience enabling it to know, better than those who adopted the Amendment and construed it before the ink from its framers' pen was dry, the purposes of the Amendment and its effect, if any, upon racial segregation in the public schools.

2. Reargument Brief—*Davis* v. *County School Board**

[A]ppellants have . . . charge[d] that, in effect, many of the seceding States perpetrated a gigantic fraud on the United States. They adopted constitutions, it is said, designed to establish general school systems which stated nothing about segregation. By doing this, it is alleged, they recognized that the Fourteenth Amendment was designed to outlaw school segregation. Their purpose was to secure readmission of their representatives in Congress. Then, the representatives having been so readmitted and the States having escaped Congressional control, their legislatures, despite their knowledge that school segregation was unconstitutional, immediately established segregated schools.

This assertion is without support in fact. It is based on the assump-

---

*pp. 154–55. *Records and Briefs*, Part 3.

tion that the legislators of many States, all sworn to uphold the Constitution of the United States, willingly and knowingly violated their oaths at once and enacted legislation in bad faith which they knew to be unconstitutional. A mere statement of such a theory is enough to show how far from the truth it must be.

Even more, the assumption has no force in logic. The legislatures that ratified the Amendment in the southern States were not composed of die-hard Confederates still devoted to rebellious causes; in almost every case, they were made up of a majority of loyalists, northern adventurers and Negroes. The governors who recommended school segregation came from as far away as Maine. Legislatures so composed would have no reason to engage in the chicanery which Appellants assume.

One further fact is important. In certain instances, these legislatures were permitted to ratify the Amendment and then to take no further action until Congress had acted to readmit their representatives. Thus in Florida, the legislature followed the advice of the governor and, after ratifying the Amendment (and the Thirteenth Amendment) and electing senators, adjourned until readmission had received Congressional approval. That was because, until Congress had acted, the action of the legislature, under the Reconstruction Act, could be only provisional. So the legislature that ratified the Amendment could not in this instance have acted in regard to schools before readmission.

Finally, what Congress had done was not kept from the States, south or north. Congress had fostered school segregation in the District of Columbia. Congressional leaders had made it clear that the Amendment was not designed to abolish school segregation. Southern leaders knew these facts: they relied on them in good faith as they were entitled to do.

We reject the obnoxious proposition advanced by Appellants and are confident that the Court will reject it. Where a legislature ratified the Amendment and thereafter established segregated schools, either on a mandatory or a permissive basis, we conclude that, without regard to intervening readmission of representatives to Congress, the legislature did not consider that the Amendment abolished school segregation.

3. Appellants' Brief on Reargument: The Constitutional Issue*

II

The statutory and constitutional provisions involved in these cases cannot be validated under any separate but equal concept. . . .

C. **The Separate but Equal Doctrine Marked an Unwarranted Departure from the Main Stream of Constitutional Development and Permits the Frustration of the Very Purposes of the Fourteenth Amendment as Defined by This Court.**

In *Plessy* v. *Ferguson*, this Court for the first time gave approval to state imposed racial distinctions as consistent with the purposes and meaning of the Fourteenth Amendment. . . .

Race for the first time since the adoption of the Fourteenth Amendment was sanctioned as a constitutionally valid basis for state action, and reasonableness for the racial distinctions approved was found in the social customs, usages and traditions of a people only thirty-one years removed from a slave society. . . .

D. **The Separate but Equal Doctrine Was Conceived in Error.**

The separate but equal doctrine of *Plessy* v. *Ferguson*, we submit, has aided and supported efforts to nullify the Fourteenth Amendment's undoubted purpose—equal status for Negroes—as defined again and again by this Court. The fallacious and pernicious implications of the doctrine were evident to Justice Harlan and are set out in his dissenting opinion. It is clear today that the fact that racial segregation accords with custom and usage or is considered needful for the preservation of public peace and good order does not suffice to give constitutional validity to the state's action. What the doctrine has in fact accomplished is to deprive Negroes of the protection of the approved test of reasonable classifications which is available to everyone else who challenges legislative categories or distinctions of whatever kind.

---

*Reprinted in Kurland and Casper, Vol. 49, pp. 481–711.

1. The Dissenting Opinion of Justice Harlan in *Plessy v. Ferguson.*

Justice Harlan recognized and set down for history the purpose of segregation and the implications of the separate but equal doctrine and evidenced prophetic insight concerning the inevitable consequences of the Court's approval of racial segregation. . . .

2. Custom, Usage and Tradition Rooted in the Slave Tradition Cannot Be the Constitutional Yardstick for Measuring State Action Under the Fourteenth Amendment. . . .

[T]he very purpose of the Thirteenth, Fourteenth and Fifteenth Amendments was to effectuate a complete break with governmental action based on the established usages, customs and traditions of the slave era, to revolutionize the legal relationship between Negroes and whites, to destroy the inferior status of the Negro and to place him upon a plane of complete equality with the white man. [P]ost Civil War reestablishment of ante-bellum custom and usage, climaxed by the decision in *Plessy v. Ferguson*, reflected a constant effort to return the Negro to his pre-Thirteenth, Fourteenth Amendment inferior status. When the Court employed the old usages, customs and traditions as the basis for determining the reasonableness of segregation statutes designed to resubjugate the Negro to an inferior status, it nullified the acknowledged intention of the framers of the Amendment, and made a travesty of the equal protection clause of the Fourteenth Amendment.

[T]he *Plessy v. Ferguson* decision is out of line with the modern holdings of this Court, for in a variety of cases involving the rights of Negroes it has constantly refused to regard custom and usage, however widespread, as determinative of reasonableness. This was true in *Smith* v. *Allwright*, of a deeply entrenched custom and usage of excluding Negroes from voting in the primaries. It was true in *Shelley* v. *Kraemer*, of a long standing custom excluding Negroes from the use and ownership of real property on the basis of race. In *Henderson* v. *United States*, a discriminatory practice of many years was held to violate the Interstate Commerce Act. In the *Sweatt* and *McLaurin* decisions, the Court broke a southern tradition of state-enforced racial distinctions in graduate and professional education—a custom almost as old as graduate and professional education itself.

In each instance the custom and usage had persisted for generations and its durability was cited as grounds for its validity. If this were the only test, ours indeed would become a stagnant society. Even if there be some situations in which custom, usage and tradition may be considered in testing the reasonableness of government action, customs, traditions and usages rooted in slavery cannot be worthy of the constitutional sanction of this Court.

3. Preservation of Public Peace Cannot Justify Deprivation of Constitutional Rights.

The fallacy underlying *Plessy* v. *Ferguson* of justifying racially-discriminatory statutes as essential to the public peace and good order has been completely exposed by Frederick W. Lehmann, a former Solicitor General of the United States, and Wells H. Blodgett in their Brief as *amici curiae* in *Buchanan* v. *Warley*, 245 U.S. 60. Their statements warrant repetition here:

> "The implication . . . of the ordinance is that unless the white and colored people live in separate blocks, ill feeling will be engendered between them and conflicts will result and so it is assumed that a segregation of the races is necessary for the preservation of the public peace and the promotion of the general welfare. . . .
>
> The ordinance, almost upon its face, . . . is a discriminating enactment by the dominant majority against a minority who are held to be an inferior people. . . . Many things may rouse a man's prejudice or stir him to anger, but he is not always to be humored in his wrath. The question may arise, 'Dost thou well to be angry?'"

Accepting this view, the Court in *Buchanan* v. *Warley* rejected the argument that a state could deny constitutional rights with impunity in its efforts to maintain the public peace:

> "It is urged that this proposed segregation will promote the public peace by preventing race conflicts. Desirable as this is, and important as is the preservation of the public peace, this aim cannot be accomplished by laws or ordinances which deny rights created or protected by the Federal Constitution" (245 U.S. 60, 81). . . .

Thus, the bases upon which the separate but equal doctrine was approved in the *Plessy* v. *Ferguson* case have all been uprooted by subsequent decisions of this Court. All that remains is the naked doctrine itself, unsupported by reason, contrary to the intent of the framers, and out of tune with present notions of constitutional rights. Repudiation of the doctrine itself, we submit, is long overdue.

4. The Separate but Equal Doctrine Deprives Negroes of That Protection Which the Fourteenth Amendment Accords Under the General Classification Test.

One of the ironies of the separate but equal doctrine of *Plessy* v. *Ferguson* is that under it, the Fourteenth Amendment, the primary purpose of which was the protection of Negroes, is construed as encompassing a narrower area of protection for Negroes than for other persons under the general classification test.

Early in its history, the Fourteenth Amendment was construed as reaching not only state action based upon race and color, but also as prohibiting all unreasonable classifications and distinctions even though not racial in character. . . .

In effectuating the protection afforded by this secondary purpose, the Court has required the classification or distinction used be based upon some real or substantial difference pertinent to a valid legislative objective. . . .

But the separate but equal doctrine substitutes race for reasonableness as the constitutional test of classification. We submit, it would be a distortion of the purposes and intendment of the Fourteenth Amendment to deny to those persons for whose benefit that provision was primarily intended the same measure of protection afforded by a rule of construction evolved to reach the Amendment's subsidiary and secondary objectives. We urge this Court to examine the segregation statutes in these cases to determine whether the statutes seek to serve a permissible legislative objective; and, if any permissible objective is found, whether color differentiation has pertinence to it. So examined, the constitutional provisions and statutes involved here disclose unmistakably their constitutional infirmity. . . .

F. The Necessary Consequence of the Sweatt and McLaurin Decisions Is Repudiation of the Separate but Equal Doctrine.

While *Sweatt* v. *Painter* and *McLaurin* v. *Oklahoma State Regents* were not in terms rejections of the separate but equal doctrine, their application in effect destroyed the practice of segregation with respect to state graduate and professional schools. . . .

In the *Sweatt* case, the Court stated that, with members of the state's dominant racial group excluded from the segregated law school which the state sought to require Sweatt to attend, "we cannot conclude that the education offered petitioner is substantially equal to that he would receive if admitted to the University of Texas." If this consideration is one of the controlling factors in determining substantial equality at the law school level, it is impossible for any segregated law school to be an equal law school. . . .

In the *McLaurin* case, the racial distinctions imposed in an effort to comply with the state's segregation laws were held to impair and inhibit ability to study, to exchange views with other students and, in general, to learn one's profession. The state, therefore, was required to remove all restrictions and to treat McLaurin the same way as other students are treated. Consequently these decisions are a repudiation of the separate but equal doctrine.

III
Viewed in the light of history the separate but equal doctrine has been an instrumentality of defiant nullification of the Fourteenth Amendment.

The history of segregation laws reveals that their main purpose was to organize the community upon the basis of a superior white and an inferior Negro caste. These laws were conceived in a belief in the inherent inferiority of Negroes, a concept taken from slavery. Inevitably, segregation in its operation and effect has meant inequality consistent only with the belief that the people segregated are inferior and not worthy, or capable, of enjoying the facilities set apart for the dominant group.

Segregation originated as a part of an effort to build a social order in which the Negro would be placed in a status as close as possible to that he had held before the Civil War. The separate but equal doctrine furnished a base from which those who sought to nullify the Thirteenth, Fourteenth and Fifteenth Amendments were permitted to operate in relative security. . . .

This is the historic background against which the validity of the separate but equal doctrine must be tested. History reveals it as a part of an overriding purpose to defeat the aims of the Thirteenth, Fourteenth and Fifteenth Amendments. Segregation was designed to insure inequality—to discriminate on account of race and color—and the separate but equal doctrine accommodated the Constitution to that purpose. Separate but equal is a legal fiction. There never was and never will be any separate equality. Our Constitution cannot be used to sustain ideologies and practices which we as a people abhor.

That the Constitution is color blind is our dedicated belief. We submit that this Court cannot sustain these school segregation laws under any separate but equal concept unless it is willing to accept as truths the racist notions of the perpetuators of segregation and to repeat the tragic error of the Plessy court supporting those who would nullify the Fourteenth Amendment and the basic tenet of our way of life which it incorporates. We respectfully suggest that it is the obligation of this Court to correct that error by holding that these laws and constitutional provisions which seek to condition educational opportunities on the basis of race and color are historic aberrations and are inconsistent with the federal Constitution and cannot stand. The separate but equal doctrine of *Plessy* v. *Ferguson* should now be overruled.

4. The Oral Argument*

ARGUMENT ON BEHALF OF APPELLANTS HARRY BRIGGS, ET AL.

By Mr. Marshall. . . .

MR. MARSHALL: . . . . [Y]ou cannot escape this point: that the [Fourteenth] Amendment was adopted for the express purpose of depriving the states of authority to exercise and enforce the existing Black Codes; that by putting it in the Constitution it was obviously intended that the states would not have power in the future to set up additional Black Codes; . . . whether it is sophisticated or simple-minded; and the part that is to my mind crucial in this case, is that until this time the appellees have shown nothing that can in any form or fashion say that the statutes involved in these cases are not the same type of statutes discussed in the debates . . . , namely, the Black Codes, and I do not see how the inevitable result can be challenged, because they are of the exact same cloth. . . .

JUSTICE FRANKFURTER: Am I wrong in thinking that you must reject the basis of the decision in McLaurin for purposes of this case?

MR. MARSHALL: You mean reject the basis of the fact that they were not allowed to associate?

JUSTICE FRANKFURTER: No. The basis was the criterion of

---

*Reprinted in Friedman, *Argument*, p. 198 ff.

those cases was whether each got the same thing. Your position in these cases is that that is not arguable, that you cannot differentiate, you cannot enter the domain of whether a black child or a white child gets the same educational advantages or facilities or opportunity. You must reject that, do you not? . . .

MR. MARSHALL: I think so far as our argument on the constitutional debates is concerned, . . . the state is deprived of any power to make any racial classification in any governmental field.

JUSTICE FRANKFURTER: So I understand.

MR. MARSHALL: But I do have to qualify it to this extent: I can conceive of some governmental action—to be perfectly frank, sir, we have discussed the point of census-taking—so they could take the census . . . so long as it affects not either group—but in any area where it touches the individuals concerned in any form or fashion, it is clear to me, to my mind, under the Fourteenth Amendment that you cannot separate people or denote that one shall go here and one shall go there if the facilities are absolutely equal; that is the issue in this case, because in the South Carolina case especially it is admitted on record that every other thing about the schools is equal, schools, curricula, everything else. It is only the question as to the power of the state. . . .

JUSTICE FRANKFURTER: [T]he point of my question is that I think we are dealing with two different legal propositions; *McLaurin* is one and what you are tendering to the Court is another.

MR. MARSHALL: The questions raised by this Court in June, as we understand it, requested us to find out as to whether or not class legislation and, specifically segregation, whether or not it, in and of itself, with nothing else, violated the Fourteenth Amendment.

We have addressed ourselves to that in this brief, and we are convinced that the answer is that any segregation, which is for the purpose of setting up either class or caste legislation, is in and of itself a violation of the Fourteenth Amendment, with the only proviso that normally, in normal judicial proceedings, there must be a showing of injury or what have you. That is our position. . . .

JUSTICE FRANKFURTER: Your argument comes down to this: If in one of the states in which there is a large percentage of Negro voters, a preponderance, where we get a situation where X state has a preponderance of Negro voters who are actually going to the polls, and actually assert their preponderance and install a Negro governor to the extent that more money is spent for Negro education, better housing, better schools, more highly paid teachers, where teachers are more attracted, better maps, better schoolbooks, better everything than the white children enjoy—and I know I am making a fantastic, if you will, assumption—

MR. MARSHALL: Yes.

JUSTICE FRANKFURTER: (continuing)—and yet there is segregation, you would come here and say that they cannot do that?

MR. MARSHALL: If it is done by the state, the state has been deprived of—

JUSTICE FRANKFURTER: That is your position; that is the legal—

MR. MARSHALL: I think, sir, that is our flat legal position, that if it involves class or caste legislation—

JUSTICE FRANKFURTER: That is the antitheses of the McLaurin . . . doctrine.

ARGUMENT ON BEHALF OF APPELLEES R. W. ELLIOTT, ET AL.

By Mr. Davis

MR. DAVIS: May it please the Court, I suppose that there are few invitations less welcome in an advocate's life than to be asked to reargue a case on which he has once spent himself, and that is particularly unwelcome when the order for reargument gives him no indication whatever of the subjects in which the Court may be interested, and, therefore, I want to at the outset tender the Court my thanks and, I think, the thanks of my colleagues on both sides of the desk for the guidance they have given us by the series of questions which they asked us to devote our attention to, and in what I shall have to say, I hope to indicate the answers which, for our part, we give to each one of them.

At the previous hearing of this case I think all counsel on both sides of the controversy, and in every case, realizing that it was an act of mercy and, perhaps, even of piety, not to increase the reading matter that comes to this Court, briefed the case in rather concise fashion. An effort was apparent, and I am sure I shared it, to condense the controversy to the smallest compass it would bear.

Now, for a rough guess I should think the motion for reargument has contributed somewhere between 1500 and 2000 pages to the possible entertainment, if not the illumination, of the Court. But I trust the Court will not hold counsel responsible for that proliferation. . . .

In Clarendon School District No. 1 in South Carolina, in which this case alone is concerned, there were in the last report that got into this record something over a year or year and a half ago, 2,799 Negroes, registered Negro children of school age. There were 295 whites, and the state has now provided those 2,800 Negro children with schools as good in every particular.

In fact, because of their being newer, they may even be better. There are good teachers, the same curriculum as in the schools for the 295 whites.

Who is going to disturb that situation? If they were to be reassorted or comingled, who knows how that could best be done?

If it is done on the mathematical basis, with 30 children as a maximum, which I believe is the accepted standard in pedagogy, you would have 27 Negro children and 3 whites in one school room. Would that make the children any happier? Would they learn any more quickly? Would their lives be more serene?

Children of that age are not the most considerate animals in the world, as we all know. Would the terrible psychological disaster being wrought, according to some of these witnesses, to the colored child be removed if he had three white children sitting somewhere in the same school room?

Would white children be prevented from getting a distorted idea of racial relations if they sat with 27 Negro children? I have posed that question because it is the very one that cannot be denied.

You say that is racism. Well, it is not racism. Recognize that for sixty centuries and more humanity has been discussing questions of race and race tension, not racism.

Say that we make special provisions for the aboriginal Indian population of this country, it is not racism.

Say that the twenty-nine states have miscegenation statutes now in force which they believe are of beneficial protection to both races. Disraeli said, "No man," said he, "will treat with indifference the principle of race. It is the key to history."

And it is not necessary to enter into any comparison of faculties or possibilities. You recognize differences which racism plants in the human animal. . . .

Let me say this for the State of South Carolina. It does not come here as Thad Stevens would have wished in sack cloth and ashes. It believes that its legislation is not offensive to the Constitution of the United States.

It is confident of its good faith and intention to produce equality for all of its children of whatever race or color. It is convinced that the happiness, the progress and the welfare of these children is best promoted in segregated schools, and it thinks it a thousand pities that by this controversy there should be urged the return to an experiment which gives no more promise of success today than when it was written into their Constitution during what I call the tragic era.

I am reminded—and I hope it won't be treated as a reflection on anybody—of Aesop's fable of the dog and the meat: The dog, with a fine piece of meat in his mouth, crossed a bridge and saw the shadow in the stream and plunged for it and lost both substance and shadow.

Here is equal education, not promised, not prophesied, but present. Shall it be thrown away on some fancied question of racial prestige?

It is not my part to offer advice to the appellants and their supporters or sympathisers, and certainly not to the learned counsel. No doubt they think what they propose is best, and I do not challenge their sincerity in any particular period but I entreat them to remember the age-old motto that the best is often the enemy of the good.

V.
Reargument: The Remedy

SEEN IN PERSPECTIVE, the consideration of remedy in the *Brown* re-argument resolved itself down to a debate between the appellants and one of the *amici curiae*, the United States government.

The southern briefs seemed unwilling to contemplate an unfavorable decision on the merits in *Brown*; and while favoring a remand to the lower federal courts in the event of such a dire eventuality, they were either uncommunicative or defiant about the path which those courts should follow. John W. Davis' brief flatly denied that either the Supreme Court or the district courts had the "judicial power to do more than to forbid compulsory or permissive segregation by State constitution or statute in the context of the particular case under review. . . . It will then be solely for the school authorities of the particular State or school district . . . to determine how they shall remold its school system upon a non-segregated basis." (p. 84 of brief.)

The Virginia brief appeared to concede greater discretion to the district courts, but its entire discussion of remedy was admitted to be fragmentary, for such discussion "assume[s] that the critical issue has been decided in a fashion contrary to the position that we urge." (p. 77 of brief.)

The brief of the United States government elaborated the gradualist approach to desegregation first adumbrated in 1952, the approach which had apparently caught the attention of several Justices from the outset. Indeed Acting Solicitor General J. Lee Rankin, representing the United States at oral argument, was the first participant in *Brown* to use the phrase which became shorthand for the path the Court eventually took: dismantling of dual school systems might permissibly be accomplished with "deliberate speed." Rankin was sharply questioned by Justice Jackson, who thought the government should articulate more precise standards to guide possible desegregation. But in a

deeper sense, Jackson remained skeptical that the entire judicial process was suited to managing the social upheaval which desegregation
would bring. Justice Frankfurter seemed more optimistic about the
prospects held out by the government position.

The NAACP was not pleased, however, by any suggestion of melio-
rism. The final pages of its brief on reargument pleaded for the invio-
late nature of "personal and present" constitutional rights.

This section concludes with some fascinating recollections of the
man whose strategy helped lead to the postponement of those rights,
yet may also have been responsible for the fact that the NAACP
ultimately triumphed in *Brown*.

1. Supplemental Brief for the United States on Reargument*

IV

**If the court holds that racial segregation in public schools is uncon-
stitutional, it has power to direct such relief as in its judgment will
best serve the interests of justice in the circumstances. . . .**

It may be contended . . . that the powers of a court of equity are
not so comprehensive where vindication of the constitutional right to
equal protection of the laws is involved. Such right, the Court has
pointedly observed, is "personal and present." *Sweatt v. Painter*, 339
U.S. 629, 635; *McLaurin v. Oklahoma State Regents*, 339 U.S. 637,
642. . . . [Thus] it is no answer to a particular plaintiff's claim to say
that at some time in the future he will receive the equality of treatment
which is his constitutional right. So . . . in the present cases, the
plaintiffs could well say that, as individuals whose constitutional rights
have been and are continuing to be violated, it affords them inadequate redress to enter decrees providing only that at some time in the
future (perhaps after they are too old themselves to enjoy the benefits
of the Court's decision) colored children as a group must be given
public education on a non-segregated basis. For these plaintiffs the
remedy of immediate admission to non-segregated schools is an indispensable corollary of the constitutional right, for to recognize a liti-

---

*Reprinted in Kurland and Casper, Vol. 49, pp. 853–1054.

gant's right without affording him an adequate remedy for its violation
is to nullify the value of the right.

On the other hand, it is also true that the constitutional issues
presented to the Court transcend the particular cases and complainants at bar, and in shaping its decrees the Court may take into account
such public considerations as the administrative obstacles involved
in making a general transition throughout the country from existing
segregated school systems to ones not based on color distinctions. If
the Court should hold in these cases that racial segregation *per se*
violates the Constitution, the immediate consequence would be to
invalidate the laws of many states which have been based on the
contrary assumption. Racial segregation in public schools is not an
isolated phenomenon limited to the areas involved in the cases at bar,
and it would be reasonable and in accord with its historic practices
for the Court in fashioning the relief in these cases to consider the
broad implications and consequences of its ruling.

The "personal and present" language appears in cases involving
education on the professional and graduate levels. Each case involved
a single plaintiff. It is one thing to direct immediate relief where a
single individual seeks vindication of his constitutional rights in the
relatively narrow area of professional and graduate school education,
and an entirely different matter to follow the same course in the
broad area of public school education affecting thousands of children,
teachers, and schools. We do not think that when the Court in those
cases characterized the right to equal protection of the laws as "personal and present," it was thereby rejecting the applicability, to cases
involving the right, of settled principles governing equitable
relief. . . .

V

**If the court holds that racial segregation in public schools is uncon-
stitutional, it should remand these cases to the lower courts with
directions to carry out this court's decision as speedily as the particular circumstances permit. . . .**

There is no single formula or blueprint which can be uniformly
applied in all areas where existing school segregation must be ended.
Local conditions vary, and what would be effective and practicable in
the District of Columbia, for example, could be inappropriate in
Clarendon County, South Carolina. Only a pragmatic approach based
on a knowledge of local conditions and problems can determine what

is best in a particular place. For this reason, the court of first instance in such area should be charged with the responsibility for supervision of a program for carrying out the Court's decision. This Court should not, either itself or through appointment of a special master, undertake to formulate specific and detailed programs of implementation. . . .

[T]he Government respectfully suggests to the Court that, if it holds school segregation to be unconstitutional, the public interest would be served by entering decrees in the instant cases providing in substance as follows:

(1) That racial segregation in public schools be decreed by this Court to be a violation of rights secured by the Constitution;

(2) That each case be remanded to the appropriate court of first instance for such further proceedings and orders as are necessary and proper to carry out the Court's decision;

(3) That the lower courts be directed on remand to enter decrees under which the defendants shall forthwith be enjoined from using race or color as a basis for determining admission of children to public schools under their authority or control; provided, however, that if the defendants show that it is impracticable or inequitable to grant the plaintiffs the remedy of immediate (i. e., at the beginning of the next school term) admission to nonsegregated schools, the court shall order the defendants to propose and, on approval by the court after a public hearing, to put into effective operation a program for transition to a nonsegregated school system as expeditiously as the circumstances permit;

(4) That for the accomplishment of these purposes, taking into view the difficulties which may be encountered, a period of one year be allowed from the receipt of this Court's mandate, with leave, however, in the event, in the judgment of the lower court, the necessities of the situation so require, to extend such period for a further reasonable time.

2. Oral Argument on Behalf of the United States—J. Lee Rankin*

MR. RANKIN: May it please the Court, I would like to deal briefly with the question of relief, and try to give to the Court our points on that problem.

THE CHIEF JUSTICE: Which problem is that, you say?

---

*Reprinted in Friedman, *Argument*, pp. 252–58.

MR. RANKIN: The question of relief. . . .

We do not regard lightly the question of presenting to this Court a policy of delaying at all the relief that should be granted to citizens of this country when constitutional rights are found to have been violated, as we feel that they have been in this case.

However, upon careful study of the entire problem, we do think there are considerations that we can recommend to this Court should be taken into account in the decision of these cases. These cases do not deal only with the particular plaintiffs. The Court knows that they deal with certain classes, in addition to these plaintiffs.

But beyond that, we think it is fair to take into account the fact that the precedents established by the Court in the decision of these cases will necessarily bear upon the educational systems of some seventeen states and the District of Columbia.

There have to be adjustments to take care of the children attending these schools, and to provide them a program of mixed schools that will be adequate; and there will also have to be the problems of the administration and the various financial problems involved. It seems unrealistic not to take into account those factors, and that some time may be involved in providing for them. . . .

We suggest a year for the presentation and consideration of the plan, not because that is an exact standard, but with the idea that it might involve the principle of handling the matter with deliberate speed.

JUSTICE JACKSON: Mr. Rankin, may I ask you a question or two about this remedy you suggest. We have no state before us, have we? We have several school districts.

MR. RANKIN: Yes, that is correct.

JUSTICE JACKSON: I suppose that even if we said that the state statutes or state constitutional provisions authorizing segregation were unconstitutional, local custom would still perpetuate it in most districts of the states that really want it; I assume that would be the case, would it not?

MR. RANKIN: We do not assume that once this Court pronounces what the Constitution means in this area that our people are not going to try to abide by it and be in accord with it as rapidly as they can.

JUSTICE JACKSON: I do not think a court can enter a decree on that assumption, particularly in view of the fact that for seventy-five years the "separate but equal" doctrine has prevailed in the cases that came before us within the recent past, indicating it still had not been complied with in many cases.

The only people we can reach with the judicial decree are the people who are before us in the case.

MR. RANKIN: That is correct.

JUSTICE JACKSON: So that if it is not acquiesced in and embraced, we have to proceed school district by school district, is that right?

MR. RANKIN: Well, this Court traditionally handles each case as it comes before it.

JUSTICE JACKSON: Yes. It means that private litigation will result in every school district in order to get effective enforcement, and that is why, I suppose, this "separate but equal" doctrine has never really been enforced, because many disadvantaged people cannot afford these lawsuits. But the judicial remedy means just that, does it not, lawsuit after lawsuit?

MR. RANKIN: Well, it is probably true in every Fourteenth Amendment case that comes before the Court, each litigant has to come and say, "My rights have been infringed, and I have to be provided a remedy."

JUSTICE JACKSON: That is right; that is the nature of judicial process. . . .

But what I do not get in your statement here are any criteria that we are to lay down to the lower court in your view to determine what shall be taken into consideration. . . .

What are we going to do to avoid the situation where in some districts everybody is perhaps held in contempt almost immediately because that judge has that disposition, and in some other districts it is twelve years before they get to a hearing? What criteria do you propose?

MR. RANKIN: If I may try to answer some of the questions that Your Honor—

JUSTICE JACKSON: It is all one question: What are the standards?

MR. RANKIN: In the first place, I do not think the country would ever be satisfied with anybody but the Supreme Court saying what the Fourteenth Amendment means; and, secondly—

JUSTICE JACKSON: We would not be, anyway.

MR. RANKIN: No. (Laughter)

Secondly, I think that this Court does not have the duty or the function to try to determine what is a wise educational policy for each one of the various school districts in the country.

JUSTICE JACKSON: I am with you there. . . .

MR. RANKIN: I think that that problem will have to be tried as these matters are constantly before the lower courts. . . .

JUSTICE JACKSON: I foresee a generation of litigation if we send it back with no standards, and each case has to come here to determine it standard by standard.

*   *   *   *   *   *   *   *   *   *   *

MR. RANKIN: We . . . take the position that it is reasonable for this Court to remand the matter to the lower court . . . , and that the lower court can properly then determine how rapidly a plan can be achieved to come within the criteria established by this Court and the requirements of the Fourteenth Amendment, and that upon consideration of that, with all diligent speed, the lower court can enter a decree accordingly, and we visualize problems, but our courts have many problems, and they deal with those problems, and they weigh the various problems against the rights involved to accomplish the result in the best manner and as rapidly as possible.

JUSTICE REED: Mention one problem, mention just one.

MR. RANKIN: Well, the question is whether or not children should attend tomorrow or the next school term; and I do not see any great problem in that for the federal district court. . . .

JUSTICE JACKSON: Suppose you have two schools; you have a school that has been used by white pupils, a pretty good school; you have a pretty poor one that has been used by colored children. What are you going to do? How are you going to decide—you either have got to build a new school or you have got to move some white people into the poor school, which would cause a rumpus, or you have got to center them all in the good school. What would the court take into consideration?

MR. RANKIN: Well, time after time the courts have said that they were not going to be bothered by the worries and difficulties of the litigants about meeting the requirements of the Constitution or other principles laid down by this Court; and I think those are the problems that have to be dealt with by the local school districts, and they would have the obligation to bring in a plan to accomplish this in accordance with the order of this Court, as rapidly as could be obtained, and the details of it would not be a problem of the Court unless it found that the plan was unreasonable, that it was a deliberate attempt to evade the order of the Court, or that it was not equitably proper. Those standards—

JUSTICE JACKSON: This is the most definite one . . . that you have been able to devise?

MR. RANKIN: We explored the possibility of more definite decrees, but experience seems to dictate that the more definite courts are, appellate courts, in trying to describe the activities of lower courts, the more often they are apt to not give them the opportunity to solve the problem in the best manner possible.

We conceived that the position and the duty of this Court is to establish the broad general principles of what could be obtained, what the Fourteenth Amendment meant with regard to equality in the attendance of schools; that there could not be a distinction because of race.

JUSTICE FRANKFURTER: Am I right in assuming, if not in inferring—I do not think I have the right to infer—but in assuming that the Government in its suggestions as to the kind of a decree, is not dealing with these cases on the assumption that what is involved are just these individual children, but you have indicated a while ago that underlying your suggestions lies the assumption that these cases will settle a widespread problem, as indicated by both Mr. Davis and Mr. Moore, involving, whatever it is, the relationship of ten million Negroes in seventeen states, and that it is not a question of putting one child in a school, but how to make a readjustment of an existing system throughout the states where this present practice prevails; is that right?

MR. RANKIN: Yes.

3. Appellants' Brief on Reargument: The Remedy

I

This Court should declare invalid the constitutional and statutory provisions here involved requiring segregation in public schools. After careful consideration of all of the factors involved in transition from segregated school systems to unsegregated school systems, appellants know of no reasons or considerations which would warrant postponement of the enforcement of appellants' rights by this Court in the exercise of its equity powers.

The questions raised involve consideration of the propriety of postponing relief in these cases, should the Court declare segregation in public schools impermissible under the Constitution. The basic difficulty presented is in the correlation between a grant of effective relief and temporary postponement. After carefully addressing ourselves to the problem, we find that difficulty insurmountable.

A. The Fourteenth Amendment requires that a decree be entered directing that appellants be admitted forthwith to public schools without distinction as to race or color.

"It is fundamental that these cases concern rights which are personal and present." *Sweatt* v. *Painter*, 339 U. S. 629, 635. . . . These rights are personal because each appellant is asserting his individual constitutional right to grow up in our democratic society without the impress of state-imposed racial segregation in the public schools. They are present because they will be irretrievably lost if their enjoyment is put off. The rights of the adult students in the . . . *Sweatt* and *McLaurin* cases required, this Court held, vindication forthwith. A *fortiori*, this is true of the rights of children to a public education that they must obtain, if at all while they are children. It follows that appellants are entitled to be admitted forthwith to public schools without distinction as to race and color.

B. There is no equitable justification for postponement of appellants' enjoyment of their rights.
Even if the Court should decide that enforcement of individual and personal constitutional rights may be postponed, consideration of the relevant factors discloses no equitable basis for delaying enforcement of appellants' rights. . . .

These infant appellants are asserting the most important secular claims that can be put forward by children, the claim to their full measure of the chance to learn and grow, and the inseparably connected but even more important claim to be treated as entire citizens of the society into which they have been born. We have discovered no case in which such rights, once established, have been postponed by a cautious calculation of conveniences. . . .

The Fourteenth Amendment can hardly have been intended for enforcement at a pace geared down to the mores of the very states whose action it was designed to limit. The balance between the customs of the states and the personal rights of these appellants has been struck by that Amendment. "[A] court of equity is not justified in ignoring that pronouncement under the guise of exercising equitable jurisdiction." *Youngstown Co.* v. *Sawyer*, 343 U.S. 579, 610.

Affirming the decree of one of the few judges still carrying the traditional title and power of Chancellor, the highest Court of Delaware epitomized equity in one of the cases now before this bar when it declared in *Gebhart* v. *Belton*, 91 A. 2d 137, 149 that

> "To require the plaintiffs to wait another year under present conditions would be in effect partially to deny them that to which we have held they are entitled." . . .

In deciding whether sufficient reason exists for postponing the enjoyment of appellants' rights, this Court is not resolving an issue which depends upon a mere preponderance of the evidence. It needs no citation of authority to establish that the defendant in equity who asks the chancellor to go slow in upholding the vital rights of children accruing to them under the Constitution, must make out an affirmative case of crushing conviction to sustain his plea for delay.

The problem of effective gradual adjustment cannot fairly arise in three of the five cases consolidated for argument. In the Kansas case, there was a frank concession on oral argument that elimination of segregation would not have serious consequences. In Delaware, court-compelled desegregation in this very case has already been accomplished. . . . In the oral argument [of the District of Columbia case] the counsel for respondents implied that he foresaw no difficulties in enforcing a decree which would abolish segregation. Surely it would be curious as well as a gratuitous assumption that such a change cannot be expeditiously handled in this nation's capital. . . .

We concede that there may well be delays of a purely administrative nature involved in bringing about desegregation. Any injunction requires time for compliance and we do not ask the impossible. We strongly urge, however, that no reason has been suggested and none has been discovered by us that would warrant denying appellants their full rights beyond the beginning of the next school year.

But we do not understand that the "effective gradual adjustment" mentioned in this Court's fourth and fifth questions referred to such conceded necessities. We proceed then, to consider possible grounds that might be put forth as reasons for added delay, or for the postponement of relief to appellants.

It has been suggested that desegregation may bring about unemployment for Negro teachers. If this is more than a remote possibility, it undoubtedly can be offset by good faith efforts on the part of the responsible school boards. On the other hand, if appellees' suggestion is based upon an unexpressed intention of discriminating against Negro teachers by wholesale firings, it is not even worthy of notice in a court of equity.

It has been bruited about that certain of the states involved in this litigation will cease to support and perhaps even abolish their public school systems, if segregation is outlawed. We submit that such action is not permissible. . . . Any such reckless threats cannot be relevant to a consideration of effective "gradual adjustment"; they are based upon opposition to desegregation in any way, at any time.

Finally, there are hints and forebodings of trouble to come, ranging from hostility and deteriorated relations to actual violence. Obviously this Court will not be deterred by threats of unlawful action. *Buchanan* v. *Warley*, 245 U.S. 60, 81.

Moreover, there are powerful reasons to confirm the belief that immediate desegregation will not have the untoward consequences anticipated. The states in question are inhabited in the main by law-abiding people who up to now have relied upon what they believe—erroneously, as we have demonstrated—to be the law. It cannot be presumed that they will not obey the law as expounded by this Court. Such evidence as there is lends no support to defendants' forebodings.

A higher public interest than any yet urged by appellees is the need for the enforcement of constitutional rights fought for and won about a century ago. Public interest requires that racial distinctions proscribed by our Constitution be given the fullest protection. Survival of our country in the present international situation is inevitably tied to resolution of this domestic issue.

The greatest strength of our democracy grows out of its people working together as equals. Our public schools are "[d]esigned to serve as perhaps the most powerful agency for promoting cohesion among a heterogeneous democratic people. . . ." Mr. Justice Frankfurter, concurring in *Illinois ex rel. McCollum* v. *Board of Education*, 333 U.S. 206, 216–217.

C. Appellants are unable, in good faith, to suggest terms for a decree which will secure effective gradual adjustment because no such decree will protect appellants' rights.

Question 5 assumes that the Court, having decided that segregation in public schools violates the Fourteenth Amendment, will, nevertheless, in the exercise of its equity powers, permit an effective gradual adjustment from segregated schools to systems not operated on the basis of color distinctions. This necessarily assumes further that reasons might be produced to justify consideration of postponement of the enforcement of the present and personal rights here involved. As we have pointed out immediately hereinbefore we are unable to identify any such reason. . . .

Though no cogent reasons were offered to support them, two suggestions of methods of postponement of relief to appellants were made to this Court in the original brief for the United States. The first of these was "integration on a grade basis," i.e., to integrate the first grades immediately, and to continue such integration until completed as to all grades in the elementary schools (Brief, pp. 30–31). The second was integration "on a school-by-school" basis (Brief, p. 31).

The first suggestion is intolerable. It would mean the flat denial of the right of every appellant in these cases. The second plan is likewise impossible to defend because it would mean the deliberate denial of the rights of many of the plaintiffs. If desegregation is possible in some schools in a district, why not in all? Must some appellants' rights be denied altogether, so that others may be more conveniently protected? . . .

[T]he only specific issue which appellants can recommend to the Court that the decrees should reach is the substantive one presented here, namely, that appellees should be required in the future to discharge their obligations as state officers without drawing distinctions based on race and color. Once this is done not only the local communities involved in these several cases, but communities throughout the South, would be left free to work out individual plans for conforming to the then established precedent free from the statutory requirement of rigid racial segregation.

In the very nature of the judicial process once a right is judicially declared proposals for postponement of the remedy must originate with the party desiring that postponement.

We submit that it would be customary procedure for the appellees to first produce whatever reasons they might urge to justify postponement of relief. Appellants then would be in a position to advise the Court of their views with respect to the matter.

4. Philip Elman—"The Solicitor General's Office, Justice Frankfurter, and Civil Rights Litigation, 1946–1960: An Oral History" (1987)*

ELMAN: . . . . I told Richard Kluger—when he interviewed me for *Simple Justice*—that this first brief we filed in December 1952 is the one thing I'm proudest of in my whole career. Not because it's a beautifully written brief; I don't think it is. Rather, it's because we were the first to suggest, and all the parties and amici on both sides rejected it after the government proposed it, that if the Court should hold that racial segregation in public schools is unconstitutional, it should give district courts a reasonable period of time to work out the details and timing of implementation of the decision. In other words, "with all deliberate speed."

The reason I'm so proud of that proposal is that it offered the Court a way out of its dilemma, a way to end racial segregation without inviting massive disobedience, a way to decide the constitutional issue unanimously without tearing the Court apart. For the first time the Court was told that it was not necessarily confronted with an all-or-nothing choice between reaffirming separate but equal, as urged by the states, and overruling *Plessy* and requiring immediate integration of public schools in all states, as urged by the NAACP. We proposed a middle ground, separating the constitutional principle from the remedy—a proposal that nobody had previously suggested and that, when we made it, both sides opposed.

It was entirely unprincipled, it was just plain wrong as a matter of constitutional law, to suggest that someone whose personal constitutional rights were being violated should be denied relief. It was saying to Linda Brown and all the other children in these cases, "Yes, you're right, your constitutional rights are being violated and ignored, you are not being allowed to go to a public school of your choice because of your race, and we agree that's unconstitutional. But we're not going to do a damn thing for you. You go back to that same segregated school you're going to. We'll take care of your children, perhaps. Or your grandchildren. But we're not going to do a damn thing for you. By the time we get around to doing something for kids like you, you will have graduated from school." That's what we were arguing, even though the Supreme

---

*Harvard Law Review, Vol. 100, 817, 1987.

Court had held again and again that constitutional rights are personal, that if an individual's constitutional rights are being violated, he is entitled to immediate relief. As a matter of constitutional principle, what we were arguing in this brief was simply indefensible.

Now, where did this idea come from? Not from Frankfurter; he never expressed anything along those lines. But it did grow out of my many conversations with him over a period of many months. He told me what he thought, what the other Justices were telling him they thought. I knew from him what their positions were. If the issue was inescapably presented in yes-or-no terms, he could not count five votes on the Court to overrule *Plessy*. Black, who was a sure vote to overrule *Plessy*, was frightening the other Justices the most. He was saying to them, "Now, look, I have to vote to overrule *Plessy*, but this would mean the end of political liberalism in the South. Politicians like Lister Hill will be dead. It will bring the Bilbos and the Talmadges out of the woodwork; the Klan is going to be riding again. It will be the end of liberalism in the South."

Burton and Minton didn't say very much. As it turned out, when the votes were finally cast, they were on the right side, but of course when they voted, they were not voting for immediate relief. Nobody on the Court ever voted for immediate implementation, for opening up all the public schools in the whole country, tomorrow morning at nine o'clock, all nonsegregated.

Q: Aren't you exaggerating? Was that really the alternative that the petitioners placed in front of the Court?

ELMAN: Yes. That was the stark issue posed to the Court by the parties—which the Justices never had to reach, because the United States as amicus curiae offered a way out, and they grabbed it. If they had not had that alternative offered to them, one that came to them with the seal of approval of both the Democratic Truman and Republican Eisenhower administrations, who knows what would have happened. It would, in Frankfurter's judgment, have been an incredible godawful mess; possiby nine different opinions, nine different views on the Court. It would have set back the cause of desegregation; it would have hurt the public school systems everywhere; and it would have damaged the Court.

Vinson was clearly for leaving the Constitution as it was. *Plessy* and separate but equal had been the law of the land for over a half-century, and he was not ready to change it. Let them amend the Constitution or let Congress do something, but Vinson was not going to overrule

Plessy. He had Tom Clark with him, at least initially in 1952. True, Clark voted the other way in the end—after "with all deliberate speed" had been added to the choices before the Court—but Clark was then with Vinson. At least Frankfurter said so. Reed kept quiet publicly, but he was certainly with Vinson.

So as Frankfurter saw it when the cases came up, he would be the fifth man. He saw Vinson, Clark, and Reed for simply affirming *Plessy;* Jackson for leaving it to Congress. On the other side, although Frankfurter wasn't sure of Minton, he had Black, Douglas, and Burton for overruling *Plessy*, with Black screaming it would be a political disaster to do so. So I began looking around for something that would get Jackson, that would hold Frankfurter, that would even get a strong majority to hold racial segregation unconstitutional but would provide some kind of cushion, something to avoid the immediate impact, some insurance against the inevitable fallout of a Court decision requiring immediate integration everywhere. So that is why I made this "indefensible" argument in point four of the 1952 brief. None of this was based on what I thought was right—I had no idea whether it would have been better educationally or politically to do it immediately—I was simply counting votes on the Supreme Court. I was trying to come up with a realistic formula that would win the case, that would overrule *Plessy*, that would knock out separate but equal, that would not damage the Court or public educational systems. It was as simple as that. I repeat: I had had no discussion about it with Frankfurter beforehand.

Q: You said you were talking with him all the way along?

ELMAN: Sure, but I had no discussion with Frankfurter beforehand with respect to the position I was going to take in point four of this brief. I just didn't want to take a chance on telling him—because of what might happen if I did. I was on very shaky legal ground. As I said, it was insupportable in dealing with individual constitutional rights, and I didn't want Frankfurter to tell me so. . . . The expression "with all deliberate speed" was used first by Holmes in a case called *Virginia v. West Virginia*. (222 US 17, 20, 1918)

Q: Was that phrase in your brief?

ELMAN: No. The phrase made its first appearance in *Brown* in [Assistant Attorney General J. Lee] Rankin's oral argument in 1953. But the idea was the same as in our brief. . . .

Well, going back to that brief in December of 1952, I had been a great hero of the NAACP and all these other people who were fighting to end racial segregation, but after that brief was filed, I wasn't a hero anymore. They thought point four was gradualism, and to them gradualism meant never. Unlike Frankfurter and me, they couldn't or didn't count the votes on the Court. When that brief was filed, Frankfurter called me up and said, "Phil, I think you've rendered a real service to your country." That's the way I felt about it then, and that's the way I feel about it now, even though many people think that "with all deliberate speed" was a disaster. It broke the logjam. It was the formula that the Court needed in order to bring all the Justices together to decide the constitutional issue on the merits correctly. Without "all deliberate speed" in the remedy, the Court could never have decided the constitutional issue in the strong, forthright, unanimous way that it did; and it was essential for the Court to do so if its decision was to be accepted and followed throughout the country.

The Justices couldn't decide at the 1952 Term. Eisenhower became President in January 1953, and Herbert Brownell became Attorney General; we had no Solicitor General for a while. Lee Rankin was running the S.G.'s office for Brownell, and Rankin was very pleasantly surprised by the caliber of the lawyers he found there. . . .

Q: What was happening that spring in the *Brown* case?

ELMAN: Well, what the Court did in the segregation cases in June of 1953 was to set them down for reargument. The Justices discussed the cases in conference, but they never took a vote; they just expressed their views. Some of their conference notes are now available, and it's not altogether clear who said what or when. Tom Clark, for example, said long afterward that, oh yes, he was for overruling *Plessy*. But that's not the way I heard it from Frankfurter.

There's no question that the grand strategist in all this inside the Court was F.F. He was writing memos to his colleagues and having his clerk, Alex Bickel, do research into the legislative history of the fourteenth amendment, the results of which he then circulated to the Court. To use the Yiddish word that Frankfurter used all the time, he was the *Kochleffel*. It means cooking spoon, stirring things up; the man stirring everything up inside the Court was Frankfurter. They couldn't decide the cases, they didn't know what to do with them, they had no majority, and they hadn't even taken a formal vote, because they didn't want to harden anybody's position.

So in the summer of 1953 before they adjourned, they set the cases down for reargument: they asked five questions of the parties, and they invited the Attorney General of the United States and the attorneys general of all the states requiring or authorizing segregation to

file briefs and present oral argument. Well, that order setting the cases
down for reargument brought misery to the Department of Justice.
The new people in the Eisenhower administration had been waiting
on the sidelines for the Court to decide. They had had nothing to do
with the cases, they had never taken a position on the issue, they
didn't want to get involved, and here the Supreme Court was asking
the Attorney General of the United States to file a brief and present
oral argument. Well . . .

Q: Excuse me, do you know how that invitation came about? Whose
idea it was?

ELMAN: It was Frankfurter's.

Q: You had nothing to do with it?

ELMAN: Oh, he might have told me about it. It came as no surprise
to me, but reargument was his idea. What he kept telling me was,
"These cases are just sitting, Phil, nothing's happening." I knew that.
Incidentally, I must emphasize to you that I never mentioned my
conversations with Frankfurter to anyone. He didn't regard me as a
lawyer for any party; I was still his law clerk. He needed help, lots of
help, and there were things I could do in the Department of Justice
that he couldn't do, like getting the support of both administrations,
Democratic and Republican, for the position that he wanted the Court
to come out with, so that it would not become a hot political issue.
When the Court announced its decision, he wanted both the present
and former Presidents of the United States to be publicly on record
as having urged the Court to take the position it had. And that's
exactly the way it worked out.

CONCLUSION

The Riddle of *Brown*

Introduction

I

THE COURT MET in conference to discuss the school cases once again on December 12, 1953—three days after the close of oral arguments, and almost one year exactly since the indecisive conference of 1952. The Justices were armed with Alexander Bickel's memorandum on the debates in the 39th Congress, and with a prefatory note from Justice Frankfurter which interpreted the document for them. The legislative debate, he argued, was "in a word, inconclusive, in the sense that the . . . Congress . . . neither manifested that the Amendment outlawed segregation in the public schools . . . , nor that it manifested the opposite."[1]

The new Chief Justice had asked few questions at the *Brown* reargument, giving no indication of his views on school segregation. But at the conference of December 12, Earl Warren quickly exhibited the traits which would make him the most influential Chief Justice of the United States since John Marshall. He was decisive, yet gracious and conciliatory in manner. Furthermore, he did not shrink from reducing abstruse constitutional issues to uncomplicated moral imperatives. This general approach to adjudication was denounced by his critics of later years as crude and oriented only to producing desired results, and there is no doubt that such an approach easily serves as a mask for personal convictions. But Warren's one-time law clerk and biographer, G. Edward White, argues that the Chief Justice's ethical preoccupation represented a consistent, if unconventional "theory of judging," which did not succumb to the view "that judges were free to do as they liked."[2]

> The ethical imperatives that guided Warren as a judge reflected his personal morality in that Warren held a set of values that he believed represented moral truths about decent, civilized life. It was inconceivable to Warren that these values would not be embodied in constitutional principles, since he believed that they

formed the essence of American democracy. Indeed, Warren felt *bound*, as a judge, to consider ethical imperatives in his adjudication; in his view, they deserved as much consideration as explicit constitutional language, and perhaps more. His principal concerns as a jurist were to discern the underlying ethical structure of the Constitution and to apply rigorously its ethical imperatives, even if such an application resulted in a failure to achieve orthodox doctrinal consistency.[3]

Never was this philosophy better suited to a case than it was to *Brown v. Board of Education*.

Warren opened the conference by proposing that no vote be taken, so that the cases could be discussed informally. He then made it very clear how he would vote. "[T]he more I've read and heard and thought," Burton's notes record him as saying, "the more I've come to conclude that the basis of segregation and 'separate but equal' rests upon a concept of the inherent inferiority of the colored race. I don't see how *Plessy* and the cases following it can be sustained on any other theory." Obviously this basis was not defensible. "I don't see how in this day and age we can set any group apart from the rest and say that they are not entitled to exactly the same treatment as all others. . . . I can't see how today we can justify segregation based solely on race."[4]

Yet if the moral imperative was absolute, the mechanics of implementation required caution. "It would be unfortunate," said Warren, "if we had to take precipitous action that would inflame more than necessary."[5] The varying conditions in the states must be taken carefully into account. "How we do it is important. . . .[M]y instincts and feelings lead me to say that . . . we should abolish the practice of segregation in the public schools—but in a tolerant way."[6]

Warren's statement struck a lofty ethical tone. But in a more practical sense it meant there was an openly declared majority on December 12 for outlawing school segregation. Douglas, Burton, and Minton repeated their earlier views; Hugo Black was absent from the conference because of the illness of his sister, but sent word that his views were the same. In reality the majority was six. While Frankfurter gave a convoluted statement at the 1953 conference, as he had in 1952, there was no doubt, we now know, as to how he would vote.

Tom Clark was ready to add a seventh vote. Taking up on the hints he had provided in 1952 (according to Douglas' notes at least), Clark indicated that he would support a decision undercutting *Plessy*, so long as relief was carefully worked out. The Court must be very deliberate, he argued, in framing the decrees which ended segregation, since there were serious "dangers of violence" in parts of the South.[7]

Justice Jackson stuck to his equivocal views. But again he indicated that he could live with a "political" decision, one which, as his law clerk later put it, made "new law for a new day."[8] Only Stanley Reed was opposed to Warren's position.

A majority of as much as 8–1 for the appellants loomed up as a result of the December 12 conference. Yet Warren clearly understood that the basic constitutional issue discussed in that meeting was inseparable from the question of how a decision abrogating segregation would be carried out. Matters of implementation were especially crucial not only to Clark and Jackson, but to Frankfurter and Black as well. Consequently, the Chief decided to hold a conference on January 16, 1954, devoted entirely to a discussion of remedy. This tactic subtly implied that the root issue in *Brown* was already resolved, yet offered an opportunity to reassure those who were wavering.

In preparation for the January 16 meeting, Frankfurter circulated a memorandum to his Brethren, assuring them that "the typewriting was done under conditions of strictest security."[9] Much of the memo reflected the consensus forming among the Justices about how to handle a judgment for the appellants. The Court was being asked, felt Frankfurter, to inaugurate a massive undertaking, "to transform" the school systems in more than a third of the states. A "declaration of unconstitutionality," therefore, "is not a wand by which these transformations can be accomplished."[10] When the wrong to be dealt with was also "a deeply rooted state policy the Court does its duty if it decrees measures that reverse the direction of the unconstitutional policy so as to uproot it 'with *all deliberate speed.*'"[11]

As to the agency which would manage the desegregation process, the "one thing one can feel confidently is that this Court cannot do it directly."[12] Frankfurter thought that the school cases should be remanded to the district courts. But he also felt that the Supreme Court should appoint, or direct the district judges to appoint, special masters for this litigation, experts who would gather the detailed factual material necessary for making individual judgments in individual states and school districts.

The Justices would have to issue a formal decree on implementation in Frankfurter's view. "A mere declaration will not do." But it was clear to him that the initial decree must "confine itself to general terms"—simply stating that "the inequalities which any segregated school system begets cannot stand," though abolition of segregation would be done "with due regard" for the principle "that school systems be not disrupted."[13]

The January 16, 1954, conference on remedy was marked by this kind of caution. The Chief Justice again advised against hasty action on desegregation, especially in the deep South, and argued that the Supreme Court should get "as little involved in administration as we can." The district courts should handle the matter, yet they needed some form of decree as a starting point. "[W]e ought not to turn them loose without guidance. . . ."[14] Justice Black agreed with a remand to the district level, but he did not believe there was much guidance the Court could usefully give. "Let it simmer. . . . It can't take too long."[15] Justice Reed too felt that desegregation must not be "a rush job,"[16] though this did not mean he had changed his mind on the constitutionality of separate schools. There was no indication in his remarks of January 16 that he was ready to outlaw them.

The rest of the Justices also counseled prudence. It was not desirable to "[throw] the Court's weight around," said Minton.[17] Jackson made a critical suggestion at this conference which his colleagues eventually adopted. He favored a total separation between the decision on the constitutional issue and the one on remedy. The Court could determine the fate of school segregation immediately, yet order another reargument devoted entirely to questions of implementation. Clark and Black endorsed this approach on the spot.

The discussion of January 16 seemed to guarantee that eight Justices would stand together on the merits. This majority was confirmed at a climactic conference, held in late February or early March. The Court voted 8–1, most probably, to forbid segregation in public education; agreement was also reached, we assume, to order a reargument on remedy. In his memoirs, Warren states that at this meeting, "we voted unanimously among ourselves to declare racially segregated public schools to be unconstitutional."[18] But Professor Schwartz's evidence indicates that Justice Reed was working on a dissent in *Brown* during these months, and that his opposition to the majority persisted into April.

Moreover, Justice Jackson gave indications in February and March that he might write a separate opinion in the case, agreeing with the majority's result, but registering disagreement with their approach.

Jackson wanted to be certain that the decision was clearly presented as a "political" one, as law adapted to shifting circumstances. More important, he remained deeply skeptical that the courts were the proper vehicle for overseeing remedial action. In February of 1954, he sketched some thoughts on the constitutional merits of *Brown*. A month later, he fleshed out his ideas into what was meant as a separate concurring opinion.

His preliminary memo noted pointedly that, "This Court must face the difficulties in the way of honestly saying that the states which have segregated schools have not, until today, been justified in regarding their practice as lawful."[19] There was after all "little . . . to show that [the Civil War] Amendments were understood in their own time to condemn the practice here in question."[20] The actions of the states as well as of the District of Columbia, buttressed by the earliest court decisions on separate schools, scarcely offered warrant for the notion that integration was "required by the original purpose and intent of the Fourteenth or Fifth Amendment."[21]

But despite the implications of some of his conference remarks, Jackson did not deny that "Constitutional generalities"[22] had the capacity to vary in content. "Of course the Constitution must be a living instrument and can not be read as if written in a dead language. It is neither novel nor radical doctrine that statutes once constitutional may become invalid by changing conditions. . . ."[23]

The equal protection clause must now be applied to an era in which great changes had occurred "in the status of the public school,"[24] but also in which the educational and cultural advance of black Americans had been nothing short of "spectacular." Whatever the situation in the 1860s or 1890s, "the mere fact that one is in some degree colored no longer creates a presumption that he is inferior, illiterate, retarded or indigent."[25] Thus the pattern of change which justified an attack on *Plessy* "is not a change in the Constitution but in the Negro population."[26]

Jackson's notion of a "political" decision was not significantly different in the end from the kind of decision which Frankfurter or Phillip Elman would have regarded as perfectly consistent with a capacious but legitimate view of original intent: one which recognized, as the government's brief on reargument had said, that "Constitutional provisions like . . . 'equal protection of the laws' express broad principles of government the essence of which is their . . . adaptability to the progressive changes . . . of the nation."[27]

But Justice Jackson's gravest concern, articulated most fully in the draft of his proposed concurrence, was how a desegregation decree could be implemented. That the lower federal courts were inadequate to the task and would find themselves overwhelmed by it seemed obvious to him. "The futility of effective reform . . . by judicial decree" was illustrated, he thought, by the very history of the separate but equal doctrine, which throughout its existence had "remained an empty pronouncment" because courts lacked the power to enforce broad legal doctrines against "persons not before them" in a particular lawsuit.[28] Jackson stated flatly that he would "not be a party to . . . casting upon the lower courts a burden of continued litigation."[29]

In this situation, he recurred to a modified version of the approach to *Brown* which had appealed to him from the start. Once the Supreme Court acted to declare educational segregation unconstitutional, the Congress should move in and take charge by legislative action of the dismantling of dual school systems. If the House and Senate had shown massive reluctance to tackle the problem in the past, this "inertia" could be explained by their "belief that the existing system is constitutional."[30] Now that the Court was ready to speak, Jackson implied, the Congress could be expected to act.

The Justice ended his draft concurrence by simply holding school segregation unconstitutional and calling for a reargument on remedy. But Philip Elman was convinced that this was the prelude to a disposition of the desegregation problem under section 5, that Jackson believed it sensible and proper to tell the original plaintiffs in *Brown*, "You go across the street and ask Congress to give you relief."[31]

Jackson may or may not have followed through on his separate concurrence, but again fate intervened to surmount this potential obstacle to unanimity. The Justice's draft was dated March 15, 1954. On March 30, he suffered a serious heart attack which confined him to the hospital until May. This ended the possibility of serious work on an individual opinion. Indeed Mrs. Elsie Douglas, Jackson's secretary, notes at the beginning of the March 15 draft that it was never "circulated to members of the Court or used in any way except in conference with C. J. Warren at Doctors Hospital."[32] At this meeting, held a few days before *Brown* was handed down, Jackson agreed to sign the Court's opinion.

Meanwhile, the only possible dissenter had been brought around. Warren worked in a low-key manner on Stanley Reed in March and April of 1954. They were frequently joined by the placatory Justice Burton. Finally, Warren told Reed, "Stan, you're all by yourself in this now. You've got to decide whether it's really the best thing for the country."[33] Reed agreed to allow the school decisions to be unanimous. The only condition he laid down for his vote, according to his law clerk George Mickum, was that the decree implementing desegregation must be measured and gradual in nature, and not attempt to rip the old system apart.

At the end of April, Chief Justice Warren called in one of his law clerks, Earl Pollock, and gave him an outline of the opinion he wanted written in *Brown v. Board of Education*, along with some specific language he wished included. Based on this outline, Pollock drafted most of what became the final opinion. The other Justices made only minor changes. At the same time, law clerk William Oliver was working on the opinion in *Bolling v. Sharpe*.

On May 17, 1954, the two opinions were read in their entirety by the Chief Justice of the United States. All of the Justices were present, including Robert Jackson. Mrs. Douglas tells us that, "He came directly to the Court from the hospital that day so that there might be a full bench when these cases were handed down."[34] George Mickum remembers seeing tears in Justice Reed's eyes as the reading was completed.

On May 20, Justice Frankfurter sent Reed a gracious note, which also clears up any doubts as to what Frankfurter's view on *Brown* had been a year earlier. "[I]f the *Segregation* cases had reached decision last Term," he stated, "there would have been four dissenters—Vinson, Reed, Jackson and Clark. . . . That would have been catastrophic."[35] Reed's ultimate willingness to go along with the majority was a signal service to the nation, Frankfurter felt. "I am not unaware of the hard struggle this involved in the conscience of your mind and in the mind of your conscience. . . . As a citizen of the Republic, even more than as a colleague, I feel deep gratitude for your share in what I believe to be a great good for our nation."[36]

In reply, Justice Reed reflected upon his ambivalence. "[T]here were many considerations that pointed to a dissent," he admitted, but "they did not add up to a balance against the Court's opinion. . . . [T]he factors looking toward a fair treatment for Negroes are more important than the weight of history."[37]

II

What was decided in the brace of cases which comprise *Brown v. Board of Education*? Professor Alfred Kelly wrote that because of *Brown*, "the 'separate but equal' doctrine of *Plessy v. Ferguson*, insofar as it applied to schools, now stood formally overruled."[38] This was obviously true in any realistic sense. But the Justices specifically refrained from using the word "overrule." In its structure and in its ostensible reach, their decision took the middle path to disposing of educational segregation, the approach stressed by appellants during the initial argument of 1952.

Chief Justice Warren began the Court's opinion by pronouncing the historical evidence "inconclusive," as Frankfurter had, and by acknowledging in essence that the Court was making new law for a new day. "In approaching this problem, we cannot turn the clock back to 1868 . . . , or even to 1896. . . . We must consider public education in the light of its full development and its present place in American life. . . ." Of course, Warren did not describe the decision as "political"; nor, on the other hand, did he characterize it as stemming from some well-understood intention of the framers to cast the fourteenth amendment in spacious generalities. Throughout, *Brown* was spare in its exposition.

The Chief Justice then came to the heart of the matter: Did racial separation in education deprive minority children "of equal educational opportunities"? In reaching his conclusion, he followed directly the logic of *Sweatt* and *McLaurin*. *Sweatt* had focused for the first time on those intangible elements which make for educational excellence, and found segregation unacceptable in law schools because it deprived black students of such intangibles. *McLaurin* condemned segregation within a graduate institution, again resorting to "intangible considerations"—the opportunity for discussion and exchange of views with other students.

There follows one of the most important passages in American constitutional law:

> Such considerations apply with added force to children in grade and high schools. To separate them from others of similar age and qualifications solely because of their race generates a feeling of inferiority as to their status in the community that may affect their hearts and minds in a way unlikely ever to be undone.

Separate but equal then had "no place" in American education, for segregated facilities were "inherently unequal."

Warren saw himself in *Brown* as deciding the issue "expressly reserved" in *Sweatt* v. *Painter:* whether *Plessy* was "*inapplicable* to public education." In fact, the explicit language of *Sweatt* had reserved judgment on a different question: whether *Plessy* v. *Ferguson* **itself** "should be reexamined."[39] This was in response to the assertion in the NAACP brief that if the Court found the validity of separate but equal *"applicable* [to public education]," *that entire doctrine* "should now be reexamined and overruled."[40]

The Chief Justice seemed to be going out of his way, therefore, to vindicate the original legal strategy conceived by Thurgood Marshall and Robert Carter, and spelled out best in the first *Briggs* brief. He was returning to the kind of reasoning which Frankfurter had denigrated so sharply in 1952, though by 1953 the appellants were no longer giving these views their highest priority.

Indeed, Warren put a finer point upon the matter than the NAACP had ever intended, exacerbating in the process the controversy which erupted over *Brown*. The structure of the opinion gave the distinct impression that segregation in elementary and secondary schools was being pronounced unconstitutional almost solely because of empirical psychological evidence which had recently surfaced, demonstrating the deleterious effects of such separation on school children. The "hearts and minds" passage is the only substantive statement in *Brown* concerning the evils of grade school segregation (followed by Judge Huxman's words in the Topeka decision, which say much the same thing). That this insight is thought to be the fruit of contemporary advances is suggested by the Court's next sentence. "Whatever may have been the extent of psychological knowledge at the time of *Plessy v. Ferguson*, [our] finding is amply supported by modern authority."

The more practical traumas of segregation which were documented at the trial level—isolation from the majority group, the tension with America's democratic culture—are alluded to only vaguely, in the opinion's fragmentary discussion of *Sweatt* and *McLaurin*. This emphasis in language undoubtedly focused attention more extensively on the tests conducted by Kenneth Clark than on the broader condemnation of the racial caste system found in Myrdal, or on the tough-talking common sense of David Krech or Brewster Smith.

The "modern authority" referred to in the text was documented in a much-discussed footnote, footnote number 11. Kenneth Clark led the list of authorities cited, though Gunnar Myrdal is also mentioned, along with Isidor Chein, and sociologist E. Franklin Frazier of Howard University, author of *The Negro in the United States* (and later of *Black Bourgeoisie*).

In later years, the Chief Justice and his law clerk, Earl Pollock, called into question the importance of this psychological analysis, maintaining that the discussion of harm in *Brown*, and the footnote which elaborated it, were meant simply as a reply to *Plessy*'s absurd contention that any sense of inferiority felt by blacks as a result of segregation was a subjective concoction of their own minds. The sole reason for footnote 11, said Pollock, "was as a rebuttal to the cheap psychology of *Plessy* that said inferiority was only in the mind of the Negro. The Chief Justice was saying in effect that we know a lot more now about how human beings work than they did back then and can therefore cast doubt on that preposterous line of argument."[41]

But the phrasing of this point in the opinion creates ambiguity, a case again in constitutional history of where the intention of the authors is not automatically revealed by the intention of their words. "Whatever may have been the extent of psychological knowledge at the time of *Plessy* v. *Ferguson*, [our] finding is amply supported by modern authority." The sentence does not strike one as censorious in nature, and in a decision of *Brown*'s gravity it is unlikely to have been meant sarcastically. On the contrary, the words convey a conciliatory purpose, especially when combined with other evocations in the opinion of changing times being the principal cause of changing principles.

There is no doubt that Warren wished to avoid a judgment cast in an accusatory tone, one which pilloried the South for clinging to practices which the Court had repeatedly upheld as constitutional. In his opinion, as in his opening remarks at conference, he was anxious to project himself as "a reasonable and concerned man with malice toward none."[42] What better way to cushion the outrage many southerners were certain to feel than by suggesting that racial separation in education was being proscribed mainly because new light had been shed upon the issue by experimental psychology? If Thurgood Marshall saw distilled in Professor Clark's doll tests "the cumulative grief of three hundred years," their actual deployment in *Brown* seemed more consistent with Justice Jackson's demand for a "political" decision. (The "hearts and minds" passage was written by Warren himself; it was among the specific sentences which he directed Earl Pollock to include in the draft opinion.)

The use of Kenneth Clark's research turned out to be a masterstroke, though in an unintended sense, perhaps. Clark himself certainly never held out his discoveries as startlingly "new" (or minimized the harshness of the southern caste system). Nonetheless, the innovative, though at that point still uncompleted work of Professor Clark and his wife was understandably celebrated for their role in ending Jim Crow education.

Yet Warren's perceived emphasis gave to the central charge against *Brown* more serious attention than it might otherwise have received, the charge that it was "sociology (or more properly child psychology), not law." This condemnation gained currency, and even academic respectability, not simply because the Chief Justice's opinion cited data from the social sciences. Use of such data was common practice in American law in 1953. The criticisms took hold because of the provisional and subjective nature of the social science materials which seemingly were stressed.

One of the first reactions to *Brown*, a journalistic forerunner of some of the scholarly critiques, came from *New York Times* columnist James Reston. "Relying more on the social scientists than on legal precedents," he said, " . . . the Court insisted on equality of the mind and heart rather than on equal school facilities." The Justices were most impressed, felt Reston, by "the testimony . . . on the effects of discrimination on personality development."[43] (Some of the more perfervid southerners detected a communist conspiracy behind footnote 11. The files of the House Un-American Activities Committee, claimed Senator Eastland, contained myriad references to scholars cited in the footnote—ten in one instance, eighteen in another.) Even those who did not regard *Brown* as an exercise in social psychology expressed some regret at its general drift. "It seems to me," said Professor Charles Black of Yale, "that the venial fault of the opinion consists in its not spelling out that segregation . . . is perceptibly a means of ghettoizing the imputedly inferior race. . . . I would conjecture that the motive for this omission was reluctance to go into the distasteful details of the southern caste system. . . ."[44]

In any event, *Brown* did not automatically outlaw the separate but equal principle in other areas of American life. Its logic did not even appear to affect these areas, focused as it was on the harm experienced by school children. Yet within a week of the decision, the Justices unanimously reversed and sent back to the lower courts "for consideration in the light of *Brown* v. *Board of Education*," a ruling upholding segregation in public parks.[45] The clear implication was that racial separation in such facilities was no longer constitutional. Within a year, the Court, merely citing *Brown*, struck down segregation of public beaches and golf courses;[46] within two years, it destroyed *Plessy*

directly by outlawing racial segregation in transportation.[47] These
unanimous decisions showed that Earl Warren and his colleagues
were serious about removing the most visible badges of slavery in
America. But the decisions also raised questions, as the Chief Justice
later did, about the centrality of his discussion of psychological harm.
They deepened the debate about *Brown's* true meaning.

One thing was certain. The great decision of May 17, 1954, was
only the first step on a long journey for American education and for
American society. Next would come the briefs and oral arguments
which led to another *Brown v. Board of Education*—to *Brown II.*

Notes

[1]Felix Frankfurter, "Memorandum for the Conference," December 3,
1953, (cover page). Felix Frankfurter Papers, Harvard Law School Library.

[2]G. Edward White, *Earl Warren: A Public Life* (New York, 1982), pp.
217, 221.

[3]*Ibid.*, p. 218.

[4]Quoted in Bernard Schwartz, *Super Chief* (New York, 1983), p. 86.
Professor Schwartz's great biography contains the most complete account of
the final deliberations leading to *Brown I.*

[5]*Ibid.*

[6]*Ibid.*, pp. 86, 86–87.

[7]Mary Frances Berry, *Stability, Security, and Continuity: Mr. Justice Burton and Decisionmaking in the Supreme Court, 1945–1958* (Westport, Connecticut, 1978), p. 156.

[8]Quoted in Richard Kluger, *Simple Justice* (New York, 1975), p. 609. The
comment was made by E. Barrett Prettyman, Jr., Jackson's law clerk during
the 1953 term.

[9]Felix Frankfurter, Memorandum of January 15, 1954, (cover page).
Frankfurter Papers, Harvard Law School Library.

[10]*Ibid.*, p. 1.

[11]*Ibid.*, p. 2, (Italics added).

[12]*Ibid.*, p. 4.

[13]*Ibid.*, p. 3.

[14]Felix Frankfurter. Notes on Conference of January 16, 1954, p. 1.
Frankfurter Papers, Harvard Law School Library. Professor Schwartz was the
first to use these valuable notes and, equally as important, to decipher them.

[15]*Ibid.*, pp. 3–4.

[16]*Ibid.*, p. 2.

[17]*Ibid.*, p. 3.

[18]Earl Warren, *Memoirs* (Garden City, N.J., 1977), p. 2.

[19]"Memorandum by Mr. Justice Jackson," February 15, 1954, p. 4. Robert H. Jackson Papers, Library of Congress.

[20]*Ibid.*, p. 6.

[21]*Ibid.*, p. 9.

[22]*Ibid.*

[23]*Ibid.*, p. 10.

[24]*Ibid.*, p. 15.

[25]*Ibid.*, p. 14.

[26]*Ibid.*, p. 13.

[27]*Supplemental Brief For the United States on Reargument, Brown* v. *Board of Education*, p. 128.

[28]"Memorandum by Mr. Justice Jackson," March 15, 1954, p. 12. Jackson Papers, Library of Congress.

[29]*Ibid.*, p. 17.

[30]*Ibid.*, p. 18.

[31]Phillip Elman, "The Solicitor General's Office, Justice Frankfurter, and Civil Rights Litigation, 1946–1960: An Oral History," *Harvard Law Review* (Vol. 100, 1987), 841.

[32]"Memorandum by Mr. Justice Jackson," March 15, 1954, (cover page).

[33]Quoted in Richard Kluger, *Simple Justice*, p. 698.

[34]"Memorandum by Mr. Justice Jackson," March 15, 1954, (cover page).

[35]Felix Frankfurter to Stanley Reed, May 20, 1954. Frankfurter Papers, Harvard Law School Library.

[36]*Ibid.*

[37]Stanley Reed to Felix Frankfurter (Undated). Frankfurter Papers, Harvard Law School Library.

[38]Alfred Kelly, *The American Constitution*, Fourth Edition (New York, 1970), p. 925.

[39]*Sweatt* v. *Painter*, 339 US 629 (1950), at 636.

[40]*Brief for Petitioner, Sweatt* v. *Painter*, p. 52.

[41]Richard Kluger, *Simple Justice*, p. 706.

[42]S. Sidney Ulmer, "Earl Warren and the *Brown* Decision," *The Journal of Politics* (Vol. 33, 1971), 689, 693.

[43]James Reston, "A Sociological Decision," *The New York Times*, May 18, 1954, p. 18.

[44]Charles L. Black, Jr., "The Lawfulness of the Segregation Decisions," *The Yale Law Journal* (Vol. 69, 1960), 421, 430.

[45]*Muir* v. *Louisville Park Theatrical Association*, 347 US 971 (1954).

[46]*Mayor of Baltimore* v. *Dawson*, 350 US 877 (1955); *Holmes* v. *Atlanta*, 350 US 879 (1955).

[47]*Gayle* v. *Browder*, 352 US 903 (1956).

I.
Countdown to May 17, 1954

AS THE SUPREME Court moved toward decision in *Brown v. Board of Education*, two of the great Justices of modern American history spelled out their thoughts on school segregation in the privacy of their chambers.

Robert Jackson's memorandum of March 15, 1954, was meant to be made public, if he followed through on a separate concurrence. But a memo written by Felix Frankfurter expressed his very personal thoughts on the issues posed by the school cases. Undated, but probably written in the weeks just after the *Brown* reargument, this document shows how difficult the decision to proscribe segregation was for Frankfurter, how well he knew that it flew in the face of his normal cautions of judicial restraint, but also how utterly convinced he was that such action was necessary, and morally correct. There is no indication that Frankfurter sent this memorandum to any of his Brethren.

The recollections of Frankfurter's close friend Phillip Elman offer some characteristically pungent and brilliant insights into the events of late 1953 and 1954.

1. Memorandum by Justice Robert H. Jackson (March 15, 1954)*

I

Since the close of the Civil War, the United States has been "hesitating between two worlds—one dead, the other powerless to be born."

---

*Robert H. Jackson Papers, Library of Congress.

Constitutions are easier amended than social customs, and even the North never fully conformed its racial practices to its professions.

One whose impressionable years were spent in public schools in a region where Negro pupils were very few and where economic, social and political motives united against segregating them is predisposed to the conclusion that segregation elsewhere has outlived whatever justification it may have had. The practice seems marked for early extinction. Whatever we might say today, within a generation it will be outlawed by decision of this Court because of the forces of mortality and replacement which operate upon it.

Decision of these cases would be simple if our personal opinion that school segregation is morally, economically or politically indefensible made it legally so. But it is not only established in the law of seventeen states and the national capital; it is deeply imbedded in social custom in a large part of this country. Its eradication involves nothing less than a substantial reconstruction of legal institution and of society. It persists because of fears, prides and prejudices which this Court cannot eradicate, which even in the North are latent, and occasionally ignite where the ratio of colored population to white passes a point where the latter vaguely, and perhaps unreasonably, feel themselves insecure.

However sympathetic we may be with the resentments of those who are coerced into segregation, we cannot, in considering a recasting of society by judicial fiat, ignore the claims of those who are to be coerced out of it. We cannot deny the sincerity and passion with which many feel that their blood, lineage and culture are worthy of protection by enforced separatism of races and feel that they have built their segregated institutions for many years on an almost universal understanding that segregation is not constitutionally forbidden.

It has seemed almost instinctive with every race, faith, state or culture to resort to some isolating device to protect and perpetuate those qualities, real or fancied, which it especially values in itself. Separatism, either by voluntary withdrawal or by imposed segregation, has been practiced in some degree by many religions, nationalities and races, and by many—one almost can say all—governments, to alleviate tensions, prevent subversions and to quell or forestall violence. It is today being practiced on a voluntary basis by minorities, who discourage or forbid intermarriage, maintain separate denominational schools, and otherwise seek to prevent contacts which threaten dilution of blood or dissipation of faith. This instinct for self-preservation is enough to account for the prevalence of segregation in several of the Northern states.

But, in the South, the Negro appears to suffer from other antagonisms that are an aftermath of the great American white conflict. The white South harbors in historical memory, with deep resentment, the program of reconstruction and the deep humiliation of carpetbag government imposed by conquest. Whatever other motives were behind these offensive reconstruction measures and whatever their necessity or merit, the North made the Negro their emotional symbol and professed beneficiary, with the natural consequence of identifying him with all that was suffered from his Northern champions. Thus, I am convinced the race problem in the South involves more than mere racial prejudice. It is complicated emotionally with a white war and white politics.

Whether a use of the power of this Court to decree an end of segregation will diminish or increase racial tensions in the South I have no personal experience or knowledge to judge, nor is that my responsibility. But I am satisfied that it would retard acceptance of this decision if the Northern majority of this Court should make a Pharisaic and self-righteous approach to this issue or were inconsiderate of the conditions which have brought about and continued this custom or should permit a needlessly ruthless decree to be promulgated.

The plain fact is that the questions of constitutional interpretation and of the limitations on responsible use of judicial power in a federal system implicit in these cases are as far-reaching as any that have been before the Court since its establishment.

II

Does Existing Law Condemn Segregation?

Layman as well as lawyer must query how it is that the Constitution this morning forbids what for three-quarters of a century it has tolerated or approved. He must further speculate as to how this reversal of its meaning by the branch of the Government supposed not to make new law but only to declare existing law and which has exactly the same constitutional materials that so far as the states are concerned have existed since 1868 and in the case of the District of Columbia since 1791. Can we honestly say that the states which have maintained segregated schools have not, until today, been justified in understanding their practice to be constitutional?

Of course, for over three-quarters of a century majestic and sweeping generalities of the Due Process and Equal Protection Clauses of the Fourteenth Amendment were capable of being read to require a full and equal racial partnership in all matters within the reach of law. . . . Yet, if these texts had such meaning to the age that wrote them, how could the identical Due Process Clause of the Fifth Amendment for half a century have tolerated slavery in the District of Columbia? And when those words were copied into the Fourteenth Amendment and the Equal Protection Clause added, why were they not deemed to assure the Negro the right to vote? . . . It was nearly two years later (1870) when the Fifteenth Amendment was added to assure equal voting rights; but, even then, with the shortcomings of the Fourteenth Amendment obvious, nothing was included as to either segregation or education. Thus, there is no explicit prohibition of segregated schools and it can only be supplied by interpretation. . . .

III

Does the Amendment Contemplate Changed Conditions?

The Fourteenth Amendment does not attempt to say the last word on the concrete application of its pregnant generalities. It declares that "The Congress shall have power to enforce, by appropriate legislation, the provisions of this Article." It thus makes provision for giving effect from time to time to the changes of conditions and public opinion always to be anticipated in a developing society. A policy which it outlines only comprehensively it authorized Congress to complete in detail.

If the Amendment deals at all with state segregation and education, there can be no doubt that it gives Congress a wide discretion to enact legislation on that subject binding on all states and school districts. Admittedly, it explicitly enables Congress from time to time to exercise a wide discretion as to new laws to meet new conditions. The question is how far this Court should leave this subject to be dealt with by legislation, and any answer will have far-reaching implications.

The Court may decide the right of a particular plaintiff in a specific case. . . . But in embarking upon a widespread reform of social customs and habits of countless communities we must face the limitations on the nature and effectiveness of the judicial process.

The futility of effective reform of our society by judicial decree is demonstrated by the history of this very matter. For many years this Court has pronounced the doctrine that, while separate facilities for each race are permissible, they must be equal. Our pronouncement to that effect has remained a dead letter in a large part of the country. Why has the separate-but-equal doctrine declared by this Court so long been a mere promise to the colored ear to be broken to the hope?

It has remained an empty pronouncement because the courts have no power to enforce general declarations of law by applying sanction against any persons not before them in a particular litigation. . . .

I see no reason to expect a pronouncement that segregation is unconstitutional will be any more self-executing or any more efficiently executed than our pronouncement that unequal facilities are unconstitutional. A law suit must be maintained in every school district which shows persistent recalcitrance. . . . That is an effective sanction in a private controversy, but it is a weak reed to rely on in initiating a change in the social system of a large part of the United States. With no machinery except that of the courts to put the power of the Government behind it, it seems likely to result in a failure that will bring the court into contempt and the judicial process into discredit.

The Court can strike down legislation which supports educational segregation, but any constructive policy for abolishing it must come from Congress. Only Congress can enact a policy binding on all states and districts, and it can delegate its supervision to some administrative body provided with standards for determining the conditions under which sanctions should apply. It can make provisions for federal funds where changes required are beyond the means of the community. . . . Moreover, Congress can lift the heavy burden of private litigation from disadvantaged people and make the investigation and administrative proceedings against recalcitrant districts the function of some public agency that would secure enforcement of the policy.

A Court decision striking down state statutes or constitutional provisions which authorize or require segregation will not produce a social transition, nor is the judiciary the agency to which the people should look for that result. Our decision may end segregation in Delaware and Kansas, because there it lingers by a tenuous lease of life. But where the practice really is entrenched, it exists independently of any statute or decision as a local usage and deep-seated custom sustained by the prevailing sentiment of the community. School districts, from habit and conviction, will carry it along without aid of state statutes. To eradicate segregation by judicial action means two generations of litigation.

It is apparent that our decision does not end but begins the struggle over segregation. Representatives of the Negroes contend with great force that if to enter white schools is a right at all it is a present and personal right and that deferred relief may be a denial of rights to those pupils who meanwhile pass school age. Counsel for the states contend that if segregation is abolished at all, the process must be adapted to varying local conditions which will require time and consideration and varying periods of adjustment. . . .

The Department of Justice concedes that uniform and immediate enforcement of a Court decree condemning segregation is impossible. It points out that school districts may have to be consolidated or divided, or their boundaries revised, and the teachers and pupils may have to be transferred. The Government points out that an essential part of the plan will involve placing white children under colored teachers, unless colored teachers are to be dismissed in some areas where they have been hired in substantial numbers. This is one of the most controversial problems of adjustment. . . .

The Government advises that the courts assume this task and that we remand these cases to the District Courts under instructions to proceed with enforcement as rapidly as conditions make it appear practicable. . . .

I will not be a party to thus casting upon the lower courts a burden of continued litigation under circumstances which subject district judges to local pressures and provide them with no standards to justify their decisions to their neighbors, whose opinions they must resist. The Department offers us no standards, and none exist in the law, to determine when and how the school system should be revamped. For the courts to supervise the educational authorities . . . seems to me manifestly beyond judicial power or functions. Our sole authority is to decide an existing case or controversy between the parties. . . . We are urged, however, to supply means to supervise transition of the country from segregated to nonsegregated schools upon the basis that Congress may or probably will refuse to act. That assumes nothing less than that we must act because our representative system has failed. The premise is not a sound basis for judicial action.

IV

The Limits and Basis of Judicial Action

Until today Congress has been justified in believing that segregation does not offend the Constitution. In view of the deference habitually paid by other branches of the Government to this Court's interpretation of the Constitution, it is not unlikely that a considerable part of the inertia of Congress, if not of the country, has been due to the belief that the existing system is constitutional. The necessity for judicial action on this subject arises from the doctrine concerning it which is already on our books.

It is not, in my opinion, necessary or true to say that these earlier judges, many of whom were as sensitive to human values as any of us, were wrong in their own times. With their fundamental premise that the requirement of equal protection does not disable the state from making reasonable classifications of its inhabitants nor impose the obligation to accord identical treatment to all, there can be no quarrel. We still agree that it only requires that the classifications of different groups rest upon real and not upon feigned distinctions, that the distinction have some rational relation to the subject matter for which the classification is adopted. . . .

But the second step in their reasoning, sometimes in reliance on precedents from slave days, sometimes from experience in their own time, was not a legal so much as a factual assumption. It was that there were differences between the Negro and the white races, viewed as a whole, such as to warrant separate classification and discrimination not only for their educational facilities but also for marriage, for access to public places of recreation, amusement or service and as passengers on common carriers and as the right to buy and own real estate.

Whether these early judges were right or wrong in their times I do not know. Certainly in the 1860s and probably throughout the Nineteenth Century the Negro population as a whole was a different people than today. . . . I do not find it necessary to stigmatize as hateful or unintelligent the early assumption that Negro education presented problems that were elementary, special and peculiar and that the mass teaching of Negroes was an experiment not easily tied in with the education of pupils of more favored background. Nor, when I view the progress that was made under it, can I confidently say that the practice of each race pursuing its education apart has been, up to now, wholly to the Negro's disadvantage. . . . Indeed, Negro progress under segregation has been spectacular and, tested by the pace of history, his rise is one of the swiftest and most dramatic advances in the annals of man. It is that, indeed, which has enabled him to outgrow the system and to overcome the presumptions on which it was based.

The handicap of inheritance and environment has been too widely overcome today to warrant these earlier presumptions based on race alone. I do not say that every Negro everywhere is so advanced. . . . But it seems sufficiently general to require me to say that mere possession of colored blood, in whole or in part, no longer affords a reasonable basis for a classification for educational purposes and that each individual must be rated on his own merit. Retarded or subnormal ones, like the same kind of whites, may be accorded separate educational treatment. All that is required is that they be classified as individuals and not as a race for their learning, aptitude and discipline.

Moreover, we cannot ignore the fact that assimilation today has proceeded much beyond where it was at the earlier periods. Blush or shudder, as many will, mixture of blood has been making inroads on segregation faster than change in law. No clear line of separation between the races has been observed. More and more a large population with as much claim to white as to colored blood baffles any justice in classification for segregation.

Nor can we ignore the fact that the concept of the place of public education has markedly changed. Once a privilege conferred on those fortunate enough to take advantage of it, it is now regarded as a right of a citizen and a duty enforced by compulsory education laws. . . .

It is neither novel nor radical doctrine that statutes once held constitutional may become invalid by reason of changing conditions, and those held to be good in one state of facts may be held to be bad in another. A multitude of cases, going back far into judicial history, attest to this doctrine. In recent times, the practical result of several of our decisions has been to nullify the racial classification for many of the purposes as to which it was originally held valid.

I am convinced that present-day conditions require us to strike from our books the doctrine of separate-but-equal facilities and to hold invalid provisions of state constitutions or statutes which classify persons for separate treatment in matters of education based solely on possession of colored blood. . . .

I favor, at the moment, going no farther than to enter a decree that the state constitutions and statutes, relied upon as requiring or authorizing segregation merely on account of race or color, are unconstitutional. I would order a reargument on the contents of our decree and request the Government and each of the parties to submit detailed proposed decrees applicable to each case.

2. Felix Frankfurter—Undated Memorandum*

Only for those who have not the responsibility of decision is it easy to decide these cases. This is so because they present a legal issue inextricably bound up with deep feeling on sharply conflicting social and political issues. The legal issue derives from the established practice of exercising judicial authority when appeal is made to vague provisions in the Civil War Amendments. . . . The inevitable result is that issues are cast in legal form for disposition by this Court that are embroiled in explosive psychological and political attitudes.

However, it is not our duty to express our personal attitudes toward these issues however deep our individual convictions may be. The opposite is true. It is our duty not to express our merely personal views. However passionately any of us may hold egalitarian views, however fiercely any of us may believe that such a policy of segregation as undoubtedly expresses the tenacious conviction of Southern States is both unjust and shortsighted, he travels outside his judicial authority if for this private reason alone he declares unconstitutional the policy of segregation.

Equally so he cannot write into our Constitution a belief in the Negro's natural inferiority or his personal belief of the desirability of segregating white and colored children during their most formative years. To attribute such a view to science, as is sometimes done, is to reject the very basis of science, namely, the process of reaching verifiable conclusions. The abstract and absolutist claims both for and against segregation have been falsified by experience, especially the great changes in the relations between white and colored people since the first World War. The inequities and hardships of a policy of segregation have in the short period of thirty odd years undergone great amelioration. The promising results of this tendency afford no ground for complacency. But it is fair to say that the pace of progress has surprised even those most eager for its promotion.

The outcome of the Civil War, as reflected in the Civil War Amendments, is that there is a single American society. Our colored citizens, like the other components which make up the American nation are not to be denied the right to enjoy the distinctive qualities of their cultural past. But neither are they to be denied the right to grow up with other Americans as part of our national life. And experi-

---

*Felix Frankfurter Papers, Harvard Law School Library.

ence happily shows that contacts tend to mitigate antagonism and engender mutual respect.

The legal problem confronting this Court is the extent to which this desirable and even necessary process of welding a nation out of such diverse elements can be imposed as a matter of law upon the States in disregard of the deeply rooted feeling, tradition and local laws, based upon local situations to the contrary. The basis of such legal compulsion, if the Constitution requires it, is a provision of the Fourteenth Amendment, whereby a State is forbidden to "deny to any person within its jurisdiction the equal protection of the laws."

But the equality of laws enshrined in a constitution which was "made for an undefined and expanding future, and for a people gathered and to be gathered from many nations and of many tongues," *Hurtado* v. *California*, 110 U.S. 516, 530, 531, is not a fixed formula defined with finality at a particular time. It does not reflect, as a congealed summary, the social arrangements and beliefs of a particular epoch. It is addressed to the changes wrought by time and not merely the changes that are the consequences of physical development. Law must respond to transformation of views as well as to that of outward circumstances. The effect of changes in men's feelings for what is right and just is equally relevant in determining whether a discrimination denies the equal protection of the laws.

3. Phillip Elman—"The Solicitor General's Office, Justice Frankfurter, and Civil Rights Litigation"

ELMAN: . . .[T]he word came that Vinson had died, very suddenly. Frankfurter was then in New England where he spent the summer. The Justices all came back to Washington to attend the funeral services. I met Frankfurter, I think at Union Station, and he was in high spirits. I shouldn't really report all this, but this is history and as he used to say, history has its claims. Frankfurter said to me, "I'm in mourning," sarcastically. What he meant was that Vinson's departure from the Court was going to remove the roadblock in *Brown*. As long as Vinson was Chief Justice, they could never get unanimity or anything close to it. If Vinson dissented, Reed would surely join him, Tom Clark probably would too, and Jackson would write that the issue should be left to Congress. Anyway, Frankfurter happily said to me, "I'm in mourning." And, with that viselike grip of his, he grabbed me by the arm and looking me straight in the eye said, "Phil, this is the first solid piece of evidence I've ever had that there really is a God."

Q: That's a piece of bittersweet agnosticism.

ELMAN: He was right. Without God, we never would have had *Brown*, a unanimous decision that racial segregation is unconstitutional. Without God, the Court would have remained bitterly divided, fragmented, unable to decide the issue forthrightly. The winning formula was God plus "all deliberate speed." God won *Brown v. Board of Education*, not Thurgood Marshall or any other lawyer or any other mortal. God intervened. God takes care of drunks, little children, and the American people. He took care of the American people and little children and *Brown* by taking Fred Vinson when He did.

Vinson was replaced by Warren. Warren had no problems with *Brown*. There was now a clear majority because, thanks to "all deliberate speed," the Court could separate the constitutional decision on the merits from what to do about it, the remedy. Jackson could go along with the simple proposition that racial segregation violates the fourteenth amendment and *Plessy* should be overruled. He could go along with that on May 17, 1954, because he thought he would have an opportunity the following year to say, "Well, we've rendered our decision. We've told the Congress what the fourteenth amendment means. Now Congress ought to enforce it."

Q: Jackson's attitude was very cautious. Did you and Frankfurter agree with him?

ELMAN: I remember arguing with Frankfurter. He was very sympathetic to Jackson. Frankfurter felt, for reasons going beyond the segregation cases, that Congress ought to exercise its section five power to enforce the fourteenth amendment, as it later did in the Civil Rights Act of 1964, long after he had moved out of the picture. So he was very sympathetic to the Jackson position.

I used to say to him, "Now look, the fourteenth amendment has been on the books since 1868, and its legislative history shows that it was adopted to remove doubts about the constitutionality of the Civil Rights Act of 1866, which had given black freedmen all the rights of white men in dealing with property and everything else. The blacks were the group for whom the amendment was written; it was intended for their protection. And since 1868, everybody else has come to the Court invoking the protection of the fourteenth amendment. Corporations and Chinese and aliens and everybody else come in and claim they've been denied equal protection of the laws. They come to the Supreme Court of the United States, and you listen to them. And if you find that their rights have been violated, you take care of them. But when the one group for whose protection the fourteenth amendment was adopted, the blacks, comes in and asks you for relief, Jackson wants you to say, 'Yes, your constitutional rights have been violated. But don't come to us. You go across the street and ask Congress to give you relief; we're not going to give you a damn thing. All we're going to do is tell you that your rights have been violated.' How can you do that?"

So that was the trouble with Jackson's position, I think. And Frankfurter was torn. Anyway, Jackson never had a chance to express it, because he died. He came out of the hospital to sit on the bench on May 17th, because he wanted the whole world to see that the Court was unanimous. Of course, you know, Reed dissented until almost the very last day. Warren went to see him. Reed didn't write anything or note his dissent, but he never agreed with the decision.

Well, on May 17, 1954, after holding racial segregation in public schools to be unconstitutional, the Court set the cases down for further reargument on the question of the relief to be ordered. By this time, Simon Sobeloff was Solicitor General, and the third brief we filed was almost an anticlimax; it was essentially the same brief we had written twice before. . . .

Q: You talked about ongoing private conversations with Frankfurter about pending civil rights cases in which you were involved as a lawyer for the government. How do you respond to what I guess might be considered post-Watergate morality—or something of that nature— that could suggest that in a sense, Frankfurter was receiving a government brief all along, from you, to which Davis never had a chance to reply?

ELMAN: Yes, I suppose there's a point there. I have no easy, snappy response to that. In *Brown* I didn't consider myself a lawyer for a litigant. I considered it a cause that transcended ordinary notions about propriety in a litigation. This was not a litigation in the usual sense. The constitutional issue went to the heart of what kind of country we are, what kind of Constitution and Supreme Court we have: whether, almost a century after the fourteenth amendment was adopted, the Court could find the wisdom and courage to hold that the amendment meant what it said, that black people could no longer be singled out and treated differently because of their color, that in everything it did, government had to be color-blind. I don't defend my discussions with Frankfurter; I just did what I thought was right, and I'm sure he didn't give it much thought. I regarded myself, in the literal sense, as an amicus curiae.

The personal relationship that existed between Justice Frankfurter and me was very close. I was his law clerk emeritus, and he regarded me as his law clerk no matter where I was and what I did. That continued to be the case until the day he died. . . .

I don't know whether I mentioned this to you, but over the years— I'm talking now not just about the two years that I was at the Court but about the entire length of our relationship from 1941 to 1965 when he died—the Justice and I would talk on the phone a good deal. He would call me almost every Sunday night at home. He would have gone through the Sunday papers, and after dinner he liked to talk, or *shmoos*, as he would say. We'd have a long, relaxed, gossipy conversation for an hour and a half sometimes. . . .

Q: Did you ever say, "I don't want to know this, I'm not supposed to know it?"

ELMAN: Well, there were certain unspoken restrictions. We never discussed a case that I had argued. Never, other than his calling up my wife afterward and telling her how good or how funny I was or what a great answer I had given to so and so. *Brown v. Board of Education*, which we fully discussed, was an extraordinary case, and the ordinary rules didn't apply. In that case I knew everything, or at least he gave me the impression that I knew everything, that was going on at the Court. He told me about what was said in conference and who said it.

As I look back now, I can see myself in *Brown v. Board of Education* as having been his junior partner, or law clerk emeritus, in helping him work out the best solution for the toughest problem to come before the Court in this century. He succeeded in the end—but it was nip and tuck—and I would like to think that I contributed an important assist.

I'll be immodest. In a letter to McGeorge Bundy dated May 15, 1964, Justice Frankfurter wrote:

> Everyone who is cognizant of the course of litigation which ended in the Supreme Court decision on discrimination in public schools knows that Phil Elman was the real strategist of the litigation. . . . [H]e was largely responsible for blocking the leaders of

the colored people who proposed a remedy which not only would not have succeeded with the Court but, what is even worse, would have had disastrous consequences to the National interest. . . . It was Phil who proposed what the Supreme Court finally decreed, namely, that the Court should not become a school board for the whole country, that the question of how non-discrimination should be brought about should be left primarily to the local school boards, and that any dissatisfaction with their plans should go to the local federal courts.

4. *Brown* v. *Board of Education* (1954)*

Mr. Chief Justice Warren delivered the opinion of the Court.

These cases come to us from the States of Kansas, South Carolina, Virginia, and Delaware. They are premised on different facts and different local conditions, but a common legal question justifies their consideration together in this consolidated opinion.

In each of the cases, minors of the Negro race, through their legal representatives, seek the aid of the courts in obtaining admission to the public schools of their community on a nonsegregated basis. In each instance, they have been denied admission to schools attended by white children under laws requiring or permitting segregation according to race. This segregation was alleged to deprive the plaintiffs of the equal protection of the laws under the Fourteenth Amendment. In each of the cases other than the Delaware case, a three-judge federal district court denied relief to the plaintiffs on the so-called "separate but equal" doctrine announced by this Court in *Plessy* v. *Ferguson*, 163 U.S. 537. Under the doctrine, equality of treatment is accorded when the races are provided substantially equal facilities, even though these facilities be separate. In the Delaware case, the Supreme Court of Delaware adhered to that doctrine, but ordered that the plaintiffs be admitted to the white schools because of their superiority to the Negro schools.

The plaintiffs contend that segregated public schools are not "equal" and cannot be made "equal," and that hence they are deprived of the equal protection of the laws. Because of the obvious importance of the question presented, the Court took jurisdiction. Argument was heard in the 1952 Term, and reargument was heard this Term on certain questions propounded by the Court.

---

*347, US, 483.

Reargument was largely devoted to the circumstances surrounding the adoption of the Fourteenth Amendment in 1868. It covered exhaustively consideration of the Amendment in Congress, ratification by the states, then existing practices in racial segregation, and the views of proponents and opponents of the Amendment. This discussion and our own investigation convince us that, although these sources cast some light, it is not enough to resolve the problem with which we are faced. At best, they are inconclusive. The most avid proponents of the post-War Amendments undoubtedly intended them to remove all legal distinctions among "all persons born or naturalized in the United States." Their opponents, just as certainly, were antagonistic to both the letter and the spirit of the Amendments and wished them to have the most limited effect. What others in Congress and the state legislatures had in mind cannot be determined with any degree of certainty.

An additional reason for the inconclusive nature of the Amendment's history, with respect to segregated schools, is the status of public education at that time. In the South, the movement toward free common schools, supported by general taxation, had not yet taken hold. Education of white children was largely in the hands of private groups. Education of Negroes was almost nonexistent, and practically all of the race were illiterate. In fact, any education of Negroes was forbidden by law in some states. Today, in contrast, many Negroes have achieved outstanding success in the arts and sciences as well as in the business and professional world. It is true that public school education at the time of the Amendment had advanced further in the North, but the effect of the Amendment on Northern States was generally ignored in the congressional debates. Even in the North, the conditions of public education did not approximate those existing today. The curriculum was usually rudimentary; ungraded schools were common in rural areas; the school term was but three months a year in many states; and compulsory school attendance was virtually unknown. As a consequence, it is not surprising that there should be so little in the history of the Fourteenth Amendment relating to its intended effect on public education.

In the first cases in this Court construing the Fourteenth Amendment, decided shortly after its adoption, the Court interpreted it as proscribing all state-imposed discriminations against the Negro race. The doctrine of "separate but equal" did not make its appearance in this Court until 1896 in the case of Plessy v. Ferguson, supra, involving not education but transportation. American courts have since labored with the doctrine for over half a century. In this Court, there have been six cases involving the "separate but equal" doctrine in the field of public education. In *Cumming* v. *County Board of Education*, 175 U.S. 528, and *Gong Lum* v. *Rice*, 275 U.S. 78, the validity of the doctrine itself was not challenged. In more recent cases, all on the graduate school level, inequality was found in that specific benefits enjoyed by white students were denied to Negro students of the same educational qualifications. *Missouri ex rel. Gaines* v. *Canada*, 305 U.S. 337; *Sipuel* v. *Oklahoma*, 332 U.S. 631; *Sweatt* v. *Painter*, 339 U.S. 629; *McLaurin* v. *Oklahoma State Regents*, 339 U.S. 637. In none of these cases was it necessary to re-examine the doctrine to grant relief to the Negro plaintiff. And in *Sweatt* v. *Painter, supra*, the Court expressly reserved decision on the question whether *Plessy* v. *Ferguson* should be held inapplicable to public education.

In the instant cases, that question is directly presented. Here, unlike *Sweatt* v. *Painter*, there are findings below that the Negro and white schools involved have been equalized, or are being equalized, with respect to buildings, curricula, qualifications and salaries of teachers, and other "tangible" factors. Our decision, therefore, cannot turn on merely a comparison of these tangible factors in the Negro and white schools involved in each of the cases. We must look instead to the effect of segregation itself on public education.

In approaching this problem, we cannot turn the clock back to 1868 when the Amendment was adopted, or even to 1896 when *Plessy* v. *Ferguson* was written. We must consider public education in the light of its full development and its present place in American life throughout the Nation. Only in this way can it be determined if segregation in public schools deprives these plaintiffs of the equal protection of the laws.

Today, education is perhaps the most important function of state and local governments. Compulsory school attendance laws and the great expenditures for education both demonstrate our recognition of the importance of education to our democratic society. It is required in the performance of our most basic public responsibilities, even service in the armed forces. It is the very foundation of good citizenship. Today it is a principal instrument in awakening the child to cultural values, in preparing him for later professional training, and in helping him to adjust normally to his environment. In these days, it is doubtful that any child may reasonably be expected to succeed in life if he is denied the opportunity of an education. Such an opportunity, where the state has undertaken to provide it, is a right which must be made available to all on equal terms.

We come then to the question presented: Does segregation of children in public schools solely on the basis of race, even though the physical facilities and other "tangible" factors may be equal, deprive the children of the minority group of equal educational opportunities? We believe that it does.

In *Sweatt v. Painter, supra*, in finding that a segregated law school for Negroes could not provide them equal educational opportunities, this Court relied in large part on "those qualities which are incapable of objective measurement but which make for greatness in a law school." In *McLaurin v. Oklahoma State Regents, supra*, the Court, in requiring that a Negro admitted to a white graduate school be treated like all other students, again resorted to intangible considerations: ". . . his ability to study, to engage in discussions and exchange views with other students, and, in general, to learn his profession." Such considerations apply with added force to children in grade and high schools. To separate them from others of similar age and qualifications solely because of their race generates a feeling of inferiority as to their status in the community that may affect their hearts and minds in a way unlikely ever to be undone. The effect of this separation on their educational opportunities was well stated by a finding in the Kansas case by a court which nevertheless felt compelled to rule against the Negro plaintiffs:

> Segregation of white and colored children in public schools has a detrimental effect upon the colored children. The impact is greater when it has the sanction of the law; for the policy of separating the races is usually interpreted as denoting the inferiority of the negro group. A sense of inferiority affects the motivation of the child to learn. Segregation with the sanction of law, therefore, has a tendency to [retard] the educational and mental development of negro children and to deprive them of some of the benefits they would receive in a racial[ly] integrated school system.

Whatever may have been the extent of psychological knowledge at the time of *Plessy v. Ferguson*, this finding is amply supported by modern authority.* Any language in *Plessy v. Ferguson* contrary to this finding is rejected.

---

*K. B. Clark, *Effect of Prejudice and Discrimination on Personality Development* (Midcentury White House Conference on Children and Youth, 1950); Witmer and

We conclude that in the field of public education the doctrine of "separate but equal" has no place. Separate educational facilities are inherently unequal. Therefore, we hold that the plaintiffs and others similarly situated for whom the actions have been brought are, by reason of the segregation complained of, deprived of the equal protection of the laws guaranteed by the Fourteenth Amendment. This disposition makes unnecessary any discussion whether such segregation also violates the Due Process Clause of the Fourteenth Amendment.

Because these are class actions, because of the wide applicability of this decision, and because of the great variety of local conditions, the formulation of decrees in these cases presents problems of considerable complexity. On reargument, the consideration of appropriate relief was necessarily subordinated to the primary question—the constitutionality of segregation in public education. We have now announced that such segregation is a denial of the equal protection of the laws. In order that we may have the full assistance of the parties in formulating decrees, the cases will be restored to the docket, and the parties are requested to present further argument on Questions 4 and 5 previously propounded by the Court for the reargument this Term. The Attorney General of the United States is again invited to participate. The Attorneys General of the states requiring or permitting segregation in public education will also be permitted to appear as amici curiae upon request to do so by September 15, 1954, and submission of briefs by October 1, 1954.

It is so ordered.

Kotinsky, *Personality in the Making* (1952), Ch. VI; Deutscher and Chein, *The Psychological Effects of Enforced Segregation: A Survey of Social Science Opinion, Journal of Psychology*, Vol. 26, p. 259 (1948); Chein, *What Are the Psychological Effects of Segregation Under Conditions of Equal Facilities?*, 3 *Int J Opinion and Attitude Res* 229 (1949); Brameld, *Educational Costs*, in *Discrimination and National Welfare* (MacIver, ed, 1949), 44–48; Frazier, *The Negro in the United States* (1949), 674–681. And see generally Myrdal, *An American Dilemma* (1944).

II.
The Debate Over *Brown*

THE CHIEF JUSTICE'S opinion in *Brown* v. *Board of Education* seemed buttressed on the findings of social psychology; yet the brief decisions on parks and golf courses and transportation suggested otherwise. A series of seminal articles in the decade following *Brown* explored these conflicting signals.

Thus Professor Herbert Wechsler of Columbia Law School argued that Warren's findings of psychological harm were central to the opinion, and seriously undermined its credibility. Professor Louis Pollak of Yale Law School (now a federal district judge) sought to rewrite the opinion in a way which would avoid these shortcomings.

Others, however, claimed that there were no shortcomings that needed addressing. Professor John Kaplan of Stanford took the view that *Brown* had in fact realized the fondest hopes of the appellants: it declared segregative categories in education, and by implication elsewhere, to be unconstitutional *per se*. Any discussion of psychological harm, therefore, was basically superfluous. Charles Black brilliantly articulated the view that if evidence of psychological harm was essential to the outcome in *Brown*, the harm was self-evident, and needed no experimental gloss put upon it. A reading of *An American Dilemma* would suffice.

In 1965, Owen Fiss, now Alexander Bickel Professor of Public Law at Yale, took the controversy in a new direction. He argued that for better or worse the Court had accepted empirical psychological findings in *Brown*, and that these findings were potentially applicable to *any* type of racial or ethnic segregation in public schools—whether such segregation was formally imposed by law or not.

1. Herbert Wechsler—"Toward Neutral Principles of Constitutional Law" (1959)*

. . . I come to the school decision, which for one of my persuasion stirs the deepest conflict. . . . Yet I would surely be engaged in playing Hamlet without Hamlet if I did not try to state the problems that appear to me to be involved.

The problem for me, I hardly need to say, is not that the Court departed from its earlier decisions holding or implying that the equality of public educational facilities demanded by the Constitution could be met by separate schools. I stand with the long tradition of the Court that previous decisions must be subject to reexamination when a case against their reasoning is made. Nor is the problem that the Court disturbed the settled patterns of a portion of the country; even that must be accepted as a lesser evil than nullification of the Constitution. Nor is it that history does not confirm that an agreed purpose of the fourteenth amendment was to forbid separate schools or that there is important evidence that many thought the contrary; the words are general and leave room for expanding content as time passes and conditions change. Nor is it that the Court may have miscalculated the extent to which its judgment would be honored or accepted; it is not a prophet of the strength of our national commitment to respect the judgments of the courts. Nor is it even that the Court did not remit the issue to the Congress, acting under the enforcement clause of the amendment. That was a possible solution, to be sure, but . . . it would merely have evaded the claims made.

The problem inheres strictly in the reasoning of the opinion, an opinion which is often read with less fidelity by those who praise it than by those by whom it is condemned. The Court did not declare, as many wish it had, that the fourteenth amendment forbids all racial lines in legislation, though subsequent per curiam decisions may, as I have said, now go that far. Rather, as Judge Hand observed,* the separate-but-equal formula was not overruled "in form" but was held to have "no place" in public education on the ground that segregated schools are "inherently unequal," with deleterious effects upon the colored children in implying their inferiority, effects which retard their educational and mental development. So, indeed, the district court had found as a fact in the Kansas case, a finding which the

*Harvard Law Review, Vol. 73, 1, 1959.
*Learned Hand, The Bill of Rights (1958), p. 54.

Supreme Court embraced, citing some further "modern authority" in its support.

Does the validity of the decision turn then on the sufficiency of evidence or of judicial notice to sustain a finding that the separation harms the Negro children who may be involved? There were, indeed, some witnesses who expressed that opinion in the Kansas case, as there were also witnesses in the companion Virginia case, including Professor Garrett of Columbia, whose view was to the contrary. Much depended on the question that the witness had in mind, which rarely was explicit. Was he comparing the position of the Negro child in a segregated school with his position in an integrated school where he was happily accepted and regarded by the whites; or was he comparing his position under separation with that under integration where the whites were hostile to his presence and found ways to make their feelings known? And if the harm that segregation worked was relevant, what of the benefits that it entailed: sense of security, the absence of hostility? Were they irrelevant? Moreover, was the finding in Topeka applicable without more to Clarendon County, South Carolina, with 2,799 colored students and only 295 whites? Suppose that more Negroes in a community preferred separation than opposed it? Would that be relevant to whether they were hurt or aided by segregation as opposed to integration? Their fates would be governed by the change of system quite as fully as those of the students who complained.

I find it hard to think the judgment really turned upon the facts. Rather, it seems to me, it must have rested on the view that racial segregation is, in principle, a denial of equality to the minority against whom it is directed; that is, the group that is not dominant politically and, therefore, does not make the choice involved. For many who support the Court's decision this assuredly is the decisive ground. But this position also presents problems. . . . Is it . . . defensible to make the measure of validity of legislation the way it is interpreted by those who are affected by it? In the context of a charge that segregation *with equal facilities* is a denial of equality, is there not a point in *Plessy* in the statement that if "enforced separation stamps the colored race with a badge of inferiority" it is solely because its members choose "to put that construction upon it"? Does enforced separation of the sexes discriminate against females merely because it may be the females who resent it and it is imposed by judgments predominantly male? Is a prohibition of miscegenation a discrimination against the colored member of the couple who would like to marry?

For me, assuming equal facilities, the question posed by state-enforced segregation is not one of discrimination at all. Its human and its constitutional dimensions lie entirely elsewhere, in the denial by the state of freedom to associate, a denial that impinges in the same way on any groups or races that may be involved. I think, and I hope not without foundation, that the Southern white also pays heavily for segregation, not only in the sense of guilt that he must carry but also in the benefits he is denied. In the days when I was joined with Charles H. Houston in a litigation in the Supreme Court, before the present building was constructed, he did not suffer more than I in knowing that we had to go to Union Station to lunch together during the recess. . . .

But if the freedom of association is denied by segregation, integration forces an association upon those for whom it is unpleasant or repugnant. Is this not the heart of the issue involved, a conflict in human claims of high dimension, not unlike many others that involve the highest freedoms. . . . Given a situation where the state must practically choose between denying the association to those individuals who wish it or imposing it on those who would avoid it, is there a basis in neutral principles for holding that the Constitution demands that the claims for association should prevail? I should like to think there is, but I confess that I have not yet written the opinion. To write it is for me the challenge of the school-segregation cases.

2. Louis H. Pollak—"Racial Discrimination and Judicial Integrity: A Reply to Professor Wechsler"*

If Professor Wechsler's criticisms were simply addressed to the form of the Court's opinion in *Brown*, one would be hard put to dispute them. Certainly the opinion is most obscure in its crucial elements. . . . Moreover, the opinion does not appear to articulate any grounds for disposing of the arguably quite different issues—segregated beaches, golf courses, buses, and parks—subsequently resolved . . . in apparent reliance on *Brown*.

But Professor Wechsler goes further. He suggests that the problem in *Brown* is not one of discrimination at all, for both races are disadvantaged and the burden of guilt surely falls more heavily on whites

University of Pennsylvania Law Review, Vol. 108, 1, 1959.

than on Negroes. The real legal issue, Professor Wechsler believes, is a claim of right of association balanced against an equal and opposite claim of right of nonassociation. Seeing the issue this way, he seems to suggest that no supportable opinion could have been written in *Brown*—or at least that writing such an opinion is a "challenge" not yet successfully met. Faced with this challenge, perhaps one who supports the judgment but confesses dissatisfaction with the opinion rendered has some obligation to draft what he regards as an adequate opinion:

> "These four consolidated cases, which come to us from three federal district courts and one state supreme court, present a single question: the compatibility with the Fourteenth Amendment's equal protection clause of state laws which require, or permit local authorities to require, segregation of white and Negro school children in compulsory public schools. The courts below all sustained the challenged laws; but there was division among them on the subsidiary issue whether it is harmful to Negro children, in whose behalf these class actions were brought, to shunt them off on racial grounds to schools which are the equivalent in every non-racial dimension of the white schools from which they are barred. (In the Delaware case, the . . . court found that, quite apart from racial separation, the Negro school was not the equivalent of the white schools.). . . .
>
> "It is . . . urged upon us that the extensive research into the history of the Fourteenth Amendment's adoption, so diligently conducted by counsel at our request, fails to disclose any intent on the part of the framers to end segregation in public schools. We think it is true, but not of itself dispositive. For one thing, it is familiar constitutional history that this Court has progressively brought within the ambit of the Fourteenth Amendment many issues and many litigants probably not contemplated by those who framed and ratified the Amendment. Moreover—and of more immediate moment—we read the history of the Amendment as contemplating an essentially dynamic development by Congress and this Court of the liberties outlined in such generalized terms in the Amendment.
>
> "Next it is argued that the precise question at issue has already been disposed of by this Court in *Plessy v. Ferguson*, 163 U.S. 537. In response it is said that *Plessy* dealt with segregation on intrastate railways, and is distinguishable. We think it is not possible to ignore this Court's heavy reliance, in sustaining the segregation challenged in *Plessy*, on what it regarded as the manifest validity of segregated public schools. But we do not doubt our power, or indeed our obligation, to re-examine grave constitutional questions in a proper case. Given the finality of constitu-

tional determinations, they must always be 'open to reconsideration, in the light of new experience and greater knowledge and wisdom.' 317 U.S. XLII, XLVII (Remarks of Chief Justice Stone on the death of Justice Brandeis). And this is especially true when the constitutional provisions at issue are themselves of an evolutionary generality. . . .

"On the issue of the reasonableness of governmentally imposed distinctions between whites and Negroes, as well as on the issue of whether harm accrues to either group through enforced separation, we have been deluged with scholarly writings. These writings supplement extensive testimony which is of record in some, but not all, of the cases before us. Learned and impressive authority is deeply engaged on both sides of these twin issues. Were it our function to assess what has been put before us, we would find ourselves unpersuaded that there are demonstrable differences other than those of pigment between whites and Negroes, or that any state policy other than the impermissible one of nourishing race prejudice (see *Hirabayashi* v. *United States*, 320 U.S. 81) underlies the requirement that the races be separated. Moreover, we would be inclined to surmise that governmental separation of the races sets in motion grievous consequences for whites and Negroes alike.

"But, assuming we were competent to make such judgments, we do not think we are called on to do so in order to determine the issues presently tendered. For we start from the base point that in the United States 'all legal restrictions which curtail the civil rights of a single racial group are immediately suspect.' *Korematsu* v. *United States*, 323 U.S. 214, 216. Certainly legislation cast in such terms is not entitled to the ordinary presumptions of validity. On the contrary there is special need for 'a searching judicial inquiry into the legislative judgment in situations where prejudice against discrete and insular minorities may tend to curtail the operation of those political processes ordinarily to be relied on to protect minorities.' Justice Stone dissenting in *Minersville School District* v. *Gobitis*, 310 U.S. 586, 606. See *United States* v. *Carolene Products*, 304 U.S. 144, 152, n.4. We could not, therefore, sustain the reasonableness of these racial distinctions and the absence of harm said to flow from them, unless we were prepared to say that no factual case can be made the other way. As indicated above, we are not prepared to say this.

"We have said that we do not think it incumbent upon us, at least for present purposes, to resolve controversies as to the justification for and impact of Jim Crow legislation. But we would be less than candid if we failed to acknowledge that denial of the degrading effects of such legislation seems to us to border on the disingenuous:

'[T]he Jim Crow laws applied to *all* Negroes—not merely to
the rowdy, or drunken, or surly, or ignorant ones. The new laws
did not countenance the old conservative tendency to distinguish
between classes of the race, to encourage the "better" element,
and to draw it into a white alliance. Those laws backed up the
Alabamian who told the disfranchising convention of his state that
no Negro in the world was the equal of "the least, poorest, lowest-
down white man I ever knew." . . . The Jim Crow laws put the
authority of the state or city in the voice of the street-car conductor, the railway brakeman, the bus driver, the theater usher, and
also into the voice of the hoodlum of the public parks and play-
grounds. They gave free rein and the majesty of the law to mass
aggressions that might otherwise have been curbed, blunted, or
deflected.

'The Jim Crow laws, unlike federal laws, did not assign the
subordinate group a fixed status in society. They were constantly
pushing the Negro further down.' C. Vann Woodward, *The
Strange Career of Jim Crow*, p. 93.

'All others can see and understand this. How can we properly
shut our minds to it?' *Bailey* v. *Drexel Furniture Co.*, 259 U.S.
20, 37. We see little room for doubt that it is the function of Jim
Crow laws to make identification as a Negro a matter of stigma.
Such governmental denigration is a form of injury the Constitution recognizes and will protect against. . . .

"We have ventured to disclose our intuitions about issues hotly
controverted by those social scientists professionally entitled to
have opinions. We would think it corrosive of the judicial function were we to translate our amateur wisdom into constitutional
imperatives. Fortunately, disposition of these cases does not require us to pursue such a ruinous course. Suffice it here to conclude that the constitutional doubts instantly generated by statutes
drawing racial lines have not been allayed. . . .

"In support of what we deem to be the well-founded contention
that governmentally imposed segregation carries with it a stigma
directed at the segregated group, plaintiffs have placed great emphasis on the aggravated onus of segregation imposed in facilities—such as public schools here at issue—which the segregated
group is *required* to utilize. We do not find it necessary to make
a present determination whether segregation by law could be
sustained in state facilities made available for the voluntary use
of its citizens—public parks, for example. That case is not now
before us. It may, however, be appropriate to observe that where
facilities are voluntary the community's asserted need to ordain
segregation seems even less weighty than in the cases before us:
for under such circumstances those for whom racial mingling is
obnoxious are under no obligation to attend. What deserves present mention, however, is that defendants likewise take comfort

from the compulsory character of school attendance laws. This factor is said to constitute a special ground for sustaining state imposed segregation. We are told that invalidation of required segregation in public schools arbitrarily elevates plaintiffs' claim of right not to be separated on racial lines above an equally weighty claim of right of others, both white and Negro, not to be compelled to mingle. But we think the contention fails. To the extent that implementation of this decision forces racial mingling on school children against their will, or against the will of their parents, this consequence follows because the community through its political processes has chosen and may continue to choose compulsory education—just as, from time to time, the nation has, through federal legislation, adopted the principle of coerced association implicit in a draft army. In neither instance can the coercion be said to emanate from this Court or from the Constitution. In any event, parents sufficiently disturbed at the prospect of having their children educated in democratic fashion in company with their peers are presumably entitled to fulfill their educational responsibilities in other ways. . . .

"Finally, we are warned that a departure from *Plessy* v. *Ferguson* will be accompanied by vast social unrest—that the principle of mandatory racial separation is so ingrained in southern life that relaxation of it will promote widespread discord between and within the races. Nevertheless, 'important as is the preservation of the public peace, this aim cannot be accomplished by laws or ordinances which deny rights created or protected by the federal Constitution.' *Buchanan* v. *Warley*, 245 U.S. 60.

"Accordingly the judgments below, except for that in the Delaware case, must be reversed. But the form and timing of the mandates appropriate in these cases present problems of such magnitude that we will for the present withhold the entry of judgments and continue the cases on our docket to permit further argument relating to these procedural questions. . . ."

A draft opinion, prepared in hindsight by one who has no responsibility to decide, is only an academic exercise designed to prove a point. The fateful national consequences of *Brown* v. *Board of Education* flow from the opinion and judgment actually rendered. Professor Wechsler, sympathetic to the result but skeptical of the rationale, is frankly uncertain of history's verdict. . . . But some are bold enough—or fool-hardy enough—to make the prophecy Professor Wechsler eschews: the judgment in the segregation cases will as the decades pass give ever deeper meaning to our national life. It will endure as long as our Constitution and our democratic faith endure.

3. John Kaplan—"Segregation Litigation and the Schools," Part II: "The General Northern Problem" (1963)*

The "Meaning" of *Brown.* . . .

To say that the Supreme Court found as a psychological and sociological fact that separate schools were harmful to Negro children and were therefore unconstitutional is to blur the distinctions among the possible rationales open to the Court. The language in the Court's opinion which can be read as implying that inequality, as distinguished from mere separation, caused the unconstitutionality must be considered in the light of the Supreme Court's treatment of segregation over the years. Since the Court apparently was not prepared flatly to overrule *Plessy* v. *Ferguson* at that time, it was necessary to show that even under the *Plessy* rule the plaintiffs in *Brown* and the other segregation cases would have to prevail. The stipulation of the parties, however, that the Negro and white schools were equal with respect to all tangible facilities limited the Court to consideration of intangibles of the type discussed in *Sweatt* v. *Painter* and in *McLaurin* v. *Oklahoma State Regents.* It was in this context that the Court found separate schools inherently unequal and the separate but equal doctrine hence inapplicable in the field of public education. One should remember that, under *Plessy,* only equality of facilities saved the segregation from being unconstitutional. The Court there was not concerned with what it regarded as unequal treatment and went to some pains to show that the Negro was being treated equally, even though he was segregated because he was a Negro. When this equality did not exist— as it did not, in *Brown*—it was the differential treatment accorded to Negroes as Negroes, not the inequality of facilities, that violated the fourteenth amendment.

A reference to the facts of the case of *McLaurin* v. *Oklahoma State Regents* makes this reasoning somewhat more clear. In *McLaurin,* all facilities were equal, indeed identical, except for the fact that school authorities on the basis of race prevented the plaintiff from normal contact with his schoolmates. Certainly, the mere fact that one person is denied the right to associate in school with other persons cannot be

---

Northwestern University Law Review, Vol. 58, 157, 1963.

said to be a constitutional violation. Unless a school authority operates only one school it must always divide the school population in some way or other and thus prevent some students from having contact with some others. In some ways a student in one school might even be harmed by his inability to associate with students in another. But even such harm would not mean that the separation was constitutionally prohibited. The *McLaurin* case merely stood for the principle that, at least in higher education, *race* might not be made the criterion for separation of one group of students from another. The practical positions of the two races in the United States made it clear that this very separation made the two groups unequal, and thus outside of the rule of *Plessy* v. *Ferguson.* In the *Brown* case, the Court merely took the view that the *McLaurin* principle was equally applicable to segregated education in the grade and high schools, and that, as in *McLaurin,* it was the racial separation, rather than any inequality of facilities or other educational benefits, that was the essence of the plaintiffs' claim. This view explains the Court's language that "such considerations apply with added force" to children in grade and high schools because of the psychological harm these children suffer. The Court was asserting that *Brown* was in a sense an easier case than *McLaurin* and *Sweatt* v. *Painter,* where this type of harm to young children was not to be expected, rather than to show that harm to Negro children or inequality of schools was the essence of the constitutional violation. To highlight this principle one might ask, "Since when are unequal schools per se unconstitutional?" The Supreme Court has never held that in the absence of some racial classification the mere inequality of one school compared with another involves a constitutional violation. In many communities one school is clearly better in terms of faculty, student body, physical facilities, and prestige, than others, yet no one has suggested that this inequality raises a federal constitutional question. If pure inequality were the essence of the constitutional violation, such schools might in some ways be much more unequal and inferior than many Negro schools segregated by force of law.

This view of *Brown* is reinforced by examining the type of evidence that was available to the Court on the question of the actual harm visited upon Negro children by school segregation. Several commentators have pointed out that though a large quantity of expert testimony was introduced as evidence in the cases and in briefs, it was by no means sufficiently definite, unambiguous, uncontradicted, or sweeping to allow the Court to find as a fact, irrefutable in all future cases, that regardless of the area or social climate, even deliberate state-imposed segregation in schools would work such harm on Negro children as to require a finding of unconstitutionality. Subsequent cases disposed of by the Court without a written opinion support this view of the *Brown* case even more clearly. These cases, striking down segregation on golf courses and in parks, where not an iota of evidence indicated the existence of the harm described in the *Brown* case, seem to indicate that it was not the inequality of facilities or the harm which caused the constitutional violation, but rather the separateness by state classification. Thus, *Plessy* held that racial classifications did not offend the Constitution so long as they did not cause some type of harm. *McLaurin* and *Brown* found the necessary harm inherent in the separation by racial classification in education, and subsequent cases have dispensed with the necessity for showing any harm at all so long as racial classifications are drawn by state authority.

4. Charles L. Black—"The Lawfulness of the Segregation Decisions" (1960)*

If the cases outlawing segregation were wrongly decided, then they ought to be overruled. One can go further: if dominant professional opinion ever forms and settles on the belief that they were wrongly decided, then they will be overruled, slowly or all at once, openly or silently. The insignificant error, however palpable, can stand, because the convenience of settlement outweighs the discomfort of error. But the hugely consequential error cannot stand and does not stand.*

There is pragmatic meaning then, there is call for action, in the suggestion that the segregation cases cannot be justified.† In the long run, as a corollary, there is practical and not merely intellectual significance in the question whether these cases were rightly decided. I think they were rightly decided, by overwhelming weight of reason, and I intend here to say why I hold this belief.

*Reprinted by permission of The Yale Law Journal Company and Fred B. Rothman & Company from *The Yale Law Journal*, Vol. 69, 421–430.
*Cf. Pollak, *Racial Discrimination and Judicial Integrity: A Reply to Professor Wechsler*, 108 U. Pa. L. Rev. 1, 31 (1959). I am indebted throughout to this Article, though the rationale I offer in support of the decisions differs from Professor Pollak's. His, however, seems to me a sound alternative ground for the desegregation holdings.
†See Wechsler, *Toward Neutral Principles of Constitutional Law*, 73 Harv. L. Rev. 1, 34 (1959). The present Article was immediately suggested by Professor Wechsler's questionings. It is not, however, to be looked upon as formal "reply," since I cover

My liminal difficulty is rhetorical—or, perhaps more accurately, one of fashion. Simplicity is out of fashion, and the basic scheme of reasoning on which these cases can be justified is awkwardly simple. First, the equal protection clause of the fourteenth amendment should be read as saying that the Negro race, as such, is not to be significantly disadvantaged by the laws of the states. Secondly, segregation is a massive intentional disadvantaging of the Negro race, as such, by state law. No subtlety at all. Yet I cannot disabuse myself of the idea that that is really all there is to the segregation cases. If both these propositions can be supported by the preponderance of argument, the cases were rightly decided. If they cannot be so supported, the cases are in perilous condition.

As a general thing, the first of these propositions has so far as I know never been controverted in a holding of the Supreme Court. I rest here on the solid sense of *The Slaughterhouse Cases* and of *Strauder* v. *West Virginia*,* where Mr. Justice Strong said of the fourteenth amendment:

> It ordains that no State shall make or enforce any laws which shall abridge the privileges or immunities of citizens of the United States (evidently referring to the newly made citizens, who, being citizens of the United States, are declared to be also citizens of the State in which they reside). It ordains that no State shall deprive any person of life, liberty, or property, without due process of law, or deny to any person within its jurisdiction the equal protection of the laws. What is this but declaring that the law in the States shall be the same for the black as for the white; that all persons, whether colored or white, shall stand equal before the laws of the States, and, in regard to the colored race, for whose protection the amendment was primarily designed, that no discrimination shall be made against them by law because of their color? The words of the amendment, it is true, are prohibitory, but they contain a necessary implication of a positive immunity, or right, most valuable to the colored race,—the right to exemption from unfriendly legislation against them distinctively as colored,—exemption from legal discriminations, implying inferiority in civil society, lessening the security of their enjoyment of the rights which others enjoy, and discriminations which are steps towards reducing them to the condition of a subject race. (at 307–8)

---

here only one part of the ground he goes over, and since my lines of thought are only partly responsive in terms to the questions as he sees them.
*83 U.S. (16 Wall.) 36 (1873); 100 U.S. 303 (1880).

If *Plessy* v. *Ferguson* be thought a faltering from this principle, I step back to the principle itself. But the *Plessy* Court clearly conceived it to be its task to show that segregation did not really disadvantage the Negro, except through his own choice. * There is in this no denial of the *Slaughterhouse* and *Strauder* principle; the fault of *Plessy* is in the psychology and sociology of its minor premise.

The lurking difficulty lies not in "racial" cases but in the total philosophy of "equal protection" in the wide sense. "Equal protection," as it applies to the whole of state law, must be consistent with the imposition of disadvantage on some, for all law imposes disadvantage on some; to give driver's licenses only to good drivers is to disadvantage bad drivers. Thus the word "reasonable" necessarily finds its way into "equal protection," in the application of the latter concept to law in general. And it is inevitable, and right, that "reasonable," in this broader context, should be given its older sense of "supportable by reasoned considerations." "Equal" thereby comes to mean not really "equal," but "equal unless a fairly tenable reason exists for inequality."

But the whole tragic background of the fourteenth amendment forbids the feedback infection of its central purpose with the necessary qualifications that have attached themselves to its broader and so largely accidental radiations. It may have been intended that "equal protection" go forth into wider fields than the racial. But history puts it entirely out of doubt that the chief and all-dominating purpose was to ensure equal protection for the Negro. And this intent can hardly be given the self-defeating qualification that necessity has written on equal protection as applied to carbonic gas. If it is, then "equal protection" for the Negro means "equality until a tenable reason for inequality is proffered." On this view, Negroes may hold property, sign wills, marry, testify in court, walk the streets, go to (even segregated) school, ride public transportation, and so on, only in the event that no reason, not clearly untenable, can be assigned by a state legislature for their not being permitted to do these things. That cannot have been what all the noise was about in 1866.

---

*"We consider the underlying fallacy of the plaintiff's argument to consist in the assumption that the enforced separation of the two races stamps the colored race with a badge of inferiority. *If this be so, it is not by reason of anything found in the act, but solely because the colored race chooses to put that construction upon it.*" at 551. (Emphasis added.) The curves of callousness and stupidity intersect at their respective maxima.

What the fourteenth amendment, in its historical setting, must be read to say is that the Negro is to enjoy equal protection of the laws, and that the fact of his being a Negro is not to be taken to be a good enough reason for denying him this equality, however "reasonable" that might seem to some people. All possible arguments, however convincing, for discriminating against the Negro, were finally rejected by the fourteenth amendment.

It is sometimes urged that a special qualification was written on the concept of "equality" by the history of the adoption of the amendment—that an intent can be made out to exclude segregation from those legal discriminations invalidated by the requirement of equality, whether or not it actually works inequality. This point has been discussed and documented by Professor Alexander Bickel, who, though he finds convincing arguments for the conclusion that school segregation was not among the evils the framers of the amendment intended for immediate correction, suggests that they intended at the same time to set up a general concept for later concrete application. Other recent writers take somewhat similar views. The data brought forward by Professor Bickel do not seem to me as persuasive, on his first point, as they do to him.* But in supporting his second point he develops a line of thought tending to establish that the legislative history does not render the segregation decisions improper, and I am glad to join him in that practical conclusion. I would add only one point: The question of the "intent" of the men of 1866 on segregation *as we know it* calls for a far chancier guess than is commonly supposed, for they were unacquainted with the institution as it prevails in the American South

---

*Actually, the question of my dissent from Professor Bickel's conclusions depends on their exact meaning. In his data I find, to be sure, a case for concluding that the relevant people did not "intend" to abolish segregation, in the sense that they had no positive and consciously formed intention of doing so. That conclusion means little when one is dealing with general language. I am not convinced that a sufficient equivalency is made out between the Civil Rights Bill and the fourteenth amendment (there being no relevant legislative history whatever on the amendment as such) to justify attaching the bill's history to the amendment for the purpose of establishing a definitely formed intent to exclude segregation from the prohibitive ambit of the amendment's general words—a totally different meaning of the predicate "did not intend." The motive for insertion of the present equal protection clause seems to me, on Professor Bickel's evidence, simply mysterious. *Cf.* Fairman, *Does the Fourteenth Amendment Incorporate the Bill of Rights?*, 2 Stan. L. Rev. 5, 41 (1949). Obviously, the development, qualification, and support of these points would call for more discussion than is warrantable in the present context, given the practical agreement in which Professor Bickel and I (as I believe) find ourselves.

today. To guess their verdict upon the institution as it functions in the midtwentieth century supposes an imaginary hypothesis which grows more preposterous as it is sought to be made more vivid. They can in the nature of the case have bequeathed us only their generalities; the specifics lay unborn as they disbanded. I do not understand Professor Bickel to hold a crucially different view.

Then does segregation offend against equality? Equality, like all general concepts, has marginal areas where philosophic difficulties are encountered. But if a whole race of people finds itself confined within a system which is set up and continued for the very purpose of keeping it in an inferior station, and if the question is then solemnly propounded whether such a race is being treated "equally," I think we ought to exercise one of the sovereign prerogatives of philosophers—that of laughter. The only question remaining (after we get our laughter under control) is whether the segregation system answers to this description.

Here I must confess to a tendency to start laughing all over again. I was raised in the South, in a Texas city where the pattern of segregation was firmly fixed. I am sure it never occurred to anyone, white or colored, to question its meaning. The fiction of "equality" is just about on a level with the fiction of "finding" in the action of trover. I think few candid southerners deny this. Northern people may be misled by the entirely sincere protestations of many southerners that segregation is "better" for the Negroes, is not intended to hurt them. But I think a little probing would demonstrate that what is meant is that it is better for the Negroes to accept a position of inferiority, at least for the indefinite future.

But the subjectively obvious, if queried, must be backed up by more public materials. What public materials assure me that my reading of the social meaning of segregation is not a mere idiosyncracy?

First, of course, is history. Segregation in the South comes down in apostolic succession from slavery and the *Dred Scott* case. The South fought to keep slavery, and lost. Then it tried the Black Codes, and lost. Then it looked around for something else and found segregation. The movement for segregation was an integral part of the movement to maintain and further "white supremacy"; its triumph (as Professor Woodward has shown) represented a triumph of extreme racialist over moderate sentiment about the Negro.* It is now de-

---

*Woodward, *The Strange Career of Jim Crow*, Ch. II *Capitulation to Racism*, at 49–95 (1957). See generally *id. passim.*

fended very largely on the ground that the Negro as such is not fit to associate with the white.

History, too, tells us that segregation was imposed on one race by the other race; consent was not invited or required. Segregation in the South grew up and is kept going because and only because the white race has wanted it that way—an incontrovertible fact which in itself hardly consorts with equality. This fact perhaps more than any other confirms the picture which a casual or deep observer is likely to form of the life of a southern community—a picture not of mutual separation of whites and Negroes, but of one in-group enjoying full normal communal life and one out-group that is barred from this life and forced into an inferior life of its own. When a white southern writer refers to the woes of "the South," do you not know, does not context commonly make it clear, that he means "white southerners"? When you are in Leeville and hear someone say "Leeville High," you know he has reference to the white high school; the Negro school will be called something else—Carver High, perhaps, or Lincoln High to our shame. That is what you would expect when one race forces a segregated position on another, and that is what you get.

Segregation is historically and contemporaneously associated in a functioning complex with practices which are indisputably and grossly discriminatory. I have in mind especially the long-continued and still largely effective exclusion of Negroes from voting. Here we have two things. First, a certain group of people is "segregated." Secondly, at about the same time, the very same group of people, down to the last man and woman, is barred, or sought to be barred, from the common political life of the community—from all political power. Then we are solemnly told that segregation is not intended to harm the segregated race, or to stamp it with the mark of inferiority. How long must we keep a straight face?

Here it may be added that, generally speaking, segregation is the pattern of law in communities where the extralegal patterns of discrimination against Negroes are the tightest, where Negroes are subjected to the strictest codes of "unwritten law" as to job opportunities, social intercourse, patterns of housing, going to the back door, being called by the first name, saying "Sir," and all the rest of the whole sorry business. Of course these things, in themselves, need not and usually do not involve "state action," and hence the fourteenth amendment cannot apply to them. But they can assist us in understanding the meaning and assessing the impact of state action.

"Separate but equal" facilities are almost never really equal. Sometimes this concerns small things—if the "white" men's room has mixing hot and cold taps, the "colored" men's room will likely have separate taps; it is always the back of the bus for the Negroes; "Lincoln Beach" will rarely if ever be as good as the regular beach. Sometimes it concerns the most vital matters—through the whole history of segregation, colored schools have been so disgracefully inferior to white schools that only ignorance can excuse those who have remained acquiescent members of a community that lived the Molochian child-destroying lie that put them forward as "equal."

Attention is usually focused on these inequalities as things in themselves, correctible by detailed decrees. I am more interested in their very clear character as *evidence* of what segregation means to the people who impose it and to the people who are subjected to it. This evidentiary character cannot be erased by one-step-ahead-of-the-marshal correction. Can a system which, in all that can be measured, has practiced the grossest inequality, actually have been "equal" in intent, in total social meaning and impact? "Thy speech maketh thee manifest . . ."; segregation, in all visible things, speaks only haltingly any dialect but that of inequality.

Further arguments could be piled on top of one another, for we have here to do with the most conspicuous characteristic of a whole regional culture. It is actionable defamation in the South to call a white man a Negro. A small proportion of Negro "blood" puts one in the inferior race for segregation purposes; this is the way in which one deals with a taint, such as a carcinogene in cranberries.

The various items I have mentioned differ in weight; not every one would suffice in itself to establish the character of segregation. Taken together they are of irrefragable strength. The society that has just lost the Negro as a slave, that has just lost out in an attempt to put him under quasi-servile "Codes," the society that views his blood as a contamination and his name as an insult, the society that extralegally imposes on him every humiliating mark of low caste and that until yesterday kept him in line by lynching—this society, careless of his consent, moves by law, first to exclude him from voting, and secondly to cut him off from mixing in the general public life of the community. The Court that refused to see inequality in this cutting off would be making the only kind of law that can be warranted outrageous in advance—law based on self-induced blindness, on flagrant contradiction of known fact.

I have stated all these points shortly because they are matters of common notoriety, matters not so much for judicial notice as for the background knowledge of educated men who live in the world. A court may advise itself of them as it advises itself of the facts that we are a "religious people," that the country is more industrialized than in Jefferson's day, that children are the natural objects of fathers' bounty, that criminal sanctions are commonly thought to deter, that steel is a basic commodity in our economy, that the imputation of unchastity is harmful to a woman. Such judgments, made on such a basis, are in the foundations of all law, decisional as well as statutory; it would be the most unneutral of principles, improvised *ad hoc*, to require that a court faced with the present problem refuse to note a plain fact about the society of the United States—the fact that the social meaning of segregation is the putting of the Negro in a position of walled-off inferiority—or the other equally plain fact that such treatment is hurtful to human beings. Southern courts, on the basis of just such a judgment, have held that the placing of a white person in a Negro railroad car is an actionable humiliation; must a court pretend not to know that the Negro's situation there is humiliating?

I think that some of the artificial mist of puzzlement called into being around this question originates in a single fundamental mistake. The issue is seen in terms of what might be called the metaphysics of sociology: "Must Segregation Amount to Discrimination?" That is an interesting question; someday the methods of sociology may be adequate to answering it. But it is not our question. Our question is whether discrimination inheres in that segregation which is imposed by law in the twentieth century in certain specific states in the American Union. And that question has meaning and can find an answer only on the ground of history and of common knowledge about the facts of life in the times and places aforesaid.

Now I need not and do not maintain that the evidence is all one way; it never is on issues of burning, fighting concern. Let us not question here the good faith of those who assert that segregation represents no more than an attempt to furnish a wholesome opportunity for parallel development of the races; let us rejoice at the few scattered instances they can bring forward to support their view of the matter. But let us then ask which balance-pan flies upward.*

---

*Professor Wechsler, in the Article to which I am in several points responding, says: "The virtue or demerit of a judgment turns . . . entirely on the reasons that support it and their adequacy to maintain any choice of values it decrees, *or, it is vital to add, to maintain the rejection of a claim that any given choice should be decreed.*"

The case seems so onesided that it is hard to make out what is being protested against when it is asked, rhetorically, how the Court can possibly advise itself of the real character of the segregation system. It seems that what is being said is that, while no actual doubt exists as to what segregation is for and what kind of societal pattern it supports and implements, there is no ritually sanctioned way in which the Court, as a Court, can permissibly learn what is obvious to everybody else and to the Justices as individuals. But surely, confronted with such a problem, legal acumen has only one proper task—that of developing ways to make it permissible for the Court to use what it knows; any other counsel is of despair. And, equally surely, the fact that the Court has assumed as true a matter of common knowledge in regard to broad societal patterns, is (to say the very least) pretty far down the list of things to protest against.

I conclude, then, that the Court had the soundest reasons for judging that segregation violates the fourteenth amendment. These reasons make up the simple syllogism with which I began: The fourteenth amendment commands equality, and segregation as we know it is inequality.

Let me take up a few peripheral points. It is true that the specifically hurtful character of segregation, as a net matter in the life of each segregated individual, may be hard to establish. It seems enough to say of this, as Professor Pollak has suggested, that no such demand is made as to other constitutional rights. To have a confession beaten out of one might in some particular case be the beginning of a new and better life. To be subjected to a racially differentiated curfew might be the best thing in the world for some individual boy. A man might ten years later go back to thank the policeman who made him get off the platform and stop making a fool of himself. Religious persecution proverbially strengthens faith. We do not ordinarily go that far, or look so narrowly into the matter. That a practice, on massive historical evidence and in common sense, has the designed

---

Wechsler, *supra* note 3, at 19–20. (Emphasis added.) Unless it chose to rely without reexamination on the sociology of *Plessy v. Ferguson*, or to follow the evasive, futile, and novel procedure of leaving the matter to Congress (see *id.* at 31–32, rejecting both these non-solutions, and on the latter point, see my forthcoming *The People and the Court*, at 137–39), what kind of an opinion could the Court have written sustaining the affirmative thesis that segregation as we know it *really is equal*—especially in view of the fact, which I suppose would be conceded, that the very least one can possibly say is that no strong presumption of validity supports racially classificatory state laws?

and generally apprehended effect of putting its victims at a disadvantage, is enough for law. At least it always has been enough.

I can heartily concur in the judgment that segregation harms the white as much as it does the Negro. Sadism rots the policeman; the suppressor of thought loses light; the community that forms into a mob, and goes down and dominates a trial, may wound itself beyond healing. Can this reciprocity of hurt, this fated mutuality that inheres in all inflicted wrong, serve to validate the wrong itself?

Finally it is doubtless true that the *School Segregation Cases*, and perhaps others of the cases on segregation, represented a choice between two kinds of freedom of association. Freedom from the massive wrong of segregation entails a corresponding loss of freedom on the part of the whites who must now associate with Negroes on public occasions, as we all must on such occasions associate with many persons we had rather not associate with. It is possible to state the competing claims in symmetry, and to ask whether there are constitutional reasons for preferring the Negroes' desire for merged participation in public life to the white man's desire to live a public life without Negroes in proximity.

The question must be answered, but I would approach it in a way which seems to me more normal—the way in which we more usually approach comparable symmetries that might be stated as to all other asserted rights. The fourteenth amendment forbids inequality, forbids the disadvantaging of the Negro race by law. It was surely anticipated that the following of this directive would entail some disagreeableness for some white southerners. The disagreeableness might take many forms; the white man, for example, might dislike having a Negro neighbor in the exercise of the latter's equal right to own a home, or dislike serving on a jury with a Negro, or dislike having Negroes on the streets with him after ten o'clock* When the directive of equality cannot be followed without displeasing the white, then something that can be called a "freedom" of the white must be impaired. If the fourteenth amendment commands equality, and if segregation violates equality, then the status of the reciprocal "freedom" is automatically settled.

I find reinforcement here, at least as a matter of spirit, in the

---

*The white inhabitants of Mobile in their corporate capacity moved to protect this particular "freedom not to associate" in 1909. See Woodward, *op. cit. supra*, note 14, at 86–87.

fourteenth amendment command that Negroes shall be "citizens" of
their States. It is hard for me to imagine in what operative sense a
man could be a "citizen" without his fellow citizens' once in a while
having to associate with him. If, for example, his "citizenship" results
in his election to the School Board, the white members may (as recently in Houston) put him off to one side of the room, but there is
still some impairment of their freedom "not to associate." That freedom, in fact, exists only at home; in public, we have to associate with
anybody who has a right to be there. The question of our right not to
associate with him is concluded when we decide whether he has a
right to be there.

I am not really apologetic for the simplicity of my ideas on the
segregation cases. The decisions call for mighty diastrophic change.
We ought to call for such change only in the name of a solid reasoned
simplicity that takes law out of artfulness into art. Only such grounds
can support the nation in its resolve to uphold the law declared by its
Court; only such grounds can reconcile the white South to what
must be. *Elegantia juris* and conceptual algebra have here no place.
Without pretending either to completeness or to definitiveness of
statement, I have tried here to show reasons for believing that we as
lawyers can without fake or apology present to the lay community,
and to ourselves, a rationale of the segregation decisions that rises to
the height of the great argument.

These judgments, like all judgments, must rest on the rightness of
their law and the truth of their fact. Their law is right if the equal
protection clause in the fourteenth amendment is to be taken as stating, without arbitrary exceptions, a broad principle of practical equality for the Negro race, inconsistent with any device that in fact
relegates the Negro race to a position of inferiority. Their facts are
true if it is true that the segregation system is actually conceived and
does actually function as a means of keeping the Negro in a status of
inferiority. I dare say at this time that in the end the decisions will be
accepted by the profession on just that basis. Opinions composed
under painful stresses may leave much to be desired;* it may be that

---

*I do not mean here to join the hue and cry against the *Brown* opinion. The charge
that it is "sociological" is either a truism or a canard—a truism if it means that the
Court, precisely like the *Plessy* Court, and like innumerable other courts facing
innumerable other issues of law, had to resolve and did resolve a question about
social fact; a canard if it means that anything like principal reliance was placed on
the formally "scientific" authorities, which are relegated to a footnote and treated as

the per curiam device has been unwisely used. But the judgments, in law and in fact, are as right and true as any that ever was uttered.

5. Owen M. Fiss—"Racial Imbalance in the Public Schools: The Constitutional Concepts" (1965)*

I

Introduction

The desire of the Negro to achieve a position of equality in American society has led to a fervent protest against segregation in the public schools. The Supreme Court responded to this protest in *Brown* v. *Board of Education* by unequivocally condemning attendance schemes that have as their declared purpose the separation of the races. In the wake of this decision attention is shifting to those public schools where segregation is not the open and declared policy of the school board, but where, nevertheless, the races remain segregated. . . .

B.

The Constitutional Principle: Equality of Educational Opportunity

If it can be established that government is responsible for the creation and maintenance of racially imbalanced schools in a particular community [even though racial separation is not required by law], the imposition of a constitutional obligation to take correctional steps depends on whether this imbalance constitutes a denial of "equal protection of the laws" in violation of the fourteenth amendment. If this question is to be resolved affirmatively, when the school board's policy is merely one of approval or disregard [of segregation], a principle requiring equality of educational opportunity must be abstracted

---

merely corroboratory of common sense. It seems to me that the venial fault of the opinion consists in its not spelling out that segregation, for reasons of the kind I have brought forward in this Article, is perceptibly a means of ghettoizing the imputedly inferior race. (I would conjecture that the motive for this omission was reluctance to go into the distasteful details of the southern caste system.) That such treatment is generally not good for children needs less talk than the Court gives it.

Harvard Law Review, Vol. 78, 564, 1965.

from the equal protection clause, for the protest against the creation
and maintenance of imbalanced schools essentially consists of a claim
that the educational opportunity afforded Negro children required to
attend such schools is unequal to that afforded children attending the
other public schools of the community. If such a constitutional principle can be established it would require the justification of unequal
educational opportunity and in the absence of such a justification,
equal educational opportunity. . . .

[In *Sweatt* and *McLaurin*, the Justices pronounced, and] four years
later, in *Brown* v. *Board of Education*, the Court reiterated [just such
a] basic principle: the educational opportunity afforded in the public
schools "must be made available to all on equal terms." . . . The
Court assumed that "the physical facilities and other 'tangible' factors"
were equal, and went on to construct out of several empirical judgments a necessary relationship between the open and declared policy
of segregation and the impairment of educational opportunity: first, a
Negro public school does not possess those qualities, enumerated in
Sweatt, that "are incapable of objective measurement" but critical in
determining the quality of the educational opportunity; second, the
Negro child compelled to go to a Negro school is deprived, even more
than in *McLaurin*, of the educationally important opportunity to engage in discussion and exchange views with white students; and third,
to separate the Negro school children "from others of similar age
and qualifications, solely because of their race, generates a feeling of
inferiority as to their status in the community that may affect their
hearts and minds in a way unlikely ever to be undone," and this has
an "effect . . . on their educational opportunities" since a "'sense of
inferiority affects the motivation of a child to learn.'" The Court then
concluded: "Separate educational facilities are inherently unequal."
The Court in *Sweatt*, *McLaurin*, and *Brown* explicitly made the empirical judgment necessary to expose the substantial inequality, and
impliedly made the normative judgment that this unequal treatment
was not justified by the accident of color or the desire of whites not
to associate with Negroes.

The constitutional status of the equal-educational-opportunity principle, not the correctness of these normative and empirical judgments,
is being asserted here. However, it has been suggested that the Court
could have decided these cases without assessing the quality of a segregated educational opportunity, that instead of employing the equal-
educational-opportunity principle the Court might have relied on the

more "neutral" or "general" principle that race is an inherently arbitrary classification. Two points are often overlooked by the proponents of this alternative explanation of *Brown:* first, that the inherently-arbitrary-classification principle is compatible with the equal-opportunity principle; and second, that regardless of the grounds on which *Brown* and its predecessors might have been decided there is no doubt of the ground on which they were decided.

The inherently-arbitrary-classification principle has taken on several different meanings, although each is consistent with the no less "general" and "neutral" (whatever those words mean) principle of equality of educational opportunity. For Professor Pollak, the principle merely creates a presumption that a law that "draws racial lines" treats the racial minority unequally. The application of this presumption would have relieved the Court from probing below the nominal level of the Jim Crow education laws and from having to rely openly on the empirical judgment that segregation disadvantages the minority. The Court would have had to rely on its "amateur wisdom" only to determine whether the presumption of unequal treatment had been rebutted and whether this unequal treatment could be justified. As such, the inherently-arbitrary-classification principle is merely a technique for facilitating the application of the equal-opportunity principle. . . .

[Another] version of the inherently-arbitrary-classification principle has been suggested by Professor John Kaplan: Any law that contains a "racial classification" is so "completely arbitrary and irrational" that it necessarily violates the equal protection clause regardless of actual or presumed harm, or unequal treatment in any factual sense. The "essence of the constitutional violation" of a law that places children of different races in different schools is not that such a law treats Negroes unequally in any factual sense, but rather that it treats "Negroes as Negroes.". . . [But] Professor Kaplan . . . leaves the critical question unanswered: Why cannot Negroes be treated as Negroes, if there is no inequality in any sense other than that they are treated as Negroes and if racial considerations are not used to justify restrictions on individual liberty? Conceivably, some laws may be so "absurd" or "irrational" on their face that they hardly partake of the quality of laws. Certainly, this was not the case with the laws at stake in *Brown:* in 1954, seventeen states and the District of Columbia had laws requiring segregation and four states had legislation explicitly permitting segregation at the option of the local authorities.

The second point often overlooked is that regardless of whether *Brown* could have been decided on "other grounds," it—as well as *Sweatt* and *McLaurin*—was decided on the basis of the equal-educational-opportunity principle. . . .

The Supreme Court's apparent willingness in *Brown* to announce the principle of equal educational opportunity and make the requisite empirical and normative judgments does not mean that the principle is without difficulty. [But cases are likely to arise under it, in various parts of the country, in which] a court will be called upon to decide whether the racial imbalance that exists in the schools of a particular community results in a systematically and substantially inferior educational opportunity for Negroes. . . .

V

Conclusion. . . .

The equal protection clause, requiring equality of educational opportunity, may in some instances be violated by the maintenance of racially imbalanced schools. The reach of these propositions cannot be ignored: they provide the framework for constitutionally permitting and sometimes requiring radical reform of the *status quo*.

III.
Bolling v. Sharpe: The Court's Commentary on Brown?

THE DISTRICT OF Columbia segregation case, Bolling v. Sharpe, had to be decided separately from Brown v. Board of Education, because it could not be argued under the equal protection clause of the fourteenth amendment. ("No state shall . . . deny to any person . . . the equal protection of the laws.") Those petitioning the Supreme Court on behalf of the plaintiffs in Bolling—black students in the nation's capital refused admission to a white junior high school—based their constitutional claims, therefore, on the due process clause of the fifth amendment. In doing so, they articulated, and the Court accepted, a modified but clearly recognizable version of the "top layer" argument first considered in Sweatt v. Painter—that all categories which segregate by race are inherently unconstitutional.

The petitioners' brief in Bolling actually fused this argument, fashioned initially for an equal protection context, with the notion of substantive due process, which, whether rightly or wrongly, had become an accepted part of American constitutional jurisprudence. The right to an education, it was claimed, "to acquire useful knowledge," was a "fundamental right" guaranteed to all citizens of a federal jurisdiction by the fifth amendment. This right was protected against unreasonable or arbitrary governmental restriction. And restrictions based upon race must meet the more stringent test of "pressing public necessity" in order to be valid, since, as Korematsu had ruled, they were "immediately suspect" and subject to the "most rigid scrutiny."

Segregation of the races did not even bear a "reasonable relation" to any educational objective; it was a deprivation of constitutional rights, which was "injurious per se."

Warren's opinion wound up relying upon the broad notion that "Negro children" in the District were being deprived of the "liberty" guaranteed by the fifth amendment, rather than mentioning the specific right to an education. This language was crafted to suit Justice Black, who was staunchly opposed to inventing new rights under the due process clause of either the fifth or the fourteenth amendment. Still, *Bolling* struck down the District of Columbia statute on the basis of its content, not because of the procedures for its enforcement. The decision was an exercise in substantive due process, or as it has been called, "substantive equal protection."

But did *Bolling* also put a definitive gloss upon *Brown*, demonstrating, as the decisions on golf courses and transportation seemed to demonstrate, that *Brown's* purpose was to outlaw segregation ipso facto, and that discussion of psychological harm was peripheral? Professor Lino Graglia of Columbia Law School is one who believes this is the case. In his book *Disaster by Decree*, he contends that "the *Brown* decision did not in fact turn on a finding of educational harm from grade school segregation, as was in effect at once admitted in *Bolling* v. *Sharpe*. . . . [T]he prohibition of school segregation [in *Bolling*] was based on a simple prohibition of racial discrimination." (Ithaca, New York, 1976, p. 29.)

Professor Owen Fiss, however, strongly disagrees with the attempt to interpret *Brown* through *Bolling*.

1. Brief for Petitioners—*Bolling* v. *Sharpe**

ARGUMENT

I

The action of respondents in excluding minor petitioners from admission to Sousa Junior High School solely because of race or color and in refusing to permit adult petitioners to enroll their children in Sousa Junior High School solely because of race or color deprives petitioners of their liberty and property without due process of law in contravention of the fifth amendment of the constitution of the United States. . . .

---

*p. 10ff. *Records and Briefs*, Part 4.

B. **The Educational Rights Which Petitioners Assert Are Fundamental Rights Protected by the Due Process Clause of the Fifth Amendment from Unreasonable or Arbitrary Restrictions.**

Minor petitioners assert *rights to enjoy the educational opportunities* provided in the District of Columbia unrestricted by reason of their race or color and adult petitioners assert rights to enroll their children in public schools in the District of Columbia, unrestricted by reason of race or color. These educational rights are fundamental rights protected by the Fifth Amendment against unreasonable or arbitrary restrictions.

This Court held in *Meyer v. Nebraska*, 262 U.S. 390, 399, 400 (1923), that:

> "While this Court has not attempted to define with exactness the liberty thus guaranteed, the term has received much consideration and some of the included things have been definitely stated. Without doubt it denotes not merely freedom from bodily restraint but also the right of the individual to contract, to engage in any of the common occupations of life, to *acquire useful knowledge*, to marry, establish a home and bring up children, to worship God according to the dictates of his own conscience, and generally to enjoy those privileges long recognized at common law as essential to the orderly pursuit of happiness of free men. . . . The established doctrine is that this liberty may not be interfered with under the guise of protecting the public interest, by legislative action which is arbitrary or without reasonable relation to some purpose within the competency of the State to effect." . . .

C. **The Official Action of Respondents Excluding Minor Petitioners from Admission to Sousa Junior High School Solely Because of Race or Color Is Immediately Suspect and Must Be Tested by Standards Laid Down by This Court to Determine Whether Petitioners' Rights Protected by the Fifth Amendment Have Been Violated.**

Segregation of the races by government fiat is incompatible with our national policy. . . . Consequently in the light of the Fifth Amendment . . . and in view of the national public policy limiting government enforced distinctions based solely on race or color, this Court has placed upon the government the burden of justifying racial distinctions imposed upon its citizens. As this Court said, speaking through Mr. Justice Black in *Korematsu v. U.S.*, 323 U.S. 214, 216 (1944)—

> "It should be noted, to begin with, that all legal restrictions

which curtail the civil rights of a single racial group are immediately suspect. That is not to say that all such restrictions are unconstitutional. It is to say that courts must subject them to the most rigid scrutiny. *Pressing public necessity may sometimes justify the existence of such restrictions; racial antagonism never can."* (Emphasis supplied.)

In the Japanese cases this Court . . . evolved certain definite standards by which government enforced racial distinctions among its citizens must be tested.

1. *The restrictions must be justified by an affirmative showing of peculiar circumstances, present emergency, or pressing public necessity.*

(a)   In *Meyer* v. *Nebraska, supra,* this Court invalidated a Nebraska statute restricting the teaching of foreign languages, as infringing educational rights protected by the due process clause of the Fourteenth Amendment. At page 402 the Court said:

> "The interference is plain enough and no adequate reason therefor in time of peace and domestic tranquility has been shown." . . .

4. *The restrictions must have a reasonable relation to an authorized purpose within the competency of the government to effect.* . . .

In *Korematsu* v. *U.S., supra,* this Court said at page 218:

> "[E]xclusion from a threatened area . . . has a definite and close relationship to the prevention of espionage and sabotage."

In the instant case, the exclusion of minor petitioners from Sousa Junior High School solely because of race or color has no reasonable relation to any educational purpose suggested by respondents, for they have suggested no purpose. It is submitted that no purpose within the competency of the government to effect can be advanced in this case.

D. Petitioners Sustain Injury as the Direct Result of the Action of Respondents in Excluding Minor Petitioners from Sousa Junior High School Solely Because of Race or Color.

The exclusion of minor petitioners from admission to Sousa Junior High School, solely because of race or color is a deprivation of *petitioners' constitutional rights to acquire useful knowledge, to choose a particular public school, and to enjoy public educational opportunities without government enforced limitations or restrictions based solely on race or color.* That injury continues and is not removed or even lessened by reason of the fact that minor petitioners "do now attend a junior high school in said District," allocated by respondents for the instruction of Negro children. Beyond question the deprivation of a constitutional right is injurious per se. See *Cummings* v. *Missouri*, 4 Wall. 277 (1866), where this Court observed that "liberty" includes "freedom from outrage on feelings as well as restraints on the person." . . .

Any deprivation of a freedom of choice solely on the basis of race or color is violative of petitioners' civil rights and thus injurious. To be compelled to attend school because of the compulsory school law, and then to be compelled to accept segregation on the basis of race or color and to have one's feelings outraged is injurious per se. The deprivation of a civil right is an injury.

2. *Bolling* v. *Sharpe* (1954)*

Mr. Chief Justice Warren delivered the opinion of the Court.

This case challenges the validity of segregation in the public schools of the District of Columbia. The petitioners, minors of the Negro race, allege that such segregation deprives them of due process of law under the Fifth Amendment. They were refused admission to a public school attended by white children solely because of their race. They sought the aid of the District Court for the District of Columbia in obtaining admission. That court dismissed their complaint. The Court granted a writ of certiorari before judgment in the Court of Appeals because of the importance of the constitutional question presented. 344 U.S. 873.

We have this day held that the Equal Protection Clause of the Fourteenth Amendment prohibits the states from maintaining racially segregated public schools. The legal problem in the District of Columbia is somewhat different, however. The Fifth Amendment, which is applicable in the District of Columbia, does not contain an equal protection clause as does the Fourteenth Amendment which applies only to the states. But the concepts of equal protection and due process, both stemming from our American ideal of fairness, are not mutually exclusive. The "equal protection of the laws" is a more explicit safeguard of prohibited unfairness than "due process of law," and, therefore, we do not imply that the two are always interchange-

---

*347 US 497, 1954.

able phrases. But, as this Court has recognized, discrimination may be so unjustifiable as to be violative of due process.

Classifications based solely upon race must be scrutinized with particular care, since they are contrary to our traditions and hence constitutionally suspect. As long ago as 1896, this Court declared the principle "that the Constitution of the United States, in its present form, forbids, so far as civil and political rights are concerned, discrimination by the General Government, or by the States, against any citizen because of his race."* And in *Buchanan* v. *Warley*, 245 U.S. 60, the Court held that a statute which limited the right of a property owner to convey his property to a person of another race was, as an unreasonable discrimination, a denial of due process of law.

Although the Court has not assumed to define "liberty" with any great precision, that term is not confined to mere freedom from bodily restraint. Liberty under law extends to the full range of conduct which the individual is free to pursue, and it cannot be restricted except for a proper governmental objective. Segregation in public education is not reasonably related to any proper governmental objective, and thus it imposes on Negro children of the District of Columbia a burden that constitutes an arbitrary deprivation of their liberty in violation of the Due Process Clause.

In view of our decision that the Constitution prohibits the states from maintaining racially segregated public schools, it would be unthinkable that the same Constitution would impose a lesser duty on the Federal Government. We hold that racial segregation in the public schools of the District of Columbia is a denial of the due process of law guaranteed by the Fifth Amendment to the Constitution.

For the reasons set out in *Brown* v. *Board of Education*, this case will be restored to the docket for reargument on Questions 4 and 5 previously propounded by the Court. 345 U.S. 972.

It is so ordered.

3. Rejoinder—Owen M. Fiss (1965)

[What cannot be] overlooked is that regardless of whether *Brown* could have been decided on "other grounds," it—as well as *Sweatt* and *McLaurin*—was decided on the basis of the equal-educational-opportunity principle. The language of the opinion, and the Court's

---

Gibson v. *Mississippi*, 162 U.S. 565, 591.

familiarity with an alternative approach, which was used to decide [*Bolling* v. *Sharpe*], leave no doubt that the Court deliberately chose the principle of equal educational opportunity even though the application of this principle required the Court to assess the total social impact of the institution of segregated education. The reasons for the choice are speculative although the fact of the choice is not. The Court may have decided that it would be unconvincing to announce abruptly that race is an inherently arbitrary classification when certain American institutions had been based on racial separation for several hundred years. Or it may have felt itself obliged to continue the debate in the terms set by *Plessy* v. *Ferguson*, namely that segregation did not disadvantage the Negro except for his choice to "put that construction upon it." Perhaps the Court simply believed that equality of educational opportunity was the principle most deeply involved in these cases and boldly stated so in order to permit that principle's fullest growth. The Court's willingness to decide summarily other cases involving noneducational facilities by citing *Brown* does not necessarily indicate a subsequent rejection of the principle; these summary dispositions can be viewed as the development of a per se rule embodying a judgment that governmental segregation in facilities other than schools—even if attendance is not compulsory—unjustifiably treats the Negro unequally. The refusal to reassess the social impact of segregation in each public facility, and in each community, does involve some rather heavyhanded treatment of state government. Perhaps such treatment can be explained by the Court's lack of respect for a political process from which Negroes have been effectively excluded and in which it is reasonable to assume racial bigotry played a significant role. It can also be explained as a concession to the interest of judicial economy and as an attempt to make the law an effective instrument of social reform.

Afterword

THE DISPARATE READINGS of *Brown v. Board of Education* pointed to conflicting interpretations of how the decision should be implemented. If *Brown* simply pronounced classifications which segregated by race inherently unconstitutional, it applied to transportation and recreation facilities as well as to schools; but it imposed a limited constitutional obligation on the segregated school systems themselves, many thought. Southern officials would merely be required to get rid of compulsory separation of the races and establish some impartial method of assigning students. The same obligation would obtain presumably when pockets of deliberate discrimination were uncovered in northern or western school systems, where segregation was not mandated for the system as a whole.

If, however, *Brown* was primarily about psychological harm and "equal educational opportunity," impartiality in student designations might not be a sufficient response to the decision. Actual integration of schools could be required, in the dual systems of the South, and perhaps in other parts of the country as well. By the early 1960s, plaintiffs in communities whose schools were not segregated by law, such as Gary, Indiana, were claiming that the so-called de facto segregation which resulted from residential patterns was unconstitutional *per se*.

But the dichotomy posed by *Brown I* turned out to be a false one in large measure. For though the second *Brown v. Board of Education* appeared to resolve the questions posed by its predecessor in a fairly conservative manner, requiring only that American education rid itself of the racial classifications and deliberate discriminations of the past, the remedial obligations imposed by *Brown II* turned out to be more complex, or the Courts subsequently made them more complex, than was originally supposed.

Brown II decreed that the perpetrators of state-imposed segregation

342

were to "effectuate a transition to a racially nondiscriminatory school system . . . . with all deliberate speed." (349 US 294, at 301.) This language nourished the assumption that neutrality in pupil assignment was all that was being asked of errant state officials. The ultimate realization of such neutrality was thought to be a well-functioning neighborhood school system.

Judge John Parker put the matter with characteristic precision when *Briggs v. Elliott* was sent back again to the lower courts.

> [I]t is important that we point out exactly what the Supreme Court has decided and what it has not decided in this case. . . . It has not decided that the states must mix persons of different races in the schools or must require them to attend schools or must deprive them of the right of choosing the schools they attend. What it has decided, and all that it has decided, is that a state may not deny to any person on account of race the right to attend any school that it maintains. . . . The Constitution, in other words, does not require integration. It merely forbids discrimination. (132 F. Supp. 776, 1955, at 777.)

Judge Parker's words were cited in rejecting the plaintiffs' claims in the *Gary* case.

Yet by the late 1960s and early 1970s, a critical change in perception was taking place. Lower federal courts, and eventually the Supreme Court, came to the conclusion that the "neutrality" represented by neighborhood schools was not sufficient to erase the discriminatory legacy of the past, that it did not constitute the equitable remedy which *Brown II* demanded.

Through a series of intricate, some would say artificial deductions, the Justices held in the *Swann* case of 1971 that only integration of southern schools, brought about by cross-town busing if necessary, could wipe away the racial classifications of the segregation era. In the *Keyes* decision of 1973, the Court applied the same logic to the pockets of discrimination found in northern and western school systems; busing was required there also to satisfy *Brown II*. These decisions led to criticisms almost as bitter as the denunciations which descended upon *Brown I*. Whether these later attacks were motivated less by racial bias than by a concern for educational values was itself a subject of intense debate. Meanwhile, constitutional scholars questioned whether the Court's demands for integration stemmed from an enthusiasm for its pure remedial logic, or from a disguised belief that all segregation was harmful to minority groups.

These complications merit their own separate study. But they cannot obscure the moral and constitutional achivement of May 17, 1954, what Judge Pollak has called "the most important American governmental act of any kind since the Emancipation Proclamation." (*The Constitution and the Supreme Court*, Cleveland, 1966, p. 266.)

Ernest Rubenstein, a law clerk to Justice Clark in 1954, was interviewed by Richard Kluger for his great book, *Simple Justice*. Rubenstein's reaction to the reading of *Brown* in open court is an appropriate way to end a study of these events. "I felt good—and clean. It was so right" (p. 708).

List of Detailed Sources

Part One

I. Sumner in *Roberts* v. *City of Boston*—59 Mass. 198. Brief is reprinted in *Charles Sumner: His Complete Works* (Boston, 1900), Vol. 3, pp. 51–100 (esp. pp. 74–76, 88, 93–96).

II. *Plessy* v. *Ferguson*

  1. Tourgée Brief—*Records and Briefs of the Supreme Court*, 163 US 537. Reprinted in Phillip B. Kurland and Gerhard Casper (eds.), *Landmark Briefs and Arguments of the Supreme Court: Constitutional Law* (Arlington, Va., 1975–), Vol. 13, pp. 27–63 (esp. pp. 37, 41, 53, 55–58, 62–63).

  2. Phillips Brief—*Records and Briefs*, 163 US 537. Reprinted in Kurland and Casper, Vol. 13, pp. 3–26 (esp. pp. 10–14).

  3. Brown Opinion—163 US 537, at 550–51.

  4. Harlan Dissent—163 US 537, at 554–55, 557–62.

III. Houston and Marshall in *Murray*—169 Md. 478. *Records and Briefs of the Maryland Court of Appeals*, Vol. 177 (October Term, 1935, No. 53). Appellees' Brief, pp. 25–27.

IV. Myrdal—*An American Dilemma*, Vol. II, pp. 575–76, 586–88.

V. *Sweatt* Brief—pp. 8–9, 12, 19–21, 26–31, 33–35, 69, 73–75. *Records and Briefs*, 339 US 629, Part 2.

VI. *Sweatt* v. *Painter*, 339 US 629, at 633–36; *McLaurin* v. *Oklahoma State Regents*, 339 US 637, at 640–42.

Part Two

I. The Doll Man

1. Clark Testimony—*Briggs* Trial, pp. 87–90, 92–93, 96. *Records and Briefs of the Supreme Court*, 349 US 294, part 2.*

2. Cahn Article—*N.Y.U.L. Rev.* (Vol. 30, 1955), 150, 161, 163–65, 159.

3. Note—*Yale Law Journal* (Vol. 61, 1952), 730, 735–37.

4. Van den Haag and Ross—*The Fabric of Society*, pp. 165–66.

5. Clark—*Prejudice and Your Child*, pp. 45–46, 195–96, 193–94.

II. The Social Scientists

1. Holt—*Brown* Trial, pp. 169–73, Part 1.

2. Krech—*Briggs* Trial, pp. 133–34, Part 2.

3. Smith—*Davis* Trial, pp. 183–87, 195–96, Part 3.

4. Brookover—*Brown* Trial, pp. 164–67, Part 1.

5. Chein—*Davis* Trial, pp. 209–10, 233–34, part 3.

6. Speer—*Brown* Trial, pp. 118, 135–37, Part 1.

III. Rebuttal

1. Buck—pp. 534–44, Part 3.

2. Kelly—pp. 518, 522–26, 528–29, Part 3.

3. Garrett—pp. 550, 552–53, 555–56, 568–70, Part 3.

4. Darden—pp. 452–55, 459, 461–62, Part 3.

IV. Mr. Moore's Antics

1. Clark—pp. 280–82, 285–86, 264–65, Part 3.

2. Chein—pp. 213–14, 235–36, 213, Part 3.

---

*Note: All other references to trial testimony or briefs in the *Brown* cases are from 349 US 294 (8 Parts). Trial testimony and briefs within the various parts are numbered separately. There is no consecutive pagination.

3. Brooks—p. 177, Part 3.

V. Preliminary Decisions

1. *Briggs*—98 F. Supp. 529, at 535–37, 540–42, 547–48.

2. *Davis*—103 F. Supp. 337, at 339–41.

3. *Brown*—98 F. Supp. 797, at 798–800.

4. *Belton*—87 A. 2d 862, at 864–65, 869–70.

Part Three

Brown

1. Appellants' Brief—Part 1, Part 7. Reprinted in Kurland and Casper, Vol. 49, pp. 27–61 (esp. pp. 32–39, 43–44, 49–52, 60).

2. Appellees' Brief—Part 1. Reprinted in Kurland and Casper, Vol. 49, pp. 70–110 (esp. pp. 78, 89–92, 94–95, 100, 102–3, 106–9).

3. Oral Argument—*Oral Arguments of the Supreme Court*, 1952 Term (Microfiche #1), Case #8. Reprinted in Leon Friedman (ed.), *Argument* (New York, 1969), pp. 18–22, 26, 29, 34–35.

II. *Briggs*

2. Appellees' Brief—pp. 19–20, 23, 25–27, 29, 33–34, Part 2.

1 Appellants' Brief—pp. 12–16, 20–26, 28–29, 31, Part 2.

3. Oral Argument—1952 Term (Microfiche #2), Case #101. Reprinted in Friedman, pp. 44–45, 47–49, 51, 55–56, 61, 63–64.

III. *Davis*

1. Appellees' Brief—pp. 12, 15–17, 21–22, 24, 27–31, Part 3.

2. Appellants' Brief—pp. 15, 23–26, 28–31, 33, Part 3.

3. Oral Argument—1952 Term (Microfiche #3), Case #191. Reprinted in Friedman, pp. 92–93, 99, 76.

IV. *Belton*

1. NAACP Brief—pp. 11–13, Part 5.

2. Oral Argument—1952 Term (Microfiche #5), Case #448. Reprinted in Friedman, pp. 164–65.

V. American Jewish Congress Brief—Part 1. Reprinted in Kurland and Casper, Vol. 49, pp. 215–39 (esp. pp. 224–26, 230–35).

Part Four

I. "whr"—Documents in this section can be found in the *Congressional Record*, 92nd Congress, 1st Session—Senate (December 8, 9, 1971), 45440–41, 45440, 45815–16.

II. Original Intent

1. Bork Article—*San Diego Law Review* (Vol. 23, 1986), 823, 824–29.

2. Sandalow Article—*Michigan Law Review* (Vol. 79, 1981), 1033, 1034–38, 1046–50, 1068–69.

III. Double Perspectives

1. Kelly Lecture—Richard Kluger Papers, Yale University Library, pp, 2, 9–17, 19–24.

2. Kelly Article—*Michigan Law Review* (Vol. 54, 1956), 1049, 1066–71, 1077–79, 1081–82, 1084, 1086.

3. Bickel Letter—cited in text.

4. Bickel Article—*Harvard Law Review* (Vol. 69, 1955), 1, 22–23, 25–26, 56–63.

5. Kelly Rebuttal—footnote, 1068.

IV. Reargument—Central Conflict

1. *Briggs* Brief—pp. 49–51, 53–58, Part 2.

2. *Davis* Brief—pp. 154–55, Part 3.

3. Appellants' Brief—Part 6. Reprinted in Kurland and Casper, Vol. 49, pp. 481–711 (esp. pp. 544, 551–53, 555–63, 578).

4. Oral Argument—1953 Term (Microfiche #4), Case #2. Reprinted in Friedman, pp. 198, 202–4, 206, 215–17.

V. Reargument—Remedy

1. United States Brief—Part 7. Reprinted in Kurland and Casper, Vol. 49, pp. 853–1054 (esp. pp. 1018, 1030–32, 1034, 1050–53).

2. Oral Argument—1953 Term (Microfiche #4), Case #2. Reprinted in Friedman, pp. 252–58.

3. Appellants' Brief—Part 6. Reprinted in Kurland and Casper (pp. 703–10).

4. Elman Article—*Harvard Law Review* (Vol. 100, 1987), 817, 827–32.

Conclusion

I. Countdown

1. Jackson Memorandum—Jackson Papers, Library of Congress, pp. 1–6, 11–23.

2. Frankfurter Memorandum—as cited in text.

3. Elman—840–41, 843–45.

II. Debate

1. Wechsler Article—*Harvard Law Review* (Vol. 73, 1959), 1, 31–34.

2. Pollak Article—*University of Pennsylvania Law Review* (Vol. 108, 1959), 1, 24–31.

3. Kaplan Article—*Northwestern University Law Review* (Vol. 58, 1963), 157, 171–73.

4. Black Article—*Yale Law Journal* (Vol. 69, 1960), 421–30.

5. Fiss Article—*Harvard Law Review* (Vol. 78, 1965), 564, 588, 590–91, 593–96, 617.

III. *Bolling* v. *Sharpe*

1. Petitioners' Brief—pp. 10, 13, 16–17, 21–22, Part 4.

2. Fiss Rejoinder—594–95.

For Further Reading

1. General: *Brown*—Its Background and its Progeny

Barnes, Catherine. *Journey from Jim Crow: The Desegregation of Southern Transit* (New York, 1983).

Bell, Derrick. *Race, Racism and American* Law (Boston, 1980).

Berger, Raoul. *Government by Judiciary* (Cambridge, Mass., 1970).

Berman, Daniel. *It Is So Ordered: The Supreme Court Rules on School Segregation* (New York, 1966).

Blaustein, Albert, and Clarence Ferguson. *Desegregation and the Law* (New Brunswick, N.J., 1957).

Carter, Dan. *Scottsboro: A Tragedy of the American South* (Baton Rouge, La., 1969).

Dollard, John. *Class and Caste in a Southern Town* (New Haven, Conn., 1937).

Garraty, John, editor. *Quarrels That Have Shaped the Constitution* (New York, 1987).

Graham, Howard Jay. *Everyman's Constitution* (Madison, Wis., 1968).

Harlan, Louis. *Separate and Unequal: Public School Campaigns and Racism in the Southern Seaboard States* (Chapel Hill, N.C., 1958).

Hill, Herbert, and Jack Greenberg. *Citizen's Guide to Desegregation* (Boston, 1955).

James, Joseph. *The Framing of the Fourteenth Amendment* (Urbana, Ill., 1956).
The Ratification of the Fourteenth Amendment (Macon, Ga., 1984).

Kellogg, Charles. *NAACP* (Baltimore, 1967).

Kluger, Richard. *Simple Justice* (New York, 1975).

Lofgren, Charles. *The Plessy Case: A Legal-Historical Analysis* (New York, 1987).

Mason, Alpheus. *The Supreme Court: From Taft to Warren*, Revised Edition (Baton Rouge, La., 1968).

Miller, Loren. *The Petitioners: The Story of the United States Supreme Court and the Negro* (New York, 1966).

Orfield, Gary. *Must We Bus?* (Washington, D.C., 1978).

Peltason, Jack. *Fifty-eight Lonely Men: Southern Federal Judges and School Segregation* (New York, 1961).

Pritchett, Herman. *Civil Liberties and the Vinson Court* (Chicago, 1954).

Ross, B. Joyce. *Joel E. Spingarn and the Rise of the NAACP* (New York, 1972).

ten Broek, Jacobus. *Equal Under Law* (New York, 1965).

Tushnet, Mark. *The NAACP's Legal Strategy Against Segregated Education, 1925–1950* (Chapel Hill, N.C., 1987).

Wilkinson, Harvie. *From Brown to Bakke* (New York, 1979).

Wolters, Raymond. *The Burden of Brown: Thirty Years of Desegregation* (Knoxville, Tenn., 1984).

Woodward, C. Vann. *The Strange Career of Jim Crow*, Third Revised Edition (New York, 1974).

2. The Judicial Process

Bickel, Alexander. *The Least Dangerous Branch*, Second Edition (New Haven, Conn., 1986).
  The Morality of Consent (New Haven, 1975).
  The Supreme Court and the Idea of Progress (New York, 1970).

Black, Charles. *The People and the Court: Judicial Review in a Democracy* (New York, 1960).

Black, Hugo. *A Constitutional Faith* (New York, 1968).

Bork, Robert. *The Tempting of America* (New York, 1990).

Corwin, Edward. *Corwin on the Constitution*, Richard Loss, ed., 3 vols. (Ithaca, N.Y., 1981–88).

Dworkin, Ronald. *Taking Rights Seriously* (Cambridge, Mass., 1977).

Ely, John Hart. *Democracy and Distrust* (Cambridge, Mass., 1980).

Frankfurter, Felix. *Mr. Justice Holmes and the Supreme Court* (Cambridge, Mass., 1938).
   Of Law and Men, Phillip Elman, ed. (Cambridge, Mass., 1965).

Freund, Paul. *On Understanding the Supreme Court* (Boston, 1949).

Jackson, Robert. *The Supreme Court in the American System of Government* (Cambridge, Mass., 1955).

Kurland, Phillip. *Politics, the Constitution, and the Warren Court* (Chicago, 1970).

Levy, Leonard. *Judgments: Essays on Constitutional History* (New York, 1972).
   Original Intent and the Framers' Constitution (New York, 1988).

Lofgren, Charles. *"Government from Reflection and Choice"* (New York, 1986).

Lusky, Louis. *By What Right?* (Charlottesville, Va., 1975).

O'Brien, David. *Storm Center: The Supreme Court in American Politics* (New York, 1986).

Perry, Michael. *The Constitution, the Courts, and Human Rights* (New Haven, Conn., 1982).

Rodell, Fred. *Nine Men: A Political History of the Supreme Court* (New York, 1955).

White, G. Edward. *The American Judicial Tradition* (New York, 1976).

Woodward, Bob, and Scott Armstrong. *The Brethren: Inside the Supreme Court* (New York, 1979).

3. Biographies and Autobiographies

Baker, Liva. *Felix Frankfurter: A Biography* (New York, 1969).

Berry, Mary. *Stability, Security, and Continuity: Mr. Justice Burton and Decision-making in the Supreme Court* (Westport, Conn., 1978).

Black, Hugo, and Elizabeth Black. *Mr. Justice and Mrs. Black: The Memoirs of Hugo L. Black and Elizabeth Black* (New York, 1986).

Black, Jr., Hugo. *My Father: A Remembrance* (New York, 1975).

Bland, Randall. *Private Pressure on Public Law: The Legal Career of Thurgood Marshall* (Port Washington, N.Y., 1973).

Douglas, William O. *Go East, Young Man: The Early Years* (New York, 1974).
The Court Years: 1939–1975 (New York, 1980).

Dunne, Gerald. *Hugo Black and the Judicial Revolution* (New York, 1977).

Frankfurter, Felix. *Reminisces*, Harlan Phillips, ed. (New York, 1960).

Friedman, Leon, and Fred Israel, eds. *The Justices of the United States Supreme Court, 1789–1969: Their Lives and Major Opinions*, 4 vols. (New York, 1969), esp. Vols. III, IV.

Gerhart, Eugene. *America's Advocate: Robert H. Jackson* (New York, 1958).

Harbaugh, William. *Lawyer's Lawyer: The Life of John W. Davis* (New York, 1973).

Hirsch, H. N. *The Enigma of Felix Frankfurter* (New York, 1981).

Hixson, William. *Moorfield Storey and the Abolitionist Tradition* (New York, 1972).

Lash, Joseph, ed. *From the Diaries of Felix Frankfurter* (New York, 1975).

McNeil, Genna Rae. *Groundwork: Charles Hamilton Houston and the Struggle for Civil Rights* (Philadelphia, 1983).

Parrish, Michael. *Felix Frankfurter and His Times: The Reform Years* (New York, 1982).

Schwartz, Bernard. *Super Chief: Earl Warren and His Supreme Court* (New York, 1983).

Simon, James. *The Antagonists: Hugo Black, Felix Frankfurter and Civil Liberties in America* (New York, 1989).
Independent Journey: The Life of William O. Douglas (New York, 1980).

Warren, Earl. *Memoirs* (Garden City, N.Y., 1977).

White, G. Edward. *Earl Warren: A Public Life* (New York, 1982).

Acknowledgments

IN ADDITION to my colleagues and my family, I owe an immeasurable debt to many people whom I have yet to have the pleasure of meeting, but who made an indispensable contribution to these pages.

I am deeply grateful to those who gave me permission to utilize documents or materials that appear in this book: Mrs. Alexander Bickel and the Harvard Law School Library for permission to use material from Professor Alexander Bickel's letter to Justice Felix Frankfurter of August 22, 1953, found in the Felix Frankfurter Papers.

Professor Charles H. Black, the *Yale Law Journal*, and Fred B. Rothman and Co. for permission to use "The Lawfulness of the Segregation Decisions."

Dr. Kenneth B. Clark and the Beacon Press for permission to use material from *Prejudice and Your Child*.

Mrs. Mary Jackson Craighill and Mr. William E. Jackson for permission to use material from Justice Robert H. Jackson's Memorandum of March 15, 1954, and other material from the Robert H. Jackson Papers at the Library of Congress.

Mr. Philip Elman and the *Harvard Law Review* for permission to use material from "The Solicitor General's Office, Justice Frankfurter, and Civil Rights Litigation, 1946–1960: An Oral History."

Professor Owen M. Fiss and the *Harvard Law Review* for permission to use material from "Racial Imbalance in the Public Schools: The Constitutional Concepts."

Mrs. John Kaplan for permission to use material from Professor John Kaplan's article "Segregation Litigation and the Schools," Part II: "The General Northern Problem."

Mr. Richard Kluger and the Yale University Library for permission to use material from Professor Alfred Kelly's talk "An Inside View of *Brown v. Board of Education*."

Judge Louis H. Pollak and the *University of Pennsylvania Law*

Review for permission to use material from "Racial Discrimination and Judicial Integrity: A Reply to Professor Wechsler."

Professor Terrance Sandalow and the *Michigan Law Review* for permission to use material from "Constitutional Interpretation."

Mrs. Cathleen Douglas Stone for permission to use material from the William O. Douglas Papers at the Library of Congress.

Professor Ernest van den Haag for permission to use material from *The Fabric of Society.*

Professor Herbert Wechsler and the *Harvard Law Review* for permission to use material from "Toward Neutral Principles of Constitutional Law."

I am also grateful to the Business Officers and Editors of the following journals:

The *Harvard Law Review* (especially Ms. Dolores Hajra) for permission to use material from "The Original Understanding and the Segregation Decision," by Alexander Bickel.

The *Journal of Negro Education* for permission to use material from "Does the Negro Need Separate Schools," by W.E.B. DuBois.

The *Michigan Law Review* for permission to use material from "The Fourteenth Amendment Reconsidered: The Segregation Question," by Alfred Kelly.

The *New York University Law Review* for permission to use material from "Jurisprudence," by Edmond Cahn.

The *San Diego Law Review* for permission to use material from "The Constitution, Economic Rights and Original Intent," by Robert Bork.

The *Yale Law Journal* and Fred B. Rothman and Co. for permission to use material from "Grade School Segregation: The Latest Attack on Discrimination."

I should also like to thank HarperCollins Publishers for permission to use material from *An American Dilemma* by Gunnar Myrdal and the Harvard Law School Library for permission to use material from an undated memorandum by Justice Felix Frankfurter, found in the Felix Frankfurter Papers.

Librarians and archivists always increase the pleasure of any scholarly endeavor. I would especially like to thank Patricia Bartkowski of the Wayne State University Library, David DeLorenzo and Judy Mellins of the Harvard Law School Library, and Judith Ann Schiff of the Yale University Library.

The marvelous professionals at the Library of Congress Manuscript Division and at its Law Library were, as always, helpful and accommodating. I owe a special debt to my friends at the University of Baltimore Law Library and at the Albert S. Cook Library at Towson State University for providing a delightful home base of operations.